The Christian Philosophy
of Jacques Maritain

The Christian Philosophy of
Jacques Maritain

Jason L. A. West

The Catholic University of America Press
Washington, D.C.

The paper used in this publication meets the minimum requirements
of American National Standards for Information Science—
Permanence of Paper for Printed Library Materials, ANSI Z39.48-1992.

Cataloging-in-Publication Data is available from the Library of Congress

ISBN (paper): 978-0-8132-3937-8 | ISBN (ebook): 978-0-8132-3936-1

Printed in the U.S.A.

Book design by Burt&Burt
The interior is set in Warnock Pro and Meta Sans Pro

To the Faculty, Students, and Staff
of Newman Theological College, Edmonton, AB.

The truest and most fraternal friendship
can exist between people
who think differently on essential matters.
It includes doubtless, then, an element of suffering,
but one which renders the friend more dear still.

Jacques Maritain, *On the Church of Christ*, 111

Contents

Preface

This work is a study of the Christian philosophy of Jacques Maritain (1882–1973). Its aim is to show that he provides a dynamic and compelling approach to philosophy in his time. Maritain was one of the leading proponents of the philosophy of St. Thomas Aquinas in the twentieth century. Unlike many other Thomists he not only engaged in historical and exegetical studies, but also developed a creative retrieval of the thought of Aquinas that addressed contemporary concerns. Although his thought is deeply rooted in this particular tradition of inquiry, he was always clear that his philosophy had to stand or fall on the merits of the arguments in its support, not on the basis of authority. Maritain is unusual among his contemporaries due to the fact that he addressed virtually every branch of philosophy, bringing Thomism into creative dialogue with new topics such as the empirical sciences, modernist poetry, and contemporary painting. This makes it very important to have an account of his thought available that presents its full range. The present work will provide a study of his contributions to the various branches of philosophy with an emphasis on his attempt to bring the disparate aspects of philosophy into a coherent whole.

It is not entirely appropriate for an introduction to a complex and multifaceted thinker to argue for a thesis. Such an approach risks limiting one's selection of material to that which supports one's conclusion or twisting the diverse approaches of a rich thinker into a uniform pattern to fit a predetermined theory. However, it would be fair to say that a prominent theme of the present book as a whole is that Maritain's diverse philosophical contributions are united in demonstrating that modern concerns with the empirical, singular, and historical are compatible with the fundamental insights of Thomism; indeed, this philosophical framework is frequently needed for an adequate account of these contemporary concerns.

Maritain's work has added interest since it has proven influential not only among philosophers and theologians, but also among renowned artists, musicians, writers, and politicians. Eric Satie, Igor Stravinsky, Georges Rouault, Flannery O'Connor, Charles De Gaulle and many others claimed to find inspiration in his thought for their own work. The continuing influence of Maritain is evident in the ongoing publication of books and periodicals devoted to his thought, the beginning of the publication of his Collected Works in English by the University of Notre Dame Press, and the continuing activity of Maritain Associations and Centers in many countries such as the United States, Canada, Brazil, Italy, France, and several others.

There are several features that make this particular contribution to Maritain scholarship unique. This book is the only one in English to present Maritain's thought on the full range of topics upon which he wrote. Further, it focuses on Maritain as a twentieth-century philosopher, rather than an interpreter of Aquinas. Questions of his relation to Aquinas and the authenticity of his Thomism, while important, are not my focus in this work. In my reading, Maritain's philosophical aims are almost always primary, while the use of ideas from Aristotle, Aquinas, or John of St. Thomas are usually instrumental insofar as they help solve the philosophical problem at hand. Accordingly, this book presents Maritain's philosophy in its own context.

Each chapter of the book deals with an area of philosophy that was typically the subject of several books by Maritain. I have generally not considered topics to which Maritain only devoted particular articles or that he addressed in correspondence. To do so would make this text far too large and would risk losing sight of the main concerns of his philosophy in a mass of detail. Finally, I have tried to be attentive to the religious context of Maritain's work and highlight overlooked contributions to theology and other areas of philosophy that are informed by his theological commitments (e.g., mysticism, ecclesiology, education, and philosophy of history). Accordingly, the present book aims at providing the reader with a comprehensive presentation of Maritain's thought and a clear vision of his philosophical viewpoint as a whole.

In view of his continued importance and the range of his philosophical contributions, a scholarly study of Maritain's thought as a whole for English readers is long overdue. This is essential since his approach to philosophy is integrative; that is to say, what is developed in one area of Maritain's philosophy has important implications for other areas. For instance, his political philosophy is rooted in his ethics, which is in turn drawn from his philosophy of the person, which is based in his theory of nature, metaphysics, and God. Consequently, this work will fill a significant lacuna in the current scholarship on Maritain.

Maritain wrote before issues of gender-inclusive language became topical. He generally used the term "man" to refer to human persons in general irrespective of gender, as in the titles of his books *Man and the State* or *The Rights of Man and the Natural Law*. I have retained his original terminology in quotations throughout the text. When speaking in my own voice I have generally followed his usage in using the term "man" when speaking of humanity in general. However, in explanations and examples I have moved interchangeably between genders. I feel that this reads more naturally than adopting other—often more artificial— conventions to express gender in an inclusive manner.

I first read Maritain seriously when I arrived at Newman Theological College as a new philosophy professor fresh from the specialized focus of graduate school. I found myself having to learn how to teach ten different philosophy courses on a two-year rotating cycle, sometimes on subjects I had barely studied myself. In this context, Maritain's works became a life preserver, providing me background and context to pull together the diverse areas I was teaching into some sort of coherent whole for my students. More specialized research was completed during a sabbatical from 2010 to 2011, which was generously supported by the college. It is a joy to dedicate this work to the fine colleagues and students that I have had during my years at Newman Theological College.

Acknowledgments

I would like to thank my colleague Dr. Ryan N.S. Topping, who read a draft of this text and made many helpful comments. Likewise, two anonymous referees for The Catholic University of America Press provided invaluable advice to improve this work. Special thanks is due to the editors John Martino and Trevor Crowell, who helped shepherd the book through the publication process. Thanks is also due to Jessica Barr, archivist at St. Michael's College of the University of Toronto, for her help in obtaining the cover photo of Maritain. I would also like to thank Dr. William Sweet and Dr. Louis Groarke for their friendship and many discussions of Maritain over the years. Finally, my wife Christine and our six children have been a tremendous support, and have been patient with my enthusiasm for this project.

Parts of some chapters were developed from material previously published in scholarly articles that have been reworked for inclusion in this new context. I would like to thank the publishers for permission to use of material from the following articles:

1. "The Thomistic Debate Concerning the Existence and Nature of Christian Philosophy: Towards a Synthesis," *The Modern Schoolman* 77, no. 1 (1999): 49–72.
2. "The Possibility of Natural Mystical Experience: The Evolution of Jacques Maritain's Position," *Philosophy, Culture, and Traditions* 8 (2012): 123–34.
3. "Gilson, Maritain, and Garrigou-Lagrange on the Possibility of Critical Realism," *Maritain Studies* 17 (2001): 49–69.
4. "The Existential Character of Maritain's Ethics," *Maritain Studies* 37 (2021): 3–11.
5. "Maritain and Dewan on The Intuition of Being and the Birth of Metaphysics," *The Wisdom of Youth: Essays Inspired by the Early Work*

of Jacques and Raissa Maritain, edited by Travis Dumsday, 147–58 (Washington, DC: American Maritain Association, 2016).

6. "Maritain on the Possibility of a Thomistic Philosophy of History," *Maritain Studies* 39 (2023): 3–12.

The Christian Philosophy of Jacques Maritain

CHAPTER 1

Background

What am I? A convert.
A man God has turned inside out like a glove.
Lettre à Jean Cocteau

Life and Context

Jacques Maritain was born in Paris on November 18, 1882, to Paul and Genevieve Maritain.[1] His father was a lawyer and was the secretary of the renowned French statesman Jules Favre, whose daughter he married. Religion had little place in Jacques's upbringing. Rather,

---

1   Maritain's life has in many ways been more thoroughly studied than his philosophical thought. This is, no doubt, due to his engaging personality, deep friendships, and fascinating life. Much of the biography available is shaped, appropriately, by Raïssa's two memoirs, *We Have Been Friends Together* and *Adventures in Grace,* trans. Julie Kernan (Garden City, NY: Image Books, 1961), as well as Jacques's *Notebooks.* The best scholarly accounts are Jean-Luc Barré, *Beggars from Heaven,* Translated by Bernard E. Doering (Notre Dame, IN: University of Notre Dame Press, 2005), and Henry Bars, *Maritain et notre temps* (Paris: Grasset, 1959). An engaging contemporary account is Julie Kernan, *Our Friend, Jacques Maritain: A Personal Memoir* (New York: Doubleday, 1975). For a brief overview see Ralph McInerny, *The Very Rich Hours of Jacques Maritain: A Spiritual Life* (Notre Dame, IN: University of Notre Dame Press, 2003). Clearly the brevity of the present account makes any attempt at completeness impossible. Likewise the summary of writings makes no claim to completeness; only Maritain's major works are included. Several other collections of essays and lecturers are available in French and English. For an exhaustive bibliography for the years covered, see Donald and Idella Gallagher, *The Achievement of Jacques and Raïssa Maritain: A Bibliography 1906–1961* (Garden City, NY: Doubleday & Co., 1962).

in keeping with the ideals of late nineteenth-century France, it was replaced with an emphasis on service to humanity. Through his mother's circle of friends and his childhood companion Ernest Psichari—who was a grandson of one of the most famous liberal writers in France during the late nineteenth century, Ernest Renan—Jacques was nurtured in a context that prided itself on a commitment to contemporary intellectual life. The concern for the poor and suffering he developed in his youth remained with him his entire life, yet he found the ideas he encountered about the purpose of life and the nature of society inadequate to settle the deep philosophical questions that tortured him.

In the year 1900 Jacques began studying natural sciences at the Sorbonne. At the university he met a young Jewish immigrant woman from Russia named Raïssa Oumansoff, who was destined to become his wife. These kindred spirits were profoundly disillusioned by the materialism they found at the university. Both were students of science with a burning desire to know the truth. Reflecting on these early years much later in life, Raïssa described her experience thus: "before all else, I had to make sure of the essential thing: the possession of the truth about God, about myself, and about the world. It was, I knew the necessary foundation for my life."[2] Jacques shared his future wife's passion for truth, as well as her conviction that the natural sciences were the basic key to all knowledge. Of course, the professors of science at the Sorbonne—who were generally positivists—would have found such ambitions puzzling, if not downright naïve.

Turning to the study of philosophy, they were still unable to fulfill the longing of their hearts. In Raïssa's view, the philosophers that they encountered at the university "despaired of *truth* whose very name was unlovely to them and could be used only between the quotation marks of a disillusioned smile."[3] The philosophical training that was offered had no higher goal than to use ideas as instruments of rhetoric, leaving students unprepared for the genuine intellectual and moral struggles they would have to face. For his part, Jacques's view of the Sorbonne

2   Raïssa Maritain, *We Have Been Friends Together*, 34.
3   Raïssa Maritain, *We Have Been Friends Together*, 61.

was even more cynical as time progressed. In his private notes we find the following judgment, which gives us a sense of his own impression:

> 10th of April 1906. Philosophers play with fire (poets also). Nothing is as comical as a course at the Sorbonne, in which an enervated professor expounds his historical views to some dunces, and discusses David Hume as peacefully as Plato. Does this seem dead to you? Fortunately, not the slightest spark flies! But just remember all that this has raised up![4]

It comes as no surprise that by the summer of 1901 Jacques and Raïssa were thoroughly disheartened and in despair. In fact, walking together one day they decided that if life, which presented such tormenting questions, could not provide answers, then it was not worth living. As a result of this deep disillusionment, they made a pact with each other to commit suicide together if they did not find any deeper meaning to life within a year: "We wanted to die by a free act if it were impossible to live according to the truth."[5]

Fortunately, their friend Charles Péguy encouraged them to attend the lectures of Henri Bergson. Bergson was an immensely popular philosopher who challenged the positivism of the French intellectual elite, offering a defense of metaphysical knowledge and an understanding of the absolute that opened their eyes to the limits of the materialist positivism common among so many of their professors.[6] This led to a period of intellectual discovery that culminated in their conversion to Catholicism and their mutual study of St. Thomas Aquinas.

After their marriage they lived with Raïssa's sister Vera, who also converted and took care of their practical affairs. The three formed a small community, and from this point on they devoted themselves to a deeply spiritual life, involving a rigorous routine of prayer and study. In 1912 the couple became members of the Third Order Benedictines

---

4   *Notebooks,* 29; also see 10n16.
5   Raïssa Maritain, *We Have Been Friends Together,* 64–68.
6   See Bergson, *Introduction to Metaphysics,* trans. T. E. Hulme (Indianapolis: Hackett Publications, 1999) and *Creative Evolution.* Translated by Arthur Mitchell. (New York: Random House, 1944).

and took a private vow of celibacy in order to commit themselves more fully to study and contemplative prayer. Raïssa, who frequently suffered from health problems, devoted much of her days to prayer and writing poetry. From this time on she had intensely mystical experiences.[7] At the prompting of her spiritual director, Raïssa began to read Aquinas's *Summa Theologiae* while she was recovering from illness. Jacques, though busy with his editorial work, began studying Aquinas shortly after her. Although he had initially thought his conversion to Catholicism might require him to give up his intellectual life as a philosopher, he soon realized his new faith actually deepened his intellectual vision.[8]

The Maritains' discovery of St. Thomas Aquinas occurred at the high point of the Thomist revival within the Catholic Church. In 1879 Pope Leo XIII published the influential encyclical *Aeternae Patris* on the restoration of Christian philosophy. In the midst of the challenges facing the Church, from rationalism to secular humanism and beyond, the Pope urged a return to the thought of St. Thomas Aquinas. The encyclical set out a two-fold project of recovery. The first aspect was a deeper study of Aquinas's writings and the development of a new modern edition. The second was a new engagement between Thomism, modern philosophy, and science. Initially this project was carried out primarily in Catholic seminaries, but by the twentieth century its influence had spread, and a new generation of non-clerical scholars, like Jacques Maritain and Étienne Gilson, began to play leading roles.[9]

---

7   Raïssa's deep interior life of prayer was captured in her notebooks, which Jacques discovered after her death and published posthumously as *Raïssa's Journal* because of the importance of their teaching on the spiritual life. For a full study of her life and thought, see Brenna Moore, *Sacred Dread: Raïssa Maritain, the Allure of Suffering, and the French Catholic Revival (1905–1944)* (Notre Dame, IN: University of Notre Dame Press, 2013).

8   In fact, while he passed his final aggregation in philosophy he did very poorly on the oral examination, while succeeding strongly on the written part. In a letter to his professor, Lévy-Bruhl, he implies the reasons he was given for this: he had "too subtle a mind" and "too refined thought." More substantially he notes the examiners disagreed with his approach to Descartes, quoting Professor Darlu, "If you adopt a philosophy that seeks things more than words, and that believes reality is inexpressible, then why enter a contest to fight with words?" Jacques & Raïssa Maritain, *Lettres Intimes*, 1901–1932, T. 1, ed. Dominique et Rene Mougel (Paris: Éditions Desclée de Brouwer, 2023), letter 12, 35n1. The full letter to Lévy-Bruhl is published in *Revue philosophique de la France et de l'etranger* 178, no. 4 (1989). See Raïssa Maritain, *We Have Been Friends Together*, 142.

9   The history of this development and the various approaches to Thomism that emerged has been studied by Gerald A. McCool, SJ. The early reception of *Aeternae Patris* is presented in

With this growing interest, opportunities arose that allowed Maritain to become not only a highly regarded philosopher, but one of the first of what we would now call public intellectuals. In fact, for much of the twentieth century, he was the leading representative of the Catholic Church in the mind of the general public. The other great lay Thomist of this time, Gilson, was better known among scholars for his work in the history of philosophy and his contributions to founding the Pontifical Institute of Mediaeval Studies in Toronto.

Clearly, Maritain's philosophy was not simply an abstract theory constructed apart from his lived experience. Rather, his thought organically grew out of the way that he lived. Maritain's philosophy was the fruit borne from his very life. As Raïssa expressed it:

> 12th April 1934.—Everything that is in Jacques's work we have first lived in the form of a vital difficulty, in the form of experience— problems of art and morality, of philosophy, of faith, of prayer, of contemplation.
>
> All this has been given to us first of all to *live*, each according to his nature and according to God's grace.
>
> (We began by knowing through experience the absence of truth. Afterwards we began to suffer for it, etc...)
>
> *This goes on.*[10]

Indeed, the Maritains' discovery of St. Thomas in the midst of the intellectual malaise of early twentieth-century Paris was to provide Jacques with his life's work: the creative retrieval of Aquinas for the world of today.

During his long life, Maritain was a master of the art of friendship and developed a wide circle of friends. Through this network he fostered the study of Thomism, not only among philosophers, but also

---

Nineteenth-Century Scholasticism: The Search for a Unitary Method, 2nd rev. ed. (New York: Fordham University Press, 1999). The second generation of Thomists who emerged at the start of the twentieth century, including Maritain, are explored in his work *From Unity to Pluralism: The Internal Evolution of Thomism* (New York: Fordham University Press, 1999).

10 *Raïssa's Journal*, 235–36. Jacques makes the same point in an essay presented in 1965 when speaking about the privilege Christians have, because in doing philosophy they draw upon an *experience* of living in a confrontation with absolute truth. See "On Truth," in *Untrammeled Approaches*, trans. Bernard Doering, Ernst R. Korn, and Heinz R. Schmitz (Notre Dame, IN: University of Notre Dame Press, 1997, 49.

among prominent artists, writers, politicians and just about everyone with whom he came into contact. Many of these people attended study circles that he and Raïssa hosted in their home. Among his close friends were his and Raïssa's godfather (the novelist Leon Bloy), the painter Georges Rouault, the poets Paul Claudel and Charles Péguy, the writer Jean Cocteau, and the pianist Eric Satie—many of the leading cultural figures in France at the time. Indeed, he also developed friendships with notable American intellectuals, such as the novelist John Howard Griffin and the writer and monk Thomas Merton. His thought also influenced politicians, such as French President Charles De Gaulle and Venezuelan President Rafael Caldera. Nor was his influence restricted to his personal friends; a composer as great as Igor Stravinsky was inspired by Maritain's aesthetics to develop the works of his neoclassical period.[11]

Like his friendships, Maritain's writing reflects his varied interests, and often the circumstances of his life. After marrying he spent two years in Heidelberg studying biology under experimental biologist Hans Driesch. He also worked on an orthographic dictionary and a "dictionary of practical life" to earn money. His first published article appeared in 1910 and developed ideas from Bergson on reason and science. By the time he wrote his first book in 1913, *Bergsonian Philosophy and Thomism*, he was a committed Thomist and launched a searing attack on his former mentor. Later in life he expressed regret for the overzealous nature of his bombastic style, one that characterized a number of his early writings, while upholding the fairness of his book's arguments.[12] In 1914 he was named adjunct professor of modern philosophy at the Institut Catholique and began teaching. In 1918 he became joint

11 On their friendship with Bloy, see *We Have Been Friends Together*, 87–113; on Péguy, 52–55. On Rouault see *Adventures in Grace*, 188–97. On Cocteau see Cornelia A. Tsakiridou, "When Art Fails Humanity: Jacques Maritain on Jean Cocteau, Modernism and the Crisis of European Civilization," in *The Renewal of Civilization*, ed. Galvin T. Colvert (Notre Dame, IN: The American Maritain Association, 2011), 152–73. On Stravinsky see Robert Fallon, "Knowledge and Subjectivity in Maritain, Stravinsky, and Messiaen" in *Jacques Maritain and the Many Ways of Knowing*, ed. Douglas A. Olivant (Notre Dame, IN: The American Maritain Association, 2002), 284–302.

12 "Preface to the Second Edition," *Bergsonian Philosophy and Thomism*, Vol. 1 of *The Collected Works of Jacques Maritain*, ed. Ralph McInerny (Notre Dame, IN: University of Notre Dame Press, 2007), 12. See also Francesca Aran Murphy, *Art and Intellect in the Philosophy of Étienne Gilson* (Columbia: University of Missouri Press, 2004), 30–32.

heir with Charles Maurras to a modest fortune left by a man who was spiritually moved by his correspondence with Maritain.[13] This liberated Jacques from having to teach in order to focus on his writing until well into the 1940s, although he still taught the occasional course. He then took the 1918–1919 academic year off to write the first volumes of a series of philosophy textbooks at the request of the French bishops. Only two volumes of this series were ever completed (*Introduction to Philosophy* and *Formal Logic*). There followed an impressive series of publications, including *Art and Scholasticism* (1920), *Theonas* (1921), *Prayer and Intelligence* (with Raïssa in 1922), *Antimodern* (1922), *Réflexions sur l'intelligence et sur sa vie propre* (1924). During this time Jacques and Raïssa began "Thomist Circles," in which a wide range of significant intellectuals and artists met at their home in Meudon to study and discuss Thomistic philosophy. Jacques also became more associated in the political movement Action Français, a right-wing monarchist party led by Maurras. Like many Catholics of the time, Maritain supported the movement, as its policies included the restoration of Roman Catholicism as a state religion. Maurras, however, was an atheist, and likely anti-Semitic, but was sympathetic to the Church simply as an instrument of social order. Consequently, Action Français was condemned on December 20th, 1926, by Pope Pius XI for its utilitarian views of religion as a force of social cohesion and for its problematic influence on youth. Maritain quickly accepted this judgment, recognizing the naiveté of his earlier political position, and rejected his prior association with the movement. This prompted him to write the first of what would become many books on political philosophy, titled *The Things that are not Caesar's* (1927). He then took a leave from teaching between 1929 and 1930 to write his magnum opus *Distinguish to Unite, or The Degrees of Knowledge* (1932). Around this time also appeared *The Angelic Doctor* and *Religion and Culture* (1930), *The Dream of Descartes* (1932), *An Essay on Christian Philosophy* (1932), *Preface to Metaphysics* (1933), *Frontiers of Poetry* (1935), *Science and Wisdom* (1935), and *Philosophy*

---

13 The inheritance was the family fortune of Pierre Villard. For this interesting correspondence, see *Notebooks*, 101–32.

of Nature (1935). This remarkably productive period culminated in his masterpiece on politics and culture, *Integral Humanism* (1936).

This often-frantic pace of writing is explained by Maritain's friend and colleague Yves Simon, who notes that Maritain received many invitations to speak and, feeling he was poor at speaking extemporaneously, wrote out his lectures word for word. Once the lecture was given, he would correct and expand it before publishing it as a journal article. Over time a group of articles on related themes would be reworked for publication as a book. This helps to explain why many of his works can seem to lack unity. *The Degrees of Knowledge*, for example, is not so much a unified monograph as a collection of papers written on related topics, as it was not conceived as a unified systematic treatise. This process is evident in a number of Maritain's best-known works.[14]

When France fell during World War II, the Maritains were fortunately in the United States, where Jacques was lecturing, and they remained there for the duration of the German occupation. This exile had a deep effect, especially on Raïssa, who struggled in English, missed France, and did not have the same kind of practical commitments that kept Jacques frantically busy. This led her to write her memoirs *We Have Been Friends Together* (1941) and *Adventures in Grace* (1945). The poignancy with which the Maritains experienced this profound crisis is movingly expressed in the opening lines of her first book:

> July 6th 1940. There is no longer any future for me in this world. Life for me draws to a close, ended by the catastrophe that has plunged France into mourning, and with France, the world, or at least all those in France and in the world who treasure the human and divine values of free intelligence, wise liberty and universal charity. Not for a long time—perhaps never again—shall our eyes behold our beloved France.[15]

---

14 Yves Simon, "Jacques Maritain: The Growth of a Christian Philosopher," in *Jacques Maritain: The Man and His Achievement*, ed. Joseph W. Evans (New York: Sheed & Ward, 1953), 9. Simon was a significant Thomist philosopher in his own right who developed his thought in a manner that generally complimented Maritain's philosophy. See *An Yves R. Simon Reader: The Philosopher's Calling*, ed. Michael D. Torre (Notre Dame, IN: University of Notre Dame Press, 2021).

15 Raïssa Maritain, *We Have Been Friends Together*, 11.

With *Integral Humanism*, and the opening of World War II, Jacques's attention and writing naturally turned more towards political affairs, as he wrote *Natural Rights and Natural Law* (1942), *Christianity and Democracy* (1943), and *Education at the Crossroads* (1943). His work on this area reflected a greater openness to the insights of modern political theory as he developed defenses of human rights and democracy from his Thomistic principles. When the Spanish Civil War broke out, Maritain refused to support Franco, in contrast to many French Catholics. As a result, his friendship with his mentor Fr. Garrigou-Lagrange, who attempted ordering him to avoid writing about politics and stick to metaphysics, was considerably strained. Moreover, there were attempts in the Holy Office to have *Integral Humanism* placed on the Index of Forbidden Books—which were only avoided when Cardinal Montini, the future Pope Paul VI, intervened personally with Pope Pius XII on Maritain's behalf.[16]

Maritain also worked actively to help war refugees to the United States and gave radio broadcasts to support the war effort, while teaching at Princeton University and lecturing widely in North America. After the war he served as the French ambassador to the Vatican from 1944 to 1947. Even in this challenging position, he found time to write one of his most profound works of metaphysics, *Existence and the Existent* (1947). Upon completing his term as ambassador he returned to his writing, publishing *Man and State* (1951), *Creative Intuition in Art and Poetry* (1953), *Approaches to God* (1953), *Reflections on America* (1957), *Liturgy and Contemplation* (with Raïssa 1959), and *Moral Philosophy* (1960).

At this time the Maritains returned to France where Jacques's beloved Raïssa was to die on July 7, 1960. After her death Jacques visited the United States and then went to live with a religious community, the Little Brothers of Jesus near Toulouse, where he was to spend the rest of his life giving conferences in philosophy to the community. Many

---

16 Philippe Chenaux, "Maritain devant le Saint-Office: Le rôle du père Garrigou-Lagrange, OP," *Archivum Fratrum Praedicatorum,* Novum Series VI (2001): 401–20.

of these were published posthumously in the collection *Untrammeled Approaches* (1973).

Maritain's thought was one of many important factors influencing the Second Vatican Council, a multi-year series of meetings of Catholic bishops and other representatives. The council developed a series of documents that changed the tone of the Church's relation to the modern world from one of hostility to one of dialogue and cooperation. During the council there were renewed attempts by political conservatives to get *Integral Humanism* placed on the Index of Forbidden Books, while progressives tended to want to leave the Thomism of the earlier generation behind. Accordingly, Maritain was somewhat alienated from many of the current trends of thought in the Church. Nevertheless, he was frequently consulted by Pope Paul VI, who was himself a self-proclaimed disciple of Maritain and translator of his books into Italian.[17] As a layman Maritain could not directly intervene in the council, but the Pope asked him for his views on topics that were to be discussed in the last sessions, and the elderly philosopher provided his views in a series of four notes in the spring of 1965. The first three related to the publication of an encyclical on truth, the notion of religious freedom in civil society, and the apostolate of the laity. The last addressed liturgical reform and private prayer; it was the longest of the notes and offered concise criticisms on the French translations of liturgical texts, as well as suggestions for ecclesiastical studies.[18] Maritain also provided the first draft of what was later published with some amendments by the pope as the *Credo of the People of God*.[19] At the conclusion of the council, Paul VI chose Maritain to receive the Church's message to intellectuals. At this point many philosophers and theologians in the Church had

17 A very good account of the friendship between Maritain and Pope Paul VI and his influence upon the pontiff's thought can be found in Catherine M. A. McCauliff, "Jacques Maritain's Embrace of Religious Pluralism and the Declaration on Religious Freedom," *Seton Hall Law Review* 41, no. 2 (2011): 596–602.

18 "Quatre memorandums," in Jacques and Raïssa Maritain, *Oeuvres completes*, vol. 16 (Fribourg: Éditions Saint-Paul, 1999), 1085–130. See Giuseppe Alberigo and Joseph A. Komonchak, eds., *History of Vatican II*, vol. V (Maryknoll, NY: Orbis Books, 2006), 548–49.

19 Gianni Valente, "Paul VI, Maritain and the Faith of the Apostles: An Interview with Georges Cardinal Cottier," *30 Days* no. 4, 2008. https://www.30giorni.it/articoli_id_17898_l3.htm.

turned away from Thomism, the liturgy and vocations were in crisis, and many had left the priesthood and abandoned their vows to religious life. These upheavals greatly pained Maritain, who responded with one of his best-selling books, *The Peasant of the Garonne* (1966), in which he lauded the council's teachings while offering a scathing criticism of their reception in the academy and the Church. Although he intended this to be his last book, he published two other, more theological works: *On the Grace and Humanity of Christ* (1967) and *The Church of Christ* (1970). Jacques passed away in Toulouse on April 28, 1973, at the age of 90, and was buried with Raïssa in Kolbsheim. In the 1954 preface written for the publication of his *Notebooks* he summed up his own appraisal of his life and vocation. It makes a fitting note on which to end this brief account of his remarkable life:

> What am I, I asked myself then. A professor? I think not; I taught by necessity. A writer? Perhaps. A philosopher? I hope so. But also a kind of romantic of justice too prompt to imagine to himself, at each combat entered into, that justice and truth will have their day among men. And also perhaps a kind of spring-finder who presses his ear to the ground in order to hear the sound of hidden springs, and of invisible germinations. And also perhaps, like every Christian, despite and in the midst of the miseries and the failures and all the graces betrayed of which I am becoming conscious in the evening of my life, a beggar of Heaven disguised as a man of the world, a kind of secret agent of the King of Kings in the territories of the prince of this world, taking his risks like Kipling's cat, who walked by himself.[20]

Christian Philosophy

Maritain's fundamental approach to philosophy can be characterized in terms of three basic qualities: it is (1) rational, (2) Thomistic, and (3) Christian. In his early *Introduction to Philosophy,* he offers a fairly standard definition of philosophy:

20 *Notebooks*, Preface.

> Philosophy is the science which by the natural light of reason stud-
> ies the first causes or highest principles of all things—is, in other
> words, the science of things in their first causes, in so far as these
> belong to the natural order.[21]

Several elements of this definition call for explanation. First of all, the term *science* is used in the classical sense of the Latin term *scientia*, rather than in the standard modern usage, according to which science is identified with the natural sciences. In this classical use of the term, something is a science when it is a body of knowledge that is derived from reasoning on the basis of indisputable self-evident first principles. Further, philosophy is said to follow from the natural light of reason in order to distinguish it from sacred theology, which argues from revealed principles held on faith that are neither self-evident to us nor demon-strated from more basic truths.

Finally, philosophy studies first causes. This is to say that philosophy is not concerned with the most evident and tangible aspects of things, but rather with their most fundamental causes and natures. This is why almost any aspect of reality can fall under the study of philosophy. The philosopher of nature, for instance, studies the same objects as the phys-icist. However, the philosopher does so in a unique (i.e., philosophical) way. The physicist will be interested in aspects of motion, how velocity relates to mass and force, for instance. In studying experimental results, it is unlikely that the physicist will ask, "What is motion?," "What is the most fundamental nature of matter?," or "Why do any material beings exist in the first place?" Of course, there is nothing to prevent the phys-icist from attempting to develop answers to such questions, but the moment she does so she is acting as a philosopher and will need to be judged by philosophical rather than scientific criteria. It is the philoso-pher who studies these most fundamental features of things, and since any aspect of reality can be approached in this way, nothing falls outside the scope of the philosopher's investigations. Yet since philosophy stud-ies everything in accordance with its own proper method (i.e., in terms

---

21 *Introduction to Philosophy*, trans. E. I. Watkin (London: Sheed and Ward, 1944), 69.

of first causes), it does not absorb the other disciplines into itself, but leaves them autonomous in their respective spheres.[22]

As the above definition implies, philosophy is an activity of reason. It is not merely a checklist of claims that happen to be true. It is a deep inquiry to the very roots of an issue in order to understand why they are true. According to Maritain, this may occur in two spheres. In speculative philosophy, such as metaphysics or philosophy of nature, the philosopher's aim is quite simply to grasp what is true. In practical philosophy, such as ethics or political theory, the aim is not merely to know the truth but to know the truth in order to be able to act upon it. Here Maritain fully endorses Aristotle's observation that we ought to study ethics not only to know what is good, but also to become good. Maritain was well aware that in our industrial and consumer-oriented society, philosophy could well look like a waste of time. He was painfully aware that many would ask what the use of reflecting upon abstract truths could be. Would it not be better to have bright young men and woman study something practical like medicine, engineering, or law?

Maritain begins his reply in a rather unusual way. Instead of providing a list of practical uses for philosophy, he insists that philosophy—especially in its speculative form—is indeed useless. This is not meant in the pejorative sense that it is good for nothing, but rather in the literal sense that it is without, or beyond, use. Philosophy is not merely an instrument to be used to attain something else. Rather, it is desirable for its own sake. As Maritain argues:

> What is the use of philosophy? Philosophy, taken in itself, is above utility. And for this very reason philosophy is of the utmost necessity for men. It reminds them of the supreme utility of those things which do not deal with means, but with ends. For men do not live only by bread, vitamins, and technological discoveries.

Rather, human beings exist for a purpose that transcends material necessities and conveniences. We exist not to earn a living; rather, we live in order to grow in virtue and the values of the spirit:

22 *Introduction to Philosophy*, 65–67.

They live by values and realities which are above time, and are worth being known for their own sake; they feed on that invisible food which feeds the life of the spirit, and which makes them aware, not of such or such means at the service of their life, but of their very reasons for living—and suffering, and hoping.[23]

It is a fatal mistake to confuse knowledge and power. Philosophy in its own right must be a disinterested activity. It is directed toward truth for its own sake. Philosophy is not a productive activity to achieve power over things. This is why it is always a deep human need. Nevertheless, philosophers, even if mistaken, provide a service to society. Every philosopher clearly articulates the views of a culture. If these views happen to be correct, they benefit us by providing explicit arguments in favor of our most deeply held convictions. But even if they are wrong—as many brilliant philosophers undoubtedly are—they are beneficial, for they act like a beacon, warning us to stay clear of the very errors they seek to defend.[24]

On occasion one can get the sense that Maritain thinks achieving certainty and agreement in philosophy is easy, but nothing could be further from the truth. While Maritain asserts that philosophy does develop a body of knowledge, he is not naive about the prospects of getting philosophers to agree. Philosophies are often as individual as fingerprints. Even those within the same general school of thought, such as Thomism, bitterly dispute among themselves a wide range of fundamental theses. For Maritain, this was the ordinary condition of philosophy and followed from its very nature. Christian and non-Christian philosophers, with hard work, may at times find a mutual understanding and do justice to one another's intellectual positions, but we should not expect complete agreement:

In this sense the tension between Christian and non-Christian philosophies can never be overcome. We may be sorry about that, but we should not be too sorry; for, in a general way, be they

23 *The Use of Philosophy* (Princeton, NJ: Princeton University Press, 1961), 6–7. Also see *Untrammeled Approaches*, 52.

24 *The Use of Philosophy*, 5.

> Christian or non-Christian philosophers, the natural condition of any philosopher seems to imply that he can be in agreement only with himself. Even this kind of agreement seems rather difficult, and due to some infrequent piece of luck.[25]

Clearly, this is not the writing of someone overconfident about philosophy's ability to secure the agreement of all reasonable people. But why do mathematics and the sciences seem able to provide definitive advances, while philosophers are still working away at the problems posed by Plato and the ancient Greeks? Maritain's reply is to develop a distinction between a problem and a mystery that he borrows from the Christian existentialist Gabriel Marcel. Some questions present themselves to us as a problem which is to be definitively solved. If one does a crossword puzzle, each clue has a right answer, and once you have solved the puzzle the questions cease to hold any fascination for the mind. Other issues, such as the nature of the human good, the meaning of suffering, or the nature of reality, do not have definitive "right" answers that settle these issues for every reasonable person. These are not problems to be solved, but mysteries to be pondered. In this sense, a mystery is not utterly unintelligible; rather, it is grasped only in a progressive and continually deepening way. A mystery is not resolved once and for all, nor is it supplanted the way a slower computer is rendered obsolete by new technology. In cases where the intelligibility of the object we ponder is too rich for the human mind to grasp completely, the aspect of mystery predominates. Although in every issue we study there is a mixture of both problem and mystery, one may play a more significant role than the other. In the sciences, it is often the problem aspect that is dominant, while in philosophy it tends to be the mystery which takes precedence: "A philosophy unaware of mystery would not be a philosophy."[26] This is why one can be a scientist without being a historian of science, whereas it is usually impossible for a philosopher

---

25 "About Christian Philosophy," in *Challenges and Renewals*, eds. Joseph Evans and Leo Ward (Notre Dame, IN: University of Notre Dame Press, 1966), 115.

26 *A Preface to Metaphysics: Seven Lectures on Being* (New York and London: Sheed and Ward, 1939), 13.

to make any headway without some awareness of the history of the discipline.[27]

In the domains of morals and politics, philosophy is needed gravely. A culture may suffer from a split between its ideals, which provide its reasons for living and acting, and the inner cast of mind of the people who happen to be in doubt and insecure about the ideals that hold sway in their community. They may still be willing to live up to these ideals and even sacrifice for them, yet be unable to offer a rational justification for them:

> Such a situation is possible; it cannot last. A time will come when people will give up in practical existence those values about which they no longer have any intellectual conviction. Hence we real- ize how necessary the function of a sound moral philosophy is in human society. It has to give, or to give back, to society intellectual faith in the value of its ideals.[28]

Consequently, Maritain does not view the philosopher's vocation as that of an isolated intellectual working out theories in an ivory tower. Rather, he sees the philosopher as someone who is deeply engaged in his culture, and yet one who can transcend this culture through a dis- interested inquiry into truth.

Indeed, Maritain's project can be seen as an attempt to restore intel- lectual faith in the value of the ideals of Thomism and Christianity. In this regard, he is sometimes dismissed as a mere partisan, someone who defended an indefensible theory, namely Thomism, out of loyalty to the Church. While Maritain was certainly a faithful Catholic, this criticism is unjust. He repeatedly asserts that we do not turn to Aquinas as a pious authority to find out what we should think. Rather, we turn to Aquinas because his views are often true, and most importantly, because the arguments he gives lead us to see that they are true.[29]

27 *A Preface to Metaphysics*, 12–19.
28 *The Use of Philosophy*, 12.
29 *St. Thomas Aquinas*, trans. Peter O' Reilly and Joseph W. Evans, (New York: Meridian Books, 1958), 19.

For Maritain the question is never "Is this what Aquinas said?" Rather, it is always "What is the truth about the issue we are studying?" Accordingly, any criticism of Thomism worth taking seriously must be based on an assessment of the arguments it offers. In fact, there is a great deal to learn from Maritain, whether one is a Catholic or not. One should not accept or reject any philosophy on the basis of labels or intellectual fashions:

> One is not a Thomist because, in the emporium of systems, one chooses it as if one were choosing one system among others just as you try one pair of shoes after another in a shoe store until you find a pattern that fits your foot better. If that were the way it was done, it would be more stimulating to cut a system to one's own measure.[30]

Such an approach would completely misconstrue the nature and purpose of Thomistic philosophy. Its aim is not merely to put ideas together into a logically coherent or even a pleasing or persuasive form. Rather, its first task is to listen to, and observe, what really is the case in order to articulate the fundamental principles that can lead us to the truth:

> One is a Thomist because one has repudiated every attempt to find philosophical truth in any system fabricated by an individual and because one wants to seek out what is true— for oneself, indeed, and by one's own reason—by allowing oneself to be taught by the whole range of human thought, in order not to neglect anything of that which is.[31]

Accordingly, it is not out of love for Aristotle or Aquinas that one is a philosophical realist. Rather, it is because one has a desire to know the real as it is that one turns to these masters of wisdom for guidance:

> Aristotle and St. Thomas occupy a privileged place for us only because, thanks to their supreme docility to the lessons of the real, we find in them the principles and the scale of values through

---

30 *Degrees of Knowledge*, xiii–xiv.
31 Ibid.

which the total effort of this universal thought can be preserved without running the risk of eclecticism and confusion.[32]

Nevertheless, Maritain clearly saw the thought of Aquinas as an exemplar of the perennial philosophy. By the perennial philosophy Thomists have generally meant three things. First, there is a set of historically ever-recurring questions about reality, knowledge, and goodness. Second, Thomism offers an always relevant and valid set of answers to these questions. Third, these answers form an integrated and coherent philosophical system that organically develops over time as it generates new insights and addresses new problems. Accordingly, other philosophers before and since Aquinas have certainly discovered truths, but the great strength of Aquinas's philosophy is that he put the truths that others taught in a piecemeal fashion together into a coherent and intelligible whole capable of organically integrating whatever new truths we might find into itself.

Although Maritain is a Thomist, he never restricts himself to offering a mere exegesis of the master's texts. This sort of work is necessary and important, but it is mere archaeology: "Thomism does not want a return to the Middle Ages."[33] Rather, Maritain presents a creative retrieval of Aquinas's thought for today. Maritain rethinks the entire philosophical tradition in light of *both* Aquinas *and* the needs of the present time. In his work one comes into contact with the great minds of the past, and in dialogue with them discovers solutions to the problems that are facing us here and now.

Maritain's turn to Aquinas is not a call to go back to the dark ages. If one of his earliest books was entitled *Antimodern*, even within its pages he noted that his view could be just as legitimately called ultra-modern. His contempt was only directed towards modern self-complacency and spiritual hypocrisy:

---

32 Ibid. He also states this point succinctly elsewhere, writing, "Not a whimsy spun out of his own brain, but the entire universe with its enormous multitude and variety of data must be the philosopher's teacher." *Introduction to Philosophy*, 96.

33 *St. Thomas Aquinas*, 18. On Thomism as the perennial philosophy, see also "Letter on Philosophy at the Time of the Council," in *Untrammeled Approaches*, 64.

But if it is a matter of saving and assimilating all the riches of being which are accumulated in modern times, of desiring renewals, and of loving the effort of those who continue to pioneer and break new ground, then I wish nothing so much as to be ultra-modern.[34]

Maritain is convinced that even in the ebb and flow of history one can grasp a wisdom that is not rooted in time but is immutable, and that this wisdom does not call for a halt to history but actually contributes to its progress. Thus, the attention he gives to Aquinas does not stem from a desire to go back to medieval times, but is a plea to see today for ourselves the very same eternal truths that were beheld by the thirteenth-century friar, so that we might come to share in a wisdom that transcends time.

Clearly, Maritain does not separate his philosophy from his faith. Being a genuine philosopher, his arguments are always open to assessment on the basis of reason alone. He is, therefore, concerned to preserve the philosophical integrity of his arguments. However, since the philosopher is also a complete person, non-philosophical factors such as the historical, social, and religious context in which he finds himself may offer insights that will help to develop his philosophy.

Maritain refined his views on the relationship between Christianity and philosophy in a debate that raged among French Catholic philosophers in the 1930s. For him this was not merely an academic debate over terminology (as even Étienne Gilson, the leading protagonist of Christian philosophy, came to think towards the end of his life). In fact, Maritain went so far as to say, "The more I think about this problem of Christian philosophy the more it appears a central point of the history of our time since the Renaissance: and probably as the central point of the history of the age to come."[35] The debate began with papers presented between 1930 and 1931, in which Émile Bréhier argued that the two concepts— "Christian" and "Philosophy"—were mutually incompatible.

---

34 *Antimoderne* (Paris: Éditions de Revue des Jeunes, 1922) quoted in *St. Thomas Aquinas,* 18. Also see *Science and Wisdom,* trans. Bernard Wall (New York: Charles Scribner's Sons, 1940), 32.

35 *Science and Wisdom,* 129.

It makes no more sense, Bréhier asserted, to speak of a Christian philosophy than it does to refer to a Christian mathematics or physics.[36] For him philosophy is based upon "clear and distinct ideas," while Christianity is concerned with what is authoritatively revealed. On this view, the idea of Christian philosophy is as nonsensical as wooden iron, to borrow Heidegger's much-quoted phrase.[37] Most of the leading Catholic intellectuals of the day took sides for or against Bréhier's thesis. Some, like Fr. F. Van Steenberghen, endorsed it in an attempt to show that the Christian was a philosopher just like anyone else.[38] The most prominent critic of Bréhier was the Thomist and historian of philosophy Étienne Gilson, for whom the concept of Christian philosophy was to become a central preoccupation reappearing in many of his writings. Gilson was a very highly regarded historian of philosophy, renowned for his writings on Aquinas and other figures of the Middle Ages. His works aimed to show that the view of a perennial philosophy throughout the major scholastics was too simplistic, and that each had unique philosophical positions. He is often seen as the leading figure in the "existential Thomist" school, due to his view that Aquinas's emphasis on being was fundamentally original and distinctive. In Gilson's view, the primary failure in the history of philosophy was essentialism, the tendency to try to explain being as if it were just another essence or concept.[39]

36 See Émile Bréhier, "Y a-t-il une philosophie chrétienne?" *Revue de métaphysique et de morale* 38 (1931): 162; and "La notion de philosophie chrétienne," *Bulletin de la Société française de Philosophie* 31 (1931): 49.

37 On this consequence of Bréhier's argument I follow the interpretation of Fr. Joseph Owens, CSsR, "Introduction," *Towards a Christian Philosophy* (Washington, DC: The Catholic University of America Press, 1990), 6–7.

38 See also Fernand Van Steenberghen, "La IIe Journée d'études de la Société Thomiste et la notion de philosophie chrétienne," *Revue néo-Scolastique* 35 (1933): 544–54; and "Étienne Gilson, historien de la pensée médiévale," *Revue Philosophique de Louvain* 77 (1979): 493–507. Van Steenberghen was an important Thomist philosopher at l'Institut supérieur de philosophie at l'université catholique de Louvain. This university was strongly influenced by Cardinal Mercier (1851–1926), who initiated a school of Thomism focused on bringing Aquinas's thought into dialogue with modern academic disciplines and the sciences.

39 The best biography of Gilson is Laurence K. Shook, CSB, *Étienne Gilson* (Toronto: Pontifical Institute of Medieaeval Studies, 1984). A good account of his thought as a philosopher and historian is Francesca Aran Murphy, *Art and Intellect in the Philosophy of Étienne Gilson* (Columbia: University of Missouri Press, 2004). The fullest account of his metaphysics is found in Étienne Gilson, *Being and Some Philosophers* (Toronto: Pontifical Institute of Mediaeval Studies, 1961).

One of Gilson's first and most interesting attempts to formulate an account of the concept of Christian philosophy is found in his renowned Gifford Lectures of 1931 and 1932, published as *The Spirit of Medieval Philosophy*. In this work he argued that if one traces the history of philosophy, one finds that it undergoes a radical transformation between the Greek and modern periods, which is to be accounted for by its contact with revelation in the Middle Ages. Through this encounter with revelation, Christians practicing philosophy were prompted by the contemplation of revelation to make properly philosophical discoveries by way of natural reason that they would never have imagined if left to their own devices.[40] In light of his historical discovery of genuine philosophical progress through insights prompted by revelation, Gilson defined Christian philosophy in the following terms:

> I call Christian, *every philosophy which, although keeping the two orders formally distinct, nevertheless considers Christian revelation as an indispensable auxiliary to reason.*[41]

This account includes two important factors. First, Christian philosophy retains the integrity of a philosophical discipline *formally distinct* from the order of revelation which is dealt with in theology. In this matter Gilson was always deeply concerned to maintain an adequate distinction between faith and reason. The second point is that revelation is an *indispensable auxiliary* to Christian philosophy. These two considerations are closely related, for while the first preserves the distinction between the philosophical and the theological, the second shows the importance of the latter for the former. Revealed doctrine may force us to rethink our philosophical positions, but these teachings remain properly philosophical in that they do not permit the use of any appeal to revelation in establishing their philosophical starting points, premises, and conclusions. For Gilson, faith does not provide the philosophical starting points; rather, it merely offers guidance through which

---

40 Étienne Gilson, *The Spirit of Medieval Philosophy*, trans. A.H.C. Downes (New York.: Charles Scribner's Sons, 1940), 12.

41 Gilson, *The Spirit of Medieval Philosophy*, 37. Emphasis in the original in this and all quotations unless otherwise noted.

philosophy is better able to make use of its own resources. Hence, revelation is not used to justify the doctrine and its procedure remains purely philosophical. Yet, this forms a new kind of philosophy, insofar as its starting points are reached in a distinctive way.[42]

It must be noted that Gilson's resolution of the Christian philosophy paradox was predominantly historical. He intended to prove that a distinctly Christian philosophy did exist in the Middle Ages. In the midst of the above debate, Maritain attempted to offer a doctrinal solution to the problem, introducing an important distinction in support of Gilson. He argued that an adequate understanding of the dilemma concerning Christian philosophy required a distinction between the *nature* of philosophy and the *state* in which it is actually embodied in historical practice. By the term "nature" he intended to signify the essence of philosophy, or what it is in the abstract. Considered in this way, philosophy is wholly rational and is specified by its formal object, that is its formal method.[43] However, Maritain noted that in order to adequately understand what Christian philosophy is, one had to also consider its state. On this point he concurred with Gilson—there was a distinctively Christian state of philosophy that became a historical reality in the writers of the Middle Ages; a philosophy that, though prompted to new discoveries by revelation, succeeds in articulating them in a thoroughly philosophical manner.[44] This is simply a philosophy that is situated in the climate of explicit faith and grace.[45]

This distinction between nature and state allows Maritain to argue that the Christian philosopher is genuinely a philosopher, while also insisting that a Christian cannot simply ignore what she knows about reality through her faith when she starts doing philosophy. This is not of as much significance in matters of science in the modern sense, where the state of the inquirer is largely irrelevant to the object under

---

42 See also Owens, "Introduction," 26.

43 *An Essay on Christian Philosophy*, trans. Edward H. Flannery (New York: The Philosophical Library, 1955), 15.

44 *An Essay on Christian Philosophy*, 18. The distinction is also discussed in *Science and Wisdom*, 79, and "About Christian Philosophy," in *Challenges and Renewals*, 109–14.

45 *Science and Wisdom*, 78.

consideration. Yet, Maritain certainly agrees with Gilson that historically some aspects of revelation prompted philosophical discoveries.

This Christian influence applies not only to the state of the individual inquirer, but to the discipline of philosophy itself as practiced in a
Christian context. There are not only Christian philosophers; there is
also a Christian philosophy. This is to say that the state of philosophy
changes in a Christian milieu, for it can no longer be taken to be sufficient to know all there is to be naturally known. Christianity recognizes
a field that can only be apprehended through revelation and theology.
This means both that the knowledge of philosophy is radically limited,
and that there is an alternative means for accessing what philosophy
cannot know. Ancient Greek philosophers such as Plato and Aristotle
may well have realized we cannot learn all there is to know about God
through philosophy. But they had no other method to appeal to in order
to know this. In this way the state of philosophy is different precisely
because it is practiced in light of Christianity.[46]

Furthermore, this Christian influence is vital when we approach
questions of wisdom, especially in the practical spheres of ethics and
politics.[47] If we are subject to original sin, then that ought to make a difference to our understanding of the moral life. If the ultimate goal of the
human person is to know God, then that fact has profound implications
for the way we understand human knowing. In fact, as we shall see in the
chapter on ethics, Maritain situates his entire approach to moral philosophy in the context of this doctrine of Christian philosophy, developing
his distinctive account of "moral philosophy adequately considered."[48]

The Christian philosopher ignores the teaching of faith at his peril,
for as Maritain sees it, Christian faith does not undermine his philosophy, but assists it to reach its own proper goal.[49] Accordingly, his
approach to philosophy remains purely rational without being separated from faith. Maritain describes it by saying,

---

46 *An Essay on Christian Philosophy*, 26–27 and 46.
47 See "About Christian Philosophy."
48 *An Essay on Christian Philosophy*, 38.
49 *The Degrees of Knowledge*, xi.

> Christian philosophy is philosophy itself in so far as it is situated in those utterly distinctive conditions of existence and exercise into which Christianity has ushered the thinking subject, and as a result of which philosophy perceives certain objects validly demonstrates certain propositions which in any other circumstances would to a greater or lesser degree elude it.[50]

However, this integration between philosophy and Christianity was, naturally, a common theme of all those who defended the concept of Christian philosophy, and it was a notable part of Gilson's pioneering defense. Maritain's distinctive contribution to the debate of the 1930s on the question of Christian philosophy shows him to be especially attentive to the unique and subjective conditions in which each philosopher finds himself. This refusal to rest content with the formal doctrine of a philosophical theory and demand that attention be given to the subjective conditions in which philosophy is practiced is one the most important and original aspects of his thought. It is precisely the Christian's lived experience of faith that provides the source of a unique advantage when it comes to philosophizing. In a late essay "Concerning Truth," Maritain begins his exploration by highlighting this theme:

> In our reflections on truth I think it is fitting to begin from the top, with supernaturally revealed Truth. This is normal from the point of view of Christian thought. It is normal, for anyone who has received the gift of faith, to begin these kinds of reflections with faith, with what is highest and most precious in our intellectual equipment. The Christian has the privilege of finding himself face to face with *absolute Truth*, of that Truth which is God Himself, and of God Himself revealing Himself.

Accordingly, a Christian approach to philosophy can never be content with merely impersonal abstractions. At its very root it is born of the philosopher's own experience, particularly his or her experience of God and the depths of the spiritual life. Having experienced these truths, they can then be conceptualized, demonstrated, and explained philosophically:

---

50 *An Essay on Christian Philosophy*, 30.

> In adhering to this absolute Truth the Christian will bring into play, spontaneously and in lived actuality, *in actu exercito*, those great things about truth which philosophy discovers on its own, when it understands for example that truth is the adequation of the intellect and the real, or that being is the proper object of the intelligence, which finds its life and its freedom in adhering to it.
>
> Philosophy knows these things *in actu signato*, in signified act or by way of conceptualization. But there is an enormous advantage in having lived, in having experienced in exercised act these great themes concerning truth before conceptualizing them philosophically.[51]

In some ways we might say that the attention Maritain consistently gives to the philosopher as a subject caught up in a particular and unique state is a leitmotif of his philosophy, and we will see it arising again and again. This is likely the reason that led him to see the problems brought up in this scholarly dispute on the topic of Christian philosophy as "the central point" of modern history and of the age to come. Indeed, his answer to this dispute highlights, in many ways, the aspect of Maritain's approach to philosophy that gave him the means to definitively bring Thomism out of the Middle Ages to compete as a viable philosophy in the contemporary world—a world whose philosophy is typically characterized by a turn towards the subject.

51 "On Truth," in *Untrammeled Approaches*, 49. See also Lawrence Dewan, OP, "St. Thomas and the Renewal of Metaphysics," in *The Vocation of the Catholic Philosopher*, ed. John P. Hittinger (Washington, DC: The Catholic University of America Press, 2010), 176–79.

CHAPTER 2

Epistemology

Rationalism dreams a great deal; because reason left to itself asks
only to sleep the sleep of the senses. It stirs in its sleep; the flash
of a human glance gleams on the side of a heap of torpor, that
mischievous genii weary with illusions. If Christian philosophy
remains more awake, if in it reason comes out of the shadows of
an "admirable science" to adhere to the real with all its strength,
it is because an ardor for being far sharper than the ardor which
springs from reason's sole resources inwardly stimulates it.

The Dream of Descartes, 160

Maritain's Analysis of Modernity

Rejecting the pretensions of modern rationalism and the Enlightenment has become commonplace and even trendy among
many philosophers in recent decades, whether it be among
the founders of postmodern thought such as Adorno, Derrida,
and Feyerabend, or among Catholic thinkers as varied as Charles Taylor, Alasdair MacIntyre, or Jean-Luc Marion.[1] Long before it became

---

1   See Max Horkheimer and Theodor W. Adorno, *Dialectics of Enlightenment* (New York: Continuum International Publishing Group, 1973); Paul Feyerabend, *Against Method*, 3rd ed. (New
York: Verso, 1993); Ulrike Oudée Dünkelsbühler, *Reframing the Frame of Reason: "Trans-Lation"*

fashionable, Jacques Maritain had offered a sustained critique of both Cartesian rationalism and the Enlightenment project that found its epitome in the work of Immanuel Kant. Maritain's position is unique in that it clearly avoids the anti-epistemological tenor which is common to many contemporary Enlightenment critics. While contemporary philosophers often use the critique of the Enlightenment to simply dismiss epistemological starting points, in order to turn more directly to social analysis and criticism or ethics, Maritain argues not for a rejection of epistemology, but for a reformulation of the entire epistemological problematic. In this way, he aims to avoid the Cartesian and Kantian framework to offer a more complete and realistic theory of knowledge than the early modern philosophers uncovered.

For Maritain the central problem of modernity has its origins in Descartes's philosophical project.[2] As every student of philosophy knows, Descartes developed a method of systematic doubt in order to arrive at a firm foundation for philosophy: those truths, whatever they may be, which cannot possibly be doubted. Appealing to the difficulty of knowing whether or not you are dreaming, he argues that we cannot trust our sense experience. After all, no matter how compelling our experience is, we might always be dreaming. He then dispenses with necessary truths of mathematics and basic realities such as color and shape, which hold even in dreams, by appealing to the possibility of an evil genius. This would be a malevolent and omnipotent being that uses all of his power to deceive me. Descartes argues such a being could deceive us even about these apparently necessary truths.[3] His method is analogous to that of a farmer who, upon finding that some of the apples in his barrel are rotten, decides to dump them all out and put back only

---

in and Beyond Kant and Derrida, trans. Max Statkiewicz (New York: Humanity Books, 2002); Charles Taylor, "Overcoming Epistemology," in Philosophical Arguments (Cambridge, MA: Harvard University Press, 1995), 1–20; Alasdair MacIntyre, After Virtue, 2nd ed. (Notre Dame, IN: University of Notre Dame Press, 1984), 51–61; and Jean-Luc Marion, On Descartes' Metaphysical Prism (Chicago: University of Chicago Press, 1999).

2   See Three Reformers: Luther, Descartes, Rousseau (New York: Charles Scribner's Sons, 1929), 53–89. Also, The Dream of Descartes, trans. Mabelle L. Andison. (NY: The Philosophical Library, 1944)

3   Descartes, "Meditations on First Philosophy" in The Philosophical Writings of Descartes, Vol. II, trans. John Cottingham, et al. (Cambridge: Cambridge University Press, 1984), 36.

those that are good. In a similar way, having found some erroneous ideas, Descartes dispenses with all of them in order to ensure that only those that are incapable of error are accepted from this point onwards. This entails a method of beginning from concepts rather than things that Descartes bequeathed to the modern world.

While Descartes certainly wanted to reinstate sense experience and necessary truths as reliable, Maritain takes issue with the entire methodology, since it severs the intellect from its proper object, the intelligible being of things. As he forthrightly puts it: "Descartes unveiled the face of the monster which modern idealism adores under the name Thought."[4] Once one began from concepts in the mind, the challenge became to build a bridge from the mind and its concepts back to external reality in such a way as to ensure genuine knowledge. In freeing thought from things, Descartes was guilty of what Maritain dubbed "the sin of angelism." Whereas the human intellect naturally formulates concepts by abstracting from its sense experience of material things, Descartes maintains that our knowledge of primary truths is intuitive in its mode, innate in its origin, and independent of things in its nature. Maritain points out that these are the attributes traditionally assigned to angelic—not human—knowing. The knowledge of human beings, unlike angels, always originates from sense experience—there is nothing in the mind which was not first in the senses.[5] Accordingly, Maritain argues that Descartes presumes the human intellect can begin from starting points better suited to angels than human beings. For him this was the problematic that dominated modern philosophy after Descartes to the time of Kant and even beyond. Kant's "Critical Project" in philosophy furthered the Cartesian move away from realism, insisting that philosophy begin from an assessment of the limitations of knowledge, and thus with an account of the mind and the appearances of things within the mind. As a result, no claims to know things in themselves are legitimate and we are left merely with knowledge of the way things appear and the laws of possible experience.

4   *Three Reformers*, 54.
5   *Three Reformers*, 57.

These were trends that reemerged in the twentieth century through Neo-Kantians such as Edouard le Roy and Léon Brunschvicg, who argued that fundamental first principles such as the law of identity and non-contradiction were merely laws of thought and language, not laws of being. But more importantly, these themes were central to the phenomenological movement initiated by Husserl. Husserl's method of ἐποχή (or "bracketing") was a contemporary development of Cartesian doubt and Kantian critique, which bracketed the thing in itself at the starting point of philosophical investigation, in order to allow for a purely phenomenological analysis of our experience.[6]

By the end of his career Maritain went so far as to argue that intellectuals who follow the Cartesian path by beginning with concepts within the mind, rather than extramental beings known through sense experience and their natures, are not really philosophers, but "ideosophers." While he admires the genius of these great intellects, they have made a fatal mistake by separating the intellect from the only light that can lead it to truth—namely, the intelligible being and nature of material things:

> Of all the thinkers—and great thinkers—whose lineage has its origin in Descartes, I contest neither the exceptional intelligence, nor the importance, nor the worth, nor, at times, the genius. In regard to them I challenge only one thing, but that I challenge with might and main, and with the certainty of being right: namely, their right to the name of philosopher (except, of course, Bergson, and perhaps also Blondel). In dealing with these children of Descartes we must sweep away this name with the back of our hand. They are not philosophers; they are *ideosophers*: that is the only name which fits and by which it is proper to call them. It is in no way pejorative of itself, it merely designates *another* way of research and thought than the philosophic one.[7]

---

6 For a detailed examination of Maritain's criticisms of Husserl, see Léon Charette, "La phenomenology et la théorie de l'abstraction selon Jacques Maritain," in *Jacques Maritain: Philosophe dans la cité* (Ottawa: University of Ottawa Press, 1985), 103–12.

7 *The Peasant of the Garonne: An Old Layman Questions Himself about the Present Time*, trans. Micheal Cuddihy and Elizabeth Hughes (New York: Holt, Rinehart, and Winston, 1968), 101–2.

His point is, of course, that philosophy has as its origin and goal knowledge of what is or what can be, whereas the ideosopher's wisdom pertains only to ideas and their interrelationships.

While Maritain is clearly a strong critic of modernity, it would be a mistake to think that he simply rejects it out of hand in order to return to medieval Thomistic orthodoxy. Nor has he any interest in superficially resurrecting old ideas under the cover of fashionable contemporary terminology. To the contrary, he appropriates the truths he finds hidden in the works of the scholastic tradition in order to apply them to the contemporary context in new, and often insightful, ways. As he often puts it, the truth is eternal and, consequently, it is always up-to-date. Furthermore, we should not overlook the fact that the problems of the philosophers he attacks so forcefully do their part to shape and form his own application of Thomistic thought in the contemporary circumstances in which he found himself.[8] Indeed, several of the main features of his epistemology—such as the distinction between thing and object, the account of the concept as a formal sign, and connaturality—are articulated in dialogue with problems in which the resources of modern philosophy were so limited they had seemed intractable. By bringing Thomism to bear on these challenges, Maritain attempted to open fresh avenues to approach them. Further, as I noted above, Maritain is by no means a forerunner of the postmodern rejection of epistemology. Rather, he argues for an epistemology that is firmly situated within metaphysics, and which begins by articulating and defending the natural metaphysics of the human mind, the classical realism found in Aristotle and St. Thomas. Yet he recovers this thought in a way that can be heard and applied in the contemporary world.

Critical Realism

Maritain referred to his epistemology as a form of "critical realism." This realism penetrates all of his philosophical inquiries, so it is appropriate

8   Nikolaj Zunic, "Method in Philosophy: Maritain's Engagement with Modernity," *Maritain Studies* 22 (2006): 44–48.

to begin our study of his thought with a careful consideration of these issues. Maritain's philosophy is realist in the sense that he argues for a view that we can accurately know the extramental world through our sense experience and concepts. Moreover, the mind not only knows external objects, but also essences, the principles of intelligibility that frame the range of potentiality that these objects can instantiate. Further, he situates epistemology within metaphysics, rather than viewing it as an independent discipline that one must pass through first in order to enter legitimately into philosophical studies.[9] He thinks that realism proposed in this way is also genuinely critical. Yet, he certainly does not mean this in the Kantian sense of critique (see chapter one), whereby we have to first prove that our knowledge is possible. Any project of that sort would be, in Maritain's view, doomed to failure, as it would ask us to demonstrate the possibility of the mind's ability to know without making use of any of the ordinary means through which it comes to know. Instead, his realist philosophy is critical in the sense that it shows how our knowledge can be philosophically justified in a manner that is rationally superior to competing idealistic accounts of knowledge. This is to say that it is not merely the naive realism of common sense, but rather that same realism purified through philosophical evaluation and justification.

Yet Maritain's defense of critical realism ran counter to the views of some of his contemporaries, even among Thomists. The Thomist historian of philosophy Étienne Gilson, for example, provided a powerful argument against the critical realism of many of the leading Thomists of the day, including Maritain. Gilson was concerned with the trend of presenting Thomist realism in a Cartesian light, in order to meet the need for a critical starting point. Gilson charged neo-scholastic authors with adding a critical epistemology along the lines of Descartes's *cogito* argument prior to any substantive philosophical investigations. Gilson's main concern was to show that this project was utterly incoherent. The lack of a critical justification of realism in St. Thomas was not merely

---

9   *The Range of Reason* (New York: Charles Scribner's Sons, 1952), 25.

a lacuna waiting to be filled. Rather, the critical project, Gilson argued, was inimical to the immediate realism of St. Thomas.[10]

For Gilson, the approach of St. Thomas and that of critical philosophy indicate two distinct and irreconcilable methods. Aquinas, following Aristotle, begins with individual things existing outside of the mind and provides an account of the mind and its acts of knowing in light of these objects. Descartes, by contrast, attempts to start with concepts, and from these he tries to prove the existence of the external world and its correspondence to our ideas. According to Gilson, the failure of Descartes's project is not merely an empirical fact in the history of philosophy; rather, that failure was inevitable, for the problem he had set himself was essentially insoluble.[11] Any attempt to begin from concepts within the mind, can only hope to end with concepts within the mind, as Kant correctly recognized. Thus, Gilson leaves us with two alternatives—Kant's critical philosophy and Thomist realism—each of which has a distinctive set of starting points which logically demand a corresponding set of equally irreconcilable conclusions. Thus, in his book *The Christian Philosophy of St. Thomas Aquinas*, Gilson writes:

> If we suppose first that things are for themselves and the intellect is for itself, that is, if we suppose that it is impossible for them to meet, then there is no bridge to allow thought to cross over to things, and Idealism is true. It is contradictory to ask whether our ideas conform to things, if things are not known to us save through their ideas. Such an argument is irrefutable, and here again Idealism is true, unless indeed the argument begs the question.[12]

---

10 Étienne Gilson, *Methodical Realism,* trans. Philip Trower (San Francisco: Ignatius Press, 2011), 88–90. Parts of this section are developed from material in my article "Gilson, Maritain, and Garrigou-Lagrange on the Possibility of Critical Realism," *Maritain Studies* XVII (2001): 49–69. For an overview of the critical realism debate see Francesca Aran Murphy, *Art and Intellect in the Philosophy of* Étienne *Gilson* (Columbia: University of Missouri Press, 2004), 142–72. A useful comparison of the difference between Gilson and Maritain is Raymond Dennehy, "Maritain's Reply to Gilson's Rejection of Critical Realism," in *A Thomistic Tapestry: Essays in Memory of Étienne Gilson,* ed. Peter A. Redpath (New York: Rodopi, 2003), 57–80.

11 Gilson, *Thomist Realism and the Critique of Knowledge,* trans. Mark Wauck (San Francisco: Ignatius Press, 1986), 114.

12 Gilson, *The Christian Philosophy of St. Thomas Aquinas,* trans. Laurence Shook, CSB (New York: Random House, 1994), 234.

As Gilson sees it, Kant's idealistic philosophy follows rigorously from its starting points, so the only alternative is to show that its starting points are not binding. This is indeed what Gilson goes on to argue: "To demand that St. Thomas refute Kant's Critique is to ask him to solve a problem which from his point of view simply cannot exist."[13] Notice that this solution is not historical but philosophical. Gilson's point is not that St. Thomas did not answer the critical question because it had not yet been posed, but rather that, given the starting points of Thomistic philosophy, such a question cannot arise in principle.

In this light it is easy to understand why Gilson would view a critical realism as an oxymoron. According to him, a "critical philosophy" was one which, by definition, started with our concepts. The point of the critique is to begin philosophizing with an investigation of the operations and concepts of the mind and then work one's way out to reality. Certainly, Gilson conceded, one might apply the term "critical" to one's realism in another sense, but the only other meaning it could have was to indicate that one's philosophy was not a naive realism—one of unreflective common sense—but rather, a rationally justified realism. But this use of the term adds nothing to the notion of realism. It is simply to say that one's realism is philosophical.[14]

As a criticism of the use of quasi-Cartesian methods to answer Kant's critical question and reach Thomistic conclusions, Gilson's argument appears to be unimpeachable. Certainly, a philosophy which begins from concepts in the mind in order to prove the existence of the object which corresponds to these concepts is incompatible with, indeed the very contradiction of, the thought of St. Thomas. However, as a criticism of the idealistic method itself, it hardly goes far enough. Gilson's position refutes realists who use idealistic methods. However, it leaves those who are happy to restrict themselves to drawing idealistic conclusions from these same principles untouched. Gilson may have closed the door to Descartes, but he leaves it open for Kant.

---

13   Gilson, *The Christian Philosophy of St. Thomas Aquinas*, 234.
14   Gilson, *Thomist Realism*, 51–52.

Maritain states his disagreement with Gilson in diplomatic terms, framing it as a merely terminological difference. But I would argue that their differences go far beyond that. Indeed, the implication of Gilson's position seems to be that one can quite legitimately philosophize as an idealist, so long as one is a thoroughgoing idealist. The reason for this view is to be found in his claim that philosophers are at liberty to choose their principles, so long as they accept the consequences of this choice. Gilson writes that "philosophers are free to lay down their own sets of principles, but once this is done they no longer think as they wish—they think as they can."[15] There is clearly a tension between Gilson's adherence to realism and his view that philosophers are at liberty to choose their own principles. This becomes evident in the "Preface" to *Being and Some Philosophers*, in which he argues that those who *believe* the philosophy they teach do not *know* it. Notice how Gilson states his case:

> The only will that should be found at the origin of philosophy should be the will to know, and this is why nothing is more important for a philosopher than the *choice* he makes of his own philosophical principles.[16]

This is exactly the approach that Gilson takes when he comes to the issue of idealism versus realism, for he argues that one cannot begin philosophizing without adopting either one stance or the other. Thus, Gilson presents us with a *choice* between the principles of idealism and realism. This entails two things: (1) that we choose prior to philosophical proof, and (2) once this choice is made, we are committed to adhere to the consequences of our initial decision.

On the surface this sounds perfectly consistent with realism. The only place for the will in philosophy is the will to know. Nothing could more accurately express the spirit of Thomist realism. Yet, Gilson's claim that philosophers can freely choose their principles would naturally lead him to reject the possibility of a "critical realism" as developed by Jacques Maritain—for this is a philosophy which claims not only to

---

15 Étienne Gilson, *The Unity of Philosophical Experience* (New York: Charles Scribner's Sons, 1937), 301–2.

16 Gilson, *Being and Some Philosophers*, ix.

refute the use of idealistic principles by would-be realists, but also to uncover the internal incoherence of those very principles.

Consequently, there are two related problems with Gilson's approach in light of Maritain's epistemology: (1) he does not provide a substantial response to idealism, and (2) he holds that a philosopher is free to adopt his own set of principles. The first follows directly from the second. More generally, both of these positions are, I think, a result of his rejection of the possibility of a critical realism. While Maritain has some kind words for Gilson's arguments against idealism, ultimately he judges his approach to be insufficient.[17] Whereas Gilson goes on to say that the philosopher chooses his principles, and that he is at liberty to choose them as he likes, Maritain would insist that a philosopher does not choose principles at all, but knows them.[18]

In his attack on critical realism, Gilson suggested two possibilities for such a project. It must either pose the same problem as Kant's, or demonstrate that there is a critical problem distinct from both Kant's and the simple reaffirmation of dogmatic realism.[19] Maritain clearly opts for the latter alternative. In his view, modern thinkers from Descartes to Kant (and beyond) put philosophy on the wrong track precisely by incorrectly formulating the critical question. As he puts it in *The Degrees of Knowledge*:

---

17 *The Degrees of Knowledge*, 76–77.

18 See Fr. Lawrence Dewan, OP, "History of Philosophy, Personal or Impersonal?: Reflections on Étienne Gilson," *Maritain Studies* XI (1995): 23ff. Fr. Joseph Owens, CSsR has developed Gilson's position into a full-scale theory of philosophical pluralism in order to further the defense of a distinctively Christian philosophy. Thus, he writes, "No philosophy can force any other philosophy to accept the philosophy's own starting points. In the genial atmosphere of today's pluralism, this is an attitude that has every right to claim universal acceptance." "The Need for Christian Philosophy," *Faith and Philosophy* 11, no. 2 (1994): 180. Among his many writings on this topic, see also Joseph Owens, "Aquinas and Philosophical Pluralism," in *Some Philosophical Issues in Moral Matters: The Collected Ethical Writings of Joseph Owens* ed. D. J. Billy and Terence Kennedy (Roma: Editiones Acadamiae Alphonsianae, 1996), esp. 449. Fr. Owens was a student of Gilson who became a prominent scholar defending and developing his mentor's vision of Existential Thomism. For a more detailed discussion and critique of Fr. Owens's account of philosophical pluralism in the context of his defense of Christian philosophy see my paper, "The Thomistic Debate Concerning the Existence and Nature of Christian Philosophy: Towards a Synthesis," *The Modern Schoolman* LXXVII, no. 1 (1999): 54–60.

19 Gilson, *Thomist Realism*, 154.

The critical problem is not: "How does one pass from *percipi* (having perceived) to *esse* (being)? Since mind is the only object attained in a way that is beyond doubt, can it be demonstrated that mind also reaches things, a reality that measures it?" No!

Accordingly, Kant's way of framing the question at the heart of the critical project is simply misguided. We cannot ask about the movement of the mind from what has been perceived to being in a context in which the only object that can be attained directly without doubt is the mind itself. The manner in which the problem has been articulated is biased and can do nothing but generate an idealist answer. The solution to this quandary is not an eclectic hybrid of Kantian or Transcendental Thomism, but a properly realist formulation of the critical question, which is what Maritain goes on to do in the conclusion of this passage:

It is, rather, to be stated in these terms: "On the different levels of elaborating knowledge, what value must be assigned to *percipere* (perceiving) and what to *judicare* (judging)? Since the mind, from the very start, reveals itself as warranted in its certitude by things and measured by an *esse* (being) independent of itself, how are we to judge if, how, on what conditions, and to what extent it is so both in principle and in the various moments of human knowledge?"[20]

The importance of this text cannot be overemphasized, for here the entire problematic of modern philosophy has been resituated. This is accomplished by showing that there is a critical problem for the realist to answer which is different from Kant's and that it concerns the value to be assigned to the knowledge gained from perception, understanding, and judgment. In Maritain's thought the apprehension of being is manifest right from the start of the intellectual life. It is futile to engage in a debate as to whether or not this is the case. The real question is how and to what extent this apprehension of real beings is justified.

Accordingly, Maritain completely repudiates any form of philosophical idealism. Any theory that denies that the mind has for its proper object the real extramental being of things is, in his view, simply

20 *The Degrees of Knowledge*, 77–78. Also see *Bergsonian Philosophy and Thomism*, 65.

impossible, even on its own terms. Kant's demand that we justify the human ability to know before accepting any claims to knowledge is not only false, but radically incoherent:

> It is absurd to demand that philosophical thought begin, even before it knows anything validly, by proving that it can know (for it could do so only if it did know). It is absurd to suppose at the very start that anything which cannot help but be judged true by the mind can, as a result of some evil genius, not be true, so that then that self-same mind might be asked to show that, as a matter of fact, it is not so. It is absurd to admit that the mind could only attain phenomenal objects and then ask it to prove that such objects are extra mental realities.[21]

Realism can thereby defend its claim that any attempt to justify our knowledge beginning from concepts within the mind, rather than real extramental beings, is methodologically doomed to failure. The incoherence in question follows whether the methodology to start from ideas is proposed in a Cartesian, Kantian, or phenomenological manner. This line of argumentation is fully sufficient to warrant the title "critical." Thus, critical realism is justified philosophically on the grounds that "The mind must rather be led consciously to recognize the fact that idealism is an absolute impossibility—impossible in itself."[22]

---

21 *The Degrees of Knowledge*, 78; see also 114–18.

22 *The Degrees of Knowledge*, 77. John F. X. Knasas has argued that Maritain in fact adopts the same method as the so-called transcendental Thomists in his refutation of idealism. These Thomists were strongly influenced by Kantian methodology and sought to begin philosophy from a conceptual framework, while opening out toward more realist conclusions than idealists would admit. Theologians such as Joseph Maréchal, Karl Rahner, and Bernard Lonergan found in the intellect's dynamism towards being the foundational factor for our conscious awareness of being. Accordingly, they made use of what they called the "retorsion argument" or "performative self-contradiction." This is an *a priori* argument directed towards showing the ineluctability of being in our intellectual experience. One cannot deny the role of being without affirming it. This argument is drawn from Aristotle's and Aquinas's defense of the principle of non-contradiction. Knasas points out, rightly, that those Aristotle had argued against were all realists. He was not arguing against modern idealists who wanted to restrict the law of non-contradiction to the mind alone. Rather, he was arguing against realists who thought that an analysis of change revealed real contradictions in the physical world. Thus, he takes the transcendental Thomist appropriation of these arguments to restrict philosophical idealism to be anachronistic and levels this criticism against Maritain as well. For Knasas, no *a priori* argument of this kind is legitimate. See John F. X. Knasas, "Transcendental Thomist Methodology and Maritain's 'Critical Realism,'" in *Jacques Maritain and the Many Ways of Knowing*, ed. Douglas A. Olivant (Notre Dame, IN: The American Maritain Association, 2002), 66–77; Joseph Maréchal, *A Maréchal*

Since any attempt to justify our knowing faculties independent of the actually successful cases of knowing we have all found in our experience is inconsistent, realism as the appropriate theory of knowledge is critically justified as the natural metaphysics of the human mind. Accordingly, Maritain's concept of critique differs radically from any form of idealism or phenomenology, insofar as it is fundamentally reflexive in nature. This means that the intellect in its act of knowing, having already known real things in the world, bends back upon itself to consider its own operations in knowing. Hence, Maritain's critical project is rooted in an assessment of already achieved instances of knowledge: first we know things, and then in light of this act we come to know our own act of knowing. Our knowledge of knowing is utterly reflexive and secondary to these everyday and scientific cases of knowledge that we all have had in differing ways before coming to philosophy.[23] The critical starting point for philosophy is not, therefore, the Cartesian *cogito*, the awareness that I think. Rather, philosophy's point of departure is the realization that what is *is*—which is to say, cognition is an awareness of being. In view of this Maritain suggests *scio aliquid esse* (I know that something exists or can exist) as an alternative to Descartes's foundational principle *cogito ergo sum* (I think, therefore, I am). Maritain's starting point involves first and foremost the object of the mind (i.e. something that exists), and secondarily a reflexive awareness on the part of the mind which bends back to reflect upon its act of knowing.[24]

Central to Maritain's realism is the view that being is the first and formal object of the intellect. He defends this strong version of realism by asking if there is something present in our cognitive awareness of each and every thing. His reply is affirmative. Anything that we consider

---

Reader, ed. Joseph Donceel (New York: Herder and Herder, 1970), 215–17, 227–28; Karl Rahner, "Aquinas: The Nature of Truth," *Continuum* 2 (1964): 69; and Bernard Lonergan, *Insight: A Study of Human Understanding,* ed. Frederick E. Crowe and Robert M. Doran (Toronto: The University of Toronto Press, 1992), 376. However, it should be noted that Maritain's reasoning here is primarily concerned with refuting Idealist philosophies by unmasking the incoherence in their starting points. Contrary to Knasas's suggestion, he does not attempt to establish an *a priori* knowledge of being apart from sense experience as a starting point for metaphysics.

23 *The Degrees of Knowledge,* 79.
24 *The Degrees of Knowledge,* 80–81.

is either a being or some mode of being. No matter what we think about—be it a mule, a geometrical point, or a glass of wine—there is implicit in that awareness the fact that what we consider is a being or a mode of being. Being is the one and only thing that is present in all of the things we cognize, at least in this implicit manner. As Maritain puts it:

> Whatever I know by my intellect, there is always some being or mode of being present to my mind. There is, however, nothing else except being which is always present in this way. If, for example, I think of a quality, a magnitude, or a substance, in all these cases alike I think of some being or mode of being; but there is nothing except being which is common to these three objects of thought, and therefore present in all three alike. We therefore conclude that being is the formal object of the intellect, that is to say, the object which it apprehends primarily and in itself (*per se primo*) and in function of which it apprehends everything else.[25]

Being is implicit in our thought about all things, thus it is a basic ground upon which all our knowledge is based. The first and formal object of the intellect is, therefore, the intelligible being and nature of material things: "Being in its own proper mystery."[26]

Maritain defends rooting his theory of knowledge in being by clarifying the relation between the knower and what is known. He addresses this through his distinction between the thing and the object.[27] For the modern philosopher it is very natural to think about the object as the thing known in contrast with the knowing subject. But this leads to a serious problem when the properties of the thing pass on to the object, as when we speak of objective truths in contrast to subjective ones. This is too simplistic and has caused considerable confusion.[28] It also leads to what Maritain calls "the tragedy of the modern noetic" in which the object of thought is separated from the thing existing in the world.[29] By

---

25 *Introduction to Philosophy,* 132.

26 Jacques Maritain, *Science and Wisdom,* 23–24. *A Preface to Metaphysics,* 12.

27 See John J. Fitzgerald, "Maritain's Critical Realism," in *Jacques Maritain: The Man and His Achievement,* ed. Joseph Evans (New York: Sheed & Ward, 1953), 61–65.

28 *The Degrees of Knowledge,* 96–97.

29 *The Degrees of Knowledge,* 97.

contrast, for Maritain there can be no question of this kind of separation between the two. The thing is the reality that is known by us, considered in its extramental status as a reality existing in its own right. The object is that very same thing, but considered in its relation to the knower as something which is known. There is no question of two realities here. The thing and the object are different aspects, or ways, of considering what is in reality identical. On the one hand we consider the thing-as-thing; on the other we consider the thing-as-object.

The modern idealist—using that term in the broad sense of one who begins from concepts in the mind rather than with things—thinks of the object as a pure object cut off from anything in which it exists. But once this happens, the whole question of how to find a bridge between the object we know and the thing it represents arises. This means that one is condemned to the Sisyphean task of rebuilding the thing starting from the object (Descartes, Locke, Kant et al.) or else denying the thing altogether (Berkeley and Hume). The solution is to avoid making the fatal mistake of separating the object from the thing in the first place. As Maritain argues:

> We must say that this is a basic mistake. Philosophical reflection has neither to reconstitute the *thing* starting with the *object* as a necessary hypothesis, nor to suppress the *thing* as a superfluous thesis. Such a thesis is even self-contradictory.

Such approaches are reflective of the phenomenological and idealist traditions respectively. If we start from the object, we will find it is not possible to reconstruct the thing on that basis. Likewise, if we reject the thing as superfluous, we will have no way to account for the diverse objects that perception and conceptualization present to us. The solution is rather to be found in a philosophical realism that affirms that the thing is given with and through its object, and that any attempt to separate them is incoherent:

> *Philosophical reflection has to affirm that the thing is given with and by the object, and that it is even absurd to wish to separate them.* On this point, a truly critical critique of knowledge, a critique that

is fully faithful to the immediate data of reflexive intuition, is in accord with common sense in providing an apology for the *thing*.[30]

For Maritain the thing and object are grasped by the mind at one and the same time by the very same perceptions. Consequently, there can be no possibility of separating them. For something to be an object is for it to be the term of a relation of knowledge for a knowing subject. But this entails that the object be more than just an object. For it to be a term in such a relation it must exist; that is to say, it must exist as a thing in its own right. This is not at all to say that the thing lies hidden behind the object. To the contrary, the thing is itself grasped as an object. At the same time, as far as the knower is concerned, the thing is more than that object, for there remains the possibility for other new objects to be grasped in it by taking up differing perspectives toward the thing.[31] Take an example of simple sense perception. I can view a cup of coffee from a distance; thus it becomes an object for me in one sense. But I can also look at it from differing perspectives, I can touch it and feel its warmth, or I can taste it and sense its bitterness. Each of these perspectives presents one and the same thing to me as diverse objects. In such a manner the thing always transcends the object without ever being different or separate from it. This awareness of the thing is implied in every act of knowing. If a mind truly attains an object it must attain its first and proper object, a real or at least potential being. This leads to the foundation of the act of knowing in being, for merely considering of the principle of identity, that each thing is what it is, requires that one posit extramental being as at least possible:

> A prime object, intelligible extramental being without which nothing is intelligible: that is the irrefutable factual datum that is thrust upon the intellect in the heart of its reflection wherein it becomes aware of its own movement towards the object. That apprehension of being is absolutely first and is implied in all other intellectual apprehensions. [32]

---

30 *The Degrees of Knowledge*, 99. Emphasis in original in first quotation but added in second. On this argument see also John C. Cahalan, "Thing and Object in Maritain," *The Thomist* 59, no. 1 (1995): 21–24.

31 *The Degrees of Knowledge*, 99.

32 *The Degrees of Knowledge*, 100.

This awareness of being is often not explicitly realized or brought to the level of conscious awareness. The child who forms the judgment "This is a glass of milk" is not necessarily a prodigy destined to become a metaphysician. The awareness of being that this common-sense judgment implies is a knowledge that lies hidden in the inner recesses of the intellect's basic activity. Although it is present right from the start of our intellectual life, it remains unformulated unless we engage in explicitly philosophical reflection upon the life of the mind: "Realism is lived by the intellect before being recognized by it."[33] Accordingly, being is present initially "enveloped or embodied" in the sensible nature, clothed within the different natures we apprehend through sense experience.[34]

To reach being as an object of metaphysics one has to pass from the mere consideration of this or that thing to another higher level, the explicit consideration of being insofar as it is being. Here, being is no longer enclosed in sensible natures, but is considered in the abstract, disengaged and isolated from particularized objects, in order to be considered in its own right in its pure intelligible values.[35] Nevertheless, it is crucial that this process has its origins in the senses: "A metaphysician deprived of the senses or their use, a metaphysician asleep or dreaming, is for St. Thomas a sheer impossibility, a monster, an absurdity."[36]

To use our understanding without the notion of being at work would be an utter impossibility. It would be like saying a knife could cut, without there being any object present that was distinct from the knife to be cut. To separate the mind from being at the outset of the philosophical project is for Maritain a form of intellectual suicide that can only end in skepticism. It is in the intellectual order what the sin against the Holy Spirit is in the spiritual order, the one act which will condemn the whole enterprise of philosophy to inevitable and irredeemable failure.[37]

33 *The Degrees of Knowledge*, 83.
34 *A Preface to Metaphysics*, 25.
35 *A Preface to Metaphysics*, 26. The precise manner in which this is done is discussed in the chapter on metaphysics.
36 *A Preface to Metaphysics*, 29.
37 *The Degrees of Knowledge*, 82; and *Introduction to Philosophy*, 132–33.

The Concept and Semiotics

Maritain develops his theory of knowledge out of a thorough analysis of the place of the concept amongst the mainstream modern philosophers. As we have seen, Descartes plays a key role in this development. According to Maritain's reading, by beginning in the mind Descartes privileged our inner experience over perception, turning the idea into what we know first and foremost. Consequently, the extramental thing was merely something that the idea resembled. This set out the great problematic of modern epistemology, which asked how to show that our ideas and concepts accurately represent things. It is impossible to overestimate the influence of this Cartesian doctrine on the minds of modern philosophers. It is seen perhaps most clearly in the work of John Locke, who holds that what we know is not things, but rather ideas that function as images resembling the things in the world.[38] With this view the problem becomes how to build a bridge between our ideas and reality. Consequently, it is of little surprise that Berkeley and Hume (in his earlier writings), would resolve the tension by denying the existence of a material thing existing independently outside the mind. For Maritain, by contrast, what the mind knows is, and must be, identical with what exists. In knowing the essence of the thing, this very essence comes to exist immaterially within the mind of the knower as a concept through the process of abstraction. For Maritain, the mind *becomes what it knows* in forming the concept which possesses existence within the mind in an immaterial and universal way, which Maritain calls by the scholastic Latin phrase *esse intentionale*. This is not at all the Lockean process of seeing the concept as a kind of picture or mirror in the mind that functions as an image of what exists outside the mind as a thing. That was the fatal mistake Maritain had detected in the works of the early empiricists and idealists. A more appropriate metaphor for what Maritain has in mind would be that of a kettle on a stove. The heat in the water is, qua heat, the very same as the heat in the stove's burner. The heat that arises in the water is not a picture or a copy of the heat that

---

38 Locke, *Essay Concerning Human Understanding* ed. Peter H. Nidditch (Cambridge: Cambridge University Press, 1975), 134.

causes it. Likewise, the concept is not the mirror image of the thing we know; rather, it is really identical with that thing formally. Accordingly, to know a thing requires becoming what one knows intentionally (i.e., immaterially in the order of thought). What we have here are two modes of existence of one and the same form.

This process originates through sense experience, through which the presentative forms which the mind abstracts allow it to form concepts which are the means by which we know things. This involves two aspects. First, through sense experience the mind has the *species impressa,* or presentative form, imposed upon it. These presentative forms are "vicars of the object." Second, it then produces within itself a *species expressa,* which Maritain calls an "elaborated or uttered presentative form." Accordingly, human knowledge begins in a passive moment where the mind receives data from the external world via the senses, but then rises and completes itself in an active moment in which the mind forms the concept through abstraction.[39] In keeping with this account Maritain defines knowing as follows:

> *In short, knowing appears to us to be an immanent and vital operation that essentially consists, not in making, but in being; to be or become a thing—either itself or other things—in a way other than by an existence that actuates a subject.*[40]

Thus the concept is identical with the thing known. More precisely, the form of the thing known is abstracted so that the very same form now exists in the mind in an immaterial manner.

Thus, knowing requires immateriality, as the form of a thing can exist immaterially in the mind as a concept or materially in the thing that it informs. This presentation of the concept is succinctly stated in Maritain's *Formal Logic.* This definition points to a number of factors that he develops elsewhere in his writings on epistemology:

> A concept (or idea) is, therefore, that which the mind produces or expresses within itself—and in which it grasps or apprehends

---

39 "On Human Knowledge," in *The Range of Reason,* 13–14.
40 *The Degrees of Knowledge,* 125. Emphasis added.

a thing. The concept or mental word answers to: 1. A necessity of human intellectual knowledge; for *to be perceived the intelligible object* must be brought in the concept to the ultimate degree of immateriality required by intellection in act. 2. The *fecundity, proper to the intellect,* which seeks naturally to manifest or to "tell itself" what it has just perceived.[41]

According to Maritain, thought requires universality because concepts are arrived at through the process of abstraction, or in Maritain's terminology "eidetic visualization," which leads the mind to apprehend the universal. However, this is not a bland process of merely cutting off the individual features of a thing; neither is it a mechanical routine performed automatically by the mind. From his earliest discussions, Maritain sees the concept as intimately bound up with the mind's intuitive grasp of individuals and as something that the knower must actively work toward. When we see this particular lamp, if we did not move beyond the individual to the universal, we would still see it, but we would be unable to *think it.* The object we sense must be purified from the individual particularities of matter through eidetic visualization, so that its intelligibility, in terms of its essence, may be known immaterially as a universal. In 1929, in the preface to the second edition of his book *Bergsonian Philosophy and Thomism,* he described the process of abstraction eloquently in the context of the mind's discovery of self-evident first principles:

> Any important progress in the sciences of nature depends on intellectual discoveries of such a kind. . . . Nothing shows with greater evidence the vitality, the intuitive energies of the power of abstracting. It is a question of calling forth a brand new Word, never yet conceived, from the dark yet fecund waters which have poured into the soul through the sluice-gates of the senses. Intellect gropes its way, strives, waits; it seeks a gift which will come to it from its nature. It must retain everything it knows about things and forget what it knows about the ideas it has already learned (especially philosophical ideas), plunge into a bath of active forgetting, render soluble and virtual and bring to a state of confused

41 *Formal Logic,* trans. Imelda Choquette (New York: Sheed and Ward, 1937), 17.

vital tension its acquired experience, sympathize with the real as it would in mimicking it. Beneath its inner active light, at some unforeseeable moment of decisive emotion, the coveted idea will be born.[42]

Clearly, it is no mere mechanical separation from particulars carried out by the machinery of the mind that Maritain intends when he speaks of abstraction or—as he more aptly calls it later in his magnum opus *The Degrees of Knowledge*—eidetic visualization.

Since, as we have seen above, to know is to become something other than oneself, this presupposes emerging above matter. The natural object of the human mind is the nature or essence of material things. Accordingly, while the senses perceive aspects of sensible matter, the mind apprehends essences. The form of the material object is abstracted from its matter so as to exist in the mind immaterially or intentionally as what Maritain calls a presentative form or, in scholastic language, an expressed species. The mind *becomes* the other by taking on this presentative form within itself:

> To know does not consist in making anything nor in receiving anything, but in existing in a way better than by the simple fact of being set outside nothingness. Knowing is an active, immaterial superexistence whereby a subject not only exists with an existence limited to what that subject is as a thing enclosed within one genus—as a subject existing for itself—but with an unlimited existence in which by its own activity it is and becomes itself and other things.[43]

Clearly, the horse or building we come to know doesn't exist in our mind according to its own natural being that it possesses in matter. Rather it exists in the minds that know it intentionally. The concept, then, possesses an intentional and immaterial existence that entails a relation to the real, or at least possible, being in the world that we know.

---

42 *Bergsonian Philosophy and Thomism*, 35. See also "On Human Knowledge," *The Range of Reason*, 9.

43 *The Degrees of Knowledge*, 120. See also Gerald B. Phelan, CSB, "Verum Sequitur Esse Rerum," in *G. B. Phelan: Selected Papers*, ed. Arthur G. Kirn, CSB (Toronto: Pontifical Institute of Mediaeval Studies, 1967), 142–45.

This intentional existence doesn't bind up the thing within the limits of its nature as a material thing; rather, it sets it free from these limits to exist in the mind.[44]

The relation of identity between the concept and what is known allows for a clearer articulation of knowing than mainstream modern philosophy has been able to achieve. Maritain explicitly rejects the Lockean doctrine that the objects of our knowledge are ideas in our mind that resemble the things in the world. Maritain will have nothing to do with this "picture" theory of knowledge. Against the empiricist tradition, initiated by Locke, Maritain notes that the concept in our mind is not that which we know (*quod*); rather, it is that by which (*quo*) we know. This is a crucial distinction, for it shows that the proper role of the concept is not to stand in place of the thing. Rather, the concept exists in our mind as both a modification of the knowing subject and as a species or presentative form by means of which (*quo*) we know the thing (*quod*). Accordingly, the concept first and foremost makes known not itself, but the reality in the world as both an object and thing.[45]

The immaterial and presentative aspects of the forms through which we know leads Maritain to consider the concept in terms of a doctrine of signs that he develops out of his reading of John of St. Thomas (or

---

44 *The Degrees of Knowledge*, 121.

45 *The Degrees of Knowledge*, 130 and 416–17. See also Thomas Aquinas, *Summa Theologica.*, I, q. 85, a. 2. This analysis of the concept is very widely held in the Thomistic tradition. One strongly dissenting voice has been John Deely. Deely gives two arguments against Maritain's use of the *quo/quod* distinction. The first is that it misrepresents John of St. Thomas's position, from which Maritain develops it. The second is that it leads to an overly simplistic view, whereby the human mind automatically and infallibly reads off the essence of things in a way which is not true to the difficulty we experience in knowing the essence of material things. See John Deely, *Intentionality and Semiotics* (Scranton, PA: University of Scranton Press, 2007), 66–71. The first objection is a purely historical one which we need not address here. The second objection, however, is false, as Maritain in fact argues that we never have full knowledge of essences. Rather, the essence is something we understand only indirectly through the properties of the thing that are better known to us through our senses:

"As regards physical realities we succeed in attaining quidditative definitions only of ourselves and of things belonging to man. And only of these things can we intelligibly attain the nature to a specific degree. For all the rest of the corporeal world, for everything that is below us, since we are unable to attain a perception of their intelligible structures themselves, we are forced to have recourse to a knowledge inductively built on sensible effects alone, one that does not provide us with the essence, but only with simple outward *signs* of it." *The Degrees of Knowledge*, 34.

For ideas as the object of knowledge in Locke's epistemology see Locke, *Essay Concerning Human Understanding*, ed. Peter H. Nidditch (Cambridge: Cambridge University Press, 1975), IV, I, 1–7.

John Poinsot). This doctrine of signs allows Maritain to explain how the concept makes the object known without itself becoming an object of knowledge in its own right, and thereby landing us in Locke's predicament, in which we don't know *this* dog, but our *idea* of this dog. Maritain defines a sign simply, saying: "A sign is that which represents something other than itself to a knowing power."[46] There are, however, different types of signs, and Maritain emphasizes John of St. Thomas's basic distinction between instrumental and formal signs. An instrumental sign is a thing that is known first in itself and secondarily serves to signify something beyond itself. We are very familiar with these kinds of signs in everyday life—the smoke in the sky that is a sign of fire, for example, or a portrait that is a sign leading the mind to think of the person it represents. In these cases the sign exists and is known in itself, and only as a result of this does it function as a sign. An instrumental sign is in the first place a thing in its own right, and only in second place a signifier. A formal sign, however, is a sign whose entire essence is to act as a sign. Maritain describes it as follows:

> A formal sign is a sign whose whole essence is to signify. It is not an object which, having first, its proper value for us as an object, is found, besides, to signify another object. More exactly, let us say it is something that, before being known as object by a reflective act, is known only by the very knowledge that brings the mind to the object through its mediation. In other words, it is not known by "appearing" as object but by "disappearing" in the face of the object, for its very essence is to bear the mind to something other than itself.[47]

It is precisely the fact that the presentative form is a formal sign of the thing that allows it to be a pure means by which we know (*quo*) and not be what we know (*quod*). Thus, when I know my dog Truffle, it is my dog that I know, not my concept "dog." Likewise when I remember my grandmother, it is not my concept that I remember; rather, I remember

---

46 "Sign and Symbol," in *Ransoming the Time*, trans. Harry Lorin Binsse (New York: Charles Scribner's Sons, 1941), 218.

47 *The Degrees of Knowledge*, 127. See also "Sign and Symbol," 223.

her herself. Nevertheless my concepts "dog" and "grandmother" function as formal signs by means of which I know the things they signify:

> The concept or mental word is not that which is known when our intellect is at work; it is the means whereby intellection takes place. And what we know by that means is the very nature or intelligible determination of an actually or possibly existing thing.[48]

Accordingly, understanding the concept as a formal sign provides the basis for the analysis of the concept as that by which something is known rather than what is known: "The birth of idea, and hence of intellectual life in us, seems bound up with the discovery of the value of meaning of a sign."[49] Further, Maritain holds that presentative forms, known conceptually, are the only realities that are truly formal signs. All other signs that we encounter are instrumental signs. This dissolves the problem of idealism, as idealism holds that what we know are ideas. But if concepts or ideas are purely formal signs, then we know reality through concepts, since in themselves concepts have no formal value. This is also why it is not surprising that it is so easy to confuse the presentative form or concept with an instrumental sign and treat it erroneously as if it were the thing that we know.[50]

Connatural Knowledge

Aside from the above analysis of conceptual forms of knowledge, Maritain also takes pains to develop the idea of connatural knowledge, which he finds present—but underdeveloped—in the writings of Aristotle, Pseudo-Dionysius, and St. Thomas. Connatural knowledge is a kind of knowledge we gain through direct experience, rather than discursive and conceptual analysis. St. Thomas, for instance, explains it by reference to the person who has the virtuous habit of chastity without knowing any of the demonstrations moral philosophers or theologians might give about chastity. Such a person must in some sense know what chastity is,

48 *The Degrees of Knowledge*, 127.
49 "Sign and Symbol," 220.
50 *The Degrees of Knowledge*, 128.

even though the moral science pertaining to chastity is unknown to him or her.[51] It is this kind of knowledge that Maritain has in mind when he speaks about connatural knowledge, which he also refers to as affective knowledge or knowledge by inclination. Connatural knowledge was a central concern for Maritain. As we have seen above, he is certainly not one to undermine the importance of abstraction and conceptual knowledge. However, he was never content with mere abstractions. Rather, he was always aware of the complexities involved in discerning how to apply universal truths to lived historical circumstances.

In fact, Aquinas uses the term *connatural* in a much wider range of senses. It is used to refer to the fact that some things have the same nature,[52] that one being is the connatural principle of the other (e.g., as citizens receive the nature of citizens from their government),[53] or that something is naturally suitable to a being so that it is drawn to that thing (e.g., as a person is naturally drawn towards the object of her appetite). Maritain, however, is focused on connatural *knowledge*. He takes this to mean a kind of knowledge that is "experimental" in nature—that is, that we acquire through experience.[54] Intellectual apprehension alone is inadequate to arrive at this kind of knowledge; it must also involve the will:

> In this knowledge through union or inclination, connaturality or congeniality, the intellect is at play not alone, but together with affective inclinations and dispositions of the will, and is guided and directed by them. It is not rational knowledge, knowledge through the conceptual, logical and discursive exercise of Reason. But it is really and genuinely knowledge, though obscure and perhaps incapable of giving account of itself, or of being translated into words.[55]

---

51   *S.T.*, II-II, q. 45, a. 2 c.

52   *S.T.*, I, q. 108, a. 1 ad 3.

53   *S.T.*, II-II, q. 101, a. 3 c. For a general study of Aquinas's use of the term see Taki Suto, "Virtue and Knowledge: Connatural Knowledge according to Thomas Aquinas," *Review of Metaphysics*, 58, no. 1 (2004): 61–79.

54   *The Degrees of Knowledge*, 263, and *Freedom in the Modern World* in *Integral Humanism, Freedom in the Modern World, and A Letter on Independence*. Rev. ed. Vol. XI of *The Collected Works of Jacques Maritain*, trans. Otto Bird (Notre Dame, IN: Notre Dame University Press, 1996), 15.

55   "On Knowledge through Connaturality," in *The Range of Reason*, 23.

A person cannot explain or defend discursively what they know merely through connaturality, yet their experience tells them that it is so. This has an important place in practical knowledge, which is ordered towards doing, whether it be moral or aesthetic. For in these cases the proof of the action is in the doing. We are all aware of plain people who live morally outstanding lives without philosophy and artists who are able to produce great works of art while being utterly incapable of formulating or discussing the aesthetic principles underlying them. Conversely, an ethicist may know all about the virtues, yet fail to be virtuous. Connatural knowledge is so important in these matters because conceptual knowledge concerns the universal, while action takes place in the realm of the concrete and individual, as well as in relationships between particular persons.

In a recent article Catherine Green has raised two objections to Maritain's view of connatural knowledge. First, it seems hard to know why connatural knowledge is any different from simple prejudice or bias. It appears that one's instinctive grasp of a moral obligation may more frequently be a matter of unconscious bias than connatural knowledge, and it is not clear how one is to tell the difference. Second, it seems there are examples of experiential knowledge that serve evil purposes (e.g., the intuitive knowledge a scam artist has for a good target), and this seems to call into question the view that connatural goodness is the basis of such moral prudential judgments.[56]

In addressing the first objection, in my view, it should be noted that Green overestimates the degree to which connatural knowledge is non-rational. She refers to it as "a-rational" and quotes Maritain to the effect that it is "not rational knowledge" and "non-conceptual."[57] In

---

56 Catherine Green, "It Takes One to Know One: Connaturality—Knowledge or Prejudice," in *Jacques Maritain and the Many Ways of Knowing,* 44. Green goes on to develop an answer to this objection drawing on Yves Simon's account of connaturality, which emphasizes the role of intentional being in a way that Maritain's does not on 46ff. See Yves R. Simon, *An Introduction to the Metaphysics of Knowledge,* trans. Richard Thompson (New York: Fordham University Press, 1990), 85–90. While this approach is compatible with Maritain's thought, it provides a solution that is highly speculative and complex.

57 Green, "Connaturality—Knowledge or Prejudice," 43–44. That these are not rational and non-conceptual see Maritain, *The Range of Reason,* 23 and 25; that they are nevertheless permeated by reason, see *The Range of Reason,* 27.

fact, Maritain presents connatural knowledge, insofar as it is a mode of knowledge, as an act of inchoate reasoning. As we saw in his critique of Bergson's notion of intuition, Maritain does not see intuitive knowledge as a result of some non-rational faculty. Here we are dealing with a way of understanding that grasps particulars in view of our whole person: what we see, feel, think, etc. When he says this is not rational knowledge, this means it does not proceed from explicitly formulated premises to a conclusion. When he says it is non-conceptual, he means we are not abstracting to universal concepts and then understanding the individual cases to fall strictly within these universals. Rather, such knowledge is experimental. It is built up case by case.

Maritain himself clearly distinguishes between "genuine essential inclinations" and "accidental, warped perverted ones."[58] So he was not unaware of the risk of an inclination being distorted by bias or prejudice. One first difference between connaturality and mere prejudice is that connaturality, as the name suggests, requires an agreement in nature between the knower and the object known. In the moral order of prudence this means the will is ordered towards the good and the object desired is good. Thus, there is a knowledge by inclination in which the moral quality of the good object and actions contrary to that good are grasped immediately. In cases of bias there is no such natural agreement. In such an instance, the agreement is rather in some accidental feature; it is not the person's natural human virtue or excellence that is developed, but some incidental good of pleasure or convenience that is at stake.

Further, while the person using connatural knowledge does not have a reasoned demonstrative argument with clearly articulated concepts to justify his action, nevertheless such arguments can be developed by a person with philosophical wisdom. This is a clear difference from the case of bias or prejudice that one may attempt to rationalize through self-serving or incoherent explanations, but that cannot be reasonably justified.[59] Maritain's position is akin to Aristotle's view that the virtuous

58 *The Range of Reason*, 27.
59 *The Range of Reason*, 28.

person does the right thing, in the right way, in the way a wise person would do it. For those who are on their way towards wisdom, but do not yet fully have it, it is enough to grasp what the right thing to do is and to do it. But the wise person, who is the model, also grasps more fully the reasons for acting in this way.

Moreover, these genuine essential inclinations are fundamentally human, not merely animal, and thus they are "reason-permeated" inclinations, "refracted through the crystal of reason in its unconscious or preconscious life."[60] Further, he notes that man is a historical animal. Accordingly, this connatural knowledge is a matter of experience acquired by individuals and cultures over time. We see this in the ongoing development of human knowledge of the natural moral law.[61] Connatural knowledge leads to dynamic schemes that become permanent moral guidelines in communities; accordingly, Maritain's notion of man is that of Aristotle's political animal, rather than a modern atomistic self.[62] Thus, there seems to be an experienced dialectic between the moral agent and the moral law in our deliberation concerning moral matters that also separates connaturality from mere prejudice. The boy who happens across a bag of candy belonging to his sister knows it is wrong to eat it without asking her permission. He grasps that to do so would be to upset her, as he would be upset if the situation were the reverse. This calls for no further demonstration or proof; his conscience is already at work. Even if he should he deny his conscience and steal her candy, he can foresee the disruption to family life and his relationship to his sister that this is likely to cause. To take more severe examples, the ordinary man walking down the streets at night who encounters a woman being raped immediately knows that this is wrong and that he should intervene or at least raise a cry to stop the perpetrator. The person who needs some demonstrative argument to be moved in such a situation is obviously deficient in terms of basic

60 *The Range of Reason*, 27.
61 *Man and the State* (Chicago: University of Chicago Press, 1951), 94.
62 On the development of the atomistic conception of the self as an isolated individual in modern philosophy see Charles Taylor, *Sources of the Self: The Making of Modern Identity* (Cambridge, MA: Harvard University Press, 1989), 195–97.

human sensibilities. Nor is it convincing to suggest that his distaste for rape is really just a matter of personal preference or cultural inhibition. Rather, such acts are at odds with our natural dispositions and affections of the healthy well-adjusted person. The example of those few who find such acts enticing is proof, not of bias, but of the foundational nature of their perversion. The fact that the ordinary moral agent does not have, or need, a rational justification of his moral beliefs is evidence, not of their irrationality, but of their essential naturalness; it is evidence that they hold a greater validity that involves more than human rationality.[63]

To the second objection, it may be noted that evil agents certainly develop an intuitive sense of how to be effective at their craft, as the experienced scam artist easily recognizes a good mark. But this sort of knowledge, acquired by experience, seems easy to distinguish from connatural knowledge, as it is based merely on the habitual character of such skills, and not on any agreement in nature between the criminal and his victim.

Since connatural knowledge enters into Maritain's philosophy in so many different areas (e.g., religion, morals, aesthetics), I will not discuss all its applications at this point. Rather, I will draw attention to its use in the relevant chapters below. At this stage, it is sufficient to have presented its general nature and indicate its importance to Maritain's philosophical project, for Maritain was never content to defend merely abstract universals; rather, he was always attentive to the way in which these universal truths were to be applied and lived in concrete historical circumstances. In this respect, his thought was, and remains, vitally modern.

CHAPTER 3

Philosophy of Nature and Science

The work which metaphysics is called upon to do today is to put an end to that kind of incompatibility of temper which the humanism of the classical age had created between science and wisdom.

The Degrees of Knowledge, xi

J acques Maritain was one of the first Thomists of the twentieth century to pay serious attention to modern science. At best, modern scholastic philosophers had been content to summarize the philosophical principles of Aristotle's physics without giving much attention to their relation to modern discoveries that had been taking place since the seventeenth century; at worst, they dismissed aspects of contemporary science on dubious philosophical or theological grounds.[1]

---

1 James A. Weisheipel, OP, "Commentary on 'Maritain's Epistemology of Modern Science' by Jean-Louis Allard," in *Selected Papers from the Conference-Seminar on Jacques Maritain's Degrees of Knowledge*, ed. Robert Henle, SJ (Notre Dame, IN: American Maritain Association, 1981), 176–77. Subsequent to Maritain's magnum opus there was a minor revival of interest in philosophy of nature. The most important authors were Maritain's student Yves Simon—see Ralph Nelson, "Yves R. Simon's Philosophy of Science," in *Acquaintance with the Absolute: The Philosophy of Yves R. Simon*, ed. Anthony O. Simon (New York: Fordham University Press, 1998), 57–82—and the Canadian Thomist Charles De Koninck, whose major works on

In the course of developing a modern Thomist epistemology Maritain recognized that such an omission was simply inexcusable in the contemporary world. Although he never offered a complete and definitive philosophy of nature, Maritain did provide an outline of what one would look like and gave special attention to the relation of the modern sciences to philosophy. Indeed, this is a theme that runs throughout many of his works. Further, for a philosopher he was well qualified for this task. He had studied biology, especially neovitalism, during his years in Heidelberg; he read widely about the developments of modern physics undertaken by Einstein, Planck, and others; and he was also aware of the progress in modern mathematics made by scholars like Reiman, Poincare, and Russell.[2]

Science and Philosophy

Maritain thought on this topic begins by defining "science in general." This is not the contemporary sense of science, but rather the classical notion of ἐπιστήμη (epistēmē) found in Aristotle. As Maritain states:

> We would contend that science is a knowledge perfect in its mode, or more precisely a knowledge in which, under the compulsion of evidence, the mind points out in things their reasons for being. For the mind is not satisfied when it merely attains a thing, i.e., any datum whatever, but only when it grasps that upon which that datum is founded in being and intelligibility.[3]

---

philosophy and science are included in *The Writings of Charles De Koninck*, Vol. I, ed. and trans. Ralph McInerny (Notre Dame, IN: University of Notre Dame Press, 2008). De Koninck's students, often referred to as "Laval School" Thomists, tend to emphasize the importance of Aquinas's Aristotle commentaries as a main source for his philosophy and the need to study philosophy of nature prior to metaphysics. They tend to criticize Maritain for placing too great a division between philosophy and the modern sciences. These views are also shared with the "River Forest" School, so named from a Dominican school of philosophy at River Forest, Illinois. The best-known works of those associated with this school are Benedict M. Ashley, *The Way Toward Wisdom* (Notre Dame, IN: University of Notre Dame Press, 2009) and William A. Wallace, *The Modelling of Nature* (Washington, DC: The Catholic University of America Press, 1996), 224–27.

2 For a good account of Maritain's early education and awareness of the sciences, see Stanley L. Jaki, "Maritain and Science," in *Understanding Maritain: Philosopher and Friend*, ed. Deal W. Hudson and Matthew J. Mancini (Macon, GA: Mercer University Press), 185–89.

3 *The Degrees of Knowledge*, 25.

For Maritain this concept of science in general is the Aristotelian understanding of sure knowledge through causes. As such, it includes all speculative knowledge and, therefore, involves two distinct areas. The first is the domain of wisdom where one strives to know things through first causes; these are the sciences of *explanation*, including the fields of philosophy of nature, mathematics, and metaphysics. The second domain is that of science in the narrow sense; namely, the contemporary empirical sciences. Maritain explains that these are sciences of *observation*, which know things through secondary causes. This area incorporates the physico-mathematical sciences and the experimental, or natural, sciences.

In the Aristotelian tradition that Maritain inherits, the philosophy of nature is the science of beings insofar as they are moveable. The greatest threat to this discipline has been the historical tendency for it to be absorbed into metaphysics in the ancient world or the natural sciences in the modern one. Whereas the ancient philosophers assimilated philosophy of nature into metaphysics, the moderns have tended to absorb it within the empirical sciences.[4] Accordingly, one of Maritain's major concerns was to definitively establish it as a distinct discipline. In light of this, he defines philosophy of nature as follows:

> It is a form of knowledge whose proper object is that which moves, mutable being as such. Thus its proper object is being, being which is analogous and which imbues all generic and specific diversifications—that is why it is a philosophy—but not being as such, or being in its own intelligible mystery, which is the object of the metaphysician. The object of philosophy of nature is being taken in the conditions which affect it in the necessitous and divided universe which is the material universe. . . .[5]

In this sense philosophy of nature is clearly distinct from, yet intimately related to, metaphysics. This integral relation is emphasized by

4   *Science and Wisdom*, 46. Compare with Charles De Koninck, "Are the Experimental Sciences Distinct from the Philosophy of Nature?" in *The Writings of Charles De Koninck*, Volume I, 443–56.

5   *Science and Wisdom*, 54–55; see also *The Degrees of Knowledge*, 176, and *Philosophy of Nature*, trans. Imelda Choquette Byrne (New York: The Philosophical Library, 1951), 126–27.

Maritain's refusal to define philosophy of nature as the study of natural bodies, for that would not emphasize the fact that we are dealing with a mode of being.[6] While metaphysics studies being *qua* being, the scope of philosophy of nature is restricted to mutable, and consequently material, being. In treating of their distinct objects, the two disciplines nevertheless remain mutually interdependent.[7]

For Maritain, the speculative sciences are distinguished by their degree of abstraction from matter.[8] Following Aristotle, he holds that matter in itself would be unintelligible without some sort of form. It is by having the appropriate form imposed upon it—the form of an oak tree, a bronze, a dog, and so forth—that a physical thing can be understood as being an entity of some kind and apprehended in a concept. The different speculative sciences each abstract from matter in a different way. Accordingly, when they form concepts and develop definitions of their objects these definitions are related to matter in different ways insofar as each is more or less removed from consideration of matter.

Philosophy of nature is practiced at the first and lowest degree of abstraction, for it studies things that require matter both to exist and to be understood. One simply cannot understand the natures of material beings without some awareness of the kind of matter involved in them. One could not know the nature of a human being without knowing that human beings have bodies, or of an oak tree without knowing that they are made out of wood, have roots and leaves of a certain kind, etc. Yet, the philosopher of nature is only interested in undesignated matter, that is the general kind of matter things of this or that species need to have to be things of that kind. Her interest does not extend to the particular material conditions of individuals, just as the medical student studying anatomy is not interested in the peculiarities of Rachel's body in the way that the physician treating her would be. That her hair happens to be blonde, that a finger was cut off in an accident, or other foibles

---

6   *Philosophy of Nature*, 119.

7   *Science and Wisdom*, 49. See also *Philosophy of Nature*, 120–23.

8   *Philosophy of Nature*, 24–31. Maritain develops this position on the degrees of abstraction out of St. Thomas's *Commentary on Aristotle's Physics*, I, lect. 1; and *Commentary on Boethius' De Trinitate*, q. 5, a.1.

are largely irrelevant to the study of anatomy—rather, the student is concerned with the general anatomical conditions of human beings in general. In a similar way the philosopher of nature abstracts from matter, yet remains concerned with the general material conditions of the objects she studies, due to the fact that the object of the study is beings in the process of change. Accordingly, Maritain refers to the realm the philosopher of nature studies as the *sensible real*.

The second degree of abstraction occurs with mathematics, which studies things that need matter in order to exist, but not to be understood. Triangles, circles, numbers and other quantities the mathematician considers only exist as material objects, but in studying them she disregards the material conditions in which they exist. To the geometer it is irrelevant whether the isosceles triangle she demonstrates from and about is made of gold, wood, or granite. One can understand the geometer's definitions and proofs without any reference to matter whatsoever, and so the truths of mathematics and geometry are unchanging and certain since they abstract from matter completely in the order of understanding.

Accordingly, experience only enters into mathematics as a "pre-scientific" consideration. That is to say, one would never have had a concept of circle or square without experience. Neither would we have a concept of number without specific collections of material things that we could experience through the senses. Once we have the concepts of number and figure, they present us with objects of thought that have no ongoing reliance upon matter to be understood. Mathematical entities, shapes, and numbered entities, can only exist in the world outside of the mind, yet as mathematical entities they do not exist in matter, but in an ideal purity as concepts within the human mind.[9] To capture these considerations Maritain calls the universe as it is studied by the mathematician the *praeter-real*.

Situating the origin of mathematics in terms of beings of reason that have their origin in abstraction from matter, Maritain naturally sides with the mathematician Henri Poincare in rejecting the logicism of Bertrand

---

9   *The Degrees of Knowledge*, 57–58.

Russell, albeit for different reasons. In the *Principia Mathematica*, Russell, along with A. N. Whitehead, argued that all of mathematics could be derived from logical axioms.[10] This logical formalism was entirely inadequate, for it was based on the false assumption that mathematics has no object beyond purely logical relations. Logical formalism would make mathematics a discipline without content, receiving any definite content it might have from physics. For Maritain, this is an unacceptably nominalist method to apply to mathematics and it is rooted in an unjustified rejection of the authentically intuitive sources of knowing. The intuition in which the mathematician knows her object is neither a purely intellectual one, nor an experimental intuition within the external senses. It differs from the intuitive basis of knowledge in either philosophy of nature or metaphysics. It is an imaginative intuition (i.e., one that produces images in the mind) of internal sense, depending on external sense only as a presupposition.[11] Whereas philosophy of nature and metaphysics both, in diverse ways, involve an intuitivity of the mind turned toward the real, in mathematics the mind is not turned toward the real directly, but toward beings of reason.[12]

However, contemporary mathematicians often lose sight of the distinction between genuine mathematical insight and mere formalism. Maritain points to set theory as a key example of this. Set theory does not make use of intuitivity, but this is because, unlike genuine mathematical knowing, it is not a form of knowledge at all. Rather, set theory is an instrument of science which constructs a new language and regulates logical operations carried out in the process of reasoning. It is a matter of pure convention. While set theory plays an important role in modern mathematics, according to Maritain it is not a part of mathematics as such, but a mere instrument or logical grammar that mathematics uses.

10 Bertrand Russell, *My Philosophical Development* (London: George Allen and Unwin, 1959), 74.

11 *The Degrees of Knowledge*, 151–52.

12 "No Knowledge Without Intuitivity," in *Untrammeled Approaches*, 345. See also Jean-Louis Allard, "Maritain's Epistemology of Modern Science: A Summary Presentation," in *Selected Papers from the Conference-Seminar on Jacques Maritain's* The Degrees of Knowledge, 154.

The genuine insight of the mathematician should never be reduced to mere mechanical organization, however helpful that latter task may be.[13]

Finally, the third and highest degree of abstraction leads to metaphysics, which studies things that do not require matter either to exist or to be understood. The metaphysician considers being in its proper mystery and, as such, considers it in a way that applies to all things, whether immaterial or material. Due to the fact that being is instantiated in some immaterial beings (God, angels, human souls after death) the consideration of matter *qua* matter is not part of the metaphysical task; rather that is left to the first degree of abstraction proper to philosophy of nature. Metaphysics studies both material and immaterial beings, but from the unique perspective of intelligible being as such. Thus, Maritain denotes the universe as it is studied by metaphysics the *transensible real*.[14]

The three degrees of abstraction help to explain what constitutes philosophy of nature and the other speculative sciences as unique disciplines; however, the relation between philosophy of nature and the natural sciences is more complex. Maritain carefully distinguishes between the tasks appropriate to both of these kinds of enquiries. To accomplish this, he draws upon the insights of the great Portuguese Dominican commentator on Aquinas, John of St. Thomas (a.k.a. John Poinsot). John of St. Thomas had argued that there can be diverse varieties of abstraction—and accordingly, different disciplines—within the same degree of abstraction. In the realm of the praeter-real studied by mathematics, for example, there is a real difference between the abstraction appropriate to geometry and the higher abstraction proper to arithmetic. Consequently, diagrams can be of great use in thinking through complex geometrical problems, whereas they can only be of any help with the simplest questions of arithmetic. Likewise, in the third degree of abstraction John of St. Thomas identified logic, ontology, and natural theology. The abstraction that defines a general order

13 "No Knowledge without Intuitivity," 326–28 and 346.

14 *The Degrees of Knowledge*, 146. See also *Science and Wisdom*, 38–39; and Jean-Louis Allard, "Maritain's Epistemology of Modern Science: A Summary Presentation," 150–52.

of knowledge is an initial one that disregards some element of material data (individual matter in physics, sensible matter in mathematics, and all matter in metaphysics). But once this initial abstraction is carried out, the mind enters into an order of intelligibility that is multidimensional.[15] This complexity allows for Maritain's discovery that philosophy of nature and the empirical sciences occur both within the same degree of abstraction, notwithstanding the former's frequent methodological reliance on mathematics.

As we have seen, for Maritain science in general is distinguished by its search to know through causes. Due to this focus any science worthy of the name seeks, not merely to pile up more and more facts about its subject matter, but to know the essences of the things it studies. However, the methods of the different disciplines, even when they study the very same object, naturally approach these essences in diverse ways. Thus, within the first degree of abstraction, that which is closest to matter, there are two distinct groups of disciplines which approach the common object of mobile being in different ways. Philosophy of nature, like any philosophy, has a general ontological thrust toward first causes and the essential natures of things, whereas the natural sciences explicitly prescind from such considerations in order to focus more directly upon the field of secondary causes and observation of phenomena. Philosophy of nature asks, "What is matter?" or "What is motion?" while the natural sciences ask, "What is the mathematical formula that will express the relation between a force exerted on a mass to its velocity?" Within and through reflection upon sense experience the mind is able to discover the intelligible, the essential structure of the things that exist or can exist. Since this can be approached in two very different kinds of analysis, we end up with two distinct bodies of knowledge: namely, philosophy of nature, making use of ontological analysis, and the sciences, making use of what Maritain calls empiriological analysis:

> When you observe any material object, that object is during your observation of it, as the meeting place of two kinds of knowledge:

---

15   Yves R. Simon, "Maritain's Philosophy of the Sciences," in *Philosophy of Nature*, 161–62.

PHILOSOPHY OF NATURE AND SCIENCE | 65

sense knowledge and intellectual knowledge. You are in the presence of a sort of sensible flux stabilized by an idea, by a concept: in other words you are in the presence of an ontological or thinkable core which is manifested by an ensemble of qualities perceived *hic et nunc*. I do not mean *thought* qualities but *sensed* qualities, objects of actual perception and observation. If you come upon a plant during a botanical excursion, you may ask yourself: what is a plant? And in that case your interest lies in the direction of ontological analysis. Or you may ask: how shall I classify this in my herbarium? Here your interest is in another type of analysis: empiriological analysis.[16]

This distinction between ontological and empiriological analysis is key to understanding Maritain's conception of philosophy of nature and its relation to the sciences. Ontological analysis resolves our concepts by ascending toward intelligible being. Here the sensible remains, since we are at the first degree of abstraction, but it is only indirectly related to our concepts. The philosopher of nature aims to approach the sensible and observable insofar as it manifests intelligible being. Accordingly, philosophy of nature, unlike the natural sciences, is "participatively illuminated by metaphysical intellection."[17] Empiriological analysis resolves our concepts by descending to the sensible and the observable precisely as sensible and observable. Here it is being which is present only indirectly. It must be present or else neither an object nor a thought would arise. In empiriological analysis, being is at the service of the sensible, especially as measurable. It remains an unknown that preserves the continuity of sensible determinations and measurements and allows us to set limits circumscribing the objects we sense.[18] Although empiriological analysis may have a theoretical foundation in the ontological principles examined by philosophy of nature, there is no need for the scientist to take up philosophy in order to do her properly scientific work; that would be like saying a carpenter would be better as a carpenter by

---

16 *Philosophy of Nature*, 74. The same point is made virtually word for word in *The Degrees of Knowledge*, 156.

17 "No Knowledge without Intuitivity," 338.

18 *The Degrees of Knowledge*, 157. See also *Science and Wisdom*, 51.

becoming an architect. The principles of the architect govern the activities of the laborers as the principles of philosophy govern the activities of scientists, leaving each autonomous, albeit intimately related, in their own sphere of inquiry. Accordingly, for the natural scientist the objective light is either that of defining through the operation of the senses in non-mathematized disciplines or the method of emperiometric analysis in those that are subject to quantifiable relations.[19]

The relation between ontological and empiriological analysis gives rise to a subtle and complex balance between the two methods. Neither can contradict each other since they pursue their object in different ways according to quite separate modes of analysis. It is this difference that makes Maritain's defense of Thomistic natural philosophy credible in an age where much of its purported natural science has been definitively overturned.[20] His position rests on the fact that the scientist and the philosopher both study the sensible real, but they do so in search of quite different objects:

> Since they have utterly different formal objects, other principles of explanation, diverse conceptual instruments, and, on the part of the knowing subject himself, quite distinct intellectual virtues or discriminating lights, the domain proper to philosophy and the domain proper to the sciences do not overlap. *No explanation in the scientific order will ever be able to displace or replace an explanation belonging to the philosophical order, and vice versa.*[21]

Since the natural sciences and philosophy of nature have different methods—or in scholastic language, distinct formal objects—it is utterly impossible for them to contradict one another. As Maritain puts it evocatively, they "do not fish in the same waters."[22] When such rivalries occur, it is an indication that philosophy is trying to take on the role of

19 *Philosophy of Nature*, 137–39.

20 See Jennifer Rosato, "Holism and Realism: A Look at Maritain's Distinction between Science and Nature," in *Reading the Cosmos: Nature, Science and Wisdom*, ed. Giuseppe Butera (Washington, DC: American Maritain Association, 2011), 21–31.

21 *The Degrees of Knowledge*, 51. The emphasis is my own.

22 "Philosophy and the Unity of the Sciences," April 7, 1953, Jacques Maritain Center, University of Notre Dame, lecture transcript, https://www3.nd.edu/~maritain/jmc/jm209.htm.

the sciences or the sciences are overstepping their proper jurisdiction to give philosophical decrees. Such cases are not questions of real disputes about things, but misapplications of the appropriate method and boundary disputes between different disciplines.

In this context it is interesting to note Maritain's subtle reply to the logical positivism of the Vienna Circle, which was so prominent in the early twentieth century. Logical positivists such as Moritz Schlick, Rudolph Carnap, Philipp Frank, Otto Neurath, and Hans Riechenbach rooted their philosophical method in an acceptance of the verification principle as a criterion of meaning. Rudolph Carnap stated this view with his customary precision, writing: "According to this view, the sentences of metaphysics are pseudo-sentences which on logical analysis are proved to be either empty phrases or phrases which violate the rules of syntax. Of the so-called philosophical problems, the only questions which have any meaning are those of the logic of science. To share this view is to substitute logical syntax for philosophy."[23] For the logical positivists, a proposition will only be literally meaningful if it can, at least in principle, be verified through some empirical method. In this way, the members of the Vienna Circle thought that they had ruled out classical metaphysical claims as neither true nor false, but meaningless. Propositions that violate the verification principle might be emotionally significant to people, but they could not be literally significant.[24]

It does not come as a surprise that a philosopher as profoundly metaphysical as Jacques Maritian rejected the program of the Vienna Circle. What is surprising, however, is the degree to which he co-opted it for his own purposes. For Maritain the logical positivists' error was to extend the principle of verification beyond any reasonable bounds by treating it as a criterion for any literally significant language whatsoever. Instead, he argues that the verification principle does succeed in telling us what it means for language to be significant to someone *as a*

---

23 Carnap, *Logical Syntax of Language* (London: Routledge, 1937), 8.
24 A. J. Ayer, *Language, Truth and Logic*, 2nd rev. ed. (New York: Dover Publications, 1952), 33–35.

scientist.[25] Its strength is to offer a clear account of meaningful scientific discourse, but it commits the folly of maintaining that this is the only kind of meaningful discourse. Logical positivists made the mistake of assuming that what has no meaning for the scientist has no meaning at all. Accordingly, they wrongly applied to all knowing a criterion of meaning that holds good in only one of its spheres.[26] The metaphysical notions of being and essence, for example, do lack meaning for the scientist; they do not bear upon his scientific work. Yet this is not to say that there is no higher viewpoint within which they are intelligible and indeed necessary. Thus, Maritain goes so far as to say that a Thomistic approach to the empirical sciences is "strikingly similar" to the views of the school of Vienna.[27]

Maritain also maintains that the general principles of philosophy of nature underlie the work of the sciences, although this dependency is indirect. The sciences do not in any way depend on philosophy for their own intrinsic development.[28] A chemist, for example, will have to assume that matter exists, that the elements they study correspond to aspects of entities in the world, etc. Certainly, the demonstration of these claims belongs to the philosopher, not the chemist. Nevertheless, the chemist quite legitimately takes these positions for granted and does not need to wait for philosophers to resolve these issues in order to proceed with his properly scientific work. It would be even

---

25 *Scholasticism and Politics*, trans. Mortimer Jerome Adler (New York: The Macmillan Company, 1940), 33–36. Stanley J. Jaki presents Maritain as arguing that positivism unduly limits science and that it does not accord with the practice of science. See also "Maritain and Science," in *Understanding Maritain*, 191.

26 *Scholasticism and Politics*, 44.

27 *Scholasticism and Politics*, 39. It is interesting that Carnap himself later qualifies his endorsement of the verification principle, saying that metaphysics lacks the "cognitive content" that would make it relevant to the work of the scientist. This later position has certain parallels to the view that Maritain had already developed. See also Yves Simon, *Foresight and Knowledge*, ed. Ralph Nelson and Anthony O. Simon (New York: Fordham University Press, 1996), 84–85; and Jude P. Dougherty, *Jacques Maritain: An Intellectual Profile* (Washington, DC: The Catholic University of America Press, 2010), 60–72. Benedict Ashley, OP has objected that Maritain's approach to the empirical sciences entails positivism. However, he provides no argument to show that positivism in the specific dimensions that Maritain would embrace is problematic other than that in Ashley's own opinion it fails to do justice to the work of modern science. Benedict Ashley, OP, "Does Natural Science Attain Nature or only the Phenomena," in *The Philosophy of Physics*, ed. Vincent E. Smith. (Jamaica, NY: St. John's University, 1961), 76.

28 *The Degrees of Knowledge*, 51–52.

more erroneous to think that philosophy is subordinate to the work of the sciences in its own internal development. Rather, since philosophy deals with first principles, it is superior to—and independent of—the sciences, irrespective of the fact that acquaintance with the sciences is often very helpful in philosophical work. He makes this point with as much clarity as anyone could desire:

> Let it be understood that there is no formal dependence of phi-losophy on the sciences. Never will a result in the scientific order, never will a scientific theory, never in short, will science suffice, by its own means, to settle a philosophical question, for such ques-tions depend on principles and on a light which are beyond the scope of science.[29]

Accordingly, there is no need to "update" philosophy of nature with each new development in the sciences. This would be analogous to thinking that the soul is metamorphosed with each change in diet.[30] Yet neither are philosophy and the sciences utterly unrelated, for the object they seek to understand is—from a material point of view—the very same. Philosophy should nourish itself upon the natural sciences that provide such a rich source of knowledge about the sensible world. Indeed, Maritain goes so far as to recommend that a philosopher become intimately acquainted with the work of one of the sciences, in order to avoid the risk of falling into letting one's philosophy become a disengaged system of mere ideas without an intimate connection to the real.

In an Appendix to *The Peasant of the Garonne*, he expresses both the complementarities and differences between philosophy and science, saying,

> Let us think of two typewriters equipped with different key-boards—or, to use another comparison, of two singers whose ear and voice would supposedly be naturally attuned to two differ-ent musical keys: the scientist singing only songs composed in G, and the philosopher only songs composed in E. If they are to sing

29 *The Degrees of Knowledge*, 54.
30 *The Degrees of Knowledge*, 54.

together, it will be necessary for the scientist to sing (more or less well) in E, and, similarly, for the philosopher to learn how to sing (more or less well) in G.[31]

Certainly, philosophy is not without relevance to the sciences since it justifies and elucidates the very principles the scientist takes for granted in the course of his work.[32] Since philosophical principles are more generic and fundamental, the philosopher can judge the work of the sciences in light of this broader vision. For his part, the philosopher will draw on the sciences to elucidate his ideas, and provide concrete illustrations of the principles and conclusions he articulates.

Within the empiriological sciences Maritain distinguishes two distinctive approaches. *Empirio-metrical* disciplines attempt to resolve the observed data into mathematical formulae and structures. *Empirio-schematic* disciplines call for an experimental form and rule of explanation, in which observation predominates and its modes of demonstration are non-mathematical.

In order to elucidate these complex relationships between the sciences and philosophy that we have found in Maritain's treatment, it will be helpful to examine how they play out in the most rigorously empirio-metrical science, namely, mathematical physics, and that which Maritain identifies as more empirio-schematic and closer to philosophy, namely, biology. The following two sections will address these disciplines in turn.

Physico-Mathematical Sciences

Maritain presents contemporary physics as a mathematization of the sensible. Like any empirical science, it begins with induction from established empirical facts. However, it studies these facts in order to subject them to a deductive form and a mode of explanation in the

---

31 *The Peasant of the Garonne*, 273.
32 *The Degrees of Knowledge*, 52.

mathematical order.[33] Accordingly, it is a discipline that straddles two degrees of knowing: the physical and the mathematical. The object which is studied may be physical, but the methodology, the intelligible light under which the physical is perceived in this discipline, is mathematical:

> They [i.e. physico-mathematical sciences] are materially physical and formally mathematical. Thus they have more affinity with mathematics than with physics as to their rule of explanation and yet at the same time are more physical than mathematical as to the terminus in which their judgments are verified. [34]

It follows from this that physico-mathematical science doesn't seek out the real nature of physical causes, since it is not an ontology of the physical. Rather, it seeks to view these causes from the formal perspective of mathematics. It interprets all of its data in terms of the measurable. Accordingly, we cannot assume that the mathematical structures that result from this study represent real causes and entities outlining the ontological structure of the world of sensible nature. So far from providing a philosophy of nature, contemporary physics could more accurately be called a mathematics of nature.[35]

Nevertheless, Maritain holds that this does not involve a separation between metaphysics and the physical sciences. Rather, ontological considerations are relevant to the study, but only obliquely: "Although it will not constitute a science of physical being as such, nevertheless it will obliquely carry along with it ontological values."[36] Maritain's point is that the scientist will never be fully satisfied with a mathematical representation of the sensible, for he remains attached to the physical real. Drawing on the thought of the French philosopher of science Émile Meyerson, Maritain argues that there is an underlying ontological drive in human reason. Nevertheless, for the scientist *qua* scientist it remains irrelevant whether the explicative entities that are constructed

---

33 See Christopher S. Morrissey, "Dialectic and Demonstration in the Philosophy of Nature," *Maritain Studies* XXIII (2007): 63–74.

34 *The Degrees of Knowledge*, 147.

35 *Science and Wisdom*, 42.

36 *The Degrees of Knowledge*, 148.

by mathematical means are real beings or beings of reason. This is a distinction crucial to the philosopher of nature, but meaningless to the scientist who is only concerned with the explicative value of these entities, particularly with a view to their predictive value as distinct from ontologically relevant claims. For the scientist, as long as the entities he works with are defined in terms of at least theoretically possible operations of measurement, then they are real. For the philosopher these conceptual structures are developed for knowing these operations, even though they remain mere concepts, beings of reason.[37]

From a philosophical point of view, then, we can see that the physicist is studying the sensible real not directly by means of the real itself (i.e., mere sensation), but by means of conceptual devices or beings of reason supplied by mathematics. This approach to physics does not arrive at the essence and causes of beings in their properly ontological reality. Rather, it reconstructs them in terms of relations of measurement and the requirements of mathematical deduction in as universal a fashion as possible:

> A physico-mathematical theory will be called "true" when a coherent and fullest possible system of mathematical symbols and the explanatory entities it organizes coincides, throughout all its numerical conclusions, with measurements we have made upon the real; it is in no wise necessary that any physical reality, any particular nature, or any ontological law in the world of bodies, correspond determinately to each of the symbols and mathematical entities in question.[38]

The beings of reason that are used in this process have varied relations to reality. Some correspond directly to experimental observations, translating observable causes and structures of the real. Beyond this, entities like the electron or atom are not merely approximations, but what Maritain calls "symbolically reconstructed real beings."[39] Further

---

37 *The Degrees of Knowledge*, 148–149. See also *Philosophy of Nature*, 62–70.

38 *The Degrees of Knowledge*, 65–66.

39 Jaki points out that given we can now observe atoms and molecules directly through electron microscopes, it would no longer make sense to see them as merely symbolic images of the primordial parts of matter. Of course, Maritain could not have known this, though his views lead

removed from real being are those constructs of Einsteinian physics that are completely beings of reason, substituting for realities. Likewise, Maritain would not be concerned by more recent critics of string theory who worry that it cannot be experimentally proven, for the ontological standing of these beings of reason has no interest for the scientist *qua* scientist. Yet, even these are founded upon the real, for they are derived from the real behavior of nature; yet they are mere beings of reason that cannot exist as such.[40]

The "New Physics" of Einstein, Plank, Bohr, Heisenberg, and others provided Maritain with a remarkable contemporary example to illustrate his views on physico-mathematical science and its relation to philosophy of nature. In Maritain's analysis the New Physics that followed from relativity theory and quantum mechanics paradoxically involved both a drive toward physical realism at the expense of the mechanistic mathematization of classical physics, and a subjecting of physics to an even more radical commitment to mathematical and geometrical reduction of empirical data.

In developing the theory of special relativity, Einstein rejected any notion of an absolute reference frame or absolute rest for measurement. Einstein explains his position using a thought experiment of a train passing an embankment or platform. He asks us to imagine someone—let's call him Joe—standing in the middle of the embankment as the train goes by at a high speed. Relative to Joe the train and the embankment are the same length. An apparatus at the very front of the train labeled A will emit a flash of light when the front of the train passes the far-right side of the embankment. Another apparatus labeled B is fixed to the back of the train and will flash a light when it passes the far-left side of the embankment. Since Joe is in the middle of the embankment it is clear that he will see both lights flash simultaneously and conclude that the flashes occurred simultaneously.

---

one to expect just this kind of progress in scientific knowledge. See Stanley L. Jaki, "Maritain and Science," 193.

40 *The Degrees of Knowledge*, 150.

Einstein invites us to compare this with the experience of a person —we can call her Mary—who is on board and standing at the center of the train. For Joe the length of the train was contracted because of its high speed in relation to him. But this is not the case for Mary who is moving at the same speed as the train. According to Einstein, for Mary it is the embankment, which appears to her as moving from right to left, that will have its apparent length contracted. This means that the two events—namely, apparatus A flashing when the right side of the embankment passes the front of the train, and apparatus B flashing when the left side of the platform passes the back of the train—cannot happen simultaneously relative to Mary. Accordingly, Einstein concludes that the events are simultaneous relative to one observer, but not to the other. The "capital result" of this thought experiment is that simultaneity is relative to a system of reference.[41]

Maritain's interest in Einstein's work was evident very early in his career; he was publishing on it as early as 1920. His first article on the topic follows Bergson's critique and accuses Einstein of logical inconsistency. However, in response to correspondence on his article Maritain rejected this position and developed an alternative assessment in light of his rediscovery of a Thomistic philosophy of nature.[42] This new presentation is offered in most detail in chapter VII of his 1925 book *Réflexions sur l'intelligence et sur sa vie propre* as well as appendices III and IV to this chapter in the second edition of the work.

In assessing Maritain's position on Einstein's view of special relativity, it is crucial to recognize that he insists that he is not criticizing the doctrine as a scientific theory. Maritain's critique is restricted to the claim that the concept of time and simultaneity that Einstein refers to is the *ontologically real* time and simultaneity. Maritain's position is that ontologically real time and simultaneity are objects of natural knowledge, which are apprehended prior to the use of any scientific methodology. They are objects upon which the scientific discussion

---

41 Albert Einstein, *Relativity: The Special and General Theory*, trans.Robert W. Lawson (New York: Henry Holt and Company, 1920), 35–37.

42 Lawrence Dewan, OP, "Maritain, Einstein, and Special Relativity," *Maritain Studies* XVIII (2002): 29–30.

itself depends, albeit indirectly. Einstein's time may be "real time" in the framework needed for physics, but not within the framework required by philosophy of nature. It is real time for the physicist since it is a being of reason with a foundation in the real, rather than a mere fiction.[43] As Maritain sees it, the doctrine of relativity's use of the concept of simultaneity is dependent upon the doctrine of the isotropy of the propagation of light, which implies that light has a constant velocity in all directions for any observer in any inertial system of reference. Einstein refers to this principle of isotropy as a "free convention."[44] Maritain, however, insists that while this principle can function within mathematical physics as a being of reason to make sense of our measurements, it is an ontological impossibility, simply because it entails that simultaneity is relative at a distance.[45]

Maritain argues that Einstein's thought experiment merely shows that it is only the events *measured in this manner* that result in the conclusion that what is simultaneous is relative. In the train example there are two relevant systems: one in motion (i.e., the train observer) and the other at rest (the embankment observer). The principle of isotropy, that the velocity of light relative to the system is the same in all directions, is a freely imposed convention. It is on the basis of this convention that Mary on the train does not receive light issued from A and from B at the same time. Accordingly, Maritain argues:

> Now, one has indeed the right to make free conventions, but not to imagine that the real is obliged to conform to them. As long as one has not demonstrated (*and indeed it is impossible*) that the convention of the invariance of light in all directions (isotropy of the propagation of light) for every inertial system whatever be its velocity, corresponds to the *real* behavior of light, the "capital result" that Einstein finds at the end of his reasoning signifies simply that *inasmuch as we hold fast by hypothesis* to the method of

43 *Réflexions sur l'intelligence* in *Oeuvres complètes de Jacques et Raïssa Maritain*, 16 vols. (Fribourg, Switzerland: Éditions universitaires, 1986–2000), t. III, Appendix IV, 224–26. All references are to this edition. Translations of this work are taken from Fr. Dewan's article cited above unless otherwise noted.

44 Einstein, *Relativity: The Special and General Theory*, 32.

45 Dewan, "Maritain, Einstein, and Special Relativity," 32. See also *Philosophy of Nature*, 148–50.

measure described above and chosen once and for all, *our appreciation* of simultaneity, the way simultaneity *appears to our senses*, is necessarily relative and varies with the movement of the observer relative to the observed events.[46]

This means that the doctrine of relativity of simultaneity to a system of reference is legitimate on the basis of a freely supposed system of measurement, one which assists us in describing appearances. However, it is problematic and unjustified when it is asserted at the level of an ontological theory.

The ontological analysis, which is carried out in philosophy of nature, has its starting point in common sense, which Maritain characterizes as "intelligence in its instinctive and spontaneous play." This leads us to see that two events are simultaneous when they take place "at the same time" or "at the same instant." The philosopher has no recourse but to begin from this spontaneous and natural attitude, clarifying and elaborating upon it. Maritain refines this insight of natural common sense philosophically, stating, "Two things are simultaneous if at a designated instant in the duration proper to a being, the one is given in this duration, and the other is given also, be it in this duration, be it in another...." He also notes the consequence of this account writing, "At the designated instant, these two things *are* or *are not*; the designated simultaneity, thus defined in that which constitutes intrinsically its essence, refuses under pain of absurdity all relativity."[47] It is crucial to emphasize that this definition may not be one that can be used in physics. It may be that the physicist needs an empirico-quantitative substitute to do his work. But Maritain insists that this is a distinct issue. No matter what substitute is appealed to in order to cope with

---

46 *Réflexions sur l'intelligence*, 248–49.

47 *Réflexions sur l'intelligence*, 252–53. See also *Theonas: Conversations of a Sage*, trans. F.J. Sheed (New York: Sheed & Ward, 1933); that scientific and philosophical approaches to time differ, 67; that mathematics understands time as an *ens rationis*, whereas real time is inseparable from matter, 71; and on Einstein's use of simultaneity, see 94ff.

the mathematization of the real, the essence of simultaneity itself at the ontological level will always remain.[48]

We should not take this to suggest that Maritain thinks the sciences are dislocated from reality, the task of discovering the way things really are being left solely to philosophy. Nothing could be further from the truth. The physicist's careful measurements do bring us in touch with the real. But he insists that the significance and meaning of the measurements that science gathers are not self-evident:

> A well performed measurement informs us about the real, certainly! (It teaches us that in such and such conditions and by means of such and such procedures, the real furnishes us such and such numbers.) But the *interpretation* of the measurement, its physical significance, depends, as was said, on the entirety of physical theory, and, in any case, on our fundamental ideas about nature.[49]

In Einstein's theory, as suggested by the train example, this interpretation rests on the fundamental principle of the isotropy of the propagation of light, which has the "remarkable property" of being an absolute velocity while every other velocity is merely relative. Within Einstein's thought this principle of isotropy is merely a postulate. It may be practical, in assisting us to make sense of the measured data, but it has not been demonstrated. Indeed, Maritain goes even further, arguing that it would be impossible to demonstrate.[50]

His position is that Einstein's "free convention" in postulating the principle of isotropy results in a dilemma. Either what we call "velocity" and "movement" signify a reality in things, as properties which are really there as the ontological basis of our measurements, or what we call "velocity" and "movement" are nothing in things, existing only as numbers or measures brought about by an observer.

---

48 *Réflexions sur l'intelligence*, 253–56. See also Jennifer Rosato, "Realism and Holism," in *Reading the Cosmos: Nature, Science, and Wisdom*, ed. Giuseppe Butera (Notre Dame, IN: University of Notre Dame Press, 2012), 28–29.

49 *Réflexions sur l'intelligence*, 262–63. See also Matthew S. Pugh, "Maritain, Instrumentalism and the Philosophy of Experimental Science," in *Reading the Cosmos: Nature, Science and Wisdom*, 32–59.

50 *Réflexions sur l'intelligence*, 272–73.

The first option makes the mistake of taking an empiriometric analysis for an ontological one, and in this case that would result in a contradiction. If velocity is a real mode of a being that presupposes and depends upon time, then the velocity of light could not be the same for two inertial systems in movement, one relative to the other, unless we assume that the Lorentz transformation, which is used to pass from one system to the other (i.e., from Joe's perspective to Mary's), is applicable to the ontologically real times as such. This means that on the hypothesis in question, the duration and simultaneity taken in their intrinsic reality as properties existing in things are relative. "But relativity and the dislocation of the real time and real simultaneity imply contradiction," Maritain writes.[51] This would amount to saying that the same voyage has different real durations; not merely one duration measured with different units, but durations that differ in their intrinsic reality:

> What is absurd is to impose on *real* time and on *real* simultaneity a relativity which is proper to relations of reason varying with the observer, and to claim that the distance which separates two events in time, or two points in space, taken in that which constitutes it intrinsically, is this or that in function of an observer, that two events are really simultaneous or really successive by reason of the movement of the observer; in short, that the change in measurement coming from the change in the observer affects the very reality of the thing measured.[52]

Since supposing real time and real simultaneity involves this contradiction, it is impossible that the real velocity of light is constant for all inertial systems for the simple fact that this would presuppose that very same relativity that has been proven to be impossible. For Maritain this entails that there must be a real velocity of light that cannot be a constant relative to different systems in relative movement. Thus, the first option in the dilemma results in an absurdity.

The second option would be to treat "velocity" and "movement" not as real properties of things, but simply as products of a measurement

---

51 *Réflexions sur l'intelligence*, 273–74.
52 *Réflexions sur l'intelligence*, 275–76.

brought about by an observer. If that is the case, the absurdities that followed from the first option do not apply, for they are only relevant to time and simultaneity taken as realities, considered as objects for the intellect existing in things.[53] This aspect of the dilemma leads Maritain to clarify the relation between the measurements demanded by the physicist's empiriometric method and the reality upon which they are founded. The position that length and duration are not qualities inherent in the external world or intrinsic properties of bodies, but mere relations between the objects of this world and an observer, is something which is *true* of the measurement of length or duration we perform, but it is *false* when it is applied to the ontological basis of this relation.

In his later work *The Degrees of Knowledge* Maritain further qualifies his position, noting that while the philosopher rightly insists that there are such things as absolute time and absolute simultaneity, he may not be able to answer very well the question of what these things are at the ontological level. Thus, we should not think that he is naïve about the prospects for a detailed philosophical ontology of nature. He states the limits of such a project clearly, stating,

> The philosopher knows that bodies have absolute dimensions, that there are absolute movements in the world, an absolute time, absolute simultaneities for events as far apart as you wish in space. Here *absolute* signifies entirely determined in itself independently of any observer. The philosopher does not try to know what they are, i.e., to discern these dimensions, these movements, these times, these absolute simultaneities (at a distance), with the aid of our means of observation and measurement. He willingly concedes that is not possible. It is sufficient for him that they be discernable by spirits, who know, without observing from a point of space or at a moment of time. The physicist makes a like renunciation and with good reason. But for him, who does not philosophize, and who is concerned with what he can measure and to the extent he can measure it, the existence of these absolutes does not count and in their place he knows and handles only relative entities reconstructed by means

---

53 *Réflexions sur l'intelligence*, 277.

of measurable determinations: *entia rationis fundamento in re* [beings of reason with a foundation in things].[54]

Accordingly, the philosopher may well prove *that* such absolutes must be, while being unable to demonstrate *what* they actually are in reality.

This analysis of Einstein's position on special relativity highlights in a very concrete way the interplay between the physico-mathematical sciences and philosophy of nature. Irrespective of these specific criticisms, Maritain holds that the New Physics provides a valuable corrective to previous physics insofar as it liberates our knowledge of nature from preconceived mathematical ideas. The fate of physics in the framework presented through Descartes and Newton was one that had been dominated by rational mechanics understood as a purely mathematical science.[55] The New Physics, however, entails that mechanics is a department of physics, reasserting that movement is a *physical*, not a *mathematical*, thing. Newton's metaphysical universalization of mechanics had pretended to explain nature in its entirety by way of extension and movement. But Maritain argues that this entails rejecting the reality of movement, which becomes entirely idealized through mathematics. In rejecting any absolute reference point in the scientific tableau of nature, one with unvarying quantitative properties or determinations, the New Physics cast off the subordination of physics to a universalized mechanist theory.[56]

Accordingly, the New Physics has correctly reclaimed physics' proper place as a physical science that utilizes mathematics. However, as we have seen above, Maritain warns that the new method would fall into a deeper error if its proper and correct scientific analyses were transported uncritically to the ontological level proper to philosophy of nature. If we were to think of the space postulated by contemporary physics as real geometric space articulating the real ontological

---

54 *The Degrees of Knowledge,* 167–68.

55 An illuminating account of this historical shift in the sciences that is in keeping with Maritain's orientation can be found in Yves Simon, *The Great Dialogue of Nature and Space,* ed. Gerard J. Dalcourt (New York: Magi Books, Inc., 1970).

56 *The Degrees of Knowledge,* 165.

properties of physical things, we would hold an incoherent view. Adopting such a position would mean that it is impossible to distinguish one geometric space from another geometric space, or to distinguish the properties of real geometric space when it is imbued from matter from the properties of that same real geometric space when it is lacking matter.[57] The difference between the degree of abstraction appropriate to geometry and that which is applicable even to mathematical physics would not be respected if this supposition were accepted.

The physicist tries to understand the secrets of matter, but the very structure of his knowledge as a physicist prevents him from attaining the nature of matter in its real ontological depth. Physics can only attain it through observable and measurable determinations which, although real, are substitutes for the essence of the things under investigation. Accordingly, the method allows for an understanding of matter only to the degree that it is mathematically symbolized.[58] This balance between empirio-metric and ontological forms of analysis is the chief contribution that Maritain has to make to our understanding of science. His discussions of physico-mathematical science help refine this understanding considerably and provide concrete instances of its application. What is vital in the above discussion of the new physics is not so much the particular details of his criticism of Einstein's physics, but the clarity it brings to Maritain's way of situating the type of knowledge acquired in the science of physics, particularly in view of its use of mathematics, in relation to the philosophical knowledge of nature and ontology. In this respect, it is a contribution to our understanding of modern science which is as innovative as it is important.

A Philosophy of Biology: Evolution

The relation between biology and philosophy is more subtle than that of physico-mathematics. Due to the complexity of living organisms and the element of spontaneity associated with the activity of living organisms,

---

57 *The Degrees of Knowledge*, 182.
58 *The Degrees of Knowledge*, 172.

the biologist tends to have less recourse to purely mechanical and mathematical methods. Accordingly, she is less likely to feel tempted to give such mathematical reconstructions of the real an ontological standing. Yet even within biology there is a place for such empirio-metric analysis. This physico-mathematical biology develops physico-chemical explanations of life dealing with the material conditioning of organisms. This branch of biology seeks to analyze life in terms of the nonliving components of biological organisms. Beyond this limited pursuit, Maritain identifies a second branch of biology that is typological or formally experimental, in which the scientist studies living beings and offers an account of their nature and functioning through inductive reasoning. Although such observations will be indirectly influenced by philosophical considerations, the experimental biologist accounts for her findings in terms of what can be observed. The methodology remains empiriological, not ontological. Finally, there is a philosophical biology that tries to arrive at ontological explanations of life. This pursuit involves offering philosophical accounts of the scientific data that are developed by the other branches of biology. In this way, this branch of biology rises from the quantitative and observational level to the level of ontological explanations and analysis.[59]

The precise nature of a philosophical biology's contributions can be seen in Maritain's discussions of the problem of evolution. Surprisingly, given his early studies in biology, this is a matter that is only touched on briefly until Maritain's late writings. The two main sources for his views are a lecture that he gave to the Little Brothers of Jesus in 1967 and his critique of Teilhard de Chardin in his book *The Peasant of the Garonne*.

Prior to these works, evolution arises only in passing in Maritain's work. In one such instance it is brought up as an example of the challenges of achieving mutual understanding between different philosophical points of view. Although the discussion is of a summary nature, it is of interest as a succinct introduction to Maritain's approach. The problem arises from the criticism of Thomistic philosophy as having a view of substance that is just an inert principle that provides for continuity

---

59 *The Degrees of Knowledge*, 210–11.

through change. On the basis of this critical appraisal, Thomism offers merely a metaphysics of presence. Likewise, the substantial form which determines a thing's species is thought to be fixed and definite, unable to contain any principle that would bring about its own transformation into another substantial form, let alone a greater one. When a substantial change takes place, the new substantial form is drawn out of the matter's potentiality. The prior substantial form is corrupted and ceases to exist the instant the new substantial form comes about. This supposedly Aristotelian approach suggests what might be more aptly termed a replacement than an evolution of the substantial form.[60]

Maritain's response is to argue that this objection rests upon a simplistic view of substance. Substance is not merely an inert substratum; rather, "it is the first root of a thing's activities." While the substance remains the same in regard to its changing accidents, it ceaselessly acts and changes through those accidents, which are to be seen as an expansion of the substance into other non-substantial modes of being. The substance may change with respect to the activities it brings about through its accidents, while nevertheless not changing *as* substance.[61]

More significant is the role of finality, acting for a purpose, in this early discussion, for it is a point that is central to Maritain's later thought on the topic. Thus, he writes:

> The new substance can be more "perfect"—imply a higher degree of nature, not only because matter (prime matter) "aspires" to the full actualization of all the forms it contains potentially, but because the new "more perfect" substance results from an atomic redistribution which, in its capacity of an "ultimate disposition," requires the "eduction" of a higher form, or because in the case of a new formal and subsisting unity, of the activities brought about in matter by the antecedent substances which "generate" it at the instant when they destroy each other (and whose forms remain virtually in the new substantial form then educed).[62]

---

60 This terminology of replacement rather than evolution is my own, not Maritain's. See "Philosophical Cooperation and Intellectual Justice," in *The Range of Reason*, 36–37.

61 "Philosophical Cooperation and Intellectual Justice," 36.

62 "Philosophical Cooperation and Intellectual Justice," 37.

This explains how a new, more perfect or complete type of substance can arise from a lower one. The key is found in the doctrine of finality: the view that matter itself is ordered toward an end or purpose in order to realize the full actualization of its potentiality to manifest itself in higher forms.

A further objection is that new living organisms must necessarily have the same specific substantial form as the organisms from which it derives. Maritain suggests two replies to this concern. The first is to construe the species in a "more dynamic" and "extensive" manner than we typically do. This would mean taking the species to include not only the traits exhibited at any particular point in history, but as also including the vital potentialities which it may exhibit:

> When I say "a more extensive manner," I mean that such large groups as those which [biological] classification terms families, orders, etc. should perhaps be considered as belonging to one and the same ontological species. When I say "a more dynamic manner," I mean that the substantial form, in the realm of life, could be considered as protruding, in its virtualities, beyond the capacities of the matter it informs in given conditions, like, for example, an architectural style or poetic idea which we might imagine as thrown into matter and working it by itself.[63]

In this more nuanced view, the substantial form would be an ontological impulse realizing itself in different intelligible structures and patterns throughout a phylum, even though evolutionary development could only take place within the limits of the potentiality demanded by the phylum or ontological species in question. The second, and complimentary, solution that Maritain suggests appeals to the action of God as the first cause of natural events. The divine creative act is capable of infusing in created beings the capacity to act as instrumental causes of producing in matter dispositions that go beyond an organism's species. This would allow that a new and "greater" substantial form could be

---

63 "Philosophical Cooperation and Intellectual Justice," 37.

brought about from the potentiality of matter that had been disposed for this new development under the creative action of God.[64]

In his later writings Maritain remains silent on the first option, presenting a substantially different alternative, and significantly develops the second. It is likely that his dissatisfaction with broadening the species to include a wider and more dynamic range came from his dissatisfaction with the work of Teilhard de Chardin. Teilhard saw the ancient crisis of Christianity to be reconciling the fact of Jesus Christ's humanity and divinity with the Trinity, while for him the modern crisis was one of reconciling the fact of Jesus Christ with "the world."[65] He tried to accomplish this task through presenting the world in a process of cosmic evolution accomplishing the fulfillment of Christ in all things. Thereby, Teilhard gave mystical significance to the scientific concept of evolution. Philosophically this resulted in a *"purely evolutive* conception where being is replaced by becoming and every essence or nature stably constituted in itself vanishes."[66] As Maritain sees it, such a view makes evolution, properly speaking, impossible. If there are not ontological species stably constituted by specific natures, then there can be no question of an evolution from one species to another. For Teilhard, "everything was in everything, and what he called evolution was no more than a kind of unwrapping."[67] I think this consideration, along with a deeper reflection concerning the utter distinctiveness of human nature, led Maritain to ignore what he had offered as a viable option in his earlier work.

In contrast to Teilhard's "everything is in everything" approach, Maritain draws on his reading of St. Thomas Aquinas to present a vision of

---

64 "Philosophical Cooperation and Intellectual Justice," 38.

65 Pierre Teilhard de Chardin, *The Phenomenon of Man*, 2nd ed. (New York: Harper Colophon, 1975), 218, 220, 223, 227, 228, 277; and de Chardin, *Man's Place in Nature: The Human Zoological Group* (New York: Harper & Row, 1966), 15, 25. Also see Pierre Teilhard de Chardin, "The Mass on the World," in *Hymn of the Universe*, trans. Simon Bartholomew (New York: Harper & Row, 1961).

66 *The Peasant of the Garonne*, 122. See Maritain's summary of Teilhard de Chardin's thought on 116–19.

67 "Toward a Thomist Idea of Evolution," in *Untrammeled Approaches*, 91.

the universe that is hierarchically structured.[68] The differences between these modes of being and their hierarchical relations are determined by the increasing modes of complexity of their action. The lowest degree of beings is inanimate bodies that only produce something by acting on each other. Above these beings are plants, since they possess immanent activities of nourishment and reproduction. Above the level of plants are those animals that possess a "sensitive soul" that allows them to possess external senses and memory. Finally, the supreme degree of life is found in the intellect, which is capable of reflecting not only upon other objects, but upon itself in its own inner life. This intellectual life also admits of degrees. In the human case knowledge, even of the intellect itself, always has its beginnings in the external world through sense experience. For human beings there can be no knowledge that does not start with images. Among angels the intellectual life is at a higher level, for its self-knowledge does not come from anything external. The angel knows itself directly through itself. Yet even though the angel's knowledge is entirely intrinsic in its origins, its knowledge is not its very being, but something distinct from it. That supreme form of intellectual life is reserved for God alone, who has the idea of Himself and this idea is His very being.[69] Aquinas's hierarchically structured vision of the universe, which Maritain thoroughly endorses, could hardly be more opposed to Teilhard's vision in which "everything is in everything."

Maritain then looks for the philosophical principles that would provide a solution to the problems posed by evolution. He finds them in his reading of Aquinas's account of the development of the human embryo. Maritain follows Aquinas, who presented the fetus as "evolving" through the states of mere life at first, then developing a sensitive life before the matter was finally disposed to receive an intellectual soul. This is in marked contrast to many contemporary theologians, who most often hold that the human soul is infused by God at the first moment of conception. Maritain ridicules this view as a convenient rhetorical ploy for arguing against the moral crime of abortion, for one

68 *Summa Contra Gentiles*, IV, 11.
69 "Toward a Thomist Idea of Evolution," 86–87.

cannot assume that reality coincides with what will allow for the simplest moral argument.[70] While Maritain certainly condemns abortion in the strongest terms and has philosophical reasons for doing so, he finds the view that the intellective soul is present from conception absurd, for it would mean that the soul is infused in a body that is not prepared to exercise the activities proper to it:

> To admit that the human fetus, from the instant of its conception, receives the intellective soul, while the matter is still in no way disposed with respect to it, is in my view a philosophical absurdity. It is just as absurd to call a fertilized ovum a *baby*. This is a complete *misunderstanding* of the *evolutive movement*, which in truth would be mistaken for a simple movement of augmentation or of growth, as if by dint of growing bigger a circle would turn into a square, or the *Petit Larousse* would become *The Divine Comedy*.[71]

Having insisted upon the evolutive development of the embryo, Maritain seeks out the philosophical principles at work in this case in order to apply them to the problem of the evolution of species. There is an important difference between two cases, for neither Aquinas nor Maritain say that the embryo is a mere plant in the first phase, becoming a mere animal and then finally a human being. Rather, they say:

> that possessing a human nature *virtually* from the very beginning—the human embryo during the first stage *lives by a vegetative life* and in the following *stage by sensitive life*. It is a being which from the very first instant *is made to be a man,* and which becomes *formally* what from the very beginning it has already been *virtually* and by that fundamental life force on which it depends.[72]

---

70 For a critique of Maritain's acceptance of Aquinas's development of the embryo, see James G. Hanink, "Jacques Maritain and the Embryo," *Life and Learning* 18 (2008): 249–62. For a thorough discussion of this issue, see also Benedict Ashley, OP, "When Does a Human Person Begin to Exist?" in *The Ashley Reader: Redeeming Reason* (Naples, FL: Sapientia University Press of Ave Maria, 2006), 329–68. Even if one rejects Maritain's embryological analysis, however, it does not follow that his application of those principles from Aquinas's philosophy of nature to the issue of evolution is mistaken.

71 "Toward a Thomist Idea of Evolution," 93; see also 104–5.

72 "Toward a Thomist Idea of Evolution," 94.

Thus, the embryo possesses a human nature *virtually*. This means that in its present state it is already actively and really disposed toward developing into a fully intellectual human being, which happens formally at the later stage, when the intellective soul is infused by God.

The key principles of this development within the human species Maritain finds in Aquinas's explanation:

> Prime matter tends toward its perfection by actually acquiring a form to which it was previously in potency, even though it then ceases to have the other form which it actually possessed before, for this is the way that matter may receive in succession all the forms to which it is potential, so that its entire potentiality may be successively reduced to act, which could not be done all at once.[73]

Prime matter is matter considered abstractly, apart from any particular or definite form. The same bit of matter may be at this moment a living human body, but at a later time after death a mere corpse and not a human being at all, and at some much later time mere dust. In each of these cases the matter is structured through a different form. The form is the basic principle that accounts for why the matter is this kind of thing rather than that one. In this text Aquinas suggests that this prime matter is open to an end or goal, to act in such a way that it may be manifested in more and more complex forms, one after the other. This is precisely what he and Maritain find in the development of the human embryo described above. Aquinas goes on to explain that in this case prime matter is in potency to the vegetative soul, which is in potency to the sensitive soul, which itself is in potency to the intellective soul.[74]

It is important to realize that Maritain is not merely drawing an analogy between embryological development and evolution. Rather, he is arguing that the philosophical principles that account for the evolutive development of the embryo can also account for the evolutive development of species. This is clearly not a step that Aquinas took, but rather a case of Maritain appropriating Aquinas's principles and

---

73 *S.C.G.,* III, 22, 4.
74 *S.C.G.,* III, 22, 7 and "Toward a Thomist Idea of Evolution," 109.

applying them creatively in a new context. However, there is a key difference between the two cases, for in the case of the embryo the human nature is present virtually throughout the process and God's activity in the process directs the living thing "to act as it is." In the case of the evolution of species the divine action is "*superelevating* and *superforming*" in moving the living being to become "better than it is." This results in the prenatal life of the being that is brought about by this divine motion actualizing a potency from matter that is a specific degree higher than that of the living being in question.[75] The philosophical principle underlying this account is very clearly developed from Aquinas's position on prime matter, which was quoted above. Further Maritain adds:

> Prime matter, under a given substantial form, tends to higher forms. Under the substantial form of an animal of a given species, matter, because it aspires to the actualization of all of its potency, tends toward substantial forms of higher species. I pointed out that if to this metaphysical tendentiality is added the dimension of time, if it spread out over time, it becomes an evolutive tendentiality.[76]

This evolution involves two distinct lines of causality. The first is what Maritain calls the superelevating and superforming divine motion. The second is the causal action of the living being itself, whose immanent activity functions through the motion of God by the self-regulating process proper to its own material nature. Maritain insists that in the evolution of species below the human being, this second line of causality influenced only in the ordinary natural way through the divine motion that is needed to sustain all being and action is sufficient. The living being's form seizes upon a newly developed capacity of matter to tend toward some higher form, and thereby makes itself better than what it is, drawing its life to a higher level and forming a new species.[77]

---

75 "Toward a Thomist Idea of Evolution," 115.

76 "Toward a Thomist Idea of Evolution," 116. This same point was made in his earlier paper quoted above, "Philosophical Cooperation and Intellectual Justice," 37.

77 In a later seminar "Concerning Animal Instinct," given and published in 1973 (and reprinted immediately following the evolution essay in *Untrammeled Approaches*), Maritain suggests that the role of divine governance in the ordinary evolution of species below man is the work of angels. He is clear that angels do not give being to any creature; that is the prerogative of God alone. Rather, the angels carry out the work of "divine governance," and thus he suggests

However, for the development of the human being, the virtualities latent in the earlier species are not sufficient to account for the emergence of humanity:

> As to the *evolution of all species* immersed in matter, once again the *dynamism of nature is sufficient by itself alone*, but this time, under a *superelevating* and *superforming* divine motion, which is still *general*, at least with regard to the world of life and species in mutation.
>
> But concerning the case which we will now examine, the case of that evolution which is completed with *the appearance of the human being, the dynamism of nature under the general divine superelevating motion activating the world of life, is no longer sufficient* by itself alone.[78]

To hold that the kind of "intelligence" found in animals could advance under its own natural capacities step by step to become human intelligence would be as absurd as to suggest that an architect could reach the moon by building higher and higher towers or that by perfecting its scenting ability a hunting dog could succeed in telling a genuine Picasso from a fake.[79]

Maritain then tries to determine the relationship between the human species as we now know it and the other, earlier species—or "primitive men"—which were an immediate preparation for it. In asking this question Maritain's concern is, of course, for the ontological species and not the mere classifications that are the biologist's direct concern. After presenting a brief survey of the scientific discussion and submitting it to philosophical analysis, Maritain notes that a clear problem emerges. Either the higher hominian belongs to a species different from the ontological species to which later man or man of today belongs, or he belongs to the same species. Science and philosophy appear to give different answers to this question: "They were not animals, declares science. They were not men, declares philosophy." In fact, Maritain points

---

they are principal agents in the historical development of evolution. See "Concerning Animal Instinct," 143–44.

78 "Toward a Thomist Idea of Evolution," 117–18.
79 "Toward a Thomist Idea of Evolution," 120.

out that both answers involve an absurdity. To say that primitive men belonged to a different ontological species from men of today entails that there are several human species that appeared in historic succession. But that is impossible, as having an intellective, spiritual, and immortal soul is the specific difference of the human species that separates it from all other animals and constitutes it as a distinct species, the only species whose bounds we can determine precisely. To say that primitive men do not form a different species from the men of today means saying that the unique human species began to exist much earlier and did not mark the end of an evolutionary process through which higher animals became, first, almost-men—preparing man for the time when the ultimate disposition of the matter would call for an intellective soul. This would mean that among those earliest humans, the animal and material preparation needed for the beginning of the human species would not be present. Again, this involves the philosophical absurdity of the intellective soul functioning as the substantial form of a body utterly unable to exercise the distinctive acts of its own form.[80]

Maritain responds to this paradox by suggesting a third alternative hypothesis. He suggests that the dilemma of whether these near ancestors of humanity were human or animals can be resolved by introducing a third term, suggesting that at the peak of a series of higher primates, in a relatively short and unique stage of life's development, there were animals who developed their psychism in ways that surpassed the level of all other animals of prehistoric times and of our own age:

> For the moment let us call them *overdeveloped animals*, or, if you prefer, *pre-men*. Then we no longer have to deal with the pair of opposed terms animal and man, but with a triplet or trio of terms: animal, overdeveloped animal, and man. The overdeveloped animal did not belong to the *animal kingdom* solely in the way that the animal endowed with reason belongs to it. Unlike man, who is formed by an intellective soul, it continued to belong to the immense category of living beings *informed by a sensitive soul or*

---

80 "Toward a Thomist Idea of Evolution," 120–21.

a purely animal soul. But he was part of the last stages disposing these particular living beings to give birth to the human species.[81]

In this way the paradox of whether man's immediate ancestors were men or animals is resolved. The overdeveloped animals would be animals in which evolution had resulted in bodies that were apt, or almost apt, to receive an intellective soul.

The final point that needs to be made is the role of God in the evolution of the human species. As I have already noted, Maritain thinks the evolution of any other species can be explained adequately by appealing to the latent potencies present in the nature of the lower species and the tendency of prime matter to manifest itself in more complex and higher forms. In the case of man, something further is required because the intellective, immaterial, and immortal soul which informs the human body cannot possibly evolve from matter alone in this way. Rather, in these particular beings, God—by a completely free act—chose a particular hominian couple or couples (Maritain opts for the former theory in a postscript added to the present essay in 1972)[82] in whom to infuse a spiritual, intellectual, and immortal soul that had been called for by the ultimate disposition of the matter of these bodies that were the ultimate product of the evolutionary process. As Maritain explains,

> So we have here, as regards the intellective soul which is the substantial form of the human being, the *creation* of this soul by an act of God implying an absolutely free and gratuitous divine choice. And on the other hand, as regards the ultimate disposition to be produced in matter, a *superelevating* and *superforming* divine motion which is no longer a general motion with regard to the world of life but, this time, *an exceptional and absolutely unique motion*, depending on the same absolutely free and gratuitous divine choice, which at one and the same time includes that motion which calls man forth by an ultimate disposition of matter,

---

81 "Toward a Thomist Idea of Evolution," 123–24. See also Charles Cardinal Journet, "Jacques Maritain Theologian," *The New Scholasticism* XLVI, no. 1 (1972): 37.

82 "Toward a Thomist Idea of Evolution," 129–31.

and the act by which man is created by the fact that God has created the soul which is the cause of his existence.[83]

This ultimate disposition of the matter involves two distinct but related
instances. In the first instance, since it is the ultimate disposition of
the matter at the term of the sensitive development of the fetus which
is to become human, this disposition supervenes in a substance (i.e.,
the fetus) that is still informed at that time by a sensitive soul. In the
second instance of nature, this ultimate disposition exists within the
substance informed by the new form and is a hominian fetus that has
already become human, informed by the spiritual soul infused by God.
In the first instance of nature the hominian nature was already virtually
human; in the second instance, it is formally human.[84]

Maritain's discussion of evolution provides an illustrative example
of his vision for philosophy of nature and how it functions in relation
to the biological sciences. Moving beyond the evidence presented by
empiriological investigations, the philosopher seizes upon foundational
philosophical principles—in this case, the tendency of prime matter
to manifest itself in increasingly higher forms. This principle is then
brought to bear upon the data in order to explain the phenomena at
a deeper, ontological level—in this case, the historical evidence of the
evolution of species. The tools of the philosopher are also brought to
bear to resolve the apparent tensions between the scientific and philosophical explanations—in this case, to address the tension between
scientists who thought that the higher hominians were already human
and the philosophical position that suggested they could not be human.

Indeed, both the discussion of simultaneity in Einstein's relativity
theory and that of evolution provide useful test cases for Maritain's general understanding of the philosophy of nature in relation to the modern
sciences. While the scientist's methodology will certainly vary as one
moves from physics to a discipline that is less quantitative and more
philosophical—like biology—the same general features of philosophy of

83 "Toward a Thomist Idea of Evolution," 125–26.
84 "Toward a Thomist Idea of Evolution," 126. See also "Concerning Animal Instinct," 140–41.

nature apply. This rehabilitation of philosophy of nature as a discipline distinct from either metaphysics or the empirical sciences is one of the most creative and distinctive contributions that Maritain made to the speculative or theoretical branches of philosophy.

CHAPTER 4

Metaphysics

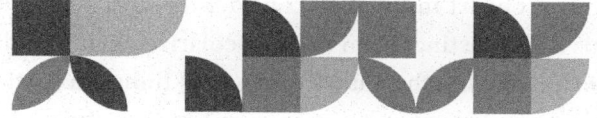

A philosopher is not a philosopher
if he is not a metaphysician.
Existence and the Existent, 19

As we saw in discussing Maritain's epistemology, being is the central point of reference in his thought. Implicit in every act of knowledge, in every statement, in every experience is the act of being. Whatever is known by the intellect presents some mode of being to the mind, that is to say, that everything is apprehended by the intellect as being embodied in some essence or nature. Being, however, is the first and formal object of the intellect, without which nothing can be thought, known, or even said.[1] Maritain distinguishes between the general notion of being that is implied universally in judgments of common sense and the awareness of being that gives birth to metaphysics as a discipline. In common judgments about sense objects like "this is a beer," being is certainly apprehended, but here it is grasped in a manner that is clothed in a sensible nature. We do not encounter

---

1 See *Introduction to Philosophy,* 132; *Science and Wisdom,* 23; *A Preface to Metaphysics,* 12; and *The Degrees of Knowledge,* 99–100.

being as a common element of all things extracted in its purity, but being enveloped in a diversity of corporeal natures.[2] Accordingly, the apprehension of being present in common-sense judgments is not the proper object of metaphysics. Being as an object of metaphysics requires reflection on being as such, being insofar as it is being. Here being is not enclosed in a sensible nature, but rather is abstracted from its particularized objects so far as possible. It is now considered in a way which is set apart in order to consider its pure intelligible value.[3] Clearly, this is also distinct from the particularized being studied by the scientist in considering the nature of physical things in motion. As we saw in the previous chapter, being as such has no meaning for the scientist and cannot enter into her properly scientific work—that is ruled out by the empiriological method into which all her results are resolved. As we have seen in previous chapters, the mind approaches greater intelligibility with each degree of abstraction. In considering material beings, we abstract from the contingent individual matter, but matter is still included in a generic way in the consideration of its objects. In mathematics and geometry, we abstract from matter entirely in our understanding of the objects we study, even though those objects—real squares and circles—only exist as material objects. Finally, metaphysics abstracts from matter altogether in the consideration of being that is inclusive of immaterial beings. However, being—in the sense that interests the metaphysician—is not attained by moving to more and more general abstractions. This would be to treat being as if it were the most universal genus. But since there is nothing to distinguish it from, such a concept of being would be empty. The present chapter will accordingly focus on the ways in which being is known through both intuition and judgment. Finally, it will provide an explanation of how the essences of things are grasped metaphysically.

---

2   *A Preface to Metaphysics*, 25.
3   *A Preface to Metaphysics*, 26.

The Intuition of Being

Throughout Maritain's work, he insists that metaphysics as a science (in the Aristotelian sense) has its origin in an intuition of being. The aspect of being of interest here is not the concrete being of common sense, the material and movable being of the sciences, nor the merely abstracted pseudo-being that prevails among logicians and essentialist or nominalist metaphysicians. Rather, the focus of attention ought to be in its most fundamental and irreducible act: the act of being. This is what is, and can only be, attained by way of intuition. Of course, philosophers notoriously appeal to intuition in various and often confusing ways. Accordingly, it is extremely important to be attentive to the precise sense that Maritain gives to the phrase "intuition of being" in this context and the way it develops over the course of his various writings on the subject.

In this respect, it is well worth noting that intuition also played a central role in the thought of Maritain's mentor and nemesis Henri Bergson. Indeed, it is no mere coincidence that we encounter a lengthy and nuanced treatment of intuition in Maritain's first book *Bergsonian Philosophy and Thomism*. Bergson had appealed to intuition in an attempt to highlight the shortcomings of the early positivism he fought against. Scientific knowledge, he pointed out, always views its object from the outside as something to be studied from various perspectives. This meant that it was a form of analysis that is by its nature restricted to a symbolic or analytic point of view. The scientist moves about the object, takes measurements, etc., and these symbolically represent the object to him.[4] Bergson contrasted this approach with an "intuitive" perspective which would move beyond an external appraisal of the object in order to come into a direct affective union with it, to see the object not from without, but from within. Bergson notes that there is at least one case we all grasp intuitively—that of our own personalities. However, he argues that through intuition we can come to view other things from within as well, through a kind of affective sympathy with

4 Bergson, *Introduction to Metaphysics*, trans. T. E. Hulme (Indianapolis: Hackett Publications, 1999), 21.

them. This is the task of metaphysics, the science that overcomes and dispenses with symbols.[5]

While Maritain will agree with Bergson on the need for intuition to go beyond the kind of analysis inherent in science, he is highly critical of the way in which Bergson characterizes this. Maritain makes his point by distinguishing a philosophical sense of intuition from a common-sense, everyday one. He explains intuition in the primary and philosophical sense as follows:

> The distinctive feature of intuition, taken in the very wide sense in which we understand it here, is that it is an *immediate* knowledge or perception, a *direct* knowledge or perception, in which the act of knowing terminates upon the thing known without any intermediary, without the interposition of a middle term,—in which it is *seen* in a word.[6]

This understanding of intuition, which is Maritain's own, is radically different from that of Bergson as it is fundamentally a direct intellectual perception of the real that terminates in a thing, while the word or concept that signifies that thing functions merely as a formal sign of it. It is the perception of the real through a concept. The second sense of intuition is how it is ordinarily understood by the non-philosopher as a hunch or gut feeling—in Maritain's words, a "form of divination." This is the sense in which we speak of the "intuitions of the heart."[7] Here it is not the immediacy of knowledge that is at issue, but the spontaneity of the subject in arriving at it. The right idea is latched onto by sympathy and we are no longer dealing with the relation between the act of cognition and the subject that is known by it. This latter sense seems to be at work in many of Bergson's examples. Accordingly, Maritain credits Bergson with correctly identifying a key weakness in the positivism of the day, and rightly seeing that the need for intuition is the proper alternative. However, he rejects Bergson's own presentation of

---

5   Bergson, *Introduction to Metaphysics*, 24.
6   *Bergsonian Philosophy and Thomism*, 149. See also *The Peasant of the Garonne*, 110, and John Hittinger, *Liberty, Wisdom, and Grace* (Lanham, MD: Lexington Books, 2003), 206–7.
7   *Bergsonian Philosophy and Thomism*, 149.

intuition as anti-intellectual, and thus an inadequate basis for a suitable metaphysical alternative.

Maritain is careful to qualify what he means by saying that intuition occurs directly without any intermediary. This does not mean that this knowledge occurs without any *subjective* intermediary. That would entail that the knowledge arises without any means of presenting the object within the knowing subject. Clearly, such a situation is impossible. If the object is not presented to the knowing agent, that agent can have no knowledge of it. Rather, as we have already seen in the discussion of epistemology, the object is present within the knowing subject as a concept or mental word that serves as a likeness of the object. The key point, to repeat what we said in chapter two, is that the act of knowledge does not terminate in this concept, as if what we knew were the mental word itself. It is, rather, that this concept is a likeness through which and in which knowledge of the real can take place. It is a means of knowing the real thing in the world; it is not the thing that is known.[8]

Yet this intuitive knowledge is complicated in the case of being, at least in the sense that interests the metaphysician, due to the fact that being cannot be attained through mere abstraction. The aspect of being that is relevant to metaphysics is the very act of existing that all things exercise in order to be. This is not something that can be attained only through a process of abstraction without falling into the Hegelian paradox in which being has been so abstracted from every particular quality that it is identical to nothing. Further, while this intuition needs to be subjected to "a rational confirmatory analysis," Maritain insists that logical analysis alone cannot give rise to it. Philosophy can neither begin nor end with confirmatory analysis, since analysis on its own lacks any insight into the real.[9] Yet it is necessary that this intuition be accompanied with rational analysis. Without it all the metaphysician would have is an intuition unconfirmed by reason that may, for all we know, not be rationally necessary. While if we rested content with the analysis—which is a perennial temptation for the philosopher—it would

8 *Bergsonian Philosophy and Thomism*, 150–51.
9 *A Preface to Metaphysics*, 3–7.

show that such an intuition is needed, the result would be incomplete. Analysis itself cannot yield the intuition of being, for it is in the intuitive perception of being alone that this arises.[10]

Yet Maritain only gradually developed his position to emphasize that an intuition of being is not only possible, but "utterly necessary to be a metaphysician at all."[11] In one of his latest works, *The Peasant of the Garonne*, he puts it more emphatically, stating, "The intuition of being is not only, like the reality of the world and of things, the absolutely primary foundation of philosophy. It is the absolutely primary *principle* of philosophy."[12] In the much earlier work *The Degrees of Knowledge* (1934), though, he discusses "metaphysical experience" as an alternative to metaphysics as a science for some individuals; he seems to deny that such intuitions are necessary for this science. In this text he writes, "Because for some men, the types of metaphysical experience of which we have just been speaking provide, on some points, a substitute for metaphysical science properly so called that does not prove that, of itself, metaphysics requires, in order to exist as a perfectly certain science and to reach being efficaciously, that it be completed by such intuitions."[13] But it is important to note that this passage occurs in the context of a discussion of mysticism, and the primary concern seems to be to argue that mystical experience is not a necessary element of metaphysics as a science. However, the term "metaphysical experience" in this context seems somewhat ambiguous, as what Maritain's later works advocate as necessary is a metaphysical—but certainly not mystical—experience.

However, in his later works, such as *Existence and the Existent* (1947) and thereafter, he advocates the necessity for an intuition of being in no uncertain terms: "A philosopher is not a philosopher if he is not a metaphysician. And it is the intuition of being—even when it is distorted by the error of a system, as in Plato or Spinoza—that makes a

---

10 *A Preface to Metaphysics*, 54–57.

11 *Existence and the Existent*, trans. Lewis Galantière and Gerald B. Phelan. New York: Pantheon Books, 1948), 19.

12 *The Peasant of the Garonne*, 111.

13 *The Degrees of Knowledge*, 297.

metaphysician."[14] Throughout his late works Maritain is uncompromising about the necessity of this intuition for the philosopher to rise to his primary task: the development of an adequate metaphysics.

But how are to we arrive at this intuition of being? Frequently he speaks of it as a "gift." Although he is careful to distinguish it from a properly mystical grace, he is clear that it remains a gift nonetheless. What he means is that there is no step-by-step procedure we can go through to ensure that we will attain this intuition. It will always be one that some people acquire while others—some of them great philosophers—do not. The reason for this is that the key to attaining the intuition of being is not to construct an elaborate philosophical system, but simply to listen to the hymn to their being that all things whisper in virtue of the fact that they exist.[15] Nevertheless, there are several approaches that can lead one to this intuition. Maritain mentions a number of examples: (1) Bergson's experience of duration, in which motion becomes a unity; (2) Heidegger's experience of anguish, in which we confront profoundly the fragility of our being as something saved from nothingness; and (3) Marcel's metaphysical elaboration of ethical experiences, in which existence loses its commonplace value so we can discover it existentially in an awareness of moral facts, like fidelity.[16] All of these cases are examples of an experience that can reach fruition in the intuitive apprehension of being. Yet Maritain insists we would make any intuition of being impossible if we rested content in the psychological or ethical aspects of these experiences. Something further is needed:

> What counts is to take the leap, to release, in one authentic intellectual intuition, the sense of being, the sense of the value of the implications that lie in the act of existing. What counts is to have seen that existence is not a simple empirical fact but a primitive datum for the mind itself, opening to the mind an infinite

14 *Existence and the Existent*, 19.

15 *The Degrees of Knowledge*, 2, and *A Preface to Metaphysics*, 52–53.

16 *A Preface to Metaphysics*, 52–53.

supra-observable field—in a word, the primary and super-intelli-
gible source of intelligibility.[17]

Certainly, the empirical elements—as well as the psychological or ethical factors—may be more readily apparent, but the metaphysician needs
to go further and see within those experiences a direct confrontation
with being *qua* being disengaged for its own sake in its intelligible and
transcendental values.[18]

These paths are all matters of experiences that can lead to an
intuition of being if seen from a metaphysical perspective. However,
Maritain suggests that this intuitionan also be prompted or confirmed
through rational analysis. His examples are the classical arguments that
show the inescapability of being: that events presuppose beings; Aquinas's argument in *De Veritate*, q. 1 a.1 that the first object of the intellect
is being, to which it reduces all of its other concepts; and a metaphysical,
rather than a merely semantic or logical, understanding of the principle
of identity, that every being is what it is.[19] These kinds of analyses are not
optional extras, but are necessary to move the mind to a recognition of
the primordial importance of being. Nevertheless, they would be empty
unless they prompted us to go further to an experiential apprehension
of being in an intuition:

> Were we content with the intuition without the rational analy-
> sis we should risk being landed with an intuition unconfirmed by
> reason, whose rational necessity therefore would not be manifest.
> Were we content with the analysis—as we are liable to be when we
> teach philosophy—though the analysis would indeed prove that
> we must arrive at the intuition of being as the goal of a necessary
> regress, it would not of itself furnish the intuition.[20]

Both the experiences and arguments given so far are philosophical. However, at times Maritain also speaks of non-philosophical

---

17 *Existence and the Existent*, 21.
18 *A Preface to Metaphysics*, 55–56.
19 *A Preface to Metaphysics*, 58–61, and *The Degrees of Knowledge*, 228–29.
20 *A Preface to Metaphysics*, 59.

experiences that can draw one into an intuition of being, "like a kind of natural grace at the sight of a blade of grass or a windmill, or at the sudden perception of the reality of self."[21] This seems to suggest that any experience, if viewed from the metaphysical perspective, might do the trick, becoming an occasion to sense the reality of being. A graphic example of this is supplied by Maritain's wife Raissa, who speaks of feeling the presence of God while riding in a car and watching the forests go by. She goes on to note that such experiences placed her in contact with a direct awareness of being: "It . . . often happened, before I knew the things of faith, that I experienced through a sudden intuition the reality of my being, of the profound, first principle which placed me outside nothingness. The violence of this powerful intuition sometimes frightened me, and first gave me the knowledge of a metaphysical absolute."[22] However, whether it is a philosophical experience or not, the key thing is to take the leap beyond ordinary circumstances, the psychological or ethical factors implicit in them, and to see that reality from the perspective of the act of being that raises it outside of nothingness. Without that intuitive awareness of being, any attempt at metaphysics would be a mere arrangement of ideas without any object, an ideosophy rather than a philosophy.

What is it that we attain in the intuition of being? The aspect of being that is the object of this intuition and that gives rise to the birth of metaphysics is

> . . . being disengaged for its own sake, in the values and resources appertaining to its own intelligibility and reality; which is to say, in that richness, that analogical and transcendental amplitude which is *inviscerated* in the imperfect and multiple unity of its concept and which allows it to cover the infinitude of its analogates and causes it to overflow or superabound in transcendental values and in dynamic values of propensity through which the idea of being transgresses itself.[23]

---

21 *Existence and the Existent*, 21.

22 Raïssa Maritain, *We Have Been Friends Together*, 116. Also cited in *The Degrees of Knowledge*, 297.

23 *Existence and the Existent*, 20. See also *A Preface to Metaphysics*, 35–50.

The one who has experienced the act of being intuitively is in a position to disengage three fundamental characteristics of it: first, the concept of being, insofar as it is the bond that runs throughout all that is, has an analogical character; second, that insofar as the concept of being is not limited to any of the Aristotelian categories of substance or accidents, but runs throughout them, it is a transcendental holding all things outside of nothingness; finally, the one who experiences the intuition of being is in a position to recognize that being is not a mere fact, but an act. Each of these points calls for further elaboration.

The being that is encountered through the intuition of being is "unimaginable." This is to say it is something that is understood by the mind, but cannot be pictured through some sort of sense image. Yet the object of this intuition is suitably named "being," as this has been conceived virtually in sensible objects long before it was isolated through a metaphysical experience intuitively as we are considering it now. But this notion of being cannot be defined; at best we can offer a simple designation that being is that which exists. But this designation is only meaningful insofar as it refers to intuitive experience of being *qua* being. As Maritain explains:

> I see it [i.e., being as the object of this intuition] as an intelligible reality which issues from the least thing and in diverse respects belongs to all things. It is as though on opening a bud there came out something bigger than the world, something that, with values and in ways essentially diverse, belongs to the bud in which I saw it first, to my self and to the very Cause of everything which exists. This being as such, the distinctive object of the metaphysician, is, however, grasped by a pure and genuine intuition only when its polyvalence or analogy, its essentially analogous value, is grasped at the same time.[24]

Maritain makes use of Cajetan's terminology to explain this analogical character of being, holding that it expresses an analogy of strict proportionality. Cajetan, drawing out the implications of Aquinas's discussion of analogy, clearly distinguished between analogy of attribution and

---

24 *A Preface to Metaphysics*, 63.

analogy of proportionality. Analogy of attribution occurs when a term is applied to many cases in reference to a primary instance. For example, the term "healthy" can be used to say "The horse is healthy," or "The medicine is healthy," or "the urine is healthy." In this case the application of the term to the horse is the primary instance, the others are derivative since medicine is called "healthy" as it is the cause of the health of the horse, whereas the urine is called "healthy" since it is a sign of the horse's health. By contrast, analogy of proper proportionality occurs when a term belongs to things in a different manner in some proportion (for instance, 2 is to 4 as 8 is to 16, since both are examples of the relation of being double), or when we speak of an action that is performed in diverse ways by diverse kinds of things (e.g., "The dog knows that it is time for dinner," in comparison with "The man knows geometry," or "The angel knows why the man is praying," or "God knows the heart of the man"). Each of these beings knows, but they know in diverse ways, each in proportion to their nature. Accordingly, names are applied to God insofar as the property indicated is a perfection possessed by creatures (e.g., goodness, justice, mercy, etc.). These properties must be present in God insofar as God is the cause of that perfection in creatures, and the perfection of the effect must be present in the cause for it to act as cause. This means creaturely perfections must belong to God, but they belong to him analogously, in a manner that is proportionate to the divine nature; he possesses perfectly and infinitely those perfections that are possessed by his effects in an imperfect and limited fashion. Accordingly, the intuition of being involves a recognition that being itself is manifested analogically throughout the entire sweep of all that is.

Being is also a transcendental. This is to say that it is not limited to the category of substance, that which subsists through itself and not in or through another, nor to any of the accidental categories of quantity, quality, relation, etc. However, it does not mean that being transcends these categories by being totally above them. Rather, being runs throughout all of the categories without being limited to any of them. Accordingly, being—as it is encountered intuitively—is richer and more pregnant with intelligible values than the idea of being immediately shows. In fact, it intrinsically overflows the very idea in which we try to objectify it. Metaphysicians recognize this applies to all of the transcendentals, each of which is as universal as being itself. Unity, for instance, is being insofar as it is undivided. Thus, in considering being, the mind apprehends its internal consistency. While a being can be divided, in doing so, it becomes a plurality of beings. Insofar as anything is, it is one. Likewise, truth is being in that has been grasped through thought. It is being insofar as it answers to a knowing mind, expressing its particular intelligibility. Finally, goodness shows that everything insofar as it is a being is metaphysically good. This is distinct from moral goodness. It implies that every being is fit to be loved in as much as it is.

Each of the transcendentals is being itself understood under a distinct aspect. Each is a primary notion that enters through looking at being from a particular angle and revealing a new intelligible mystery that is consubstantial with being. These transcendentals are in reality identical; none of these different modes of being add anything in reality to being itself, for beyond being there is utterly nothing at all. Hence they are, in traditional language, "convertible." The distinction between these intelligible infinites is simply conceptual; in reality they are fundamentally the same. Thus, from this one idea of being is included a reality and from this single and unique reality several ideas follow, for through this reality I apprehend something that is one and the same outside my mind as one, true, and good.[25]

Finally, being is also dynamically active. Scholars have long pointed out that Aquinas's Latin term for being, *esse*, is not a noun, but a verb. Implicit in this linguistic choice is the notion that being is active.[26] In this respect, Maritain, emphasizes the intimate connection between being and goodness. The affirmation of being entails an affirmation of inclination or tendency. To exist involves a superabundance that exceeds itself and passes over, as we have noted above, into goodness.

---

25 For Maritain's explanation of being as transcendental, see *A Preface to Metaphysics*, 66–67.

26 A good account of this theme in Aquinas's metaphysics is W. Norris Clarke, SJ, "Action as the Self-Revelation of Being: A Central Theme in the Thought of St. Thomas," in *Exploration in Metaphysics: Being, God, Person* (Notre Dame, IN: University of Notre Dame Press, 1994), 45–64.

The metaphysical goodness is a justification of being. It entails that each being has a certain right to exist simply because it is good. Good implies merit, as well as glory and joy. Thus, a fundamental character of being is its generosity, its tendency to overflow with goodness to communicate itself and its goodness to others.[27]

Maritain appeals to two scholastic formulas to articulate the philosophical basis of his evocative analysis. The first is that of John of St. Thomas, "inclination follows upon every form"; the second is that of Cajetan, "desire follows upon every being." He understands these to mean that wherever there is a being there is tendency and love. This is verified on two distinct planes. First, insofar as the superabundance of every being is regarded from the point of view of its overflow, in which it acts upon and thereby shares itself with others and in relation to that which receives this superabundance. Upon this insight follows the position of Aristotle, that very being tends toward the good. Maritain's examples are that rain is good for vegetables and truth is good for the intellect. Thus, we find within vegetables a natural inclination towards rain, while the intellect has a natural inclination for the truth. More broadly, God is the good of all things, and thus there is an inclination in all things to God as an end or goal.

From this insight Maritain recognizes within being itself a tendency to expand and pass beyond itself in order to communicate a surplus. Thus, every natural agent has a tendency to perfect others by transitive action, or to perfect itself ontologically through the immanent action within itself. Thus, rain waters the garden (transitive), causing the vegetables to grow (intransitive). This occurs in an incommensurably higher way in those beings that have the capacities of knowledge and love. In these cases the subject perfects itself through these actions. The superabundance of knowledge expresses the perfection of being which exists in a particular way, that is, which becomes the other through an intentional mode of existence (as discussed in the previous chapter). The superabundance of love "utters the generosity of a being which tends in a particular fashion, which overflows towards something, itself or

27 *A Preface to Metaphysics*, 68–69.

others in virtue of a supra-subjective existence....—existence as gift." [28]
Accordingly, Maritain distinguishes the natural or radical love that is an
ontological tendency implicit in all beings to act for the ends that follow
upon its nature, from the elicit love that is the love or intelligence for
truth suitable to intellectual creatures.

Being as Apprehended in Judgment

Drawing on Aquinas's metaphysics Maritain sees two distinct, co-
dependent aspects to any created real being or substance. First, there
is the being of that thing, the act that makes it exist. Second, there is
its essence, which determines what kind of thing that entity is going to
be. Both of these aspects are found in every real being. As we saw in
chapter two, in coming to know a material being the mind in its first
act abstracts the essence, so that this essence or form exists in the mind
immaterially, but remains in the thing materially. However, this gives
rise to a problem. As we have said, being is not an essence; in fact, it is
what is precisely contrasted with the essence. But if the mind attains
knowledge through abstracting an essence from matter, it would appear
that being cannot be known. [29]

Obviously, Maritain is far from willing to admit this conclusion.
Rather, he suggests that in order to grasp how the mind attains its
knowledge of existence we need to be attentive to the way in which
judgment works in relation to the activity of abstraction. In typical cases
judgment performs an existential function. Abstraction or eidetic visualization draws the essence from the thing to exist immaterially and
intelligibly in the mind. Accordingly, this first operation comes to terms
with what the thing is. Judgment, on the other hand, affirms or denies
that what has been abstracted is the case. It asserts that it is so, and

---

28 *A Preface to Metaphysics*, 70. The theme of being as a tendency to act for the good is developed
from page 68 to 71.

29 *Existence and the Existent*, 22–23, and *A Preface to Metaphysics*, 67–68. See also John Hittinger,
Liberty, Wisdom, and Grace, 204–5.

thereby reunites existence with the essence in the knowing agent by affirming the extramental existence of the essence.[30]

In judgment a subject and a predicate that differ conceptually in the mind are asserted to be identical in the thing they signify existing outside of the mind. To use one of Maritain's examples, the notion "George Bernard Shaw" is different from the notion "dramatist." Yet in the judgment "George Bernard Shaw is a dramatist," what is signified by these distinct objects of thought is identified in the order of real being. This consideration leads to the recognition of the existential function of judgment. As Maritain writes,

> Thus, the proper function of judgment consists in making the mind pass from the level of simple essence or simple object signified to the mind, to the level of thing or subject possessing existence (actually or possibly), a thing of which the object of thought (predicate) and the subject of thought (subject) are intelligible aspects. . . .
>
> . . . The judgment restores to the transobjective subject the unity that the simple apprehension [i.e., abstraction] (by laying hold of different objects of thought in it) has shattered. That unity could not hold precedence in the mind since, quite to the contrary, the mind undoes it only to reconstitute it afterwards. It held precedence outside the mind, in existence (actual or possible) which, insofar as it is possessed, is outside the order of mere representation or simple apprehension.[31]

According to Maritain, judgment reunifies essence with the existence from which it had been abstracted in the first act of the intellect. Thus, it is in judgment that the mind comes into contact with being in the sense that the metaphysician is interested in being disengaged for its own sake from the sensible nature in which it is clothed. The mind affirms and intentionally experiences existence in judgment in a way that makes existence the consummation of the mind's act of intelligibility.

---

30 *Existence and the Existent,* 16.

31 *The Degrees of Knowledge,* 103 and 104. Maritain also quotes this text in *Existence and the Existent,* 17.

There have certainly been objections to Maritain's use of an intuition of being as the sole entry point to metaphysical reflection.[32] The classical objection is clearly formulated by Joseph Marechal in *Le Point de depart de la métaphysique*. The concern is that Maritain seems to require moving from an experience given in sensation to a judgment about the act of being (*esse*) disengaged from material bodies. Yet the data does not show that being can actuate anything other than physical bodies.[33] It is true that Maritain refers to the beings (*ens*) apprehended in everyday common sense as "clothed" in a sensible nature, whereas the metaphysician begins by distinguishing the act of being in a judgment in its transcendental and analogical values. However, this need not entail that we have at this point shown that being really does actualize some immaterial entity in the way that Marechal's objection assumes. Rather, it simply involves recognizing that this entity is not merely present, but sustained in reality by an act that is transcendentally and analogically related to all other entities that exist, be they material or possibly immaterial. For Maritain's intuition to lead us to metaphysics all that we need is an awareness of the fact that this being is like all others in some way, in being ontologically dependent on being, yet is utterly distinct from all others in another way.[34] At that point being (*esse*) can be disengaged through reflection on the existential function of judgment for metaphysical analysis.

A further, and quite different, objection has been raised by Lawrence Dewan, OP, who argues that there is no hard and fast distinction between the way being is apprehended in common sense and the way it is attained in metaphysics as a science. In contrast to Maritain's emphasis on judgment as the path to being, Fr. Dewan argues that there is a

---

32 I do not address here the rather dismissive general objection that appeal to intuition in philosophy is mere poetry. For a clear response to this based in Maritain, see Hittinger, *Liberty, Wisdom, and Grace*, 206–11. For a defense of Maritain against the view that metaphysics has its starting point in a negative judgment of immateriality of a neutral character, or what Wippel argues is the role of *separatio* in Aquinas's thought, see Matthew S. Pugh, "Maritain, The Intuition of Being, and the Proper Starting Point for Thomistic Metaphysics," *The Thomist* 61, no. 3 (1997): 405–27.

33 Joseph Marechal, *A Marechal Reader,* trans. Joseph Donceel (New York: Herder and Herder, 1970), 146.

34 See *Untrammelled Approaches,* 25–26, and *A Preface to Metaphysics,* 56.

quasi-quidditative knowledge of being in abstraction. Accordingly, he maintains that the ordinary awareness of being is already pregnant with the principles that lead us to metaphysical conclusions. For Fr. Dewan, the intuition of being that is the birth of metaphysics is not being as discovered through reflection upon judgment, but rather the being that is found in "the drawing of the first metaphysical conclusion." [35]

However, this would not be an intuition in Maritain's sense at all, since the drawing of a conclusion must involve a process of deductive inference—which is precisely what Maritain distinguishes from intuition. As we pointed out above, in *Preface to Metaphysics* Maritain does suggest that we can confirm or even be led towards the intuition of being through rational analysis; yet while rational analysis is indeed necessary, it is not sufficient, for it must be completed through the experience of intuition. Maritain seems to be suggesting that the rational analysis and the intuition are co-dependent.[36] This seems to rule out the possibility of locating the intuition of being in the drawing of the first metaphysical conclusion, without abandoning the sense of intuition that is at work in Maritain's thought altogether.

Yet Fr. Dewan's main concern is to argue for the continuity between our ordinary experience of material beings and the conclusions we arrive at through developing metaphysical knowledge. In his view, Maritain separates the beings considered in the everyday experience of common sense from being considered in the science of metaphysics too harshly.[37] In Maritain's defense, however, it is important to note that this is a distinction of two aspects within one and the same thing. A glass of milk is considered to exist in one way by the child who wants a drink and in another way by the metaphysician who wishes to know. Nevertheless, what is known by both is the same existent thing, albeit objectified in two quite different ways. Moreover, Fr. Dewan suggests that the ordinary experience of being and the first operation of the intellect,

35 Lawrence Dewan, OP, "Jacques Maritain, St. Thomas, and the Birth of Metaphysics," *Maritain Studies*, vol. 13 (1997), 16.

36 *A Preface to Metaphysics*, 59.

37 Dewan, "Jacques Maritain, St. Thomas, and the Birth of Metaphysics," 15.

abstraction, contains within it the principles that have the power to demonstrate metaphysical conclusions. These principles have just not been made explicit or applied yet.

Here I think it is important to emphasize that although Maritain distinguishes abstraction from judgment very clearly, he also insists that both are acts of the *entire intellect*. We are, once again, distinguishing in order to unite. This means that for Maritain, being is apprehended in the different acts of understanding, but in different ways. In *Existence and the Existent* he explains,

> Essences are the object of the first operation of the intellect, or simple apprehension. It is judgment which the act of existing confronts. The intellect envelopes itself and is self contained, is wholly present in each of its operations . . . it apprehends and judges in the same instant. It forms its first idea (that of being) while uttering its first judgment (of existence), and utters its first judgment while forming its first idea. I say, therefore, that it lays hold of the treasure which properly belongs to judgment, in order to envelop it in simple apprehension itself.[38]

This is clearly more nuanced than a simple division that equates being confronted in simple apprehension or abstraction as common-sense knowledge, and being apprehended in judgment as metaphysical. The two acts of the intellect function together in producing the intuition of being that is the seed of all genuine metaphysical knowledge. The intellect, Maritain continues,

> . . . visualizes that treasure in an initial and absolutely original idea, in a privileged idea which is not the result of the process of simple apprehension alone, but of the laying hold of that which the intellect affirms from the moment it judges, namely, the act of existing. It seizes upon the eminent intelligibility or the super-intelligibility which the act of judging deals with (that of existence), in order to make of it an object of thought.[39]

---

38 *Existence and the Existent*, 23.
39 *Existence and the Existent*, 23.

In the intuition of being, both operations of the intellect are intimately involved. Judgment is placed in the role of rendering explicit what is contained in simple apprehension. This is made very explicit in Maritain's last discussion of the topic in a conference he gave in 1967 and that was subsequently published, entitled "Reflections on a Wounded Nature." In this essay he points to two distinct concepts of being that have different origins and meanings. Yet they are nevertheless intimately related. He explains this in a very important passage in one of his last essays, writing,

> There is a concept of being (our second concept of existence), which arises in the mind *after* the intuition of being, by a turning back of simple apprehension, or of intelligence as formative of ideas, onto that intuition; all of this happens on a certain level, the level of metaphysical intellection (even in the case of someone who does not realize what is going on, in the case of a poet for instance).

Here Maritain is introducing a concept of being that arises from an intuition of being, where there is an attempt to express it reflexively in conceptual terms by way of a metaphysical intellection, even if this apprehension remains merely connatural, as in the example of a poet. This is distinguished from a different way of conceptualizing existence that occurs before—or independently of—the intuition of being, which is merely a bare and common-sense, abstractive notion of being, in which the concept of being is simply the widest possible concept:

> And there is another concept of existence (our first concept of existence), which is formed in the mind *before* the intuition of being has welled up within it: I mean on the level of the first degree of abstraction, which is the level on which man's thought moves ordinarily and in the first place. This concept of existence is of abstractive origin, not judicative, and, yes, it precedes the intuition of being, and is in no way an integral part of it. It remains completely foreign to it.[40]

---

40 "Reflections on a Wounded Nature," in *Untrammeled Approaches*, 221. Seeing being as related to the different acts of the intellect in various ways also allows Maritain to reply to Gilson's concern that if being is known through judgment, there is no place for an "intuition of being." See also Étienne Gilson, *Being and Some Philosophers* (Toronto: Pontifical Institute of Mediaeval

This is certainly a stronger distinction between common sense apprehension and metaphysical knowledge than Fr. Dewan accepts. On his view, the principles of metaphysics are implicitly contained in the ordinary experience of beings known through the first operation of the mind by abstraction. There is some truth to this. However, I don't see how it suffices as a philosophical refutation of Maritain's view. In fact, Maritain explicitly admits that as long as one remains at the level of abstraction, the awareness of being remains implicit.[41] One could just as easily say that these same principles are contained implicitly in human sense experience, for without sense experience there would be no way for us to know about them. Yet the metaphysician is interested in making our knowledge explicit. Nevertheless, the question remains: "How is that latent potentiality of metaphysical principles made known explicitly?" I fail to find a clear answer to that question in Fr. Dewan's critique.[42]

For Maritain, by contrast, we have a clear answer insofar as the intuition of being serves to moves us beyond the level of rational analysis that is concerned only with conceptual coherence, and forces us to disengage being from our awareness of the particulars of sense experience and the mind's grasp of the natures of material things, by bringing us into contact with the metaphysical dimensions of being through experience. This decisive encounter leads us to make explicit a full understanding

---

Studies, 1952), 216–27. For an excellent account of this aspect of Maritain's thought, see Joseph Owens, CSsR, "Maritain's Three Concepts of Existence," 298–99. Gilson's main critique is that an intuition of being would entail a direct intuition of God's very nature, which is utterly impossible for a created intellect. See Étienne Gilson, "Propos sur l'etre et sa notion," in *San Tommaso e il pensiero moderno*, ed. Antonio Piolanti (Citta Nuova: Pontificia Accademia Romana de S. Tommaso d' Aquino, 1974), 8. This approach is further developed by John F.X. Knasas, "Gilson vs. Maritain: The Start of Thomistic Metaphysics," in *The Future of Thomism*, eds. Deal W. Hudson and Dennis W. Moran (Notre Dame, IN: University of Notre Dame Press, 1992), 169–83. In my view this line of argument has been definitely refuted by James G. Hanink, who points to types of experiences that originate in sense experience but allow for an intellectual awareness that extends beyond the merely material order (for instance, the experience of an irreducible singularity such as a rose, or our experience of our own acts of knowledge and free choice). See James G. Hanink, "In Defense of The Intuition of Being," in *Distinctions of Being: Philosophical Approaches to Reality* (Washington, DC: The American Maritain Association, 2013), 167–80.

41 "Reflections on a Wounded Nature," 222.

42 I should note, however, that Fr. Dewan's focus is on the degree to which Maritain's presentation coincides with that of St. Thomas. The abundance of texts that he supplies from Aquinas is certainly helpful and deserves careful study. However, my only concern in this discussion is whether Maritain's argument is a defensible philosophical position in its own right.

of being in its analogical, transcendental, and dynamic character as we articulated it in the previous section. Finally, the metaphysical dimensions of being are rendered explicit by the mind's reflection on its acts of judgment. In most judgments the idea or concept comes before the judgment. The judgment "Truffle is a dog," for example, presupposes the concept "dog." The idea of being is unique, for in judgments like "I am" or "things are," it follows the judgment and is arrived at through it. It is important to keep in mind that linguistic analysis is not adequate to arrive at the intuition of being. These existential judgments do not merely apply a predicate to a subject:

> It is, rather, the subject itself that this judgment affirms or posits in the mind, as that subject itself is posited outside the mind, in extra-mental reality; and to produce this judicative act, by really *thinking* it, is, for the intelligence, in the very heart of the spiritual intimacy of its own operation, to grasp intuitively, or *to see*, the being, the existence, the extra-mental *esse* of that subject. This is what I call the intuition of being.[43]

In this text the existential character of judgment is made explicit. Judgment does not merely assert the predicate of the subject, but rather also asserts that it *is*. In this manner, it brings being into view of the intellect, and this encounter of the mind with the act of being is the only authentic point of departure for metaphysics. In short, to reject the intuition of being entails limiting the mind to sense data and strictly logical inferences from that data, thereby cutting it off from any authentically intellectual apprehension of reality as such.

Metaphysical Knowledge of Essence

Metaphysics is not, however, limited to knowing the fact that something is—it is also concerned with what things are. This entails that it must explore both the being and the essence of things. As we saw in the previous chapter, philosophy and the sciences each are able to know the essence of things, albeit in different ways. The nominalism Maritain

---

43 "Reflections on a Wounded Nature," 220.

decries in much modern philosophy, however, has led to a tendency to turn away from knowledge of the essence of things and reduce all cognition of what things are to a matter of induction, comparison of individual cases, and statistics. This is to say that only the empiriological method employed by science can come to know what things are.

Maritain, however, insists that there is a twofold knowledge of the essences found in things. The first he calls *dianoetic* intellection, and the second, *perionetic* intellection. Dianoetic intellection moves through what is sensed in order to understand the essence of the thing. The sensible properties that we experience become signs of the essence itself. There are two kinds of dianoetic intellection. The first is proper to philosophy and allows us to understand the essence of a thing through an awareness of its properties. In this way we gradually come to know what a bird is through experience of the diverse members of the species, which leads to a progressively deeper awareness of the common features of members of the diverse species that make up this genus. The second is the domain of mathematics and grasps the relevant essences through abstraction and reflection on what has been experienced. Here the accidents are of little help, as it makes no difference to the geometer whether the triangles she demonstrates about are made of gold or bronze or wood.[44] However, it is important to recognize that in neither case do we attain knowledge of essences directly and through themselves, as if sense experience allowed our minds to automatically read off the essence of the material things that we encounter mechanically, through the mind's "taking a look" at the nature. That sort of knowledge of things from within is better suited to angels than human beings. Yet, we can come to know the essence of material things through dianoetic intellection. This process does indeed attain knowledge of the essences of material things, but it does so by way of the signs that manifest these essences, which are the properties of those things: "The hunt for definitions passes through the thickets of experience."[45] We certainly do not come to know a thing by a direct intellectual intuition of its essence.

44 *The Degrees of Knowledge*, 216–17.
45 *The Degrees of Knowledge*, 216.

Rather, we come to know a thing in its essence through the properties that signify that essence to the knowing mind. To put it another way, the essence is the term—not the principle—of our inquiry. This sort of knowledge of essence, through dianoetic intellection, is proper to philosophy. It is the kind of intellection of essence that is the concern of the metaphysician and the philosopher of nature.

Perinoetic intellection, on the other hand, is a "circumferential" form of knowledge. It, too, grasps something of the essence, but from the outside. It is the kind of knowledge that is attained through the empiriological methods of modern science, which we discussed in the previous chapter. Into this category falls the study of things through inductive and statistical methods. Here we are dealing with a knowledge by signs that stand in place of the essential natures, rather than signs that manifest those natures, which are the ones that are of interest to the philosopher as such. Maritain explains this distinction with considerable clarity, writing,

> There is, on the one hand, the knowledge of essences (substantial) by "signs" or accidents (properties) which manifest them, at least in their most universal notes (*dianoetic intellection*). On the other hand, there is the knowledge of essences by the "signs" of which it will be a question below and which are known *in place of* the natures themselves, which in this case remain inaccessible in their formal constitutive (*perinoetic intellection*).[46]

In both cases we are apprehending the essence through signs. However, in the case of dianoetic intellection, these signs are the common properties of the species which reveal the essential nature of the thing we study, albeit indirectly. In the case of perinoetic intellection these signs are used to stand in place of the essence. Of course, this does not

---

46 *The Degrees of Knowledge*, 219. This distinction is explored and contrasted with the view of William Wallace, OP, who rejects it, arguing that it entails too strong a distinction between philosophical knowledge and the natural sciences and that it leads to an unduly positivistic view of these sciences in Catherine Peters, "Dianoesis and Perinoesis in the Natural Sciences," in *Facts are Stubborn Things: Thomistic Perspectives in the Philosophies of Nature and Science*, ed. Matthew K. Minerd (Washington, DC: The American Maritain Association, 2019), 69–79. Maritain's views on the knowledge of natural science and their relation to positivism are explored in chapter 3. See William A. Wallace, *The Modelling of Nature* (Washington, DC: The Catholic University of America Press, 1996), 224–27.

amount to denying the reality of the essence, but rather of hiding it more than revealing it. Here we are dealing with clusters of accidents that are grasped insofar as they can be observed or measured. In this case the essence is not known by signs that manifest it, but by signs that hide it.[47]

Beyond these two forms of cognizing the essence of a thing, Maritain also recognizes what he calls *ananoetic* intellection. This is the analogical apprehension of the nature of being that follows upon the intuition of being. It is through a form of cognition that the analogical and transcendental character of being is apprehended. As we have seen, being is the first concept of the intellect, and that in which it resolves all of its objects of thought. This leads Maritain to recognize the transcendental and analogous character of being. As he explains it in *Preface to Metaphysics:*

> I see it [i.e., being as the object of metaphysics] as an intelligible reality which issues from the least thing and in diverse respects belongs to all things. It is as though on opening a bud there came out something bigger than the world, something that, with values and in ways essentially diverse, belongs to the bud in which I saw it first, to my self and to the very Cause of everything which exists. This being as such, the distinctive object of the metaphysician, is, however, grasped by a pure and genuine intuition only when its polyvalence or analogy, its essentially analogous value, is grasped at the same time.[48]

Furthermore, it is impossible to add anything to the concept of being that would distinguish it from other things, for anything that was beyond being would be utterly nothing. However, there are distinct modes of beings. For example, some things exist as substances in their own right, while others are accidents that modify these substances and depend on them in order to exist. Socrates exists through himself, but the whiteness of Socrates's skin exists in, and depends upon, Socrates.

More importantly, some ways of existing are co-extensive with being itself. It is here that ananoetic intellection comes to the forefront.

---

47 *The Degrees of Knowledge,* 220.
48 *A Preface to Metaphysics,* 66.

Such ways of existing are present as an aspect of all things that have being. Following a long-established scholastic tradition, Maritain calls being and these attributes that are co-extensive with being transcendentals. Such attributes are not limited to one specific mode of being in the way that the Aristotelian categories such as quantity, quality, relation, etc., are. Rather, they run throughout all things that exist in any way whatsoever. They are functions of being as such. [49]

As we have seen earlier in this chapter, Maritain articulates these attributes as follows: (1) being itself; (2) unity, which is being insofar as it is undivided (a being can be divided, but then we have two beings as a result, not one); (3) the true, which is both being in relation to the mind that confronts the real becoming the other in the mode of intentional being, and being insofar as it is intelligible in its own right; and (4) the good in the metaphysical sense, which is being understood as the term that love can delight in and that can move the will through the very fact that it is. [50] We use these different terms to highlight these conceptually distinct aspects of being: actuality, indivisibility, intelligibility, and desirability. Thus, what they signify in the order of reality is one and the same entity, although we must have recourse to distinct terms and concepts in order to understand this entity adequately. We distinguish the properties conceptually in order to more clearly understand that what the terms signify is united in reality. [51]

It is of fundamental importance that these transcendentals are not mere universals. To understand being as simply the most universal of genera would be to fall into the Hegelian error in which being is a mere abstraction. To think of being this way is to strip away any individual difference from our concept of existence. But if we do this, the logical consequence is, as Hegel recognized, the paradoxical position that being is identical with nothing. [52] On the contrary, the concept of

---

49 *The Degrees of Knowledge*, 224.

50 *The Degrees of Knowledge*, 225. For some reason, Maritain does not mention the traditional transcendental of unity in this text. It is included in the later work *A Preface to Metaphysics*, 69.

51 *A Preface to Metaphysics*, 69.

52 Georg Wilhelm Friedrich Hegel, *The Science of Logic*, trans. George di Giovanni (New York: Cambridge University Press, 2010), pt. I, §132–33.

being—like the other transcendentals—is implicitly and actually multiple. It applies to absolutely everything whatsoever there is in existence. Accordingly, the transcendentals have a vital unifying role to play: "It is remarkable that men really communicate with one another only by passing through being or one of its properties."[53] However, the concept of being, as understood transcendentally, is also one in a certain respect, for it does not completely abstract from its various analogates. It is disengaged from them, without being conceivable apart from them. Consequently, a transcendental concept is essentially analogous. It does not have a primary univocal sense which is then transferred to another broader context.[54]

In the case of the transcendentals, we are able to know they apply by analogy universally throughout the realm of the material world that we experience, and that they must apply to any being that could possibly exist whatsoever. This means that they must also be instantiated in any immaterial entity that might exist, be it God, an angel, or the soul after death. Further, Maritain holds that we know this of any possible being whatsoever, prior to demonstrating the existence of such entities. Because of the primacy of being as act, anything that exists must be a being, true, and good. This holds just as much for immaterial entities as material ones. Accordingly, it is appropriate that, having elaborated Maritain's understanding of being as analogous and transcendental, we turn to his arguments in support of the existence of God and his understanding of the philosophical elaboration of the Divine nature.

---

53 *Art and Scholasticism*, trans. Joseph W. Evans (New York: Charles Scribner's Sons, 1962), 32.
54 *The Degrees of Knowledge*, 227–28. *A Preface to Metaphysics*, 67.

CHAPTER 5

Natural Theology

> For man there are as many ways of approach to God as
> there are wanderings on the earth or paths to his own heart.
> *Approaches to God*, xi

B eing a convert to Catholicism and a thorough-going Thomist, it should be no surprise that Maritain defends the possibility of philosophical proofs of the existence of God. However, he is reticent to call them proofs, as the contemporary sense of this term is narrow and unduly restrictive. Rather, in keeping with Aquinas's own understanding of his arguments as "ways" to God, Maritain tends to refer to "approaches" to God.[1] Yet this is not to say that he is reluctant to admit that it is possible—and indeed, vitally important— to have a fully rational basis for our belief in God. Yet the arguments we develop even at the highest reaches of metaphysics do not disclose God's nature to us in its fullness. What they show is not God's very act of being, but merely that we must affirm his existence. Even this knowledge of God's existence is ananoetic in nature; this means it is knowledge by analogy and as such it remains an indirect knowledge

---

1 *Approaches to God*, trans. Peter O'Reilly (New York: Harper and Brothers, 1954), 17.

inferred from our experience of the world.[2] Accordingly, philosophical arguments concerning the existence and nature of God do not limit the divine to the scope of the human intellect. By contrast, in knowing things proportionate to itself, the intellect submits itself to them, but it also subjects those objects to the limits of our understanding and the methods we use to verify and know them. This is not the case in our demonstrations about God. Obviously we do not measure, touch, or manipulate God in order to know him better:

> To demonstrate the existence of God is neither to subject Him to our grasp, nor to define Him, nor to seize Him, nor to manipulate anything except ideas which are inadequate to such an object, nor to judge anything except our own proper and radical dependence. *The procedure by which reason demonstrates that God exists, puts reason itself in an attitude of natural adoration and of intellectual admiration.*[3]

Our efforts to demonstrate God's existence only show what we must affirm of him, while leaving the nature of the existence that we affirm of God shrouded in mystery. This is what led Maritain to speak of the "majesty and poverty of metaphysics" in his preface to *The Degrees of Knowledge*. Speaking of the science of metaphysics he writes, "Its majesty? It is wisdom. Its poverty? It is human science. It names God, Yes! But not by His Own Name. For it is not possible to paint a picture of God as it is to draw a tree or a conic section."[4]

In this chapter I focus on what is unique in Maritain's treatment of the question. While he gives much consideration and weight to the classical five ways of St. Thomas Aquinas, he also makes some original contributions to this question as a philosopher in his own right, and it is

2   *The Degrees of Knowledge,* 236.
3   *The Degrees of Knowledge,* 239. Emphasis added. Also quoted in *Approaches to God,* 24–25. The spiritual implications of the five ways suggested here are fruitfully explored in Part I of Reginald Garrigou-Lagrange, OP, *Providence,* trans. Dom Bede Rose, OSB (Rockford, IL: Tan Books, 1998).
4   *The Degrees of Knowledge,* 1.

upon these that I wish to focus here.[5] The first of these are his articulation of a pre-philosophical approach to God, which he finds underlying the natural thrust of human reason in its ordinary condition throughout human history and cultures. In terms of philosophical argumentation for God's existence, Maritain, as I have said, expounds Aquinas's arguments; however, he also develops his own arguments based upon an analysis of the conditions entailed by our own experience of human thought. Moreover, in view of the challenge the contemporary mind has with metaphysical argumentation, he also provides a provocative account of the ways in which the firsthand experience of practical reasoning can lead us toward an awareness of God's existence. The discussion of God's existence also points to his nature as an eternal and perfectly good being who is the effective cause sustaining all beings and their acts. Consequently, it is important to look at Maritain's innovative understanding of the relationship between evil and God's eternal plan for the world.

A Pre-Philosophical Approach to God

One of Maritain's important contributions to this topic is his recognition that prior to any sophisticated philosophical reasoning, the natural dynamic of human thought can lead us to an awareness of God's existence. This is not a question of a logical demonstration or argument. Rather, it is the intuitive movement of the mind to God. This is not to say that every individual will go through this process or accept its result. It is a natural progress of the human mind to God. It is neither a direct intuition of the divine, which would be super-human, nor is it simply a matter of deductive logical reasoning. Rather, it is a matter of natural reasoning. It originates in an intuitive grasp of existence as the primordial reality of beings that change, going in and out of existence, that

---

5 Forty pages out of a hundred in *Approaches to God* are devoted to Aquinas's five ways. While his reading of them is insightful in number of ways, and they do constitute arguments he philosophically accepts, they are very familiar and have been the subject of numerous detailed studies. Readers interested in an in-depth understanding should consult John F. Wippel, *The Metaphysical Thought of Thomas Aquinas: From Finite Being to Uncreated Being* (Washington, DC: The Catholic University of America Press, 2000).

leads the mind to see the necessity of a being that is utterly necessary. This is a process people generally apprehend prior to any contact with philosophical methods.[6] Nevertheless, it yields genuine knowledge that is virtually metaphysical. That is to say, it is capable of being formulated in a metaphysically rigorous manner even though this may not yet have been achieved.

For Maritain this process can be understood in terms of three fundamental stages. The starting point is an experience of an intuition of being.[7] This is the vital seed out of which our knowledge of God's existence develops. We must apprehend the act of existing that gives rise to every act and perfection, for it is through this that all the intelligible structures of reality are actuated. This intuition recognizes both my own existence and the existence of other things. Without it our philosophical reasoning inevitably becomes an insular schema concerning merely the relations between ideas without any contact to reality. The intuition of being is, in the first place, the awareness of others independent of me; it is recognition that these others are things beyond my control. Each of them is something to which I am subjected, whether I like it or not. In this awareness I realize that each thing is something that exists and acts in its own way autonomously: it asserts itself, it makes a difference, I am subject to it. From this consideration I am led to recognize my own fragility. Things assert themselves over me, acting upon me in ways I have no control over. They are in so many ways a threat to me, and from their point of view I am a threat to them.

This awareness of fragility and threat brings us to a new awareness, highlighting the fact I am subject to forces beyond my control. This leads to the recognition that inevitably I, too, will die, that my very being is a "Being-with-nothingness." My manner of existence entails my own eventual destruction, and so it is with all of the material beings that surround me.

The final aspect of this intuition is the realization that the being of things that are beyond my control (which is nonetheless

6   "A New Approach to God," in *The Range of Reason*, 90.

7   Maritain's understanding of the intuition of being is discussed in detail in chapter four.

Being-with-nothingness for these are beings that are born, exist for a time, and corrupt or die) presupposes Being-without-nothingness, a self-sufficient and necessarily existing being. If beings exist there must be some being that is absolute and free from all corruption and death.[8] This course of natural reasoning is nothing other than working out the implications implied in the intuition of being; it is simply the intuition of being fully realized.

From this experience of the intuition of being follows a second stage in which I realize that my own fragility is common to all the things that surround me. Being-with-nothingness implies Being-without-nothingness, "But the universal whole of which I am a part is itself Being-with-nothingness, by the very fact that I am part of it."[9] It follows that, since this universe that surrounds me does not exist through itself, the Being-without-nothingness that I have discovered must exist apart from it. It must be another whole, a self-sufficient and independent being that actuates all other beings and which exists through itself. In recognizing the very dynamism implicit within the intuition of being, one is led to see that absolute being transcends the entire natural universe and to confront the reality of God.

Maritain made no pretenses to be presenting an original path to God in articulating this thought. To the contrary, he called it "human reason's eternal way of approaching God."[10] In fact, he summed up the strategy underlying this approach to God succinctly: "This pre-philosophical knowledge can also be described as a spontaneous application of the principle: no artifact is possible without a maker."[11] Throughout this discussion we see again Maritain's commitment to a philosophy that is not only a matter of abstract thought and argument, but one that evolves naturally from the dynamic character of the human person's

---

8   This argument is presented in a very similar way in *Approaches to God*, 18–20; "A New Approach to God," in *The Range of Reason*, 90; and "God and Science," in *On the Use of Philosophy* (Princeton, NJ: Princeton University Press, 1961), 60. See also Olivier Lacombe, "Jacques Maritain Metaphysician," *The New Scholasticism* XLVI, no. 1 (1972): 24–29.

9   *Approaches to God*, 20.

10 *Approaches to God*, 20.

11 "God and Science," 60.

encounter with reality through lived experience in a wide variety of ways.

Speculative Approaches to God

Maritain not only explored the intellect's spontaneous and natural dynamism towards God, but he also developed philosophical arguments for God's existence. In doing so he placed himself consciously within a long philosophical tradition. Indeed, he takes up a number of arguments that had been developed by others, notably St. Thomas Aquinas's five ways. For the reasons stated above, I do not intend to explore those arguments in detail here. However, a few points are worth making, as Maritain's arguments are developed in a way that is in keeping with Aquinas's methodology. Of special importance is the fact that all of the proofs that Maritain would accept take their starting point from experience or from the effects of God that we encounter in the world. They then reason back to God as the only adequate cause of these effects. If the effects exist, then God, too, must exist. In a way we could say they are all variations on the principle, noted above, that no artifact is possible without a maker.[12]

Maritain developed two speculative philosophical arguments for God's existence. (He called them "speculative" in the sense of arguments that are ordered simply towards the truth, in order to distinguish them from approaches that rest upon practical reasoning that is bound up with human action—arguments that we will investigate in the next section.) Maritain developed two closely related arguments for God's existence. The first was presented in *The Degrees of Knowledge* (1932) and the second in *Approaches to God* (1953). Surprisingly, both arguments take their starting point from the human experience of thought. This is surprising, since such a point of departure might be thought to be closer to the approach of St. Anselm or Descartes than anything to

---

12 It should be noted that while Maritain's sixth way does not argue from sense experience, it does still argue from effect to cause. Nor does a start in sense experience seem fundamental to Aquinas's arguments. The fourth way, for instance, about the degrees of truth or goodness in things, moves from an effect to God as a cause, but not an effect known directly by sense experience.

be found in the Thomistic tradition with which Maritain identifies.[13] Anselm famously argued from the definition of God as "that being than which none greater can be conceived" to the claim that God must exist or he would not be the greatest being that can be conceived, after all. Likewise, Descartes began from a concept of God as an all-powerful and perfect being to argue that only an all-powerful and perfect being could be the cause of an idea like that, and, consequently, such a being must really exist. Thomists, including Maritain, reject these approaches arguing that from a concept nothing about the real existence of the thing signified by that concept can possibly follow. To exist in the mind as a concept is one thing; to exist in the real world as a being in one's own right is quite another. It is helpful to keep this point in mind when examining Maritain's arguments in order to see how he distinguishes his approach from the tradition inaugurated by St. Anselm that he rejects as misguided.

In *The Degrees of Knowledge* Maritain presents an argument for God's existence that takes its starting point from the philosopher's experience of his own thought. The philosopher comes to understand his thought "reflexively"; that is to say, first he thinks about some object or other, and in light of that he comes to turn his attention back upon the act of thinking itself. This act of thought presents itself as an ontological quality having a real existence that is at the moment utterly certain and undeniable. Yet at the same time, the act of thought is distinguished from the objects in the external world that I generally think about. The real being of this entity is one thing; my act of thinking about it and forming a concept of it is another. Accordingly, "two incommensurable orders" are discovered (i.e., real and intentional (viz. conceptual) being), that have no univocal relation between them, but can only be compared through their analogical participations in being.

Beyond the real existence of his thought and its distinction from the things in the world the philosopher is also aware that his thought

---

13 Joseph Bobik has argued that arguments with a similar starting point in the internal experience of thought can be found in Aquinas, particularly *S.T.*, I, q. 79, a. 4 c. and *De Spiritualibus Creaturis*, a. 10 c. See Joseph Bobik, "The Sixth Way of Aquinas," *The Thomist* 42, no. 3 (1978): 373–99.

is, in many ways, a mystery—and that, among the world of bodies, it emerges as a stranger in a strange land. Our thought is subject to time and error, forgetfulness, distractions, and emotional upheavals. It is not transparent to itself and so often its objects remain unclear to it. This awareness of thought's servitude leads the philosopher to know that thought taken in itself and in its own pure and formal manner has aspects of a transcendent order whose ultimate term cannot be merely human, but divine. Human thought, impeded as it is by so many challenges, is not pure thought, but is rather a witness to the privileges of pure thought. Pure thought in its absolute form is its own object. It is absolutely spontaneous and self-sufficient. For pure thought to exist would be to think not about some other thing, but about the act of thinking itself: receiving nothing from other things, but making them.[14]

Any philosopher will, however, immediately realize that he is not thought; rather, he *has* thoughts. If he has thought without being this thought, then it seems to follow that he derives that thought from something beyond himself. This thought must itself have a cause, since the principle of causality is not merely a feature of sensible things, but is rather a necessity involved in being itself. Consequently, it applies to all that exists or can exist. The philosopher experiences the insufficiency of his own thought in itself, and this insufficiency cannot be thought without knowing that this thought depends upon some other. This is not merely a dependency on the material conditions of the philosopher's body or the limits of the circumstances surrounding it. Rather, what is needed is something that actuates that thought and brings it into existence within the individual. This cause cannot merely be another limited thought, for it, too, would be just as dependent on something beyond itself. This would be to open the door to an infinite series of causes, and that is just to say there is no reason of being at work at all. Accordingly, Maritain concludes:

> There must, therefore, be a thought which is thought, and which is the first cause of my thought. From it must be excluded absolutely

---

14 *The Degrees of Knowledge*, 236–37.

any relation as a stuff or any material causality whatever with regard to my thought. It is a cause which compenetrates with its pure efficiency the whole being of my thought, and is absolutely separated in its essence from that same thought (which thus really remains my thought). It is absolutely uncaused Thought itself which causes in me and with me my act of thought. I already glimpsed the proper conditions of such thought which has itself as its existence and as its object. Now I know these privileges are those of an existent real.[15]

As I noted above, this argument bears a certain resemblance to Descartes's argument in *Meditation III*, insofar as it begins from the first-person experience of thought and argues that the only adequate cause of this thought is God. However, the similarities are superficial since Descartes's proof rests upon the assumption that being is univocal. For Descartes the inference to God rests upon the assumption that the objective reality an idea possesses in my mind must have a cause with as much formal reality in the external world.[16] Maritain's argument, however, rests upon the view that there is a fundamental difference between these two modes of being. Indeed, he describes them as two "incommensurable orders" and argues that they are analogically related. This means that irrespective of the similarities in structure, the two arguments are based on a completely different principle. Furthermore, Descartes's argument, like that of Anselm, rests upon the content of our thought about God. It is the fact that my idea of God is infinite and perfect that gives the argument any traction it might have. By contrast, Maritain's argument depends only on the claim that I have any thoughts at all and that these thoughts do, in some way, actually exist as thoughts, irrespective of whether or not what they signify exists outside of the mind. Accordingly, the argument depends upon the validity for intentional existence as a whole, which is what necessitates the inference to the divine mind. This is why Maritain can defend his own approach, while arguing that Descartes's argument was inadequate.

---

15 *The Degrees of Knowledge*, 238.
16 This is the argument of Descartes's third Meditation.

Nevertheless, I think there are two fundamental challenges for Maritain's argument. The first is there seems to be little justification of his inference from our limited experience of thought to the need for "Pure Thought." A consideration of our limited and derivative thoughts may lead us to the recognition of the possibility of a pure thought, but why should it require such thought to exist? Answering this question is the role of the causal argument that Maritain introduces, but it is hard to see that we need to appeal to some pure thought to act as a cause here. Each thought is fundamentally a qualitative accident of a human person, caused by the mind and its encounter with things. It is unclear why this is not a sufficient explanation of our cognitive experience.

However, one might claim the argument presented in *Degrees of Knowledge* is really not much more than an adaptation of Aquinas's first way to a particular instance of motion, namely, human thought. In that argument, Aquinas argued from the observation of motion. However, motion in this context is not understood as local motion, but rather the reduction of potency to actuality. Any actualization of a potency is an instance of motion in that sense of the term. Although he does not use the language of act and potency, Maritain's focus on the individual act of thought can be seen as a narrowing down of Aquinas's original argument to a specific example of a potency being actualized. Viewed in this way, it seems legitimate to say that Aquinas's proof starts from a very broad principle and that Maritain simply applies that very same principle to the example of thought.

In this perspective the argument developed in *Approaches to God*, which Maritain names a "sixth way," is more innovative than the earlier attempt at a proof for God's existence, although it is clearly a development of the earlier argument. In fact, he introduces the argument by admitting that for a long time he had thought it was a mere "research hypothesis," but gradually became convinced that it was rationally valid and certain. Again, Maritain distinguishes a pre-philosophical approach that is intuitive in nature from the complementary and subsequent philosophical or scientific approach that is a metaphysical justification elaborated through logical argument. This later philosophical approach begins with recognizing an intuitive experience that emerges from the

life of thought proper to the intellect and subjecting it to a phenomenological and ontological analysis.

The experience in question is simply the one that everyone experiences from time to time—although it is more frequent among those
with an intellectual disposition—of being enraptured in the consideration of a truth. Maritain describes this experience evocatively, writing,

> I am busy thinking. Everything in me is concentrated on a certain
> truth which has caught me up in its wake. This truth carries me off.
> All the rest is forgotten. Suddenly I come back to myself; a reflec-
> tion is awakened in me which seems to me quite incongruous,
> altogether unreasonable, but whose evidence takes possession of
> me, in my very perception of my act of thought: *how is it possible
> that I was born?*[17]

What he means by this question is really, *How can it be that there was
a time at which my thinking intellect did not exist?* Maritain notes that
the intellect develops in two different ways. Firstly, it develops in what
can be called "life proportioned to man." This refers to the mind's development in the midst of our ordinary social and physical activities. It
involves a series of events in time that are bound up with sense and
imagination that the intellect enlightens through its act of understanding. Secondly, the intellect develops in a way that can be called "life
proportioned to the intellect." In this case the mind is focused purely
on thought abstracted from sensation or the imagination in order to
contemplate intelligible objects themselves. It is in this mode of thought
that the intuition Maritain highlights occurs. Then it is possible to be
struck by the strangeness of saying what is now engaged in the act of
thought was once merely nothing and did not exist. "Where I am now
in the act of intellection and of consciousness of my thought, was there
once nothing? That is impossible; it is not possible that at a certain
moment what is now thinking was not at all, was a pure nothing. How
could this have been born into existence?"[18] This tension is not a logical contradiction; rather, he suggests it is a lived contradiction and

17   *Approaches to God*, 70.
18   *Approaches to God*, 70–71.

compares it to being in a room with a person for hours who then tells you he has just entered a moment ago; he knows by direct experience what has been said is impossible. The claim that I who am now in the act of thinking has always existed is imposed on me once I consider it in this experience. Yet as soon as I draw back from that experience of thought, I realize that I was born just like everyone else. Even though I obviously have no memory of the event, I recognize with certitude that I am like all other human beings in this respect.

This creates a dilemma: on the one hand, my experience of thought presents me with the absurdity that at one time I did not exist, while on the other hand the reality of my birth demands that I did begin to exist. For Maritain the only possible solution to the dilemma is to suggest that my thought must have pre-existed my birth in some other way. This, he argues, could only happen in the mind of God. My thoughts must have existed in a personal way in the divine mind before I was created. My current experience of thought is then understood as a participation in the eternal God:

> There is only one possible solution: I, who am thinking, have always existed, but not in myself or within the limits of my own personality—and not by an impersonal existence or life either (for without personality there is no thought, and there must have been thought there, since it is now in me); therefore I have always existed by a suprapersonal existence or life.

Here Maritain has articulated the basic inference that underlies his "sixth way." My subjective experience of being caught up in thought seems to free me from the experience of time, and seems hard to reconcile with the fact that there was a time at which I did not exist. The only way out of this paradox, according to Maritain, is to appeal to the divine mind in which every human agent, including myself, has existed from all eternity:

> Where then? It must have been in a Being of transcendent personality, in whom all that there is of perfection in my thought and in all thought existed in a supereminent manner and, who was, in His own infinite Self, before I was, and is, now while I am, more I

than I myself, who is eternal, and from whom I, the self which is thinking now, proceeded one day into temporal existence. I had (but without being able to say "I") an eternal existence in God before receiving a temporal existence in my own nature and my own personality.[19]

This remarkable position is developed entirely from the intuitive order. It consists in tracing out the implications involved in our direct intuitive experience of our own thought that led to the recognition that it must be a participation in the eternal, something that can only be the case if it is a participation in the infinite and eternal mind of God. Maritain develops this pre-philosophical intuition into a philosophical justification for the existence of God in the philosophical manner set out below.[20]

The first step in his argument is to realize that the intellect is above time. Time is a measure of change and consequently depends upon the movement of material beings that change, coming into and passing out of existence. Maritain certainly admits that the activities of the human intellect occur in time and are subject to time. But this is entirely extrinsic to thought as such. These conditions are purely a result of the material character of the senses and the imagination that our thought is inextricably bound up with throughout this life. Thoughts in themselves are not subject to the flux of impermanence and change. Rather, they transcend time, existing in a duration that is "a deficient imitation of eternity." As Maritain explains it,

This duration is composed of instants superior to time, each of which may correspond to a lapse of time more or less long, but is in itself without flow or movement or succession—a flash of permanent or nonsuccessive existence. Such is the proper duration of thought. Thought as such is not in time.[21]

In this way, this argument for God's existence begins from the distinction between the spiritual and the temporal, and the realization that

19 *Approaches to God*, 72–73.
20 The argument is presented in *Approaches to God*, 72–74.
21 *Approaches to God*, 72.

what is spiritual must in some sense transcend time as it applies to physical bodies.

It seems that Maritain's inference at this step in the argument is open to criticism. It is a widely acknowledged fact that truth is atemporal. This was famously pointed out in Aristotle's discussion of statements about future contingents such as the proposition "There will be a sea battle tomorrow." Philosophically it seems that since the truth of a proposition is atemporal, the proposition about the sea battle must already be true or false, before the battle has even happened.[22] However, it seems that in the course of this argument Maritain has transferred the characteristic of atemporality that belongs to the truth itself, to the thinking agent who contemplates a truth. But what is the basis for such a claim? It appears to be nothing more than the subjective psychological experience of the irrelevance of time when one is deeply engrossed in thinking. Here again, we need to recall, as we did in discussing his argument from *The Degrees of Knowledge*, that thoughts are merely accidents of thinking subjects. While the Thomist will no doubt admit that the intellect is immaterial, thinking (as any act) is an act of the whole person, as Maritain goes on to insist. Accordingly, it does not seem obvious that we can attribute the timelessness that is rightly associated with the truth of propositions to the agent who thinks those propositions without some further rationale.

In this respect we can note that the very next step in the argument is to acknowledge that thought is exercised by a person, a self composed of flesh and spirit.

This step in the approach to God emphasizes the unity of the person as a whole. Thought is an action, and like any action it emanates from the person as a whole. Indeed, thought is the most personal of all human actions. It is an act of the whole person, of a self that is composed of body and soul. But again, if this is the case, how is it that the doubt about my existence having a beginning can arise, since I am not only a thinking thing but an incarnate spirit?

---

22 Aristotle, *De Interpretatione* I, ch. 9.

The third step in the argument is to show that the self has a beginning in time, but not an absolute beginning. Even though the self began in time, like any other material thing, it did not begin absolutely. This pre-existence of the self is found in both the material and immaterial orders. As a body the child existed before birth (i.e., in terms of the earlier discussion of embryology the child is virtually present) in the cells and physicochemical materials of its ancestry from which that self was born. Insofar as the person is spiritual, exercising the spiritual activity of thinking, it could not have existed before itself, since mind can only come from mind and thought from thought. It follows that this aspect could only come from an existence superior to time:

> The self is born in time. But insofar as it is thinking it is not born of time. Its birth is supratemporal. It existed before itself in a first existence distinct from every temporal existence. It did not exist there in its proper nature (since it began to exist in its proper nature by being born in time), but everything that there is in it of being and of thought and of personality existed there better than in itself.[23]

The person is born in time as a result of the physical body the human soul informs. However, there is some sense in which the spiritual aspect of the person must preexist the birth of the body in time, since thought as such is not bound to the temporal and is, by its very nature as thought, a sharing in the eternal.

The final step is to see that the thinking self cannot have been without a beginning in time unless the self were a participation in a transcendent first existence. Maritain holds that my thought and spirituality existed before my physical existence in the mind of God. Everything in temporal existence emerges here as a participation in the first existence. Thus, the divine must contain all things within itself in some eminent way. Consequently, the first existence is the "infinite plenitude of being," transcending by its very nature all other existent things. Thus, reflection on the nature of our thought leads us to assert ". . . the principle which

---

23 *Approaches to God*, 74.

no concept can circumscribe—Being in pure act, from which comes every being; Thought in pure act from which comes every thought; Self in pure act from which comes every Self."[24]

In order to complete this approach to God it is necessary to show how things exist in him before he causes them to exist in their own act of being.[25] Maritain rejects any Platonic or Hindi suggestion that the thinking self would pre-exist in its own proper nature or have some independent existence of its own prior to its physical birth. Rather, these things pre-exist insofar as they are known by God and made present by him to the divine intellect. Following Aristotle and Aquinas, Maritain maintains that the divine essence itself is the object of the divine intellect. Accordingly, all things pre-exist in the divine mind insofar as they are participations in or likenesses of the divine essence:

> In God they are the divine essence as revealing its participability. They live there, but without existing in themselves, by a life infinitely more perfect than the existence which they have in their proper natures. They live, in God who knows them by the very life of God. They exist in the divine thought by the very existence of God which is His act of intellection.[26]

This is a principle that applies equally to all things, be they persons or inanimate things. Before they exist in themselves as substances, they exist in God as participations in the divine essence and are eternally known in that essence. This means that I who exist today have always existed in God. Maritain is careful to point out that this does not mean that we were exercising the act of thinking in God before our present life or that we actively collaborated in the divine thought. Instead it means that the thinking creature that I now am existed before itself eternally in God. Of course, I was not exercising the act of thinking there; rather,

---

24 *Approaches to God*, 74.

25 Maritain refers us to *Summa Theologiae*, I, q. 18 a. 4, from which he develops his answer to this problem.

26 *Approaches to God*, 75.

I existed insofar as I was thought by God, living by a suprapersonal and divinely personal life, the life of the divine intellect thinking itself.[27]

Practical Approaches to God

Maritain suggests two ways in which one can approach God through the activities of the practical intellect.[28] These are through poetic experience, which results from the struggles undergone in creating a thing of beauty, and the choice of good in the first act of a person's freedom. These are not philosophical demonstrations but experiential encounters that belong to a pre-philosophical order.

Maritain highlights a parallel between artistic creation and the approach to God.[29] In creating, the artist is caught up and bound by a sense of the absolute. Maritain grants that this is not the Absolute per se, but only with respect to the beauty of the work to be created. The artist is drawn by a beauty that passes into her work and motivates her act of creation. What is this beauty? This beauty is a transcendental—sharing a deep kinship with being, goodness, and truth—which was discussed in the previous chapter. Beauty allows things to show their relation to the infinite and gives joy to the human spirit. It is the reflection in things of their creator, and it is one of the names of God. God is subsistent Beauty, from which the being of all things arises. If this is the case, then it stands to reason that through her devotion to created beauty the artist will be drawn to God, who is the principle of all beauty. The intimate acquaintance with created beauty in the work

---

27 *Approaches to God*, 74–76. It is interesting to note that Maritain concludes his reflections with a brief summary of the similarity and difference between his view and that of the ancient Hindu texts, especially the *Katha Upanishad* and *Yoga-Sutra*.

28 In fact, he also suggests a third practical approach through the testimony of the "friends of God." In some ways this is the most important and powerful approach, as Maritain states, "An act of true goodness, the least act of true goodness, is indeed the best proof of the existence of God." See *Approaches to God*, 93. However, I have chosen not to discuss it at any length since there does not seem to be much to say about it from a philosophical perspective; while being a reasonable approach to God, its persuasiveness functions on a different level than that of philosophy.

29 *Approaches to God*, 79–84.

of art she creates prepares the artist for God and can culminate in a kind of "connatural" inclination towards God.[30] As Maritain explains,

> Knowledge, not rational and conceptual, but affective and nostalgic, the knowledge through connaturality which the artist has of beauty in his creative experiences, is *in itself* (I do not say for him or for his own consciousness) an advance toward God, a spiritual inclination in the direction of God, an obscure and ill-assured beginning of the knowledge of God—vulnerable, indeed, on all sides because it is not disengaged in the light of intelligence and because it remains without rational support.[31]

Maritain tends to refer to this as poetic experience. In his aesthetics, he will often use the term "poetry," drawing on the original Greek sense of *poiesis* (to make), and using it in the sense of something made through creative intuition. Thus, it often is used as a synonym for the term "artistic." This poetic experience is distinct from mystical experience. Every artist is bound up with the created world and the relations between beings, whereas mystical experience is focused on the principle of all beings that transcends the created world. The obscure knowledge through connaturality that is proper to the artist's experience comes from emotions intimately bound up with the artist's own subjectivity. Mystical experience, if it is supernatural, arises from a charity that transcends emotion or, if it is natural, from purely intellectual concentration. Nevertheless, poetic experience in approaching created things is unconsciously parallel to the mystical approach to God. Both are cases of lived analogies of the affective—rather than purely rational—knowledge the contemplative has of God. As Maritain's close friend, the painter Georges Roualt, said of his own artistic experience, "The artist discards all theories, both his own and those of others. He forgets everything when he is in front of his canvas." Here the artist is completely focused on the idea of the work to be made, and implicitly of the knowledge and beauty to be expressed through it. At this point the

---

30 See the discussion of connatural knowledge in chapter two.

31 *Approaches to God*, 80.

activity of the artist resembles the activity of God.[32] Artists can be, and often are, unaware of the religious dimension of the analogy they are living, and so it often is lived in terms of a reverence to created beauty without clearly realizing the metaphysical depths that are implied by this experience.

The second practical approach to God that Maritain considers is moral in nature. While Maritain admits that one can come to God by seeing the necessity of his existence to establish aspects of morality such as inviolable moral laws or inalienable rights, he prefers to focus on an analysis of moral experience which, he argues, can give rise to a "moral knowledge of God." The experience he suggests is the one in which a person makes their first deliberate choice of the good for a moral reason. He considers the example of a child who refuses to tell a lie not because of a fear of punishment or because it is against the rules, but for the simple fact that it is wrong. Here Maritain notes,

> At this moment the moral good with all its mysterious demands, and in the presence of which he is himself and all alone, is confusedly revealed to him in a flash of understanding. And in choosing the good, in deciding to act in such a way because it is good, he has in truth, in a manner proportioned to the capacity of his age, "deliberated about himself" and chosen his way.[33]

This choosing one's way through a choice of the good in one's first morally responsible act establishes a general orientation of one's life, though it obviously does not determine the direction of specific future actions.

This first act of freedom in favor of the good is quite complex and involves an implicit dynamism between the will and the intellect, from which Maritain draws three main consequences. First, since the will here turns away from evil because it is evil, it is clearly necessary that the intellect apprehends the difference between good and evil and recognizes that what is good should be done for the very reason that it is good. This means that the motive for this act is one that goes beyond

---

32 *Art and Scholasticism*, 60.
33 *Approaches to God*, 85. See also *The Range of Reason*, 91.

all questions of mere convenience or desire. Second, as we have said, the goodness of this first free act surpasses any merely empirical considerations in order to address explicitly what *should* be the case. This means that we are dealing with an action that is done simply because it is good. But that implies an order of agreement between our actions and our nature—that is to say, it entails that there is a law of human acts that transcends all merely empirical facts. Accordingly, this first knowledge of the good is connatural. Third, this law involves both an obligation to act in a way that is good and a realization that the only way my act *can* be good is by being in conformity with this moral law. The obvious consequence of this is that this law depends on a reality that is superior to everything else and which is Goodness itself. To fulfill the function it has—in the first act of freedom—done for the sake of the good, it must be subsistent and separate from all other things. In order to act in conformity with this good, I must direct my life towards it as both *the* Good and *my* Good. Thus, this first act of freedom, when it is good, is an action towards God as the separate and transcendent Good regardless of whether the person is aware of it or not. Such a person is ordering his acts toward God as the ultimate end of his life in actual fact, even if he has not made this explicit to himself:

> He thinks of what is good and of what is evil. But by the same token he knows God, without being aware of it. He knows God because by virtue of the internal dynamism of his choice of the good for the sake of the good, he wills and loves the Separate Good as ultimate end of his existence. Thus, his intellect has of God a vital and nonconceptional knowledge which is involved both in the practical notion (confusedly and intuitively grasped, but with its full intentional energy) of the moral good as formal motive of his first act of freedom, and in the movement of his will toward this good and, all at once, toward the Good.[34]

Thus, Maritain argues that through the will's movement toward the good there is an implied knowledge of goodness. Since the choice of the good in this first act of freedom involves a choice of my good and

---

34 *Approaches to God*, 87.

the orientation of my life, it entails a reference to the supreme and separate Good, namely, God. This is so even in the case of the avowed
atheist, who performs a good act. She orients her life towards the Good
and, thereby, to God under the aspect of goodness—and this holds true
regardless of whether or not she is aware of this fact. Accordingly, the
moral life itself provides a connatural knowledge of God, even if this
should remain inchoate and unrecognized. It is simply the implicit
dynamic of the choice of the good in one's first act of freedom.

Evil and God's Eternal Purposes

It is all too obvious, however, that not all human choices are good.
Indeed, one of the perennial dilemmas faced by Christian philosophers
is the relationship between the brute fact of evil in the world and the
commitment to the view that God has from all eternity seen and planned
what will take place. Maritain clearly saw this as the philosophical problem to which his efforts had made the most significant contribution.[35]
He developed his views on the topic in four major works through his
career. He devoted his Aquinas Lecture *St. Thomas and the Problem
of Evil* to the topic at Marquette University; a chapter of his seminal
metaphysical book *Existence and the Existent* returned to the topic and
is in some ways his broadest treatment of the subject; his later seminar
conferences on the issue defended his position against criticisms made
to his earlier work and were published as *God and the Permission of Evil*;
and finally, his book *The Sin of the Angel* looks at the implications of the
fall of the angels for his philosophical theory of evil's place within God's
providence. In this treatment I will follow the order of presentation that
Maritain offers in *Existence and the Existent*, since it seems to be the
broadest approach, and because in this work the issue is situated in the
context of the more fundamental problem of the relation between our
fallible liberty and God's absolutely immutable eternal plan for creation.

---

35 "If in my philosophical work there has perchance been some actual contribution (however
imperfectly it may have been able to be presented) to the progress of thought, and to the
researches which announce a new age of culture, it is indeed, so I am persuaded, the one
with which this little book has to deal." *God and the Permission of Evil*, trans. Joseph W. Evans
(Milwaukee: The Bruce Publishing Co., 1966), viii; see also 113.

Details from the other works that provide deeper explanations of this or that point of his doctrine will be incorporated into the discussion insofar as they clarify his position in the relevant places.

Maritain's approach to the problem needs to be understood in the context of the scholastic dispute over freedom and evil between the followers of the Dominican theologian Domingo Báñez and those of Jesuit Luis de Molina. Although we cannot do justice to the incredible subtleties involved in the original texts and the various interpretations they have been given here, some summary of the two traditions is needed to situate Maritain's discussion in its proper context. Báñez developed a defense of the Thomistic position that God's knowledge is causal. This is necessary to avoid saying that contingent actions, such as the free choices of human beings, would cause God to know something (a position which would undermine God's immutability and perfection). Rather than being informed by things happening in time, Báñez argued, God's knowledge is an efficient cause of every contingent singular being and action right down to the movements of the human intellect and will. Nevertheless, God causes things to happen in accordance with their nature and thus he wills that necessary things happen through necessity, while free things happen through the free acts of the creature. The human act remains a free one since the will is an effective cause of the action, even though it is only a secondary cause of the act, utterly dependent on a first cause: namely, God's will. Twentieth-century proponents of Báñez's thought, such as Fr. Reginald Garrigou-Lagrange and Fr. Jean-Hervé Nicolas, went further, arguing that evil actions required an antecedent permissive decree from God in order to occur.[36] Maritain's major concern with this approach is that it seems to risk making God responsible for evil. Although Báñez and

---

36 See Domingo Báñez, *In Iam Partem divi Thomae*, qq. 1–64 (Salamanca, 1584), q. 14, a. 13 and q. 49, a. 2; and Reginald Garrigou-Lagrange, *Predestination*, trans. Bede Rose (St. Louis: B. Herder Book Co., 1939). Fr. Jean-Hervé Nicolas wrote an extended three-part article criticizing Maritain's views on the problem of evil in "La permission du péché," *Revue Thomiste* LX (1960): no. 1, 5–37; no. 2, 185–206; and no. 4, 509–46. Maritain's response is found in *God and the Permission of Evil*, 44–66. There are several more recent defenses of both Báñez and Molina in the literature.

his followers are quite concerned to insist that this is not the case, it has always been somewhat mysterious to critics how it can be avoided.

Molina's position avoided this consequence by asserting that God's knowledge need not always be causal. Rather, he insisted on differentiating distinct kinds of knowledge in God in order to identify what he termed "middle-knowledge." This is called "middle" as it stands between God's knowledge of necessary truths and knowledge of his own creative acts. The objects of middle knowledge are counterfactuals that arise from freedom: if person P were in situation x, then P would do y. The doctrine of middle knowledge holds that there are true counterfactuals of this form for all possible actions of all possible free creatures. It follows that God knows all the ways that I, or anyone, could possibly act in any situation that could possibly arise. These counterfactuals are prior to God's creative will and it is in light of his knowledge of them that God ultimately decides what to create. God knows all future contingent events that will actually arise by combining his middle knowledge with knowledge of what he actually created. By knowing all the possible actions of all possible creatures in all possible situations and combining this with a complete knowledge of all things that were actually created, there would be true knowledge of what would actually happen at every moment.[37] While this has the advantage of emphasizing free will and avoiding making God responsible for evil acts, proponents of Báñez's theory argue that it makes God's knowledge passive with respect to creatures.[38]

Maritain's position can be seen as an attempt to revise the Báñezian theory in order to avoid its traditional shortcomings without falling into accepting the kind of "hands-off" God presented by the Molinists. Throughout the discussion he is concerned to preserve two key doctrines above all else: (1) God is not the cause of evil in any way, either directly or indirectly; and (2) the first cause of the absence of grace that

37 Luis de Molina, *On Divine Foreknowledge: Part IV of the "Concordia,"* rev. ed. (Ithaca, NY: Cornell University Press, 2004).

38 *God and the Permission of Evil*, 16.

leads to the commission of actual evil is from us.[39] Maritain tries to hold to these basic axioms throughout his presentation, arguing as follows:

Relation between Time and Eternity

In keeping with the classical theism embraced by Thomists, Maritain understands divine eternity not merely as the claim that God has always existed and always will exist. Rather, eternity means that God transcends time and is not subject to any sort of succession. Time is a measure of the succession that measures and orders the changes within created being, so it has no place in the divine nature. Yet every moment of time that ever was or will be is present to God's eternity, not merely as an object God knows, but rather, as a "physically" present being in itself.[40] Consequently, eternity contains and measures all time by possessing it in an indivisible way:

> God does not foresee the things of time, he sees them; and he sees in particular the free options and decisions of the created existent which, in as much as they are free, are absolutely unforeseeable. He sees them in the very instant when they take place, in the pure existential freshness of their emergence into being, in the humility of their own instant of coming forth.[41]

This means that even future events are present in eternity with all the events that led up to them and the consequences that will follow from them. Yet they are present to God's eternity without any succession.

Liberty of the Created Existent and the Line of the Good

The discussion of this topic is dominated by two key points. First, no created cause acts except under the impetus of the "super-causality" of the first cause, self-subsisting being, or God. This is to say there is a causal hierarchy in which God's primary causality is exercised through

---

39 *God and the Permission of Evil*, 6, citing *S.T.*, I-II, q. 79, a. 1 and *S.T.*, I-II, q. 112, a. 3 ad 2.

40 *Existence and the Existent*, 86. Maritain appeals to John of St. Thomas on this point, citing *Cursus Theologicus*, Tome II, q. X, disp. 9, a. 3, pp. 80–102.

41 *Existence and the Existent*, 87.

an order of secondary causes that nevertheless allows for the secondary causes to be truly efficacious as causes. Aquinas's typical example is that of a painter, who is the main cause of a painting; the brushes the artist uses are also causes of the painting in a secondary way, as we can see when a defective brush causes a blemish in the work in spite of the artist's skill. Second, freedom of choice consists in an active indetermination of the will, which itself actuates the motive that directs it. This means that while God remains the first cause of any active dimension of the will, God activates the will to exercise its act in keeping with the free nature of the human person without determining it in any particular way. The choice that results is genuinely left to the free person to decide. It follows that this liberty of created persons can only be exercised to the degree that there is an influx of the transcendent causality of God, which moves every created being to act according to its own nature, yet the acts that result from that influx are genuinely free through the cooperation or non-cooperation of human persons. As Maritain explains,

> Consequently, in the existential subordination of causes, the created existent possesses the whole initiative of good, but this initiative is second; creative Liberty possesses the whole initiative of the good and its initiative is first. There is not in the world a shadow of beauty, a trace of actuality, a spark of being of which the subsistent Being itself is not the author.[42]

When it comes to good actions there is a primary initiative on the part of God acting as a cause of the act and a secondary, but nevertheless really efficacious, initiative on the part of the free creature. To return to Aquinas's example of an artist painting with a brush, clearly the artist has the first initiative; without the motive power of the hand, the brush would not produce a work of art. Yet the brush itself really makes an effective contribution to the painting, which is easily seen by the fact that a painter takes pains to ensure that he is using high-quality tools. In the case of good actions, then, God has the first initiative as the source of all being, action, and goodness. The free creature cooperates

---

42 *Existence and the Existent,* 88.

with this creative action on God's part and contributes to the action taken place insofar as he chooses to cooperate with this divine impetus. To this point Maritain's presentation does not differ substantially from the traditional Thomist explanation of Báñez or his twentieth-century defenders. Sadly, however, human actions are not universally good, and it is in the case of evil actions that the creativity of Maritain's thought within this Thomistic framework begins to surface.

Dissymmetry between the Line of Good and the Line of Evil

As we have seen, any consideration of action in the line of good has to be understood in terms of both being and the causes of being. In the line of evil, however, everything has to be understood in terms of nothingness or nihilation. It is for this reason that there is a fundamental dissymmetry between good and evil actions, and our explanations of how they are caused cannot be the same. A good action results in being or action, while an evil act results in only nothingness, corruption, and loss.[43]

This has to be understood in terms of the widespread Augustinian view that evil is a privation of a good that ought to be present. Maritain is very clear that this does not mean that evil is not real, or that it is in any way unimportant. In fact, he insists that evil as a privation is very real as a "wound or mutilation of the being." Nevertheless, evil is a parasite; it can only exist in and through the good, just as a wound can only occur in a living body. In his lecture *St. Thomas and the Problem of Evil* Maritain argues:

> Evil is therefore efficacious through a good that is wanting or is deflected, and whose action is to that extent vitiated. What is thus the power of evil? It is the very power of the good that evil wounds and preys upon. The more powerful this good is, the more powerful evil will be,—not by virtue of itself, but by virtue of this good . . . If evil appears so powerful in the world of today, that is because

the good it preys upon is the very spirit of man,—science itself and moral ideals corrupted by bad will.[44]

Clearly, we cannot explain how evil arises in the same way that we explained the good, for in the case of goodness the primary initiative for the action is always on the side of God, to whom we freely respond. Yet God is in no way the cause of evil. So the explanation must be fundamentally different.[45]

Liberty of the Created Existent and the Line of Evil

In order for there to be an evil in the order of action—a privation of the order due to the action—there must be a prior defect in the order of being, since action follows the being of things. In the case of moral evil this results in an apparent paradox. In the case of the action of persons this defect has to be located in the will, since it is the will that causes the evil action. But it must be a free and voluntary defect of the will, since it is the evil of a free action that we are trying to explain. If it were a defect in the very nature of the will itself, it would not be a voluntary defect at all. Accordingly, this defect or privation in the will must be caused by the will itself, not by nature. On the other hand, however, it seems that if this is a defect of the will in its free activity, we have already a freely performed evil action, and we would be caught in the vicious circle of explaining the evil of a free action by the evil of a free action.[46]

Maritain resolves this paradox by appealing to a distinction St. Thomas Aquinas makes between two moments in the evil action that

---

44 *St. Thomas and the Problem of Evil*, trans. Mabelle L. Andison (Milwaukee: Marquette University Press, 1942), 2–3. An excellent explanation of Maritain's account of the discrepancy between the line of good and evil actions in relation to his doctrine of evil as nihilation is found in Bernadette E. O'Connor, "Insufficient Ado about the Human Capacity for Nothing, Too Much Ado about the Human Capacity for Being and Maritain's Dissymmetry Solution," in *Aquinas & Maritain on Evil: Mystery and Metaphysics*, ed. James G. Hanink (Washington, DC: The Catholic University of America Press, 2013), 155–69. Several essays in this volume address Maritain's arguments on evil from varying critical and affirmative viewpoints. I mention O'Connor's particularly as she is concerned with explaining Maritain's argument, while most of the other essays are engaged in criticism or comparative evaluation of Maritain's arguments.

45 *God and the Permission of Evil*, 9–10. For Maritain this was the point on which the classical Thomists, such as Báñez, were weak. They tried to explain everything, even evil, from the perspective of being, and consequently goodness. See also *God and the Permission of Evil*, 14.

46 *St. Thomas and the Problem of Evil*, 23–25; *Existence and the Existent*, 89–90.

are in an order of ontological priority. In the first moment, there is—through the will's freedom—an absence or "nihilation," which is not yet a privation or evil in the proper sense of the term. Rather, it is a mere lacuna. This absence is the failure of the will to consider the rule or norm upon which the proper ruling of his act depends. In the second moment, the will produces its free act in a manner that is disordered by the lack of its appropriate rule and is "wounded with nothingness" that is the inevitable result of this lack of consideration.[47]

This distinction allows Maritain to avoid the vicious circle he had noted, for the first moment of the act is not yet a moral evil nor even an act in the strict sense, but a pure lack of consideration. There is no evil here, for there is no duty for the will to consider the rule generally, and it would be impossible to do so all of the time. There is only a duty to consider the rule in the moment of the relevant action where the will makes its free choice. The carpenter does not err in failing to pay attention to the ruling stick, but only in failing to pay attention to it when he should: namely, in the act of cutting the wood. Likewise, it is only in the second moment—in which the will fully commits itself by choosing, where some action or being is produced—that evil in the proper sense arises. Even though the non-consideration of the rule was not an action or evil, it was in that first moment free, for the failure to consult the rule depended upon the freedom of the agent. The will has not acted and because it has not acted, it has not looked at the rule. Further, this non-consideration is something that is both real and free.[48]

Maritain's position is that the will's failure to consider the rule in the first moment of the act is the first cause of every evil action. At this point we confront the fundamental dissymmetry between the line of good and that of evil. In the case of good acts, as we saw, the first cause of the act was the transcendent creative liberty of God. In the case of evil

---

47 See St. Thomas Aquinas, *De Malo*, q. I, a. 3.; *St Thomas and the Problem of Evil*, 24–25; *God and the Permission of Evil*, 20–24; and *Existence and the Existent*, 90.

48 *God and the Permission of Evil*, 35. This point is important to recall when confronting criticisms of Maritain's speaking of God's activation of the will as "nihilated" or "shattered" by the person who does evil. Such language is obviously metaphorical, as the will does not shatter God's action by acting contrary to it, but simply by the amoral non-advertence to the moral law.

acts, the first cause of the act is entirely the liberty of the created person in not considering the rule that ought to govern his action:

> The first cause (which is not an acting or efficient cause, but is dis-acting and de-efficient), the first cause of the non-consideration of the rule, and consequently of the evil of the free act that will come forth from it, is purely and simply the liberty of the created existent. The latter possesses the free initiative of an absence (or "nothingness") of consideration, of a vacuum introduced into the warp and woof of being, of a nihil; and this time this free initiative is a first initiative because it does not consist in acting freely or allowing being to pass, but in freely not-acting and not-willing, in freely frustrating the passage of being.[49]

Accordingly, there is a fundamental difference between good and evil actions. The free person never acts entirely alone when acting in the line of good, for he has need of Good as the first cause for all the being and goodness he produces. But the free person is entirely alone and has no need of God in freely "nihilating"—and thereby doing—evil. The created will has the first initiative of this absence of considering the appropriate rule.

As the Gospel itself says, "Without me you can do nothing."[50] Maritain notes that this passage applies both to the line of good and the line of evil. In the line of good it means that we can do no good without God. However, in the line of evil it means that if we act without God we can do nothing, we can perform this action or thing that is the nihilation of the good that ought to be present.[51]

---

49 *Existence and the Existent*, 92. See also *God and the Permission of Evil*, 48. Stephen A. Long objects that Maritain's theory of nihilation of the divine act as the first cause of evil imports a positive initiative of action that contravenes God's free initiative as the first cause of every act. As will be clear from the following pages, I think that Long has underestimated the degree to which Maritain roots the first cause of evil not in an action, but in a morally neutral failure to act through a non-consideration of the relevant moral rule. See Stephen A. Long, "Providence, Freedom and Natural Law," *Nova et Vetera*, English edition 4, no. 3 (2006): 557–606. Extremely helpful background to this dispute can be found in Michael D. Torre, *Do Not Resist the Spirit's Call: Francisco Marín-Sola on Sufficient Grace* (Washington, DC: The Catholic University of America Press, 2013). Torre provides a very thorough explanation of the influence of Marin-Sola upon Maritain on this important question.

50 John 15:5.

51 See *Existence and the Existent*, 92; *St. Thomas and the Problem of Evil*, 35–36; and *God and the Permission of Evil*, 33.

Shatterable Divine Activations and Unshatterable Divine Activations

The starting point for understanding free action is the activation of God that provides the initial and gratuitous impetus towards goodness, whether through acting directly on the will or else through anything in the world that incites the will towards the good. This divine activation provides the will with the possibility of doing good. The will, however, can choose to nihilate this divine activation by taking the free initiative of not considering the rule that a good act must follow in the situation that confronts it. It is this free initiative that introduces "the vacuum in the woof and warp of being" that was mentioned in the previous step. In this case the free person nihilates and makes sterile the divine activations it has received. Yet it does so not by actively destroying them, but in a purely passive way, by not acting in accordance with them:

> Therefore if, in the world, we find moral evil and free evil acts, the reason is that there are shatterable divine activations. In other words, the reason is that the First Cause sends down into free existents activations or motions which contain within themselves, in advance, the permission or possibility of being rendered sterile *if* the free existent which receives them takes the first initiative of evading them, of not-acting and not considering or nihilating under their touch. And if it is true that every created liberty is by nature a fallible liberty (since it is not its own rule) . . . then we can understand that in accordance with the natural order of things, before the *unshatterable* divine activation, by which the will to good of creative Liberty infallible produces its effect in the created will, the divine activations received by the free existent must first be shatterable activations.[52]

Looking at the divine activation needed for the free action of a created existent to take place, Maritain notes an important distinction in this text. God's action in the free creature begins with a "shatterable activation," an impetus from God towards the good that is intrinsically

---

52 *Existence and the Existent*, 93–94. Shatterable and unshatterable divine activations are Maritain's terms for what St. Thomas had called sufficient and efficacious grace. See also *Existence and the Existent*, 104.

capable of being "shattered." Here it is important not to let Maritain's language of "shattering" or "nihilating" these divine activations lead us to think that this involves some positive action on the part of God or the created agent. This language is used to highlight the initiative of the freedom of the creature in doing evil, but it would be a grammatical fallacy to take it to imply that this involves some positive act. Rather, this shattering or nihilation takes place through our deficient initiative, our failure to respond to the divine activations that can and should move us to do the good. We have freely introduced nothingness by our failure to act in accordance with the divine activation within us, and this non-act shatters that very activation simply by freely not responding.

If we do not become an impediment in this way to the work of God within us and we allow the free passage of this influx from God, then these shatterable divine activations transform into unshatterable divine activations. This is the decisive moment at which God's resolution bears fruit in us, and our will unfailingly acts freely to produce the good to which all the divine activations and all the will's own inner dynamism had tended. What is important to note here is that the shatterable activation comes to fruition in an unshatterable one through itself, not through any act added on the part of the created existent. This is to say that God begins to move the will through activating it in a manner that the will can initially reject or shatter. If the will does not do so, this divine influx grows to an unshatterable activation of the will and results in a good act; this transition from a shatterable to an unshatterable activation is not caused by any act on the part of the free creature, but rather by God in view of the creature's not having acted to shatter the initial impulse. The sole contribution the human will makes is a negative one not to nihilate the shatterable divine activation within it:

> Not to nihilate under the divine activation, not to sterilize that impetus, not to have the initiative of making the thing we call nothing, does not mean taking the initiative or demi-initiative, or the smallest fraction of the initiative of an act; it does not mean acting on one's own to complete, in any way whatever, the divine activation. It means not stirring under its touch, but allowing it free passage, allowing it to bear its fruit (the unshatterable activation)

by virtue of which the will (which did not nihilate in the first instance) will act (will look at the rule efficaciously) in the very exercise of its domination over its motives, and will burst forth freely in a good option and a good act.[53]

Maritain goes on to explain that these acts arise within the creature through God's love for them. Yet the divine will can be understood in two different ways when it comes to willing free actions. Here Maritain appeals to a traditional distinction between God's antecedent and consequent will. The antecedent will, which Maritain calls "primordial," "original," or "naked" will, is God's will considered without any consideration of particular conditions or circumstances.[54] It designates what God wills in general or in abstraction from the actual states of affairs. It is in this sense that God wills that each person never sins, even though in fact they sometimes do. The consequent will, which Maritain calls "circumstanced" or "definitive" will, is the will of God considered as it takes into account particular conditions and circumstances and which allows free existents to commit evil and reject their supratemporal end. The circumstance that is relevant here is the free nihilating through which the freedom of created existents "evades His influx and renders the divine activation sterile." Accordingly, the free existents who attain their ultimate end do so because God willed it prior to any deliberation or good action on their part through his definitive will. Those who miss their ultimate end do so because they have freely evaded what God had willed through his primordial will. This is permitted because of the free initiative of nihilating that they have to do evil.[55]

Divine Knowledge of the Free Acts of the Created Existent

Maritain strongly insists on the traditional Thomistic doctrine that God's knowledge is totally independent of created things. The object of God's understanding is the divine essence itself, not created beings.

---

53 *Existence and the Existent*, 99–100. Also see *Existence and the Existent*, 95n9.

54 *Existence and the Existent*, 102.

55 *Existence and the Existent*, 103–4.

In this narrow sense, along with St. Thomas Aquinas, he could endorse Aristotle's view of God as thought thinking itself. This is important because it eliminates the possibility that God's knowledge of created things is in any way passive or dependent upon things. Created things change, but God's knowledge of them does not. In fact, Maritain goes so far as to insist that God's knowledge would not have been changed even if he had chosen not to create, as the poet's knowledge of a poem is the same whether she chooses to say it aloud or simply reflect upon it in her mind.[56] Rather than looking out to the surrounding world to know objects as we do, God knows all things in Himself as their primary cause. He knows the free created being and all of its possibilities in his own essence by his creative knowledge, just as the creature freely makes existent that which it creates. In such a case all of the contingency is found in the term of this creative knowledge:

> God knows the multitude of finite beings as so many participa-
> tions in that essence. He passes through the infinite to reach the
> finite. But he reaches the finite itself and does so in a necessarily
> exhaustive understanding since it is that very act of knowing which
> makes things be.[57]

God's knowledge reaches to every last aspect of the creature in its exercise of existence—since it creates all that is in them—and this act of creation occurs through this very knowledge: "It sees contingent existence because it causes it, and because, by making it *known*, it makes it *be*."[58]

This theory fits with the account of God's initiative when the free being acts in the line of good. All that is comes into being through the activation of God, which takes place through his knowledge. The good act is known to God because all that is found in it derives ultimately from God's transcendent causality of it. But the case of evil is more problematic. How does God know the evil of the free will? In answering

---

56 *Existence and the Existent*, 105–6.
57 *Existence and the Existent*, 107–8.
58 *Existence and the Existent*, 108.

this question Maritain appeals to two central principles. The first is that God is in no way a cause of moral evil. The second is that there is no direct idea of evil in the divine intellect. The first is a clear and essential teaching of faith. The second follows from the fact that a divine idea indicates a way that a creature can participate in the divine essence, so it is a cause of being or source of intelligibility in a manner which would exclude evil. God's pure innocence entails that he has no direct idea of evil, but knows evil indirectly in its true reality as a privation or nihilation that wounds being and, therefore, occurs in the good that it feeds upon. That is to say that God knows evil through having a complete knowledge of the good, not by knowing some thing as evil, since evil is merely a privation within what is good.[59]

God permits—but does not cause—evil in two ways. The first is the permission of the possibility of evil, which is found in the shatterable divine activation which created liberty can choose to frustrate. The second is permission for the "effectuation" or commission of evil. Here Maritain argues, innovatively, that this occurs in the moment when created liberty has actually nihilated the shatterable impetus through non-consideration of the rule, but before having acted. This is essential to his argument, for it means that God's permission to effectuate evil *follows upon* the free nihilating of the shatterable divine activation and *is not included in it.*[60] Thus, the free initiative of nihilation that precedes the evil act is entirely the initiative of the free agent and God plays no role in it whatsoever.

The consequence of this is that God knows evil not in his own essence, where it in no way dwells, but as a consequence of his knowledge of creatures, in whose freedom the nihilation and privation takes place:

> But what is not causable nor caused by Him, that of which He is absolutely not the cause, like the evil of the free act and like the free nihilating which is its precondition, these God does not know

59 *Existence and the Existent*, 109.
60 *Existence and the Existent*, 110. This is the key difference between Maritain's view and that of Báñez.

in the divine essence considered alone, but in the divine essence in as much as created existents are seen therein, and in as much as in *them* is seen that nihilating and privation of which their freedom is the first cause. In other terms, He knows that nihilating and that privation *in* the created existents whom He knows *in* His essence.[61]

In this way God knows the pure absence involved in evil without causing it and without having received anything from the creature. It is not the creature that specifies the divine knowledge of it. Rather, God knows the non-being and nihilating in the actually nihilating will of the free existents. Through knowing the good that is present there, God also knows the good that ought to be present there but is not. God knows this privation in the free existent that he knows in the divine essence.

God's Eternal Plan and the Free Existents

God's plan for the created world was set from all eternity, but it is important to be clear what eternity means here. Eternity is not a special kind of divine time or just a matter of God going through time forever. "It is a limitless instant which indivisibly embraces the whole succession of time. All the moments of that succession are physically present in it."[62] From the perspective of God's eternal vision all moments of time are always immediately and directly present. In knowing his essence, he knows all things of which he is the first cause and sees them in an eternal ever-present instant.

In understanding the way that God's causality plays into this plan for the world that has been established throughout eternity, it is important to accurately situate the place of freedom within it. These creatures have their place within establishing that plan not through their freedom to act, which is all from God, but through their power to be first causes in nihilating. This does not mean they escape or alter the eternal plan of God, which would be impossible. Rather, free existents have their part to play in this plan, because in establishing it through his effectuated will

---

61 *Existence and the Existent*, 111.
62 *Existence and the Existent*, 113–14.

God takes into account the freedom of creatures and their initiatives of nihilating.[63]

It is important to avoid any illusion that the divine plan is a kind of scene set up ahead of time, where creatures merely play out the parts assigned to them by God:

> We must purge our thought of any idea of a play written in advance, at a time prior to time—a play in which time unfolds, and the characters of time read, the parts. On the contrary, everything is improvised, under the eternal and immutable direction of the almighty Stage Manager. The divine plan is the ordination of the infinite multiplicity of things, and of their becoming, by the absolutely simple gaze of the creative knowledge and the will of God.[64]

The eternal plan once fixed from all eternity is immutable; nevertheless, it was freely chosen by God and, therefore, it could have been different. Further, creatures have a role of first initiative in the divine drama of the eternal plan in virtue of their free nihilating and bringing about evil. Unless by some miracle the creature receives from the outset an unshatterable impetus to the good, the initiative of nihilating or not nihilating depends entirely on that free creature. If the creature does not choose to nihilate and considers the rule appropriate to its action, this is confirmed by God's circumstanced will moving the creature to the good and is part of the eternal plan immutably. But if the free creature takes the initiative "of the thing that is nothing," this is seen in the free existent by God from all eternity, and God's circumstanced will permits the evil act of the creature and ordains it from all eternity to achieve a higher good as part of the eternal plan. Thus, the eternal plan is immutable, presuming God's free choice to act and create this world. Yet it is not a fixed script, but takes account of the free acts of creatures within it. These free acts do not alter the plan; rather, the plan takes account of the first initiatives of nihilating that is undertaken by creatures: "Let no one say that man alters the eternal plan! That would be an absurdity.

---

63 *Existence and the Existent*, 114.
64 *Existence and the Existent*, 116.

Man does not alter it. He enters into its very composition and its eternal fixity by his power of saying, No!"[65]

Maritain's natural theology, even more so than most of his philosophy, is very much within the Thomist tradition. Many of the views he develops on these issues are explanations of the texts of Aquinas or those of his great commentators. The present chapter has endeavored to focus on areas where Maritain has something particularly original to say. This is why some areas that are important to natural theology, such as the use of analogy to philosophically elucidate the divine nature, do not receive much attention in these pages. In addressing the key question of natural theology—the existence of God—we see that Maritain's approach is innovative in a number of ways. Importantly, he insists on the viability of a pre-philosophical approach to God. This is a form of spontaneous reasoning that naturally presents itself in human experience, but which is not fully worked out in the rigorous logical manner that is demanded by philosophy. Nevertheless, he holds that this path to God is nonetheless certain and sufficient to meet the needs of the human condition. In terms of philosophical arguments, he presents innovative arguments in both the speculative and practical order. In the speculative order Maritain discovers a way to God from our experience of thinking, which avoids the pitfalls of any form of idealism. Rather, he asserts that the experience of thought implies that it is a participation in something timeless, and thus we as thinking beings must have existed before our birth in some manner in the mind of God. In the practical order he shows that both the artist's experience of beauty in fashioning her work and the choice of the good in the first act of freedom imply that one is acting for God regardless of whether or not the agent is explicitly aware of this fact. Finally, on the perennial issue of the relation of evil in the world to God's eternal plan, Maritain provides an innovative solution, insisting that God plays a different role in bringing about good acts than he does in evil ones. This fundamental difference leads Maritain to argue that only the human agent is the first cause of evil, through the ability to nihilate the shatterable divine impetus that ought to reach

---

65 *Existence and the Existent*, 118.

fruition in an unshatterable divine motion and ultimately a good act. Thus, the responsibility for evil is solely on the side of the human agent, while preserving the intimate agency of God as a cause within every act whatsoever. Accordingly, he provides an answer that remains faithful to the two fundamental principles of any possible theodicy: the absolute innocence of God, and the responsibility of human agents as the first cause of the evil and the loss of grace.

Maritain's theodicy returns us to the consideration of his articulation of the basic approaches of the mind to God. He insists that in rediscovering the basic value of existence, we not only rediscover God, we rediscover love. Within the intuition of being, I not only grasp being, for I cannot do this without an inchoate awareness of my own existence or self. Accordingly, I encounter my own subjectivity as subjectivity. But this is clearly not an object of thought; rather, it is the deeper living center from which my thought springs forth, and it only attains through love its own supreme level of existence, which is existence as self-giving. Thus, our encounter with existence leads us to God and to our truest selves through recognition of the "basic generosity of existence."[66] Thus, implicit in our awareness of God through being is our call to perfect ourselves through love, and to turn from nihilating the divine act within us towards cultivating it and cooperating with its fundamental generosity.

66 *The Range of Reason,* 91–92.

CHAPTER 6

Contributions
to Revealed Theology

If to know is what you want—and knowledge must be desired—
study metaphysics, study theology. If divine union is what you
want, and you succeed in attaining it, you will know a great
deal more, but precisely in the measure that you go beyond
knowledge . . . Beyond knowing? That is to say, in love; in love
transillumined by the Spirit, compenetrated by intelligence and
wisdom. *For now my exercise is in loving alone.*
Degrees of Knowledge, 371–72

aritain was by vocation and inclination a philosopher, and
he frequently insists that he does not write as a theologian. Nevertheless, as we have seen over and over, Maritain
rejects the attempt to separate philosophy from the context
of Christian faith. In his view, situating philosophy in terms of Christian
revelation does not undermine its philosophical nature, but nourishes
it. While he never attempted to develop a comprehensive theological
vision—and rather, accepted this from the Thomistic tradition and
especially John of St. Thomas—he did make important contributions to

theology. Especially in his later works, his attention turns to more spe-cifically theological topics. His last books address explicitly theological subjects, such as the consciousness and knowledge of Christ, and the sanctity of the Church.[1] The reason for this new emphasis is not clear. Perhaps it is due to the impact of Raïssa's death and Maritain's enter-ing a quasi-hermetic life with the Little Brothers Jesus; it also is surely influenced by his concern about the way the Second Vatican Council was being received in the Church. Yet this attention to revealed theology is not a late aberration in Maritain. His work from the very beginning was a Christian philosophy, that is, a philosophy that was carried out in dialogue with revelation and theology. Indeed, the second part of his magnum opus, *The Degrees of Knowledge*, is a sustained treatise on mystical theology. In his later work he often offers detailed reflec-tions on theological topics presenting them as hypotheses for further development, rather than attempting to provide definitive solutions. He approaches theological questions from the perspective of a philosopher: moreover, a philosopher deeply learned in the Thomistic theological tradition, yet who was attentive to contemporary theological concerns. This unique combination of qualities allowed him to make creative con-tributions to the theological issues he explored.

---

1   Michael D. Torre has argued that, for all his protests to the contrary, Maritain is better char-acterized as a theologian than a philosopher, since the vast body of his work is at the service of faith. Torre admits that philosophy occurs throughout these works, but argues that its purpose is generally theological. Although Torre is right to emphasize the theological context of Maritain's thought, I do not agree with his conclusion that Maritain is best portrayed as a theologian. Firstly, there is a comprehensive philosophy to be found in Maritain's work. However, there is nothing like a comprehensive and worked-out theology to be found there. Maritain's theology is, in comparison, decidedly sketchy and focused on topics that happened to spark his interest, or which had to be treated to fully understand some aspect of his philosophical work. Even when he is addressing an explicitly theological topic like ecclesiology, Maritain himself characterizes his work as that of a "philosophical research worker" in the vineyard of the theologian. This is to say, he brings a philosophical method and perspective to his treatment of theological questions. Finally, Torre's position requires not only the claim that Maritain was unaware of what he was really up to in his work, but would require a fundamental rejection of his notion of Christian philosophy as well. If Maritain were a theologian rather than a philosopher, his very theory of Christian philosophy would be decidedly incoherent. Since this is the framework within which virtually everything he wrote was written, it would also call into question his entire intellectual project. Torre does not seem to note this last implication of his position, which I take to be decisive. See Michael D. Torre, "To Philosophize for the Faith: Jacques Maritain's Intellectual Vocation," in *The Vocation of the Catholic Philosopher: From Maritain to John Paul II*, ed. John Hittinger (Washington, DC: The Catholic University of America Press, 2010), 110–31.

The present chapter aims to articulate the main lines of his thought on the theological topics that he treated in some detail. I make no claim to address every theological subject that he addressed, nor to do so with exhaustive thoroughness. Rather, I have only highlight the topics on which he offered sustained reflections. After considering the nature of theology and its place in the structure or "typology" of knowledge, I go on to consider three theological issues that Maritain gave considerable attention: namely, mystical experience, Christ's knowledge and consciousness, and the holiness of the Church. There are many other areas of theology to which Maritain made interesting contributions. Accordingly, I restrict my choice to areas where Maritain developed substantial or book-length treatments of a theological issue, excluding topics that he only considers in individual articles. This means ignoring much of importance. For instance, his treatment of eschatology is fascinating, suggesting that the lost condemned to hell might eventually experience some form of natural happiness through the prayers of the saints and souls in purgatory, their punishment consisting in the loss of the infinitely higher supernatural happiness of the blessed.[2] In at least one other case, his treatment of the Jewish people in view of Christianity, Maritain devoted a significant amount of effort. However, I have decided not to address it here since his accomplishments have been already widely studied in texts readily available to English readers.[3] The fact is that Maritain raised innovative and important points in many areas of theology, but it is impossible to study all of them in a book of this nature. Indeed, a thorough discussion of all his work in theology should be the subject of a complete book in its own right. My aim in this chapter is to highlight some areas of theology upon which Maritain made important contributions that are integrally related to the unity of his thought as a whole. This accounts for my selecting the topics

2   "Beginning with a Reverie," in *Untrammeled Approaches*, 3-26, passim.

3   See Bernard Doering, *Jacques Maritain and the French Catholic Intellectuals* (Notre Dame, IN: University of Notre Dame Press, 1983); *Jacques Maritain and the Jews*, ed. Robert Royal (Notre Dame, IN: University of Notre Dame Press, 1993); and Richard Francis Crane, *Passion of Israel: Jacques Maritain, Catholic Conscience and the Holocaust* (Scranton, PA: University of Scranton Press, 2010).

of mysticism, Christ's consciousness and knowledge, and the Church. It is to be hoped that others will be inspired to delve into this largely neglected area of Maritain's thought.

Theology as a Science

In order to understand Maritain's approach to these theological topics, it is important to be aware of his understanding of the nature of theology as a science.[4] As we saw in the introductory chapter, Maritain situates philosophy as the highest of the sciences accessible to unaided natural reason. This is because of its object, which is the study of all things and their first causes through the natural light of human reason. Yet philosophy is not the highest of all the sciences. That honor belongs to theology, which is the highest science because it partakes of God's own knowledge. Following St. Thomas Aquinas, Maritain understands theology as the science of God.

Setting aside natural theology, which is simply the culmination of metaphysics (which knows God analogically insofar as natural reason allows), theology's premises are truths formally revealed by God: namely, the dogmas of the faith. This includes both the infallible teachings of the Church that are drawn from scripture and what has been virtually revealed. This refers to what is not directly revealed, but is logically entailed by revelation. The theologian can draw out these claims through applying reason and true philosophical doctrines to what has been revealed. Yet Maritain strongly insists theology cannot be reduced to the mere application of philosophy to the data of revelation. Rather, the material object—the subject matter, so to speak—of theology is God. What the theologian ultimately wants to learn about is not scripture, or the teachings of the councils or the great theologians, but God himself. The theologian studies all things, but what distinguishes his study from those of other disciplines is that all things are studied in relation to God.[5] It is for this reason that theology is most deserving of the name wisdom.

---

4 See Maritain, *Science and Wisdom*, 25; and Aquinas, *S.T.*, I, q. 1, a. 2.
5 *S.T.*, I, q. 1, a. 7.

Since theology is superior to the work of the philosopher, theology is within its rights to judge the conclusions of philosophy; indeed, it has an obligation to do so, just as philosophy judges the other sciences. Yet, this does not mean theology does the work proper to philosophy; rather, this is simply a negative role, rejecting false philosophical doctrines. Philosophical premises are, of course, held on their own naturally known merits, independent of theology. Otherwise, philosophy would be absorbed into theology. Philosophical premises have to stand the full scrutiny of reason and critique. So philosophy is not governed positively in its own domain by theology. Neither does theology give philosophy its starting points. There is, accordingly, a clear distinction between philosophy and theology. But as Maritain typically insists, a distinction does not mean that what is distinguished exists separately; rather, they are distinguished in one sense in order to be more clearly united in another manner. Indeed, as should be clear by now, he strongly rejects the Cartesian separation of philosophy from theology.[6]

Maritain's entire defense of Christian philosophy, which we examined in chapter one, cuts against this modern tendency to separate the two disciplines. Their spheres must be kept distinct without denying their interpenetration at key points. If we look at the relation, this time from the point of view of the theologian, we find that philosophy enters directly into the theological task. The theologian makes use of philosophy; indeed, traditionally philosophy was termed the "handmaid of theology."[7] While this use of philosophy within theology is not philosophy's intrinsic function—which is simply to prove its own proper conclusions—from the theological perspective it is vital. This unity in difference allows us to see that although philosophy is in one sense subordinate to theology as a higher science, in another sense it is independent, since it has its own subject matter that its principles are adequate to study on its own.

Maritain argues that theology uses philosophy and that this is important to the theological process. But does theology need philosophy? To

---

6   See *Introduction to Philosophy*, 84; and *The Dream of Descartes*, 69–86.
7   *S.T.*, I, q. 1, a. 5 ad. 2.

understand Maritain's reply to this question, it is important to note that what we have said so far about the superiority of theology and its prerogatives refers to that discipline formally considered in itself. However, Maritain also realizes it is important to consider the discipline in its actual state as practiced by very fallible and wounded human beings. In light of this distinction, we can see that Maritain replies in the negative. Philosophy is not absolutely necessary for theology, because theology takes its principles directly from what God reveals. Nevertheless, he insists that in practice, given the limits of the human intellect, philosophy is generally needed by the theologian. Thus, philosophy usually precedes theology in proving the preambles to the faith, since philosophy is easier for us to know, even though the truths of theology are better known in themselves.[8] In his early work Maritain argues that in its role as an instrument of theology, philosophy does three things: First, it defends the foundation of the faith within apologetics as part of theology (for example, by showing how miracles and the empty tomb show the reality of Christ's divinity or by assisting in the refutation of objections to the faith). Second, philosophy assists in teaching the mysteries of the faith by providing analogies drawn from creatures. For instance, theology appeals to a philosophical account of the mental word and the philosophical understanding of person in developing a theological elaboration of the Trinity. Finally, it aids in refuting opponents of the faith. For example, theology makes use of the doctrines of quantity and substance that are taken from philosophy in order to refute those who say teaching on the Eucharist is incoherent.[9]

In his middle period, Maritain expanded this second function of philosophy within theology, of providing analogies drawn from creatures for the theologian to use. He argues that there is a need for a new principle that would bridge the gap between metaphysics and supernatural contemplation borne of theological faith. It is necessary that before we rise to the heights of supernatural contemplation, the mysteries of

---

8 See *Introduction to Philosophy*, 86; and "Reflections on Theological Knowledge," in *Untrammeled Approaches*, 244–45.

9 *Introduction to Philosophy*, 87.

the faith be made known to us, however partially, through communicable propositions. We cannot experience these realities without having first had them made known to us.[10] Although God himself is made known to us in faith, we do not yet attain to him as he is in himself and to the blessed. Rather, God becomes an object for our understanding only through an ananoetic mode of knowing. The lowest level of this is the analogical naming of the divine perfections that arises through natural theology or metaphysics. However, in light of God's revelation, a new form of analogy—what Maritain refers to as the "superanalogy of faith"—comes about. The use of the notions of generation or filiation in our theology of the Trinity, the notion of three persons having the same nature, of the divine person being made flesh and having both a human and divine nature, are examples of the superanalogy of faith coming into play. Metaphysics could not recognize these truths and it does not fall to philosophy to demonstrate them. However, once they have been revealed by God, the knowledge of the philosopher is very helpful in articulating the meaning and coherence of that revelation. Maritain explains this, writing,

> Let us say it is a superanalogy. The mode of conceiving and of signifying is just as deficient in it as in metaphysical analogy, but what is signified—revealed, i.e., stripped of the veils proper to our natural knowledge, but presented or shown *under other veils*—is this time the deity as such, God as He sees Himself, and who gives Himself to us—obscurely and without our laying hands on Him yet, since we do not see Him.[11]

In this superanalogy of faith the uncreated object that the theologian seeks to know better is and remains suprarational, while the created analogates through which the analogy is accomplished remain conceptual and human. It is because of this superanalogy of faith that the

---

10 *The Degrees of Knowledge*, 256.
11 *The Degrees of Knowledge*, 257.

concepts applied in revealed theology are not merely metaphorical. Rather, they intrinsically and formally designate truths about God.[12]

In his very last works, often bearing on theological themes, Maritain went even further in articulating the functions philosophy might contribute within theology. In these works, he spoke of philosophy as a "research worker" functioning in collaboration with theology.[13] Looking at a properly theological topic with a philosophical perspective or "habitus" could raise fresh problems for investigation and offer new hypotheses for the resolution of old ones:

> It [i.e. philosophy] has also for function,—at least if in the head of a philosopher it is itself strengthened by faith,—to enter, yes, into the proper terrain of the *sacra doctrina* [i.e. sacred doctrine or theology] in order to make there itself an effort of reason and to propose there eventually to the competent doctors new views, I say by the title of *research worker*, and of *research worker* freer than the theologian himself.[14]

The philosopher is freer in this domain than the theologian, as he does not have the same need to be constantly attentive to the authoritative texts. This is a much more robust view of philosophy's contribution than the traditional function as "handmaid" to theology admitted. It is not just that the theologian picks up concepts and ideas from philosophical works, but rather that the philosopher can apply philosophical concepts and methods directly to theological problems.[15] Furthermore, this use of philosophy by the theologian is not to its detriment, as the doctrine of Christian philosophy makes clear. Nor is it an optional extra for the Christian philosopher—or indeed, for the progress of theology

---

12 *The Degrees of Knowledge,* 257–58. In light of this Maritain would categorically reject the view that all language about God is metaphorical in order to assert that there are also truthful analogical statements about God. Metaphorical affirmations are literally false but true in some extended sense (e.g., "God is a lion" suggests his strength and power), while analogical statements are literally true though in a qualified way (e.g., "God is just" is true, but to be understood without the limitations found in human cases of justice).

13 Georges Cottier, OP, "J. Maritain: Un philosophe travaillant comme 'research worker' au service de la theologie," *Notes et Documents* 62 (2001): 49–52.

14 *On the Church of Christ: The Person of the Church and Her Personnel,* trans. Joseph W. Evans (Notre Dame, IN: University of Notre Dame Press, 1973), v.

15 "Reflections on Theological Knowledge," 267.

itself. Maritain argues that this engagement with theology is proper to philosophy, since it is a form of wisdom. Further, having being as its natural object, philosophy must apply itself in its own way to this higher form of knowledge, which is the proper task of theology to elaborate in order to find its own completion.[16] Far from inhibiting philosophy, these encounters with theology perfect it in its own order, leading it to elaborate a more complete understanding of things than it would be able to do otherwise.

Mystical Experience

One of the aspects of Maritain's great work *The Degrees of Knowledge*, which strikes readers unfamiliar with his philosophy as strange, is that it begins with a discussion of philosophy and science only to end in a sustained reflection on mysticism. For Maritain the discussion of mystical theology is essential, as a central point of his book is that the methods and structures suitable to one form of knowing cannot be arbitrarily imposed on a different degree of knowledge. Accordingly, an account of the knowledge of God through a direct experience of his acting upon us is a fitting complement to the discussion of the natural knowledge of God acquired through metaphysics and the academic discipline of theology.

It is important to be clear from the outset that when Maritain speaks of mystical experience, he is not referring to religious sentiment or feelings, even quite powerful ones. In fact, the first chapter addressing mystical experience begins:

> Let it be agreed once and for all that, in the present instance, we understand the word "mystical experience" not in a more-or-less vague sense covering all sorts of more-or-less mysterious or preternatural facts, or even simple religious feeling but, rather, in the sense of an *experimental knowledge* of the deep things of God, or a *suffering of divine things*, an experience which leads the soul through a series of states and transformations until within the very

16 "Reflections on Theological Knowledge," 268.

depths of itself it feels the touch of divinity and "experiences the life of God."[17]

The "suffering of divine things" is a translation of Aquinas's phrase *pati divina*, which was itself taken from the Latin translation of Pseudo-Dionysius. The sense is that the things of God are imposed on the soul by God, rather than by the more active process that is involved in natural cases of knowing.[18] Thus, Maritain understands mystical experience to be "an experimental knowledge of the deep things of God."[19]

Mystical experience—although it is the highest—is only one of three forms of wisdom involved in knowing God. The first and least form of wisdom is metaphysical wisdom or natural theology. This wisdom functions entirely in the natural order and moves from ordinary sense experience of physical things to God. Metaphysics uses concepts derived from created things and applies them to God, purifying them of the limitations they have in creatures through analogy. Clearly, in virtue of the very method it uses, this form of wisdom does not attain the divine essence in its fullness or directly.[20]

The second mode of wisdom is the academic discipline of revealed theology, the science of revelation. Theology applies the methods of reason, but is based in faith. Its proper method is not the light of reason alone, but reason enlightened through faith. Its certitude is superior to metaphysics, as philosophy is based on human reason (which can err), while faith is founded on God's action (which cannot fail).

Unlike metaphysics, theology's object is not God as expressed through creatures, nor God as first cause of creatures, nor even less is it revelation. The proper object of revealed theology is God in the guise of mystery: that is, in his essence and inner life. The theologian strives to know this so far as we can in this life using all the resources of revelation and grace. God's inner life can be accessed in three ways: (1) in the

---

17 *The Degrees of Knowledge*, 263.

18 See Heather McAdam Erb, "'Pati Divina': Mystical Union in Aquinas," in *Faith, Scholarship and Culture in the 21st Century*, ed. Alice Ramos and Marie I George (Washington, DC: The American Maritain Association, 2002), 73–96.

19 *The Degrees of Knowledge*, 247.

20 *The Degrees of Knowledge*, 264.

vision of blessed or the knowledge that the saints who are now with God have of him through seeing him directly, (2) in the theological virtue of faith, which incorporates what sacred scripture reveals, and what the Church teaches, about his inner Trinitarian life, and (3) in the science of theology, which explains and draws out the implications of scripture and the Church's teaching. Each of these attains the same object, God in his inner life, but they do so in different ways.

It is essential to be clear about the differences between metaphysics, revealed theology, and mysticism. In metaphysics analogy is the form and rule of knowledge; consequently, God is not attained in virtue of his own inner life. Rather, God is made known in accordance with the limits of the human mind through the mirror of the created world. It is important to avoid any misconceptions about the role of philosophy here. Metaphysical knowledge is not in any way a preparation for mystical knowledge of God. They function in fundamentally different orders; metaphysical wisdom is a thoroughly natural form of knowledge, while mystical wisdom has its source and sustenance in the supernatural order. As we mentioned in the previous section, theology is not merely the application of philosophy to revelation, as that would subordinate theological wisdom to philosophy. Rather, theology illumines the revealed data of scripture and tradition by a faith that is intrinsically connected to reason, moving along with reason and making use of philosophy as an instrument for its own ends. Thus, the theologian is free to make use of philosophy as she sees fit.[21]

The third way to wisdom is through mystical experience or, as Maritain puts it, following St. Thomas and Pseudo-Dionysius, "suffering divine things."[22] There are two main aspects to this: first, the sanctifying grace that puts us into relationship with God as an object of our love and understanding, and second, the indwelling of the Blessed Trinity within our souls. Authentic mysticism occurs through the operation of sanctifying grace within us. As 2 Peter 1:4 states, grace makes us sharers

---

21 See the chart in *The Degrees of Knowledge*, 269.

22 On Aquinas's use of this phrase from Pseudo-Dionysius, see Urban Hannon, "Studying and Suffering Divine Things: St. Thomas Aquinas on Hierotheus," *Medieval Mystical Theology* 31, no. 2 (2022): 80–90.

in the divine nature. We become divine through participation in the divine nature by way of sanctifying grace. Yet, this leads to a paradox, for how can the finite soul formally participate in the divine nature, which is infinite? Grace brings the finite soul into relation with the infinite God, allowing God himself to become the soul's object. Formal participation in God through having God in his essence is impossible, but it is possible in the sense of having the Godhead as its *object*:

> Thomists give this answer: the soul is thus rendered infinite in the order of its *relation to the object*. A formal participation in Deity, which would be impossible were it a question of having Deity for its essence (for it is a pure absurdity that that which is not God should receive as its essence the very essence of God), is possible if it is a matter of having Deity as object. For a being which is not God to be raised up, in its very basic structure and in the energies from which its operations proceed, so as to have as the object of its understanding and love God Himself as He sees and loves Himself, that is indeed, impossible to the forces of nature alone. Yet no absolute impossibility can be detected in it. Grace bestows upon us, in a supernatural manner a radical power of grasping pure Act as our object, a new root of spiritual operation whose proper and specifying object is the Divine essence itself.[23]

As we have said, God is ontologically present in the soul as an object. The term "object," in this context, is used in its rational and philosophical Aristotelian and Thomistic sense. In this sense there is no reason to be concerned that treating God as an object would be unfitting, given the transcendence of the Godhead. This manner of presence is importantly different from God's universal presence throughout the universe, which Maritain and St. Thomas explain as a presence through causality,[24] so that God is present to all things as their first cause. But, in the case of mystics, God is present as the term the soul is inwardly turned towards. The soul is converted and ordered to God as an object of loving

---

23 *The Degrees of Knowledge*, 271. See also John of St. Thomas, *Cursus theologicus in Summam theologicam D. Thomæ* (Madrid: Vives, 1883), I-II, q. 110, disp. 22, a. 1.

24 *S.T.*, I, q. 8, a. 1.

knowledge. This is a fruitful and "experimental" knowledge, by which Maritain means knowledge by experience or acquaintance.

This leads to the next aspect of the mystical life: namely, the indwelling of the divine persons of the Trinity within our soul. Through knowledge and love the indwelling of the divine persons puts us in possession of God and unites us to him not merely as a remote object; it renders him not only intentionally present, but also really present within us. Maritain holds that sanctifying grace is an entitative habit, a seed of the operation which is the Beatific vision;it really makes present the Trinity within us. Accordingly, the life of grace is eternal life begun:

> Eternal life begins here and now. It begins here below and should grow unceasingly till the dissolution of the body in such a way as to realize by mystical experience and infused contemplation themselves, as far as possible on this earth, in the night of faith, in which *what we shall be has not yet appeared*, that possession of God to which sanctifying grace is essentially ordained.[25]

On this point Maritain follows the teaching of his mentor Fr. Reginald Garrigou-Lagrange, OP, who led retreats for members of the Thomistic circles that met at the Maritains' home in Meudon, and to whom the chapter on mystical experience and philosophy in the *The Degrees of Knowledge* is dedicated. In a massive study entitled *The Three Ages of the Spiritual Life,* Fr. Garrigou-Lagrange argued forcefully for the view that the heights of contemplation discussed by the saints, such as St. John of the Cross and St. Teresa of Ávila, were not a privileged path for the few, a vocational peculiarity of those in religious orders explicitly dedicated to this aim. Rather, he insisted that infused contemplation, the height of mystical prayer, is the summit of the ordinary path to holiness. Maritain could not have been more faithful to the views of his former spiritual guide than when he wrote, "Thus it is clear that mystical experience and infused contemplation are, indeed, seen to be the normal, rightful end

---

25 *The Degrees of Knowledge*, 275.

of the life of grace. They could even be said to be the summit towards which all human life tends."[26]

A typical objection to this doctrine asks why, if contemplative prayer is the normal summit of holiness, so few people—even among the saints—seem to attain it. Maritain, however, insists on two things. The first is that the contemplative path is not the prerogative of a special few. The second is that contemplation can be manifested in a plurality of ways and is not necessarily realized only in the purest form as described by the great mystical theologians. Those who are engrossed in the active life due to their temperament or vocation may still experience contemplation in which there is a "tempered exercise" (*un exercice attempéré*) of the gift of wisdom. People engaged in the active life, yet living the virtues and receiving the gifts of the Holy Spirit, will have a participation in mystical contemplation and may achieve an anticipation or "inchoate" form of properly mystical prayer at its height. In this manner, they have the ultimate disposition to infused contemplation.[27]

Sanctifying grace and the indwelling of the divine persons are the ontological foundations of mystical experience, its first principles. However, there remains a further question to be determined: What are the more immediate principles of mystical experience, and how is this experience realized? Maritain's answer to this question is twofold. First, the mystical is a suprahuman mode of knowing and, second, it is a connatural mode of knowing. Mystical experience is truly a suprahuman way of knowing God, since the natural principles of our nature are not sufficient to account for it. Our natural and human mode of knowing is through concepts drawn from sense experience. Insofar as we know God in a natural manner, it is by analogy.[28] Even faith, through which we do reach God in his inner life, remains a mediated form of knowing—"enigmatic," as St. Paul had put it. For faith only tells us truths about

---

26 *The Degrees of Knowledge*, 275. See also Reginald Garrigou-Lagrange, *The Three Ages of the Spiritual Life*, Vol. II, trans. Sister M. Timothea Doyle (Rockford, IL: TAN Books, 1989), 323–24.

27 *De la vie d'oraison*, 2nd ed. (Paris: l'Art Catholique, 1925), 81–82. See also James Arraj, *Mysticism, Metaphysics and Maritain* (Chiloquin, OR: Inner Growth Books, 2011), 62–64.

28 "Natural Mystical Experience and the Void," in *Ransoming the Time*, trans. Harry Lorin Binsse (New York: Charles Scribner's Sons, 1941), 260.

God's inner life, allowing us to see Him "as through a glass darkly."[29] Not even faith brings us face to face with the divine in a direct experience. To know God as directly as possible in this life requires a movement from above, a special inspiration of the Holy Spirit. Thus, the immediate principles of mystical experience are what have been traditionally called the "gifts of the Holy Spirit" in the Christian tradition, which make the soul completely mobile under God's inspiration. As Maritain poetically explains, "We are like little children to whom a supernatural art, a pencil to write in heaven, has been given. God Himself must put His hand on our hand and guide the stroke."[30]

It is in light of this participation in God's nature that Maritain can speak of our mystical experience of God as a form of connatural knowledge. As we saw in chapter two, connatural knowledge arises from an agreement in nature. This is a major element in Maritain's account of our knowledge of morality and the knowledge of the artist. Connatural knowledge comes into play when the agent does not have scientific knowledge. She cannot offer a fully worked-out justification or deductive argument for her position, yet she *knows* whereof she speaks because of a connatural agreement, a knowledge by acquaintance, with the object to be known. The moral philosopher has scientific or philosophical knowledge about the virtue of chastity, for example. She can demonstrate that adultery, for example, is wrong and give complete justification. However, another way of knowing the virtue of chastity is to simply possess the virtue, to live by it. Such a person will have connatural knowledge of the virtue by possessing it within herself through an affective experience of the relevant good, without necessarily having to possess the kind of scientific knowledge of the philosopher or theologian. In the case of mystical union, there is a connaturality with reality that is cannot be conceptualized by the agent. In this case the reality of God is grasped insofar as it is non-conceptualizable, while at the same time being grasped as "the ultimate goal of the act of knowing in its perfect immanence." Here God is apprehended as an interiorized

29 1 Cor. 13:12.
30 *The Degrees of Knowledge*, 276.

goal in which knowledge is fulfilled. This connaturality with the reality of God cannot be objectivized in a concept, and yet it remains the goal of objective union. This is a form of connaturality unique to mystical experience and distinct from the prudential experience of the moral life, the natural contemplation of philosophers, or poetic experience. It is a "possession giving not-knowing."[31]

But how can we explain mystical experience through connaturality? Wouldn't that imply that we were connatural with God? Would Maritain not be making the mystic in some sense equal to God? From what we have said already, the answer is clear. Yes, the human person is rendered connatural to the divine nature through sanctifying grace, which is manifested in the love through which we are united to God:

> What is it that makes us radically connatural with God? It is sanctifying grace whereby we are made *consortes divinae naturae* [sharers in the divine nature]. And what makes this radical connaturality pass into act; what makes it flower into the actuality of operation? Charity. We are made connatural to God through charity. Charity is not just any kind of love. It presupposes sanctifying grace, of which it is the property, and it lays hold on God as He is really present within us as a Gift, a Friend, an eternal life-companion. However, it wins to God immediately as God, in His very deity, in the very intimate and absolutely proper life with which He will beatify us. Charity loves Him in Himself and by Himself.[32]

This connatural union with God through charity is characteristic of supernatural Christian life at its highest point. But how are we to understand the spiritual experiences of the non-Christian? Looking to other traditions—notably, the spiritual traditions of India—there are reports of spiritual experiences that seem to resemble Christian mysticism. This raises the question of whether there can be any natural spiritual experience of God. Is any genuinely mystical experience possible apart from the Christian virtue of faith?

---

31 "The Natural Mystical Experience and the Void," 263.
32 *The Degrees of Knowledge*, 277. See also *S.T.*, II-II, q. 45, a. 2.

Maritain holds that there is a natural spirituality involved in any intellectual work, even that of the scientist or mathematician. This is legitimate, since the exercise of the intellect and the will always involves a spiritual element. Whether one is a peasant or an artist, there is a hidden spirituality involved in imposing the form of reason on physical things.[33] This is most evident in the work of the poet and the philosopher as their activities are primarily intellectual and, when authentic, aspire to the spiritual. Thus, while he denies that metaphysics is the gateway to the contemplative life, Maritain nevertheless holds that there is a mystical aspiration at the heart of every authentic metaphysics.[34]

It is clear, then, that Maritain admits a kind of spirituality involved in everyday activities and the work of intellectuals. But this is spirituality only in a particular or restricted sense. It does not address the more significant question of whether there is an authentic, natural mystical experience. Maritain admits that there seems to be a sense in which there is a natural spirituality and a natural contemplation and a natural mystical desire. This natural spirituality, though not mystical itself, can be pressed into service by mystical desire and present itself as if it were mystical, though it remains counterfeit. It is true that if the phrase "mystical experience" is given a vague, all-inclusive sense, then one could agree that there is a natural mystical experience, but this would remain more or less meaningless. The question is really whether there is an authentic mystical experience in the strict sense: (1) that it is not a counterfeit or illusion, and (2) that it bears on God himself, making us experience the divine reality through an experiential knowledge of God in the natural order.

Maritain's answer to this more precise formulation of the question was to develop over time. In one of his first discussions in *Réflexions sur l'intelligence* Maritain unequivocally answers no, stating, "A natural mystical contemplation is a contradiction in terms."[35] He takes a similar

---

33   *The Degrees of Knowledge,* 283–84.
34   *The Degrees of Knowledge,* 284–85. See also "The Natural Mystical Experience and the Void," 261.
35   *Réflexions sur l'intelligence,* 135.

position in *The Degrees of Knowledge*, ruling out any natural mystical experience as impossible. In these works, it is important to note that he is speaking of mystical experience as an experimental knowledge of divine things.[36] Later consideration of the Indian tradition of mysticism studied by his friends, such as Olivier Lacombe, convinced him that there might be an indirect form of natural mysticism through experience of the substantial being of the soul.[37]

However, the main lines of his argument in *The Degrees of Knowledge* remain unchanged, at least insofar as we speak of an experimental knowledge of God. In this work Maritain argues that if a natural mystical experience were possible, then the whole distinction between nature and grace would be undermined. As we have seen, there are three key aspects necessary for genuine mystical experience. First, grace infuses a new spiritual nature in us. Second, the indwelling presence of the Trinity makes possible an experience of the divine reality and God's inner life. Finally, the gifts of understanding and wisdom inspired by the Holy Spirit raise the intellect to know in faith the object of faith itself in a supernatural manner through connatural charity, making this experience of God a reality. These supernatural elements are needed for both the possibility and the real manifestation of any authentic supernatural experience of God:[38]

> To admit in any degree whatsoever, even in simplest inchoative form, a genuine experience of the depths of God's being on the natural level would necessarily mean either to confuse our natural intellectuality (specified by being in general) with our intellectuality as it flows from grace and is specified by the Divine Essence itself; or to confuse the presence of God's immensity (whereby God is present in all things in virtue of his created efficiency) with His holy indwelling (whereby He is present in a special way, as object, in souls that are in the state of grace); or, again, to muddle up in the same hybrid concept, the wisdom of the natural order

---

36 By "experimental knowledge," Maritain means knowledge based upon direct experience.

37 On Lacombe's influence on the development of Maritain's views see Arraj, *Mysticism, Metaphysics and Maritain*, Chapter 3.

38 *The Degrees of Knowledge*, 286.

(metaphysical wisdom), and the infused gift of wisdom; or, finally, to attribute to the natural love of God what belongs exclusively to supernatural charity. In any event, it would be to confuse what is absolutely proper to grace with what is proper to nature. There is no "immediate grasp" of God in the natural order. A mystical contemplation (i.e., an authentic one) in the natural order is a contradiction in terms. A genuine experience of God's inner depths, a felt contact with God, a *pati divina*, can take place only in the order of sanctifying grace and through sanctifying grace.[39]

To this strong rejection of any natural mysticism one might object that God is supremely intelligible in himself, and that he is spiritually present in our minds. Thus, it would seem that some natural experience of his presence would make sense and account for mystical experience. Maritain, however, argues that this presence is not sufficient. A genuine mystical experience requires that God be present in us not merely in a vague manner, but *as an object*. For God to be present in us as an object, it is necessary that we be made proportionate to Him. But this is not possible at all in the natural order, since the only way a finite being can be made proportionate to the infinite God is through sanctifying grace, turning us toward God as an object. A further objection could be drawn from St. Thomas Aquinas's position that every creature loves God more than itself, since God is a higher good. This seems to imply that there is a natural love of God that is distinct from the theological virtue of charity. Why would this not suffice for a connatural knowledge of God? Maritain explains that such a knowledge would not be connatural, since connaturality requires agreement in the same nature. We cannot be connatural with the supernatural unless we are made supernatural ourselves. Consequently, it is undeniable that connaturality with God through charity presumes a supernatural love. This presupposes sanctifying grace in order that God as an object of love be made present to us as a gift and a friend whose life we share. This can only arise from a supernatural faith that attains God in his essence and inner life:

39 *The Degrees of Knowledge*, 287.

The natural love of God has none of these characteristics. Even supposing it capable of making us love God efficaciously above all things (and this is not the case with our fallen nature), this love, which proceeds from our essence as creatures infinitely far removed from Pure Act, and which cannot constitute a friendship properly so called between man and God, nor achieve God as really present within us as a gift, a love, in fine, which can only love God through the mediation of the transcendental good (as supreme and subsistent Good)—since it is ruled by an analogical knowledge in which God is known only through the mediation of transcendental being (as First Being)—this natural love of God is incapable of rendering us properly connatural to things divine, incapable of providing a knowledge of God through connaturality, a mystical experience of the depths of God.[40]

A final—and significant—objection is the testimony of mystical experience of God from Muslim, Buddhism, Brahmanism, and other traditions. Such experiences cannot come from the theological virtue of faith in the Christian sense, so it seems there must be a natural mystical experience. In *The Degrees of Knowledge*, Maritain argues that if these cases are genuine, then they arise from divine grace and infused contemplation at work in these people in a modified way, apart from the Christian sacraments and a visible acceptance of revelation. Accordingly, he maintains that cases of authentic mystical experience do occur in other traditions, but that these are not natural experiences; rather, they are ones where God's work of grace remains hidden. The unbaptized, although not in union with the Church, do participate in the proper work of the Church and can receive the supernatural life and belong to the Church invisibly without knowing it:[41]

> Because there is a sheep-fold, the shepherd who keeps it is also the shepherd of those *other sheep* who, without knowing it, receive of His fullness but who have not yet heard his voice. Because the Church has received the treasure of supernatural revelation in its

---

40 *The Degrees of Knowledge*, 288–89.

41 *The Degrees of Knowledge*, 290. For a detailed discussion, see also *On the Church of Christ*, Chapter 10.

entirety, it allows us to honor everywhere the various traces or marks or scattered fragments of that revelation.[42]

In response to these phenomena Maritain calls for a revitalization of studies of comparative mysticism that would avoid a facile syncretism and help to uncover the authentic visitations of God in the various mystical traditions, "for nowhere is He left without witnesses." What Maritain envisions is not a watering down of mysticism to the lowest common denominator, but rather an evaluation of other schools of mysticism in terms of the benchmark of Christian experience, in order to determine what is authentic in them.[43] This point has become even more important to be aware of in the ecumenical and interfaith contexts of a post-Vatican II Church. The theological point upon which he insists is that when such genuine experiences occur in the absence of the theological virtue of faith, they are not natural, but they remain the work of God's grace—every bit as much as those experiences that occur within the Christian tradition.

In view of the position he argues so forcefully in *The Degrees of Knowledge*, it is surprising to find that in 1938, just six years after its first publication, Maritain presented a paper, later published as "The Natural Mystical Experience and the Void," appearing to admit the possibility of natural mystical experience. A similar point was also made, albeit briefly, in Appendix V to the subsequent editions of *Degrees*.[44] In fact, Maritain had been influenced by just the kind of studies of comparative mysticism that he had called for—notably, those of his friend Olivier Lacombe on Indian mysticism—which he considered in light of his reading of Fr. Gardeil's discussion of our knowledge of the self in the landmark work *La Structure de l'âme et de l'expérience mystique*. These influences led Maritain to reconsider the possibility of an intellective, rather than affective, connaturality that might, through the rigorous practices of Brahmanist spirituality, lead to a genuine mystical

---

42 *The Degrees of Knowledge*, 292. The ecclesiological significance of this approach is discussed at length below in the section entitled "The Holiness of the Church."

43 *The Degrees of Knowledge*, 292.

44 *The Degrees of Knowledge*, 471.

experience of the natural order. Yet, upon closer reading it is clear that this was not in any way a rejection of his earlier position so much as a supplement to it. Indeed, in this essay he subtly shifts from his earlier definition of mystical experience as an "experimental knowledge of the deep things of God" to a broader, more inclusive definition: "...in general by the phrase 'mystical experience' I mean a *possession-giving experience of the absolute.*"[45] There are two key differences in the definitions. The first and most obvious is that mysticism is now defined in relation to the absolute rather than God. Second, it is now defined, perhaps more accurately, as a "possession-giving" experience.

This is important as it highlights that, in now admitting an authentic natural mystical experience, Maritain is not overturning his earlier position, but extending it. He is as clear in this presentation as he was in his earlier work that a genuine mystical experience is not a natural culmination of philosophical contemplation. Further, he reserves the affective connaturality that had been the focus of his work in *The Degrees of Knowledge* to the heights of Christian mysticism as presented in the complementary teachings of John of the Cross and John of St. Thomas. Accordingly, it is reasonable to infer that he never changed his views about what he wrote regarding that supernatural experience of God. What is new here is an "intellectual connaturality": "a natural contemplation which by means of supra- or para-conceptual intellection attains a transcendent reality, of itself inexpressible in any human mental word. There we have the typical mode of knowing in the natural mystical experience."[46]

Maritain begins his argument by adopting St. Thomas's position that we know the soul only through a reflection on its operations. We do not know our own soul immediately or directly; rather, we encounter it through its acts of understanding and willing. In reflecting on these we can turn our attention towards the principle of these acts. However, if we do so, Maritain insists we only encounter the *existence* of the soul,

---

45 "The Natural Mystical Experience and the Void," 256. Also, when discussing this issue much later he writes: "I call 'mystical' experience, in general, any experience *fruitive of the absolute.*" See *On the Church of Christ*, 95.

46 "The Natural Mystical Experience and the Void," 264.

not its essence or nature. Thus, in our self-reflection we can be led to a true experience of the soul's singular existence (its act of being or *esse*). This is a direct experience of the soul's being. As he puts it:

> Such an experiential apprehension of the soul, not by its essence but by its acts, can be said to be immediate in this sense, that the reality it attains is not known by any other intermediary than its own actuation . . . Thus we truly have an experience of the singular existence of our soul: I mean to say, by and in its operations, and our concept of ourselves is an experimental concept.[47]

This experience, however, tells us nothing about the soul's nature. All that we know is that the soul, whose existence we have experientially encountered, is the principle of the acts that we have observed; these operations are the only possible content of my concept of myself. Further, as I give more attention to the existential experience of my soul, less is given to the diverse phenomena that have led to this reflexive apprehension of it.[48] In this experiential encounter with the soul's own singular existence, Maritain finds an account that could reframe the experiences of Brahmanist mystics who claim to reach the absolute through an experience of Atman or "the Self." Accordingly, he asks if it is not possible that this penetration beyond the soul's operations, much like the Brahmanist's escape of the apparent ego, might not lead to an encounter of the absolute self: "This mysticism, reduced to its essential kernel, would above all be a metaphysical experience of the substantial *esse* [being] of the soul by means of negative, or rather annihilating, intellectual connaturality."[49]

In applying his philosophy of self-awareness to the mystical tradition of Brahmanism, Maritain is clear that there cannot be an experiential knowledge of the soul's nature. Rather, he insists that what those who practice this spirituality encounter is the substantial being of their souls, through a drastic purification of ordinary self- awareness through

---

47 *The Degrees of Knowledge*, 471–72. See also "The Natural Mystical Experience and the Void," 270.
48 "The Natural Mystical Experience and the Void," 271.
49 "The Natural Mystical Experience and the Void," 272.

reflexive knowledge of the soul's operations. For most of us this experience is clouded through the phenomenal multiplicity of the operations, by means of which the soul is manifested to us. This purification is an attempt to move beyond the operations to the substantial existence of the principle that underlies them. Describing the Brahmanist mystic's practice in this context Maritain says,

> Risking everything to gain everything, and thanks to assiduous exercise reversing the ordinary course of mental activity, the soul empties itself absolutely of every specific operation and of all multiplicity, and knows negatively by means of the void and the annihilation of every act and every object of thought coming from outside—the soul knows negatively—but nakedly, without veils— that metaphysical marvel, that absolute, that perfection of every perfection, which is *to exist*, which is the soul's own substantial existence.[50]

This negative and apophatic experience makes use of the void and abolition. In this experience the substantial existence of the soul is known as what is unknown. This is analogous to the supernatural mystic who knows as unknown the Godhead. In this case the void or annihilation is a vital act in which the annihilation is consummated "and silence is made perfect."[51] Beginning with the knowledge of the soul's existence through its acts, the natural mystic annihilates those acts through this turn back to the void and thereby encounters the soul's substantial being, encountering it as a reality that is inexpressible by any concept, ineffably singular and unique. In this it contrasts with supernatural mystical experience:

> Instead of saying: *amor transit in conditionem objecti* [love passes over into the condition of the object], in this case we should have to say: *vacuitas, abolitio, denudatio transit in conditionem objecti* [the void, abolition, uncovering passes over into the condition of the object]. Here is the most purely existential experience possible, and it is an experience by means of not knowing. In the

50 "The Natural Mystical Experience and the Void," 274.
51 "The Natural Mystical Experience and the Void," 275.

supernatural mystical experience, the void is a condition of contemplation (a condition actively prepared by the soul and, much more, is sovereignly positive: it is the union of love under the inspiration of the Holy Spirit. In the case under discussion, the void is not only a condition but also a formal means of the experience).[52]

In the natural mysticism found here the void becomes the formal means by which one is able to experience the substantial existentiality of the soul.

However, at this stage it is unclear why we would say that this is a natural *mystical* experience. Would it not make more sense to refer to this encounter with the substantial existence of the soul as a metaphysical experience? This is an especially important question given Maritain's own lengthy discussion distinguishing metaphysical from mystical experience. Moreover, in that account he argued forcefully that metaphysical experience does not entail or naturally culminate in mystical experience.[53] Should we not then treat this experience of the soul as a paradigm of metaphysical experience rather than a form of natural experience? To do so, however, would be to fail to recognize the fact that substantial existence (*esse*) is fundamentally transcendent and polyvalent; it can be limited only by the essence that possesses it. However, in this case we know nothing of that essence. Accordingly, Maritain argues that in knowing the substantial existence of the soul, at the same time the mystic attains indistinctly "both this same existence proper to the soul and existence in its metaphysical amplitude, and the sources of existence." In encountering the existence of one's own soul, one also encounters in an indirect manner the fact that this soul emanates from and is suffused by an influx from which it attains all the reality and perfection it possesses: "This influx is not experienced in itself, of course, but rather in the effect which it produces [i.e., the substantial existence of the soul], and itself in and through this effect."[54] In view of this explanation, Maritain argues that the experience advocated by Brahmanism

---

52 "The Natural Mystical Experience and the Void," 275.
53 *The Degrees of Knowledge,* 295–98.
54 "The Natural Mystical Experience and the Void," 279.

seems to be a genuine mystical experience of the natural order insofar as it is a possession-giving experience of the absolute. The absolute that he encounters is the substantial being of his own soul, and in and by this he encounters indirectly the divine absolute through God's "presence of immensity," infusing and sustaining the being of his own soul. Maritain cautions that it is important to carefully distinguish the absolute in the form of the self from the divine absolute, and criticizes Brahmanism for frequently confusing these two senses of the word *atman* that it uses to designate both the human self and the supreme Self. However, with that qualification in mind he argues that this approach offers an authentic example of a natural mystical experience without undermining the account of mysticism offered in *The Degrees of Knowledge* or the fatal confusion of nature and grace that he leveled at any natural mysticism. There is no danger of that confusion here, since this natural mystical experience does not make the non-Christian mystic proportionate to the divine nature. What is encountered directly is not "the deep things of God," but rather the substantial being of the soul, and it is accomplished not through the means of sanctifying grace making the soul connatural to the divine through love, but through the soul's own act of self-reflection, which occurs entirely in the intellectual order.[55] Maritain overlooked this possibility in his earlier work due to the fact that at that time he had only considered the affective connaturality appropriate to mystical experience of "the deep things of God."[56]

Maritain's discussion of mysticism shows why no philosophy can raise to the level of a direct experience of God as a philosophy. For that to occur, as it does in the case of the Christian contemplative, the mystic must be made connatural with God through love. This can only occur through the twin principles of sanctifying grace and the indwelling of the Trinity within the soul. Since the methods of other mystical traditions do not admit of this grace, those experiences are to be explained not as natural forms of mysticism, but as cases where Christ's grace is at work without being made known explicitly to us or the mystics

---

55 "The Natural Mystical Experience and the Void," 284.
56 "The Natural Mystical Experience and the Void," 279–80n18.

themselves. However, as we have seen, Maritain does suggest the possibility of a kind of intellectual connaturality that would make a natural mystical experience possible in the case of Hinduism, where the mystic comes to a unique experience of the singular being of his own soul in a way that opens him to the divine source of that being. This is not a rejection of his earlier teaching on the uniqueness of Christian mysticism, but rather an extension of it through realizing the role that this direct and unique experience of the soul can play in coming to an authentic experience of the divine.

The Consciousness of Christ

Maritain turned to the topic of Christ's consciousness and knowledge in his last book, *On the Grace and Humanity of Christ*. However, it was a topic upon which he and Raïssa had reflected and discussed for many years. The book is divided into two studies that were presented as "research meetings" in 1964 to the Little Brothers of Jesus in Toulouse. Part one gives a theological summary of the different stages of Christ's life and provides a basis for part two, which is far longer and focuses on questions related to Christ's knowledge and consciousness.

The difficulty Maritain seeks to address is raised by Aquinas's treatment of Luke 2:52: "He grew in wisdom, in age and in grace before God and men." Aquinas rejects the obvious implication of the passage, namely, that Christ learned new things through his life and grew in grace. Rather, he argues that Christ's wisdom and grace only grew in relation to its external manifestations and effects, not with respect to the grace and knowledge of Christ himself.[57] Aquinas's concern was to preserve the unity of the human and divine natures in Christ and ensure the glorification of Christ as man. For Maritain, as for many commentators, however, the result was to deny the obvious meaning of the Gospel text. However, he suggests that this problem arose because Aquinas did not possess the necessary philosophical tools that modern psychology

---

57 *S.T.*, III, q. 7, a. 12.

provides concerning human consciousness, even if we must apply these to Christ in a transcendent and unique way.[58]

The discussion of Christ's consciousness is considered in terms of the scholastic doctrine adopted by both Aquinas and Maritain that Jesus's soul, throughout his mortal life, exists in the two simultaneous states of *comprehensor* and *viator*. In general the state of being a *viator* or "wayfarer" refers to someone in the condition of the normal mortal journey towards God. A *viator* is someone on the way towards beatitude. A *comprehensor*, one who has beheld or understood, refers to someone who has completed the journey, beholding God in eternal life. Thus, it seems that by definition one cannot be a *viator* and *comprehensor* at the same time. Aquinas reconciles this tension by suggesting that Jesus's intellect experienced beatitude by fully seeing God, but that the normal effects of this were not yet possessed by Jesus, as his soul was passible and his body was both passible and mortal.[59] Maritain expands on this point, arguing that while Christ was truly a *comprehensor*, having the beatific vision of God from the moment his soul was created, he did not possess the complementary perfection that is connatural to this vision, namely, the state of glory. Thus, he suggests that in becoming human Christ renounced many of the privileges of the divinity. Jesus, although possessing the beatific vision, did not have the corresponding state of glory. The state of *comprehensor* would not fully govern Jesus's humanity until he died on the cross, bringing an end to his state as a *viator*.[60] As a *viator* Jesus lives a fully human life on the path to glory and beatitude, experiencing the normal progress of intellectual and

58 *On the Grace and Humanity of Jesus*, trans. Joseph W. Evans (New York: Herder and Herder, 1969), 48–49.

59 See *S.T.*, III, q. 15, a. 10. See also *S.T.* I, q. 12. a. 7, where Maritain notes Aquinas refers to Jesus as *"perfectus comprehensor."*

60 *On the Grace and Humanity of Jesus*, 86 and 137–38. Maritain takes it for granted that Christ experienced the beatific vision. Today Thomists dispute the claim that Christ possessed this during his passion. The most prominent defense of this position is found in Jean-Pierre Torrell, OP, "S. Tomas d'Aquin et la science du Christ," in *Le mystère du Christ chez saint Tomas d'Aquin: Textes choisis et présentés par Jean-Pierre Torrell, O.P.* (Paris: Cerf, 1999), 198–213. In favor of the traditional view is the argument that Christ's passion is the cause of our resurrection and attainment of the beatific vision. But, if Christ did not have the beatific vision in his passion, then this could not cause us to attain it, for there cannot be more in the effect than there is in the cause.

human development like all human beings. This entails that the effects of the beatific vision and Jesus's infused knowledge are not absolute, but limited in accordance with his experiential knowledge, which develops naturally with maturity. However, Jesus is able to have a limited participation in the beatific vision even as a *viator* through infused knowledge mediating between his full knowledge as *comprehensor* and his more limited knowledge as *viator*.[61]

How can this be possible? It is at this point that Maritain's theory of consciousness is critical. He distinguishes between three levels of consciousness that are found in all human beings. The first is, in fact, an aspect of our unconscious—or as Maritain terms it, "infraconscious"— which refers to all natural human functions, tendencies, instincts, etc. These remain below the level of conscious awareness as natural events that occur without any direct act of volition by the agent. Above this level is conscious awareness, which Maritain defines as "a knowledge wholly experimental and felt, which of itself is obscure and inexpressible in concepts."[62] The final aspect of consciousness Maritain calls "supra-conscious," which includes the "agent intellect" and "the sources of the intuitive activities of the spirit."[63]

Maritain's unique contribution here is the element of supracon-scious which is critical to his account of how Christ's knowledge can be both completely perfect and growing over his earthly life. Before looking at its application to Christ, it is worth exploring his understanding of the ordinary case of supraconscious in human experience. As we have seen, it is identified with the agent intellect, which is a scholastic term for the aspect of the intellect that actively forms concepts and analyzes experiences. The supraconscious is also at work in our intuitive judgments, which germinate without our conscious awareness until they arise as if from hidden springs. Aside from the case of Christ, Maritain appeals to the supraconscious in his late work to explain both the creative intuition

---

61 *On the Grace and Humanity of Jesus*, 102n22.
62 *On the Grace and Humanity of Jesus*, 116.
63 *On the Grace and Humanity of Jesus*, 55.

of the poet and the contemplative experience of the mystic.[64] However, his interest in consciousness goes back to the 1930s, when he began to develop his appreciation and critique of Freud; this early discussion of the topic provides a foreshadowing of his view of the supraconscious that helps us to see its role in the human psyche more clearly.

While admiring the way Freud highlights the importance of unconscious processes and the empirical psychology that he used to corroborate his claims, Maritain is, unsurprisingly, highly critical of Freud on a number of issues. Crucial among these, for present purposes, is the doctrine of sublimation. According to Freud, erotic energy is given limited expression. Sublimation is the process by which this energy is diverted into other—typically more socially acceptable and useful—activities, such as artistic expression. Since Freud considers tendencies entirely from the side of the subject, he cannot find any essential difference between them. Due to this unfortunate fact, Freud merges all of the various unconscious drives and tendencies found in human experience into one fundamental type, namely, instinct. The differences between these tendencies are explained away as various disguises or transformations of instincts. Accordingly, Maritain notes that Freud sees the "higher states" (in Maritain's view) of poetic inspiration and mystical love as mere "transformations and masks of instinct." Such states are simply manifestations of a sensuality that has been repressed and diverted from its normal means of expression. As Maritain sums up Freud's teaching: "All human inebriation is specifically sensual."[65] From Maritain's perspective this is to lump together experiences that are in reality essentially distinct. Nevertheless, he argues the Freudian term "sublimation" is a legitimate one, but that it needs to be used in a different sense. The "inebriation" of the poet or the mystic is "specifically distinct" from instinct. Yet, this does not mean that it is completely set apart from instinct. While it would be wrong to explain these higher

---

64 *Creative Intuition in Art and Poetry* (New York: Pantheon Books, 1953), 66ff. *The Peasant of the Garonne: An Old Layman Questions Himself about the Present Time*, trans. Micheal Cuddihy and Elizabeth Hughes (New York: Holt, Rinehart, and Winston, 1968), 228n103. See also James Arraj, *Mysticism, Metaphysics and Maritain*, 83–89.

65 "Freudism and Psychoanalysis," *Cross Currents* 6, no. 4 (1956): 319.

states entirely in terms of the lower state of instinct, it would be equally absurd and inhuman to separate them from it entirely.[66] Unlike those of other animals, the instincts of the human person are formed by reason and are, consequently, more indeterminate. For example, the instinct of a hungry wolf when it spots a nearby rabbit is quite direct; it will hunt. By contrast a hungry man or woman, when presented with food, may choose to fast for the sake of God or diet for the sake of health rather than simply eat. Even if he is not dissuaded by such rational considerations, he may choose not to eat because the food available is just not to his taste or in order to offend the host. Hence, Maritain suggests adopting a rather un-Freudian definition of sublimation from Gustave Thibon:

> We can define sublimation—true sublimation—as "a sort of ascendant reflux of instinct in the direction of the immaterial sources of the human being, as the qualitative integration of sensible rhythms into the melody of the interior life. Subjectively, it is accompanied by a feeling of equilibrium, peace and inner plenitude, by a sense of liberation from the bondage and discord of the lower appetites and by a spontaneous transparency, as it were," of the depths of the spirit.[67]

This process of sublimation at work in the higher states of poetic and contemplative experience is an early treatment of what Maritain will later come to call the supraconscious. It is also suggestive of the way the supraconscious informs our conscious judgments, influencing instinct in the direction of the immaterial sources of the human being and its transcendent goals.

In Christ, however, the supraconscious functions in a different way, for it has been "divinized by the beatific vision." Thus, Christ's supraconscious is transcendent in a way that no other human being's could ever be in this mortal life. Accordingly, there is a "partition" between it and Christ's consciousness which prevents, for the most part, the glory of that vision spilling over into Christ's experiential knowledge. This

66 "Freudism and Psychoanalysis," 319.
67 "Freudism and Psychoanalysis," 320.

partition is bridged, albeit incompletely, by Christ's infused knowledge. As Maritain puts it:

> But when I speak of the world of the Beatific Vision or of the divinized supraconscious in the soul of Christ, I am speaking of the world absolutely proper to the soul of Christ alone,—world transcendent,—seat from which the Holy Spirit spreads His plenitude over the entire being of Christ,—a domain infinitely superior to the "supraconscious of the spirit" which forms naturally a part of that which I am calling the world of consciousness.[68]

This divinized supraconscious is the aspect of Jesus's intellect that enjoys the state of being *comprehensor*, while his ordinary consciousness, which Maritain refers to as the "here-below of the soul," was in the state of *viator*. The failure of this divinized supraconsciousness to be explicitly present to the consciousness of Jesus as a *viator* is not a result of its being too obscure, but rather of the beatific vision it enjoys, which is too radiant and profound to be comprehended fully by the power of a human intellect in the state of *viator*. Its brilliance is captured by Christ's consciousness only in proportion to his intellect's maturity:[69]

> I think that there was also a certain incommunicability between them, which caused that the content of the supraconscious heaven of the soul was retained, could not pass into the world of consciousness, or of the here-below, except, as I indicated in the first approach, by mode of general influx, and of comforting, and of participated light. In short there was, so to speak, a partition between the world of the Beatific Vision and that of the conscious faculties—but a translucid partition which let pass, through the light of the infused science which participated in the evidence of the vision. . . .Through a glazed window we do not see the sun but its light and its heat pass.[70]

Consequently, Jesus's awareness of the various aspects seen in the divinized supraconscious through his human life admits a gradual

---

68 *On the Grace and Humanity of Jesus*, 55.
69 *On the Grace and Humanity of Jesus*, 55n8.
70 *On the Grace and Humanity of Jesus*, 59–60. See also 68, 83–84.

growth over time, culminating with his death on the cross, at which point Maritain argues the partition between his intellect's supraconscious and consciousness was rent.

Maritain's contribution to Christology is to account for the divinization of Christ's human intellect in a manner that is more realistic and fully human than the scholastic view of the mind had allowed Aquinas to do. His use of contemporary theories of consciousness, and especially his recognition of the supraconscious, allowed him to explain how Christ could genuinely be both *comprehensor* and *viator*. Here we find him attentive to the light cast by modern psychology upon the subject and creatively integrating these insights into scholastic theology, modeling the role of what he would call a philosophical "researcher worker" entering into theology's own problems from the philosopher's point of view.

The Holiness of the Church

Maritain's account of the Church in his late works is quite far ranging. He comments on everything from papal infallibility, to the Inquisition, to the liturgy, to the customs of clerical dress. The main contribution his ecclesiological discussions make, however, is the proper understanding of the person of the Church and the relation between this and the personnel who carry out her mission here on earth. Indeed, the subtitle of his book *On the Church of Christ* is "The Person of the Church and Her Personnel."[71] It is to this theme that the present discussion of his ecclesiology is limited.

This problem presents itself in very simple terms. Christians profess in the Nicene Creed belief in the "one, holy, Catholic, and apostolic" Church. Yet, how can we reconcile this claim that the Church is indefectibly holy, with the fact that so many sins have been committed in her name? In fact, Maritain concludes his book with several chapters

---

71 It is important to note that Maritain's ecclesiology is deeply indebted to that of Charles Cardinal Journet. Journet's magnum opus was a multivolume work entitled *The Church of the Word Incarnate*. He was a close friend and collaborator of Maritain. Their recently published correspondence comes to six large volumes. On this distinction see Charles Journet, *The Church of the Word Incarnate*, trans. A. H. C. Downes (London: Sheed & Ward, 1955), 304.

devoted to the histories of atrocities committed by the Church's personnel: the crusades, the persecution of the Jews, the Inquisition, the condemnation of Galileo, and the execution of Joan of Arc all receive detailed attention. Were he writing today, no doubt the sex abuse of minors by clergy and the experience of indigenous peoples would also have been addressed within this framework. How can an institution that has been implicated in these matters be proclaimed holy? The position that Maritain defends has become thoroughly widely adopted in the Catholic Church, namely, that while the members of the Church are all sinners, the Church is without sin. Yet, his way of explaining and justifying this position is innovative and has proven very influential in the official documents of the Church, and in the various papal apologies that have been issued.

As I have suggested, Maritain addresses this problem by distinguishing the person of the Church from her personnel. The foundation of his teaching on this point is his view of the Church as a *person*. In fact, he sees this as an implication of St. Paul's teaching that the Church is the body of which Christ is the head. Maritain argues that the Church is a person in the proper sense of the term. It is not a mere analogy meant to suggest that the Church is a community with a moral or legal "personality." Rather, the Church is a true person. Further, the Church in heaven, in purgatory, and here on earth is one and the same person considered in three different states; it is not three different persons. This is a unique supernatural privilege of the Church, distinguishing it essentially from any other form of human community. Although the Church is similar to other human communities—like a nation—in having a common history, customs, and a shared set of goals and interests, there is a fundamental difference, as no other community has a divine mission or any promise of lasting forever and being assisted constantly by God.[72]

The foundation of ontological personality, according to Maritain's Thomistic metaphysics, is subsistence. The Church is fundamentally distinguished from other communities in having a twofold subsistence

---

72 *On the Church of Christ*, 18.

that is at once both natural and supernatural. The Church has a natural subsistence rooted in the human persons who are her members, just like any other human community. However, the Church also has a supernatural subsistence insofar as she is the unified whole of the organized group of persons who live through her life. This supernatural subsistence presupposes the natural one, for if the persons who are members of the Church all ceased to exist, there would be no Church. But this supernatural subsistence also transcends the natural one. He goes so far as to write: "However profound and however essential the differences between the two cases may be, she is a *person* (common or collective) as Peter and Paul is a *person* (individual)." Although the Church subsists naturally through the subsistence of its many members, as a complete whole that is one and universal, of this multitude the Church also has a true and ontological personality that goes far beyond the merely analogical moral personality we associate with corporations or nations (for a society such as a company or association is not a real substance but a proper accident): "She is herself a person in the proper and primary sense of the word, a person who renders worship to God, who proposes to us truths revealed by Him, who sanctifies us by her sacraments, who speaks, who teaches, who acts."[73] Through being animated by grace, the Church bears the image of Christ. Through this image the many members of the Church who live her life are "clothed with an individual configuration," so that by way of the individuality of this image of Christ it can subsist as if it were an individual. The individuality of Christ's image that the Church bears is an analogue to the individual substantial nature each human person possesses. And so, in calling the Church of Christ into existence through this image God grants her a subsistence that makes the Church a subject or person as a whole composed of various human beings.[74]

The body of the Church is the multitude of human people who are its members; its soul is the grace through which the Church lives. It follows from this that we are members of the Church precisely insofar as

---

73 *On the Church of Christ*, 18–19.
74 *On the Church of Christ*, 20–21.

we live in and through that grace. The sinner's action separates himself from the Church's supernatural life. He may indeed remain a member of the Church through a dead faith, a merely intellectual acceptance of the truths about God he recognizes. However, insofar as he is a sinner he moves away from the Church and acts on his own accord:

> To the extent that a man who has been baptized in the Church sins, to that extent he slips away from the life of the Church; if he installs himself in the state of sin (while keeping the faith, which without charity is "dead faith") he remains still a member of the Church, but then the life of the latter no longer passes in him. To the extent that he lives by grace and by charity, he lives also by the life of the Whole of which he is a member, and which is the mystical Body of Christ and the Bride of Christ.[75]

Here the contradiction between the holiness of the Church and the sinfulness of its members' actions is resolved. The Church herself is necessarily without sin because her life and soul are grace and charity in their fullness. The members of the Church are sinners insofar as they slip away from grace and, in doing so, slip away from the life of the whole, the Church, of which they are members. To the extent that a person lacks grace and charity, that person withdraws from the life of the Church. The person of the Church herself has no part in these sins and she does not share in the guilt of the actions of her members.

In order to explain how this occurs Maritain examines the actions of the Church's personnel, those bishops and priests who make up her hierarchy more closely. In discussing this he notes that these agents can act through two basically different types of causality. A person acts as a proper or principal cause when he acts through his own will. This is most evident in the case where a person takes the first initiative of evil. In such a situation it is the creature, not God or the Church, that initiates the evil action. A person may also act as an instrumental cause,

---

75 *On the Church of Christ,* 11.

acting under the first action and inspiration of God; when he does so, he acts in the voice and person of the Church.[76]

Central to understanding this view is the very precise and narrow understanding of those actions that can properly be attributed to the Church as such. This only applies if the personnel of the Church are acting as an instrumental cause, and we can only know this for certain when the very person of the Church acts (1) in the sacramental order, or (2) through its teaching of the ordinary or extraordinary magisterium.[77] In other cases, such as personal prudential advice, the application of moral teaching to concrete circumstances, administrative decisions, and so on, the actions of the Church's personnel have no such guarantee. In these cases we are dealing with actions not "of the Church" but an act or decision of her personnel, even though the language of historians and commentators may frequently attribute these actions inaccurately to the Church. Strictly speaking, we can only say there is an "act of the Church" or a "decision of the Church" when the Church is acting on earth through the instrumentality of her ministers, either in conveying grace through the sacraments or through an exercise of the teaching authority given by Christ. Maritain compares these cases to the action of a professor's secretary. When the secretary reads a report written by the professor to a conference, we have no doubt he captures the thought of the professor herself. However, when he tells a visitor that the professor does not have time receive the visitor, it may be contrary to the wish of the professor, such as in the case where the visitor has information that will assist her research.[78]

In most cases, however, we are presented with cases where it is challenging or impossible to distinguish the aspects of an action that may proceed from instrumental causality that stems from God and the elements of proper causality that derive from the minister or from the historical and cultural context by which he is influenced. Accordingly,

---

76 *On the Church of Christ,* 57. See also Bernard Doering, "Jacques Maritain on the Church's Misbehaving Clerics," *Cross Currents* 52, no. 2 (2002): 247.

77 *On the Church of Christ,* 235. See also Journet, *The Church of the Word Incarnate,* 21–23.

78 *On the Church of Christ,* 233.

it is incumbent upon us to recognize that the call to serve the Church—
even formally, through holy orders—provides no guarantee of holiness,
or even the beneficial achievement of a person's additional clerical functions, beyond the effectiveness of the sacramental offerings and truth of
the official teaching of the Church.

The teaching of Journet and Maritain that the Church is sinless,
but has sinful members, has become virtually canonical in Catholic
circles. Yet it has its objectors. Theologian Karl Rahner, SJ, argued
that patristic authors, such as Augustine, while admitting a sense in
which the Church is holy now, understood this credal statement more
eschatologically. With the high Middle Ages and modernity, there was
a growing urgency to see the Church as holy in the present. Consequently, he argues that this led to a reification of the Church that risked
separating the Church from her actual members.[79] In a similar vein,
Yves Congar, OP, responded to Journet's distinction between a sinless
Church and sinful members by asking, "Is this not to reify a formal point
of view?"[80] Drawing on these insights, renowned ecclesiologist Joseph
Komonchak has argued that Maritain's doctrine of the personality of
the Church undergirds the view that the Church is sinless in spite of its
sinful members. Accordingly, he holds that Maritain reifies the Church
and fails to give sufficient weight to its social origin. Reification, in this
sense, is a tendency to misrepresent social ontologies as if they existed
independently of the social realities that form them. When we encounter powerful and stable social institutions we instinctively tend to reify
them, treating them as if they were independently existing things. By
contrast, Komonchak argues that since such social realities are brought
about through human intentionality, "their objectivity is constituted by
subjectivity."[81]

---

79 Karl Rahner, "The Sinful Church in the Decrees of Vatican II," in *Theological Investigations*, vol. 6 (Baltimore: Helicon, 1969), 271–73.

80 Yves Congar, *L'Église: Une, sainte, catholique et apostolique* (Paris: Cerf, 1970), 136–37.

81 Joseph A. Komonchak, "The Epistemology of Reception," in *Reception and Communion Among Churches*, ed. Hervé Legrand, OP, Julio Manzanares Marijuan, and Antonio García y García, OFM (Washington, DC: The Canon Law Department, Catholic University of America, 1997), 188–89.

In response to this criticism, I think two things can be said in Maritain's defense. First, while it is understandable that one might see Maritain's account of the Church as a person as an obvious example of reification, this accusation fails to give any weight to the supernatural origin and constitution of the Church. Komonchak fails to show that he sees any difference between the Church and purely natural—or even conventional—forms of associations. This can be seen from the fact that his example is the particular symposium at which he was giving his paper, which existed prior to its occurrence only in the intentionality of its participants. However, this seems to imply an unacceptably nominalist view of the Church. It overlooks the very fact that Maritain insists upon, that the Church is constituted not by social action alone, but by God's grace, the "soul" of the Church, which animates it. Second, it is not clear that the distinction between a sinless Church and sinful members rests upon the doctrine of the Church as a supernatural personality. Rather, it seems that this view of Maritain's is a corollary of his reading of Journet's ecclesiology, not a logical presupposition of it. The real basis of the distinction seems to be Journet's and Maritain's very narrow interpretation of what counts as an act of the Church, namely, conferring the sacraments and proclaiming the Church's official teaching. This is certainly far more restricted than the account of the Church's nature developed by Congar and endorsed by Komonchak.

A further concern that has arisen in relation to the holiness of the Church in recent years is clericalism. This is the mistaken view that a priest is holy simply in virtue of his office and state in life. Maritain was concerned that the seeds of clericalism were present in some theological understandings of the priesthood. In response to this he insisted that the "sacerdotal state" that one enters on receiving the sacrament of holy orders and becoming a priest is a "functional state" to transmit the grace of the sacraments. When we speak of the "sanctity of the priesthood" it is the sanctity of this function, not necessarily of the way of life, that we are addressing. In assessing the thought of the influential French School of spirituality, Maritain finds in its founder, Pierre de Bérulle, a tendency to trade on the ambiguity between the sanctity of the functional state and the state of life of the priest.[82] This is to forget the fundamental distinction between the person of the Church and her personnel. Moreover, it would see the priest as acting as an instrumental cause of Christ, placing him in a loftier state than the ordinary Christian with respect to everything he might do or say in virtue of his ordination.[83] To the contrary, Maritain insists that the priest's state of life is no different from that of the ordinary Christian when it comes to his personal holiness, or his ability to carry out his responsibilities beyond conferring the sacraments or conveying the Church's magisterial teaching:

> If the function of the priest confers on him authority *in the order of salvation* that the Church uses to announce the divine truth to mankind, to transmit to them the grace of the sacraments, on the other hand it confers on him *in the order of the social-temporal* absolutely no superiority over lay people as such, by reason of which he would enjoy in this particular order some privilege of government, as if he were in a more perfect state of life.[84]

It follows from this that the priest or bishop can obviously act as a proper cause, falling into sin, even in those areas that affect his ecclesial responsibilities aside from those functions that constitute the essential core of the Church's mission, namely, the sacraments and the magisterium.

Maritain's profound contribution to ecclesiology is not his recognition that the Church's members sin, while the Church herself remains holy. This is clearly a doctrine he receives and develops from Journet. Rather, what is innovative is his way of explaining this truth of the faith. Most important in his account as a philosopher dealing with this theological problem is his recognition of the Church as a person. This allows him to explain how the multitude of members can act through either proper causality on their own accord, or through instrumental causality by placing themselves in the hands of the Holy Spirit. This philosophical elaboration of the personality of the Church and the actions of her

82 "Apropos of the French School," in *Untrammeled Approaches*, 425.
83 "Apropos of the French School," 436.
84 "Apropos of the French School," 439–40. Doering, "Jacques Maritain on the Church's Misbehaving Clerics," 250–52.

ministers makes some important contributions to this essential problem that deserve further exploration.

Maritain's writings on theology are sporadic and often uneven. Nevertheless, this is in keeping with the role of "research-worker" that he envisioned for himself in this area. Approaching theological problems and teachings from the perspective of a philosopher, he found himself free to pose solutions and present explanations that stemmed from his own unique perspective. Accordingly, his suggestions in this area involve considering traditional teachings in an original way by introducing the philosophical dimension. We can see this dynamic in his willingness to admit a natural mystical experience in Brahmanism, a view that was only made possible by allowing for an experience of the substantial being of the soul through which God might be encountered in some fashion. It is also seen in his reformulation of Freudian psychology to recognize the supraconscious and apply this to the very difficult problem of Christ's knowledge. Finally, we can see the value of the philosophical "research-worker" in the field of the theologian in Maritain's treatment of the Church as a person and the analysis of causality as he applies it to the actions of the Church's personnel. Clearly, Maritain was not a theologian, nor did he claim to be. Yet by applying his philosophical acumen in these areas, he was able to open up new paths of enquiry that deserve a broader audience than they have received thus far.

CHAPTER 7

Moral Philosophy

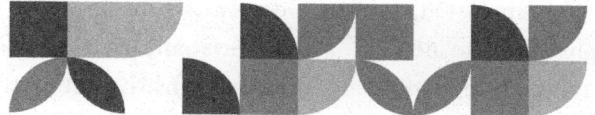

The absolutely primary love can and must be fixed in Him whose
good we wish more than our own good—and that is possible,
and even, in one sense, easy, since according to Christian faith
He is our friend, in the supernatural order of charity.
Moral Philosophy, 78

n turning to moral philosophy we move to the domain of practical
philosophy. Here we are no longer only seeking the truth to know, but
rather we wish to know the truth in these areas in order to do what
is good. As a result, the Christian state of philosophy is profoundly
important. In these areas, "Christianity has transfigured everything."[1]
Even on topics in which pagans and Christians seem to agree, the foundational understandings of basic truths are often different. For example,
both agree that contemplation is the highest human activity. However,
Christianity introduced innovations even in this area. First, Christianity
held that love is better than intelligence. While intelligence is nobler
than the will, when it comes to the things that we know and love, these

---

1 *Scholasticism and Politics*, trans. Mortimer Jerome Adler (New York: The Macmillan Company,
   1940) 165.

exist in us immaterially by knowledge—but by love they attract us to them according to their own mode of existence and dignity. Hence, in this life it is better to love things above us than to know them.[2] Second, Christianity has given contemplation, the highest form of human activity, an entirely new sense. The contemplation of philosophers is only concerned with their own intellectual perfection, and does not go further than the intellect. But the contemplation of the saints is also a love of the one contemplated, namely, God. Thus, love becomes an instrument enlightening the intellect. Third, Christianity has transformed the notion of action. It recognizes not only the transitive action that carries over to affect others directly, but especially emphasizes the importance of immanent action in which thought is the work to be done; if communicated, this thought demands to be perfected in goodness in order to serve the good of others. Finally, Christianity has recognized that contemplation is not the specialized work of a chosen few. In contrast to Plato, Aristotle, and the Stoics, who saw wisdom as limited to a few sages—if possible to attain at all—for Christians wisdom is seen as a call to all human persons, for all are called to divine love and wisdom:

> All without exception, are called to perfection, which is the same as that of the Father who is in heaven; in a manner either close or distant, all are called to the contemplation of the saints, not the contemplation of the philosophers, but to loving and crucified contemplation. All without exception. The universality of such an appeal is one of the essential features of Christianity's *catholicity*.[3]

Consequently, it is clear that as we enter into a consideration of the practical matters of moral, political, and social life, the relation between faith and reason becomes more nuanced and dynamic.

Moral Philosophy Adequately Considered

As we saw in chapter one, Maritain insists on both the distinction between philosophy and theology, and their mutual complementarity.

---

2   See *S.T.*, I, q. 82, a. 3 and II-II, q. 27 a. 4.
3   *Scholasticism and Politics*, 168. The points on contemplation are discussed on pages 165–68.

Faith informs the work of a Christian philosophy, but it does not usurp it. For Maritain this balance is maintained by distinguishing the nature of philosophy as a discipline in the abstract, and the state in which it is concretely practiced in human history. In the case of speculative philosophy this is relatively straightforward, as the Christian state of the discipline affects only the method in which it is practiced. In the case of practical philosophy—particularly ethics and politics—however, the case is otherwise. Revelation provides information that the moral philosopher needs to adequately develop a doctrine of morals as a science. Thus, the question arises as to whether in the concrete state of our actual human circumstances there can be a philosophical ethics.

A purely philosophical ethics would be adequate if human beings existed in a state of pure nature. However, in the actual state we find ourselves in, that of a fallen and redeemed nature, philosophy alone can never be a sufficient guide to our moral life. In this state purely philosophical ethics can prescribe good actions (e.g., do not steal, do not lie, etc.). But this is not sufficient for a *science* of morals:

> But the prescription of certain good acts is not enough to form a practical science, a true science of the use of freedom, a science which prescribes not only good acts, but which also determines how the acting subject can live a life of consistent goodness and organize rightly his whole universe of action. For it is the subject himself who needs to be made good.[4]

According to Maritain this type of moral philosophy in our actual condition would aim to be a practical science, but it would be inadequate to its object and thus, not really practical at all. Indeed, it would be a form of essentialism, providing a merely theoretical system to establish a state of goodness in human nature treated as a separated essence, a "creature of possibility."[5] But this would be a human being quite different from human persons as they actually exist in the state of a fallen and redeemed nature. Such a science would assign, as our last end, God loved

4 *Science and Wisdom*, 162.
5 *Science and Wisdom*, 162, 185.

efficaciously above all things by a natural love. However, in our current state of wounded nature, we are either unable to love God continually in this way or we are raised by grace to do so. In neither case would God be loved efficaciously above all things through a natural love.[6] To rise to a level of science, a purely natural moral philosophy lacks two things. First, it is unable to know the true ultimate end that human beings are actually ordained toward, since this is supernatural. Second, it cannot know the integral conditions of human existence, since these involve both the fall and the state of grace.[7] Since moral science is practical and aims to guide action, it must deal with the concrete state human beings are actually in, and not a mere possible essence of human nature. But in order to treat of the human condition as it really exists, it is necessary to draw on the higher truths only found through revelation and theological reflection. This is the only way for the ethicist to know the true human end. Certainly moral philosophy cannot adequately direct human actions toward this supernatural end; the principles of a merely natural ethics are insufficient to reach it, since it is a merely philosophical discipline.[8] This is why moral philosophy must be subalternated to theology if it is to consider its object adequately:

> This moral philosophy adequately considered remains philosophical in its origin and method, but since it is concerned to guide human beings in their real existential conditions, it must take into account aspects known only through theology. And thus are we brought face to face with a philosophy that is Christian in a pre-eminent and altogether strict sense: a philosophy which cannot be proportioned to its object unless it makes use of principles received from faith and theology, and is enlightened by these latter. Here is a practical philosophy which remains a philosophy and proceeds according to the proper mode of philosophy, yet which

---

6   *Science and Wisdom*, 163.

7   *An Essay on Christian Philosophy*, trans. Edward H. Flannery (New York: The Philosophical Library, 1955), 63. It is interesting to note that Maritain also says that a moral philosophy developed in the context of one of the major non-Christian world religions such as Judaism, Islam or Hinduism, while likely to be deficient in some ways, can be expected to be "less basically deficient" than one that tries to be merely rational and philosophical. *On the Philosophy of History*, 39.

8   *Science and Wisdom*, 165.

is not purely and simply a philosophy. Here is a philosophy which must of necessity be a superelevated philosophy, a philosophy sub-alternated to theology, if it is not to misrepresent and scientifically distort its object.[9]

Subalternation is a technical term in Thomistic philosophy. It involves more than a mere subordination of one discipline to another. In this context it refers to a state in which a science cannot be a true science unless it makes use of truths proven in a higher discipline as its princi-ples. Typical examples are the way physics makes use of principles that have been proven in mathematics or the way the optician will use as principles truths that have been demonstrated in geometry. In a similar way moral philosophy can only become fully adequate to its object if it draws on the higher lights of moral theology to know accurately the true end of the human person and the real existential condition of human life.[10] This remains philosophical, for although faith is a necessary con-dition for moral philosophy adequately considered to be established, it plays no formal role in demonstrating its conclusions.[11]

This dynamic is not merely outlined as a mere sketch of a possi-ble framework for Christian moral philosophy; rather, on Maritain's reading, it has been actually realized when one studies the impact that Christianity has made upon moral philosophy historically. On his view the key contribution of Christianity to moral thought was the "strange novelty" that God himself was not merely the supreme value that is good for himself and in himself, but that human happiness consists in actually possessing him as the supreme object. Acting for God is not only good in itself, but it is also good for us. Christianity proclaimed the unique message that God in his intimate life is the only end in which our desire for happiness can be fulfilled, and that this fulfillment is a real possibil-ity. The happiness that Christianity envisioned was not the incomplete happiness that is always progressing, but Beatitude—an absolute and complete happiness. This realization (that happiness through really

9   *An Essay on Christian Philosophy*, 40.
10 *Science and Wisdom*, 186–87.
11 *Science and Wisdom*, 198.

possessing God as the object and fulfillment of our desires is actually possible) is something that is revealed through faith; it could not possibly be known by reason. It is the words of Christ to the two thieves that died with him, assuring the repentant thief that this day he would be with him in paradise, that historically opened the human mind to this realization, not the arguments of Plato or Aristotle.[12] Christianity proclaims two things: first, that the human person is called to an absolutely complete and saturating happiness that only the possession of God himself could realize, and second, that this beatitude is of the supernatural order through a gift of grace; it does not and cannot arise from human nature. Without the benefit of Christian revelation, God loved above all other things could be recognized as the *absolute* ultimate end of every creature, but the possession of God could not be seen as the human person's ultimate *subjective* end. If left to the order of nature, there would be an infinite and unbridgeable abyss between the absolute ultimate end and the subjective ultimate end or the happiness of the human being. Aristotle, for all his brilliance, did not recognize this crucial distinction between the good and happiness; it was a crucial factor of morality that was left to Christianity to clarify:[13]

> The astonishing tidings brought by Christianity were that in fact, and by the free superabundance of divine generosity, the separation, the cleavage of which we have just spoken between the absolute ultimate End and the subjective ultimate End does not exist for man. The subjective ultimate End or the beatitude of man consists in an immediate and indissoluble union with the absolute ultimate End.[14]

It is also crucial to recognize that this does not mean that we are motivated to love God for our own subjective happiness. Rather, Christianity professes we are to love God because he is the supreme good in and of

---

12 *Moral Philosophy*, trans. Joseph W. Evans (New York: Charles Scribner's Sons, 1964), 76. The scriptural reference is made by Maritain, referring to Luke 23:43.

13 *Moral Philosophy*, 76–77. See also Ralph Nelson, "Moral Philosophy Adequately Considered," in *Jacques Maritain: The Man and His Achievement*, ed. Joseph W. Evans (New York: Sheed & Ward, 1953), 141–43.

14 *Moral Philosophy*, 77.

himself. Our happiness is the consequence of this love, not the reason for it. Maritain explains this in the course of commenting on the view of the great Renaissance Thomist Cardinal Cajetan, "I wish God to be mine, but not for me":

> Christian hope makes me wish that God be mine, but it is not for me or by reason of myself, it is not for love of myself that I wish God to be mine; it is for God and for love of God, for I love God more than myself and more than my happiness. Christian morality is a morality of beatitude, but first and foremost it is a morality of the Divine Good supremely loved.[15]

Accordingly, Maritain views his account of moral philosophy adequately considered not merely as a theoretical possibility, but an actually realized practice embodied in the history of moral inquiry in its response to the Christian message.

In reply to Maritain's position two criticisms have been frequently made, both of which Maritian either anticipated or replied to in light of critics. One criticism that has been put forward by writers like Ralph McInerny is that Maritain's view means that a purely philosophical ethics is impossible given the human condition.[16] However, this is a misrepresentation of Maritain's position. In fact, he explicitly states that his view does not reject the possibility of a purely natural ethics. Rather, he holds that a natural ethics actually exists. While this natural ethics is fundamental, it does not form a complete science of human action on its own. He explicitly argues that such an ethics can prescribe good actions. Maritain's position is not that there is no purely philosophical ethics. This view is wrongly attributed to him, but it is in no way a consequence of his argument. Rather, he holds only that such an ethics would not rise to the level of a science adequate to guide human life successfully to its true end.[17]

---

15 *Moral Philosophy*, 79.
16 McInerny argues, *contra* his reading of Maritain, that there is an adequate, purely philosophical science of morals to be developed out of Aristotle. Ralph McInerny, *The Question of Christian Ethics* (Washington, DC: The Catholic University of America Press, 1983), 16–20.
17 *An Essay on Christian Philosophy*, 62, and *Science and Wisdom*, 162.

The second and more difficult objection is that by accepting principles from theology and revelation Maritain's moral philosophy,
adequately considered, really collapses into moral theology, from which
it is indistinguishable. This objection was raised during Maritain's own
lifetime by Fr. Santiago Ramirez, OP, and it has been recently reaffirmed
by Denis J. M. Bradley in his major work *Aquinas on the Twofold Human
Good*. Ramirez argued forcefully that Maritain's conception of moral
philosophy was hopelessly incoherent. In appealing to revealed principles, such a pursuit would become formally indistinguishable from
moral theology in the strict sense.[18]

Maritain explained the difference between the two by appealing to
the scholastic distinction between formal objects. In scholastic terminology, the formal object is the method or perspective the inquiring
agent takes towards the thing he or she is studying. It is typically distinguished from the material object, which is the content or subject
matter that is studied. For instance, both philosophy and theology study
the ethics of human conduct and, accordingly, have the same material
object. But they are distinct because they study that common object
in view of different methods, or formal objects. According to Maritain
the formal object can be determined both as thing and as object. In
moral philosophy adequately considered, the thing or reality it is aimed
at bringing clearly into human cognition is the conformity of human
liberty to its rule or its ordination to the true ends of human life. Its
formal object or formal subject (i.e., the particular manner in which
it approaches the thing it studies and the way it arises in cognition) is
human acts considered in the ways in which they can be directed toward
these ends. This means that a moral philosophy adequately considered
needs to both articulate the rules and ends of human liberty, and articulate—in at least broad terms— ways that human acts can be oriented
toward those ends.

18 Santiago Ramirez, OP, "De Philosophia Morali Christiana," *Divus Thomas* 50 (1936): 87–140,
181–204. On Ramirez, see Bradley, *Aquinas on the Twofold Human Good: Reason and Human
Happiness in Aquinas's Moral Science* (Washington, DC: The Catholic University of America
Press, 1999), 506–14.

These factors are common to both moral theology and moral philosophy adequately considered, since the only true last end for the human person as we really exist is a supernatural one, namely, the beatific vision. It is, however, the formal determinant of the object as object that uniquely distinguishes moral philosophy adequately considered from its theological counterpart. This formal object as object is human acts that can be ordered and regulated by human reason when it is suitably completed. This is, for Maritain, the proper characterization of moral philosophy once it has been subalternated to moral theology. In contrast, moral theology itself is concerned with the regulation of human acts in light of what is divinely revealable. The distinction is between a finite science that has been "uplifted and completed" and a science that participates, through revelation, in the infinite science itself.[19] Moral theology studies human action from the standpoint of revelation directly, while moral philosophy adequately considered is directly concerned with knowing human action insofar as it is human and created; while it is aware of the supernatural character and context of human action, this is not its direct study, but rather the contextual framework within which it studies the natural ethical life of human persons.[20] Thus moral philosophy adequately considered is primarily concerned with the natural ends and temporal activities of human life. These ends are exalted—but not taken away—by man's ordination to a higher supernatural end.[21]

Maritain replied to this criticism by pointing out two things. First, in the framework of subalternation, moral philosophy adequately considered does not directly resolve the principles it takes from the higher science of theology to revelation itself; that task is left for moral theology to perform.[22] It takes the principles it borrows from theology as "simple data" in the same manner as it uses the mathematical or

19 *An Essay on Christian Philosophy*, 70–71.
20 *An Essay on Christian Philosophy*, 80. See also *Science and Wisdom*, 100, 174, and 184.
21 *Science and Wisdom*, 177 and 182.
22 *An Essay on Christian Philosophy*, 87–88.

empirical truths it borrows from the other sciences.[23] Second, what is borrowed from moral theology is not integral to the arguments made within moral philosophy adequately considered, but is merely a "necessary complement."[24] Although it borrows principles from theology, these principles are not radical and originative of moral philosophy adequately considered, but perfective and completive of the moral philosopher's knowledge.[25] This is a fundamental difference, for it means that the principles that are borrowed from theology do not undermine the entirely rational and philosophical character of the knowledge that is developed within a moral philosophy adequately considered. Rather, the application of data from revelation merely completes and perfects the knowledge of the Christian moral philosopher. Bradley points out that it is hard to see how the truth about man's last end could be a mere "complement" to moral philosophy, arguing that this is by Maritain's admission the "first principle" of moral philosophy adequately considered.[26] However, this is to ignore Maritain's previous insistence that truths received through subalternation from theology are not originative principles that enter directly into its work of demonstration. Rather, they are related only indirectly to this; these principles are borrowed merely to contextualize the moral philosopher's knowledge in a way that helps to stabilize it scientifically. Presumably, the awareness of our last end is referred to as a "first principle" in the sense of importance, not in the sense of being the "first" originative basis of the demonstrations offered by the moral philosopher.

Bradley also provides a detailed reply to Maritain's arguments in support of Ramirez's position that Maritain's moral philosophy adequately considered is really just a truncated moral theology. He argues that moral philosophy adequately considered can only be a subalternated science in an "analogous" sense. Unlike the physicist who borrows principles known by the mathematician, the moral philosopher takes

23 *An Essay on Christian Philosophy*, 87.
24 *An Essay on Christian Philosophy*, 87.
25 *An Essay on Christian Philosophy*, 89.
26 Bradley, *Aquinas on the Twofold Human Good*, 502. See also *Science and Wisdom*, 158.

principles that—even for the theologian—are merely "believed." The moral theologian does not know the last end of the human person, but accepts it as a consequence of her faith. Although Maritain insists the philosopher does not resolve these principles in faith, Bradley insists that it makes no difference which discipline does it; the principles will be received as "mere hypotheses." Otherwise, moral philosophy adequately considered would be resolved through its subalternation into revealed theology, and that would mean, by Maritain's own admission, that it was a theology.[27] However, this reply seems to fail to take into account Maritain's understanding of subalternation. In fact, Maritain does not say the principles that are received through subalternation by the philosopher are "mere hypotheses", and for good reason. The complex theory of subalternation would hardly be needed to form a hypothesis. In fact, Maritain refers to what has been received as "simple data."[28] Such truths can only be called hypotheses in an extended sense. In no way does it imply that the truth of the claims is in question. From the perspective of the Christian philosopher the principles are received through subalternation to moral theology as certain truths. It does not pertain to the philosopher's task at all to question or investigate the truth of these claims; that is taken as given on the basis of theology, whose practioners have received them through theology's own subalternation to the science of God and the Blessed.[29] It does not fall to philosophy in any way to judge these conclusions of a discipline that is its superior.

Bradley is, in a sense, correct to point out that since the theologian must resolve these principles into revelation they are, for her, matters of faith. His argument appears to be compelling on the surface; after all, isn't something accepted through faith a mere belief? If so, how could it be treated as a principle of a scientific demonstration without

---

27 Bradley, *Aquinas on the Twofold Human Good*, 498–99.

28 Although Maritain does use the term "hypothesis" at times to describe these claims, these are "hypotheses guaranteed from elsewhere and certified by a higher source; that is to say, they are true principles." *Science and Wisdom*, 197.

29 See *S.T.*, I, q. 1, a. 2 in which Aquinas argues that theological science subalternated to the science of God and the Blessed and *S.T.*, I, q. 1, a. 5 in which he argues that this makes it more certain than other disciplines based on merely human reason.

compromising its philosophical character? However, within the Christian perspective that Maritain is explicating, even this relation to faith is not sufficient to reduce propositions accepted through faith and received by way of subalternation to the status of "mere hypotheses" whose contraries might turn out to be true. Although Maritain does not make the point in this context, the Thomistic doctrine that faith cannot be false is highly relevant. In fact, faith is more certain than science, since it follows from a cause that cannot err, namely, God revealing, whereas human science is always subject to the potential of error.[30] It makes little sense for a Christian philosopher receiving a principle that she accepts as a more certain truth than any she could prove in her own discipline to treat that principle as a "mere hypothesis" in the way that Bradley suggests. Bradley assumes there is a contradiction between the Christian philosopher taking these principles received through subalternation to theology "on trust" and Maritain's conviction that they are relevant to attaining philosophical knowledge. But in fact, this confusion results from Bradley's own conflation of truths of faith with "mere hypotheses." Such a view is simply not Thomistic and it is one which Maritain would, quite plausibly, not have accepted for good reason.

In fact, as we have seen, Maritain does not treat the principles received from theology by the Christian philosopher as hypotheses at all, but as simple data. Rather, he holds that these principles would be hypotheses for the non-believing philosopher. He argues that since the theological truths it makes use of do not enter into its own proper activity, "the theological truths received by moral philosophy adequately considered present themselves to the non-believing philosopher as superior hypotheses from which one starts to work."[31] This is a claim that Bradley finds incredulous. The non-believer might well recognize the role theology plays for the Christian, but he holds that none have accepted theological principles as data or superior hypotheses for

---

30 *S.T.*, II-II, q. 1, a. 3 and q. 4, a. 8.
31 *Science and Wisdom*, 197.

philosophy. Bradley holds there is no reason for the non-believer to accept these as a reasonable basis for his own philosophy.[32]

Indeed, he has a point here. The truths of faith have to be accepted on the basis of an act of the will, through belief and not knowledge. However, it is important to remember that Maritain's non-believer is not a rabid atheist or even an agnostic. From his perspective, these skeptical positions are scarcely philosophical at all. Maritain argues that one does not typically come to atheism by means of rational argumentation. Considerations such as the sufficiency of scientific explanations of the natural world are at best secondhand defenses. Rather, the real origin of atheism is, he feels, a moral decision to exclude God from the primary values of existence: a decision which he aptly describes as "an act of faith in reverse gear".[33] Clearly, he is not so naïve as to think that such intellectuals would come to accept these principles without a complete change of beliefs; he is aware such philosophical conversions are rare. Rather, Maritain's view of philosophy is far more robust. His non-believing philosopher is a non-Christian theist who knows that God exists through philosophical proofs and understands, as Aristotle understood, that man's highest activity is contemplation of God. From such a perspective the acceptance of the influence of some basic truths from moral theology about man's last end appears less absurd. Although non-believers obviously cannot be offered a compelling proof of principles drawn from faith, they might yet accept them as hypotheses that help them to resolve internal incoherencies in their philosophy. Aristotle's ethics, for example, has been subject to deep controversy over his understanding of the human good. Commentators have been unable to agree as to whether it consists in pursuing the highest good of contemplation of God as much as possible, or whether it consists in a more pluralistic pursuit of a variety of goods.[34] As we have seen, in Maritain's view an incomplete understanding of the human person's

32 Bradley, *Aquinas on the Twofold Human Good*, 500–501.
33 *The Range of Reason*, 105–6.
34 See, for instance, John M. Cooper, "Contemplation and Happiness: A Reconsideration," *Synthese* 72 (1987): 187–216, and Richard Kraut, *Aristotle on the Human Good* (Princeton, NJ: Princeton University Press, 1989).

relation to God, which is available to an unaided philosophy, leads into such intractable disputes. If the acceptance of theological conclusions as hypotheses that complement philosophy provided a resolution of this and similar tensions that otherwise have not been able to be resolved, that may well provide a strong support in their favor for the non-believing philosopher.[35]

Natural Law and Moral Obligation

One of Maritain's essential contributions to moral theory is his analysis of the natural law. For Maritain the natural law is the locus of moral obligation. It is understood in view of certain observations that Maritain takes to be obvious: that there is a human nature the same in all persons, that we are endowed with intelligence and we act understanding what we are doing, that we determine for ourselves the ends that we will in fact pursue, etc. Having a determinate nature, we also have ends that correspond to our nature. However, human beings are unique because, having intelligence and free will, we must bring ourselves into accord with the ends demanded by our nature. This leads Maritain to define natural law as:

> An order or disposition which human reason can discover and according to which the human will must act in order to attune itself to the necessary ends of the human being. The unwritten law, or natural law, is nothing more than that.[36]

The natural law, then, is not a mysterious code or quasi-mystical grasp of the moral law. Natural law is, rather, simply the ordinary functioning of an organism in a way that is likely to achieve the fundamental

---

35 I have in mind something along the lines of Alasdair MacIntyre's discussion of the concept of "epistemological crisis." He argues that those from rival traditions can reach consensus about the superior rationality of one position when they find that the rival tradition has principles that answer problems that arise within its own intellectual framework in a more compelling fashion than the resources of its own tradition provide. See *Whose Justice? Which Rationality?* (Notre Dame, IN: University of Notre Dame Press, 1988), 169 and 361.

36 *The Rights of Man and Natural Law,* trans. Doris C. Anson (New York: Charles Scribner's Sons, 1943), 61. See also *Natural Law: Reflections on Theory & Practice,* ed. and trans. William Sweet (South Bend, IN: St. Augustine's Press, 2001), 27; "On Knowledge through Connaturality," 26; and *Man and State* (Chicago: University of Chicago Press, 1951), 86.

ends toward which that organism's nature tends. It is the proper way each thing should achieve "the fullness of being in their behavior."[37] In the human case this progress toward the determinate final end of our nature is characterized by intelligence and freedom. Here in the human instance the functioning that *should* take place implies not merely a descriptive account of what we expect, as a flower should grow when watered, but a moral obligation.[38] Accordingly, the natural law that governs human activity is necessarily the moral law. While it is "written" in the hearts of each person, this is a biblical metaphor. It is not to be taken to mean that it is a ready-made code fully present in each person's conscience. This would suggest that everyone knows it explicitly. That this is—sadly—not the case is only too obvious. It is, rather, known with more or less difficulty due to all sorts of factors. The natural law is an unwritten law and it has been disclosed only progressively through the history of human action and culture.[39]

This progressive awareness of the natural law leads one to a consideration of how the natural law is to be known. Maritain most frequently treats of this in terms of his doctrine of connatural knowledge. The natural moral law is learned and first known connaturally through our experience of it. This connatural knowledge is preconceptual. This is not, of course, to say that the natural law is contrary to reason, but that we become aware of it in our experience prior to rational discourse about it. Maritain notes that we may know philosophically a great deal about the virtue of prudence. We can define it, demonstrate why this or that act is in accordance with, or contrary to, prudence. But even with this knowledge we may not possess prudence as a virtue. Such knowledge may remain purely intellectual. On the other hand, a person can possess this virtue without any knowledge of moral philosophy at all. Such a person obviously knows the virtue of prudence, since they

---

37 *Natural Law: Reflections on Theory & Practice,* 29.

38 Contemporary philosophers are likely to object that this mode of reasoning exemplifies the naturalistic fallacy of inferring a moral obligation from a statement of fact identified by David Hume. This concern is addressed in William Sweet and Cristal Huang, "The Metaphysical and Epistemological Foundations of Natural Law in Jacques Maritain," *Philosophy and Culture* 33, no. 9 (2006): 3–98.

39 *The Rights of Man and Natural Law,* 62–64.

can act reliably in accordance with the virtue, and the sound moral philosopher would recognize that the person's acts generally accord with what philosophy says they should be. Maritain refers to this type of knowledge as connatural knowledge and it is the source of our knowledge of natural law:

> My contention is that the judgments in which Natural Law is made manifest to practical Reason do not proceed from any conceptual, discursive, rational exercise of reason; they proceed from that *connaturality or congeniality* through which what is consonant with the essential inclinations of human nature is grasped by the intellect as good; what is dissonant, as bad.[40]

Maritain draws three fundamental consequences from this awareness that the natural law is known through connaturality. The first is that the natural law, strictly speaking, only includes precepts that are capable of being known immediately through inclination, without the need to appeal to a conceptual and rational medium. The natural law is not only natural in what it commands as law, but it is also naturally known. Second, since the precepts are known by inclination they are known in an "undemonstrable manner." Accordingly, prior to any philosophical reflection and analysis, people find that they are not able to provide a rational justification of their most basic moral beliefs. For Maritain, this is no indication that these beliefs are irrational or invalid. To the contrary, it is an indication that they are essentially *natural*. It points to the fact that they have a greater validity than mere arguments and exemplify a rationality that is more than merely human. Finally, the natural law presents something greater than human reason for the simple fact that human reason does not cause the natural law to exist or to be known. It is not human reason but the uncreated Reason of God that is at work in establishing the natural law and making that law known.[41] It was the

---

40 "On Knowledge through Connaturality," 27. See also *Natural Law: Reflections on Theory and Practice*, 34–35.

41 "On Knowledge through Connaturality," 27–28. See also *Man and State*, 90–91.

MORAL PHILOSOPHY | 217

failure to recognize this foundation in God that led to the emaciation of natural law in the modern theories of Grotius and Locke.[42]

However, Maritain's approach through connaturality has frequently been dismissed in the recent literature on natural law.[43] The major criticism has been that his position, which holds that we do not come to know the natural law through concepts and reasons, leaves it vague what kind of knowledge is at stake here. At best it is unclear; at worst it is antirational. In his critique of Maritain, Fulvio Di Blasi argues that while his intentions were good, Maritain gives into "overly poetic and insufficiently rigorous interpretations of Thomistic philosophy." Di Blasi holds that Maritain's defense of connaturality shows a "fear" on his part of intellectual and conceptual knowledge.[44]

I would argue, however, that such critiques of Maritain fail to properly situate the role of connaturality within his theory of moral knowledge. For Maritain connaturality is the source of our first contact with natural law in our moral experience. As such, it is pre-philosophical and experiential in nature. This is not to say that knowledge through inclination or connaturality is the *only* way of knowing the natural law

---

42 Maritain's assessment of modern natural law theories is presented carefully by William Sweet, "Maritain's Criticisms of Natural Law Theories," *Maritain Studies* 12 (1996): 33–49.

43 It is, for example, dismissed in John Finnis's influential work *Natural Law and Natural Rights* (Oxford: Clarendon Press, 1980), 255. This is surprising, as Finnis's conclusion that natural law is the proper foundation for natural rights is a thesis that Maritain championed. A recent summary of twentieth-century developments in American approaches to natural law makes no mention of Maritain; see Susan F. Parsons, "Concerning Natural Law: The Turn in American Aquinas Scholarship," *Contemplating Aquinas: On the Varieties of Interpretation,* ed. Fergus Kerr, OP (Notre Dame, IN: University of Notre Dame Press, 2006), 163–83. Similarly, noted natural law expert Jean Porter, for instance, argues that it is difficult to know what to make of this form of knowledge, which is not conceptual and not articulated by reason. Jean Porter, *Nature as Reason: A Thomistic Theory of Natural Law* (Grand Rapids, MI: Eerdmans Publishing Company, 2004), 36. Recently, Stephen L. Brock has provided a nuanced critique of Maritain's account of connaturality, finding it to be preferable to that of Finnis, but finding an ambiguity in Maritain's account, which seems to suggest that connaturality occurs through the will rather than the intellect, and which would conflict with Aquinas's frequent insistence that we can only desire through the will what the intellect recognizes as good. Stephen L. Brock, *The Light That Binds: A Study in Thomas Aquinas' Metaphysics of the Natural Law* (Eugene, OR: Pickwick Publications, 2020), 119–20. It does not seem to me obvious that Maritain holds connaturality occurs through the will prior to any intellectual awareness. What it occurs prior to is the specifically philosophical use of reasoning and analysis. Thus, I take it that what Maritain has in mind is a mixed act involving both pre-philosophical intellectual activity—in an instinctive and intuitive manner—and the will, though he is admittedly unclear on this point. See above, 52–55.

44 Fulvio Di Blasi, *God and the Natural Law: A Rereading of Thomas Aquinas* (South Bend, IN: St. Augustine's Press, 2006), 179.

and that the human person is limited to this. Rather, it is to say that it is our indispensable first point of contact with the natural law. In fact, his entire presentation of connaturality contrasts it with the kind of knowledge the philosopher properly has of morality. Clearly, what Maritain envisages is two ways of knowing the natural law. There is a primordial natural way through inclination, which is not conceptual, non-discursive, and discovered in our lived moral experience when we recognize and act upon the good as good. However, there is a secondary and dependent way in which we can know the natural law through rational philosophical argumentation and analysis. Maritain decidedly does not restrict our moral knowledge to what is known connaturally, rejecting philosophical and discursive knowledge of the natural law. Rather, he situates this as consequent to, and dependent upon, a prior experience of that law through connatural inclination. The true rationale for this alternative model of knowing is not "fear" of the intellectual, but the basic and obvious experience of human persons who grasp the moral law with uncanny accuracy and unity even in the absence of such philosophical reasons.

Much like he had argued that epistemology was dependent upon a prior experiential knowledge of truth that the ordinary person finds in the knowledge she has attained through a common-sense approach to experience, so, too, Maritain argues that moral philosophy is a reflective discipline that articulates, justifies, and analyzes prior knowledge one has obtained in the moral life. After offering his defense of connaturality and an analysis of the consequences that follow from it, Maritain writes,

> Philosophers and philosophical theories supervene in order to explain and justify, through concepts and reasoning, what, from the time of the cave-man, men have progressively known through inclination and connaturality. Moral philosophy is *reflective* knowledge, a sort of after-knowledge. It does not discover the moral law. The moral law was discovered by me before the existence of any moral philosophy. Moral philosophy has critically to analyze and rationally to elucidate moral standards and rules of conduct whose

validity was previously discovered in an undemonstrable manner, and in a non-conceptual, non-rational way.[45]

Moral philosophy, for Maritain, is a conceptual and fully rational endeavor. His point is, however, that we do not begin to learn authentic morality first and foremost by way of philosophy. Rather, moral philosophy presupposes a robust connatural knowledge of the natural moral law upon which to reflect and develop its rational analyses. This resonates with Maritain's continued insistence that philosophy must be lived.[46] His position is also markedly opposed to the tendency of modern philosophy to cut itself off from the uncritical knowledge acquired in ordinary circumstances, which, according to Maritain, should typically provide philosophy's starting points. In order for the criticisms of Maritain's theory of connatural knowledge to stand, we would have to take his position to be that the only way to know the natural law is through connaturality. However, he is clearly opposed to any such position. Rather, he argues that connaturality is our first rudimentary, but certain, knowledge of natural law and philosophical reasoning provides a second reflective means to know this same law. This view seems to do full justice to the role of reason in moral inquiry, while providing a role for affectivity that allows him to avoid a lifeless rationalism. Accordingly, any suggestion that his use of connatural knowledge renders knowledge of the natural law to be vague or beyond the bounds of rational inquiry is unwarranted.

Jean Porter suggests an alternate interpretation of Maritain, arguing that the role he assigns to connaturality shows that Maritain did not view the natural law as something that could be inferred from a metaphysical consideration of human nature.[47] However, this also fails to realize the reflective character of the philosophical articulation of natural law. Clearly, Maritain holds that our initial knowledge of the

---

45 "On Knowledge through Connaturality," 28.

46 There are potentially interesting connections here between Maritain's understanding of a lived philosophy and Wittgenstein's notion of a form of life. See for example, *Philosophical Investigations*, trans. G. E. M. Anscombe (Oxford: Basil Blackwell, 1963), §241, and perhaps more notably, Pierre Hadot's *Philosophy as a Way of Life* (London: Wiley-Blackwell, 1995).

47 Jean Porter, *Nature as Reason*, 36.

natural law arises from inclination and not by a philosophical analysis of human nature in light of a fully developed metaphysics. However, our philosophical understanding and defense of natural law ethics does precisely this. Having experienced the natural law in our moral life we then go on, through a metaphysical analysis of human nature, to articulate more precisely what the natural law is and to defend it against criticisms.

Maritain explicitly distinguishes between ontological and gnoseological elements of the natural law. His treatment presupposes that human beings have a common nature as intellectual creatures and that there are fundamental ends natural to us in virtue of our essence as human beings. The natural law in its ontological consideration is simply the kind of functioning that is best suited to obtain the essential ends that we must achieve to be successful as human beings in virtue of our human nature. The natural law is, then, simply the normal functioning of the creature to achieve its proper ends. These are revealed through observing the creatures' activities and their actual success or failure in achieving those ends:

> The first basic element to be recognized in natural law is, then, the *ontological* element; I mean the normality of functioning which is grounded on the essence of that being: man. Natural law in general [as we have just seen] is the ideal formula of development of a given being.[48]

The natural law functions as an ideal because it is grounded in the intelligible necessities implicit in human nature's universal structure. It is ontological, since that nature is an ontological reality that exists within each human being. In this way it is present as an ideal in the very being of every existing person.[49]

In terms of the second, gnoseological, element in natural law Maritain notes that knowing this law is no easy matter. In fact, he goes so far as to say that the only self-evident principle that everyone infallibly holds

---

48 *Natural Law: Reflections on Theory and Practice*, 29.
49 *Natural Law: Reflections on Theory and Practice*, 31. See also *Man and the State*, 85–87.

in common is that we must do good and avoid evil. Anything beyond this is known with greater or lesser difficulty and by varying degrees. Further, this first principle that all know is a preamble to the natural law; it is not a part of the natural law itself. Rather, natural law is the body of precepts that follow from this first principle in a necessary manner. However, when people attempt to arrive at a demonstrative knowledge of the natural law, all kinds of errors are possible. Notoriously, various individuals and cultures approve what others find repugnant. However, Maritain argues that this plurality does not undermine the natural law any more than mistakes in addition undermine the truth of mathematics or the views of primitive peoples about the stars and planets undermine astronomy. In this context it is vital to recognize that our connatural knowledge of the natural law is merely a cognitive entry point, a first— albeit successful—groping toward moral knowledge. This connatural knowledge needs to be developed, both individually and collectively, to come closer to the greater adequacy of the ontological standard of the natural law. Knowledge of the natural law evolves historically, becoming more rationally adequate, as people come to terms with it in facing the various moral situations they encounter.[50]

Moral Obligation and the First Act of Freedom

Having addressed the foundation of moral obligation in the natural law, it is necessary to treat the choice of the last end of human conduct. Maritain highlights this in his discussion of the immanent dialectic of the first act of freedom. For Maritain our first act of genuine freedom, when it acts for the good simply because it is good, involves a basic orientation of the human person towards God, even if that is not consciously recognized at that point in the agent's life.

---

50 *Natural Law: Reflections on Theory and Practice*, 32–33. While the law itself and knowledge of it are distinct, the gnoseological element is fundamental, for according to the standard definition of law found in Aquinas, a law is not a law unless it is promulgated. Also see *Man and State*, 89–94. For an interesting explanation of how such mistakes can occur, see his analysis of the acceptance of incest in some cultures. He argues that such a prohibition is not natural at the level of our animal instinct, yet it is natural at the level of reason. *An Introduction to the Basic Problems of Moral Philosophy*, trans. Cornelia N. Borgerhoff (Albany, NY: Magi Books, 1990), 162–69.

Many free acts do not meet this criterion of genuine freedom. Such a choice is a radical decision that marks the first beginning of one's moral life. This occurs when a child reflects on his or her choice and decides to do the right thing, not because of fear of punishment, the distress she would cause to loved ones, the praise she might receive, or any sort of calculation of this sort. Rather, she chooses something that is good simply because it is good. This is a moral decision in which the human self is completely committed. Accordingly, the choice to do good simply because it is good implies the question "What do you live for?" While this is not asked explicitly, it is contained unconsciously within the deliberation and action that takes place:

> When he thinks: "It would not be good to do this," what is confusedly revealed to him, in a flash of understanding, is the moral good, with the whole mystery of its demands. He is face to face with this mystery, and he is all alone.[51]

Maritain sees this act of freedom choosing good for its own sake as deeply pregnant with spiritual vitality.

In his treatment of this action of choosing good for its own sake he draws out three fundamental implications, each of which is the basis of one that follows upon it:

1. This choice is not made for any empirical motive. It transcends all merely consequential calculations;

2. Consequently, this choice regards a law of human action that transcends all factual considerations and consequences. In order for the act to be good, it must conform to this law.

3. Since this law in the actual world of existence brings with it the requirements of an order dependent upon a reality superior to everything (for in being motivated by it we give it priority over any merely pragmatic calculations), it must point to Goodness itself—a thing good in virtue of its very being, not by conformity with anything beyond itself.[52]

51 "The Immanent Dialectic of the First Act of Freedom," in *The Range of Reason*, 67.

52 "The Immanent Dialectic of the First Act of Freedom," 68–69, and *Introduction to the Basic Problems of Moral Philosophy*, 134–35.

In this way Maritain reasons from the choice of a good for its own sake to the existence of a transcendent moral law, which he holds implies the existence of a Separate Good, the Good which is sought as both *the* good and *my* good:

> The initial act which determines the direction of life and which—when it is good—chooses the good for the sake of the good, proceeds from a natural élan which is also, undividedly, an élan by which this very same act tends all at once, beyond its immediate object, toward God as the Separate Good in which the human person in the process of acting, whether he is aware of it or not, places his happiness and his end. Here we have an ordainment which is actual and formal, not virtual—but in merely lived act (*in actu exercito*), not in signified act—to God as ultimate end of human life. This is the third implication of the act of which I am speaking.[53]

The knowledge of God that is contained within this first act of freedom is typically unconscious and not articulated. It is one that is contained within the actual practice of the agent as a presupposition of the principles guiding his action: "He knows God without being aware of it." This is a genuine knowledge of God, because in the agent's choice of the good for its own sake, he necessarily wills and loves the Separate Good as the ultimate end of his own existence. Accordingly, the intellect must have a living—albeit non-conceptual—knowledge of God within his practical notion of the good and as the formal motive of his first act of freedom, as well as in the movement of his will toward the particular good sought. Since this act is motivated by a real, if inarticulate, love of the Separate Good, it is at the same time motivated by—and a movement toward—this Good.

In keeping with his methodology of a moral philosophy adequately considered, Maritain turns to the prospects for his theory from the perspective of the theological teaching about the concrete historical condition in which human beings find themselves. This movement toward God in the first act of freedom could only be real if it were an act of willing and loving God above all things. From the perspective of

---

53 "The Immanent Dialectic of the First Act of Freedom," 69.

Christian theology this is potentially problematic, for God can only be willed and loved above all things through grace. While such an action might be naturally possible in a state of "pure nature," theologically we hold that human beings do not, and never have, existed in a state of pure nature. Rather, we live in the context of grace, and are impeded by the reality of original sin. Given our fallen nature and in keeping with Catholic faith, Maritain holds that the human person wounded by original sin cannot efficaciously love God above all things without grace. To deny this would be to fall into the heresy of Pelegianism which held that one could do the good needed to attain salvation independently of divine assistance. In this first step of the moral life, with one's own natural capacities alone, one is bound to fall. In such a condition apart from grace, one does not choose the rational good, but one's own will's desire for assertion to achieve a "private good" that fulfills the desire for one's own self-realization. Yet, Maritain insists in the order of real concrete existence that no one, Christian or not, is left without the resources of grace necessary to make this choice, freely choose the good for its own sake, and thereby love the Supreme Good above all things:

> In actual fact if grace has left the house, it nevertheless keeps on knocking at the door. The sin of one who has not been healed by *gratia sanans* (healing grace) and therefore turns away from the good in his first act of freedom is not a free act which is inevitably defective—because grace offered to him made it avoidable; it is because he refused this grace that he was not healed by it.[54]

Accordingly, Maritain holds that grace is available to all people irrespective of their moral condition, culture, or tradition. Whether one knows Christ or not, it is only possible to initiate one's moral life properly through the grace of Christ. Without that grace, one would only turn away from the ultimate end: God loved above all things, God as discovered in the good loved for its own sake.[55]

---

54 "The Immanent Dialectic of the First Act of Freedom," 73. See also *Introduction to the Basic Problems of Moral Philosophy,* 139–41.

55 While this account bears some resemblance to Rahner's notion of the Anonymous Christian, I think that resemblance is superficial. For Rahner a non-Christian becomes an anonymous Christian through a complete acceptance of himself as he is. Since this condition is in fact

Maritain's explanation of the immanent dialect of the first act of freedom is a remarkable example of what he means by moral philosophy adequately considered.[56] In his discussion he shows how a merely philosophical analysis would be limited by ignorance of the essential facts of the matter, which is the actual historical state of the human person under original sin. As a Christian philosopher he offers a rational analysis of the first act of freedom, and then shows the meaning of this theological fact of original sin for the philosophical analysis. Accordingly, his doctrine is at one and the same time rigorously philosophical, while being attentive to the theological dimensions without which that rational analysis would be deceptive.

Having established his position, Maritain goes on to consider a theological objection. The author of Hebrews says that it is impossible to please God without faith, for one who approaches God has to know that he exists and that he rewards those who seek him. This text could be taken to suggest that seeking God through a merely implicit knowledge would not be sufficient to achieve God. Maritain replies by distinguishing conceptual knowledge from practical knowledge. He holds that the non-believer who approaches God through choosing the good for its own sake, and is aided in doing so by grace unbeknownst to herself, has a practical knowledge of God that is revealed in her action even if she cannot express this in concepts or would deny such an expression if asked. Maritain holds that this practical knowledge of God is rationally

---

graced, as no person is left utterly bereft of grace, in a full acceptance of himself a man is also accepting Christ. Karl Rahner, "Anonymous Christians," in *Theological Investigations*, Vol. 6, trans. Karl-H. and Boniface Kruger (Baltimore: Helicon Press, 1969), 394. Also see *Karl Rahner in Dialogue: Conversations and Interviews, 1965–1982*, ed. Paul Imhof and Hubert Biallowons, trans. Harvey D. Egan (New York: Crossroad, 1986), 207. Among the problems with Rahner's position is a separation of salvation from the personal act of faith. Maritain avoids this challenge when he treats the Second Vatican Council's re-interpretation of the traditional dogma that "There is no salvation outside of the Church" (see *Lumen Gentium*, 16). He argues that it entails that non-Christians and non-Catholic Christians who have in them the grace of Christ are invisibly within the visible Church. This sounds much like Rahner, but in his explanation Maritain appeals to his notion of the supraconscious, through which the human mind—in a supraconceptual way—grasps truths that are too supreme for verbal articulation and which remain largely in the realm of the unconscious. In this way a person attached to another religion, or even an atheist, can have the grace of Christ in him without knowing it, for though in a supraconscious state he has *faith* in him through the depth of his moral life and his volition of the good. See Maritain, *On the Church of Christ*, 101–2.

56 "The Immanent Dialectic of the First Act of Freedom," 75.

possessed by the intellect in the lived act (*in actu exercito*), even if it is only in an unconscious way:

> The particular form of knowledge whose natural workings I have analyzed reaches its object within the unconscious recesses of the spirit's activity and is a merely practical and volitional knowledge of God. Such a knowledge is neither implicit nor explicit, but, although inexpressible, is a knowledge actual and formal, through which the intellect knows in a practical manner the Separate Good per *conformitatem ad appetitum rectum* (through conformity to right appetite) and as the actual terminus of the will's movement.[57]

Although this practical knowledge is unconscious and non-conceptual, it is a genuine and not merely implicit knowledge of God. When the act is vivified by healing grace, and is successful in pursuing the good for its own sake, it is not only a knowledge of God, but of God as Savior, the rewarder of the one who is seeking for the good itself that is seen. Further, He is seen not only as the good in the abstract, but as my good. Accordingly, the non-believer who acts for the good for its own sake is but a "pseudo-atheist." Her lived act professes a genuine knowledge of God as the supreme and Separate Good towards which this agent's life is directed as her ultimate end, irrespective of lack of faith that she professes.[58]

Prudence and the Moral Act

As we have argued above, Jacques Maritain is a strong defender of the natural moral law. However, he also steadfastly rejects any attempt to reduce ethics to a set of moral rules that can be derived from natural law. As the previous section has shown, he is also keenly aware of the complexity and moral drama found in the existential contingencies of

---

57 "The Immanent Dialectic of the First Act of Freedom," 76–77.

58 "The Immanent Dialectic of the First Act of Freedom," 83–85. See also "The Meaning of Contemporary Atheism," in *The Range of Reason*, 103–17. Fr. Dewan critiques Maritain for following Cajetan by doubting a child's having explicit knowledge of God in the first act of freedom, finding a greater degree of confidence in this fact in St. Thomas on this point. See Fr. Lawrence Dewan, OP, "Natural Law and the First Act of Freedom: Maritain Revisited," in *Wisdom, Law, and Virtue* (New York: Fordham University Press, 2008), 221–41.

particular choices. Instead, in his work we find a nuanced account of the virtue of prudence, which applies the precepts of the natural law to particular situations. We also find Maritain insisting that the appropriate animation of ethical action springs not from the law, but from love.

Without denying the reality and due importance of natural law, Maritain's metaphysical existentialism leads him to insist that the natural law is never sufficient to meet the exigencies of determining action. Accordingly, the authentically metaphysical basis of his ethics is thoroughly existential (in the Thomistic sense) and must include the prudential governance that guides human action, for an account of human nature and its ends informs us only of the range of possibilities for human goodness, without showing how to actually achieve them.

In arguing for this claim I will begin by briefly situating Maritain's ethical discussion in the context of his metaphysics. I will then explore his understanding of natural law and its limitations when it comes to governing action. Finally, the place of prudence as the virtue that applies the natural law to the particular will be explained. From this the role of existence and love as the interconnected basis for the foundations of ethics in Maritain's thought will be made clear.

Maritain describes his philosophy as being both a Thomism and an existentialism. In discussing existentialism, his aim is not to present Thomism in light of the fashionable thought of mid-twentieth century France. This phenomenology from Heidegger and Sartre is, for Maritain, but a scholasticism corrupted at its root, though he admits it may have some value in "manuring the soil for a new germination of authentic metaphysics."[59] By contrast, he offers his thought as an authentic existentialism in that "it gives primacy to the intuition of existential being, and rejects any attempt to construe the philosophy of being as a philosophy of essences. The unique pre-eminence of this existential realism is its "confrontation of the act of existing by an intelligence determined never to disown itself."[60]

59 *Existence and the Existent*, 7n1.
60 *Existence and the Existent*, 2.

This Thomistic Existentialism is rooted especially in the fundamental distinction between the act of existence and essence. The essence or nature of a thing is that which the thing is, and by which it presents us with its various attributes, while its existence is the fact of its being posited outside of nothingness, seen in the very reality that we encounter it. In order to exercise this act of existing my nature must be that of a subject that is able to unfold that which it is (i.e., its nature concretely understood) in the world of existence and action. Accordingly, the first cause (i.e., God), has bestowed on it not only its various determinations and a capacity to *receive* existence and various attributes, but also an ability to *exercise* existence through action, and thus play a role among all other beings that are outside of nothingness.

This very succinct summary of the argument of the revised appendix IV of *The Degrees of Knowledge* points out that there are two basic metaphysical principles in the individual subject: one, the nature or essence that determines the range of possibilities and the natural end of the thing; the other, the act of existing through which the nature is determined to be a particular acting subject. This metaphysical analysis entails at the level of ethics a twofold mode of consideration, one that takes place on the abstract or universal level of the human essence—that is, the natural moral law—and another that takes place at the level of the concrete existent—that is, prudence. Each of these will be discussed in turn.

As we have seen above, the natural law is understood in view of certain observations that Maritain takes to be obvious: that there is a human nature the same in all persons, that we are endowed with intelligence and we act understanding what we are doing, that we determine for ourselves the ends that we will in fact pursue, etc. Having a determinate nature, we also have ends that correspond to our nature. However, human beings are unique because, having intelligence, we must bring ourselves into accord with the ends demanded by our nature. As we have explained at length above, this leads Maritain to define natural law as:

An order or disposition which human reason can discover and according to which the human will must act in order to attune itself to the necessary ends of the human being. The unwritten law, or natural law, is nothing more than that.[61]

The natural law, then, is not a mysterious code or quasi-mystical grasp of moral truth. Natural law is, rather, simply the ordinary functioning of an organism in a way that is likely to achieve the fundamental ends toward which that organism's nature tends. It is the proper way each thing should achieve "the fullness of being in their behavior." In the human case this progress towards the determinate final end of our nature is characterized by intelligence and freedom. Here in the human instance the functioning that "should" take place implies not merely a descriptive account of what we expect, as a flower should grow when watered, but a moral obligation. Accordingly, the natural law that governs human activity is necessarily the moral law. While it is "written" in the hearts of each person, this is a biblical metaphor. It is not to be taken to mean that it is a ready-made code fully present in each person's conscience. This would suggest that everyone knows it explicitly. That this is—sadly—not the case is only too obvious. It is, rather, known with more or less difficulty due to all sorts of factors. The natural law is an unwritten law and it has been disclosed only progressively through the history of human action and culture.

However, since the natural law is drawn from human nature and its natural teleology, it is universal in character. It covers the general ways that lead to or inhibit flourishing. Accordingly, what it offers us is a knowledge of what actions are inherently contradictory with the human good and the wide panorama of actions that can be conducive to that good. But this knowledge has its limits. For even if we could arrive at an exhaustive and certain knowledge of the natural law, this would be insufficient for us to know what we are obliged to do here and now. Many things that are permissible in general may be wrong to do in certain circumstances. For instance, there is nothing wrong with playing golf, but for myself, who is a father of six with a wife who works at home raising our children, to spend Saturday on the links after a week away at work would impose an undue burden upon her. These kinds of circumstantial and intentional contexts are resolutely unique—individual and unrepeatable. It follows that knowledge of the natural law on its own is not sufficient for us to be assured of moral action.

Beyond this knowledge, then, we need a way to reliably apply the broad universal principles of the natural law, which apply equally to everyone, always and everywhere, to our own particular personality, set of responsibilities, and relational situations. In this respect it is important to be aware that just as there are degrees of knowledge in the speculative sphere, so, too, there are degrees of practical knowledge. In speculative matters these differentiations are determined through the different modes of abstraction that give rise to the speculative sciences, philosophy of nature, mathematics, and metaphysics. Each discipline is more intelligible insofar as it is further removed from matter. With respect to practical knowledge, the modes of understanding are differentiated insofar as they are closer to the particular contingent act to be done.

Maritain's treatment of the application of the natural moral law to particular cases is nuanced. He clearly agrees with Aristotle and Aquinas that there is a difference between the knowledge possessed by the moral philosopher and that held by the non-philosophical person who is nevertheless a good person. This means that the virtue of prudence (i.e., right reason in acting) can be possessed without speculative philosophical knowledge.

In his discussion of practical knowing Maritain distinguishes between (1) speculatively practical knowledge, which characterizes the philosophical knowledge of morality; (2) practically practical knowledge, which possesses an intermediate form of abstraction, grasping what is to be done not only in general but with a focus upon the typical type of cases that arise; and (3) the prudential act, which reliably chooses what is good in the concrete case in view of the experienced demands of the moral law. Accordingly, there is an order of more general to more specific in the sphere of morality:

By the very fact that practical knowledge is like a continuous movement of thought inclined toward concrete action to be posited in existence, its practical character, present from the beginning, is progressively intensified and, in prudence, becomes wholly dominant.[62]

Speculatively practical knowledge and prudence do not tend to raise any special problems, as this reflects the more common division between the knowledge of ethics possessed by the philosopher and that which is possessed by the non-philosophical, but moral, agent. What is new in Maritain's presentation is the account of practically practical knowledge, which is a kind of halfway house between these two.[63]

Whereas speculatively practical knowledge directs action to be done only remotely, practically practical knowledge gives more proximate direction to action, though it is not yet dealing with the immediate action to be done here and now. The distinction is between theory and what we might call today "best practices." Maritain's example is the division between theoretical and practical medicine or the difference in focus between the moral theology of St. Thomas Aquinas and that of St. Alphonsus Liguori or of St. John of the Cross.[64] We could also think of the difference between knowing the rules of football and knowing a team's playbook. The playbook deals with how one is to act within the rules of the game in order to most effectively deal with the kinds of situations that typically arise. At times Maritain will point to the kind of knowledge of morality derived from a great novelist like Dostoyevsky or Austen as an example of practically practical knowledge.[65] A strong novel leads us to moral knowledge, not through an abstract justification, but by presenting us with dramatic situations in which we see the moral law at work in concrete situations. However, if we are dealing with

62 *The Degrees of Knowledge*, 481.

63 See Ralph McInerny, "The Degrees of Practical Knowledge," in *Art and Prudence: Studies in the Thought of Jacques Maritain* (Notre Dame, IN: University of Notre Dame Press, 1988), 70.

64 *The Degrees of Knowledge*, 488.

65 The tension between a theoretical morality and lived practice is a central preoccupation of Dostoyevsky's *Crime and Punishment*. The character Fanny Price has been pointed to as a notable example of choosing virtue over societal expectations in Austen's *Mansfield Park*.

a great novel, these concrete situations in part speak to the universal human condition.

The distinction between a speculatively practical and a practically practical knowledge of ethics concerns whether the discipline is appealing to remote or proximate principles to determine what is to be done. Maritain explains this distinctive character of practically practical knowledge, saying:

> The mode which is *practical and compositive,* not only in respect to the conditions of the object known, but also *in respect to the very structure of the means of apprehending and judging,* characterizes not only *prudence,* which immediately governs the act to be done *hic et nunc* by a judgment and command appropriate to the absolute individualization of the concrete case, but it also characterizes (although to a lesser degree) a *science* of human action whose object, unlike that of prudence, is to organize universal truths, and yet which proceeds to do so, not *per principia remota operationis* [through remote principles of action] as moral philosophy (which it presupposes) does, but *per principia proxima operationis* [through proximate principles of action]. Consequently, it must depend on practical principles in its fundamental equipment and it its very knowledge-value; its means of knowledge must be fundamentally impregnated with practicality and it will yield that completed and assured truth proper to science only when it presupposes in him who teaches it an authentic experience of the concrete term to which it directs those who are taught.[66]

The natural law in itself provides the broad norms of action that direct the moral life remotely. For Maritain, at this remote level we merely have a rule; it does not yet take the form of a command.[67] Accordingly, Maritain distinguishes the notion of norm as a rule or "pilot-norm" from the norm in the sense of a law or command or "precept-norm." In the first sense, the norm as rule, we have the basic condition required for an act to be good. In order to be good an act must be in conformity with the relevant pilot-norm.

---

66 *The Degrees of Knowledge,* 487.
67 *An Introduction to the Basic Problems of Moral Philosophy,* 142.

The norm seen as a command derives from the broader pilot-norm. The recognition that this norm is obligatory for me to act upon requires that we take into account the particular circumstances in which we act. It is within the action itself that the obligation to conform to the relevant general norm arises.[68] The general types of situations we find ourselves in lead to a recognition of directive norms that are proximate to the action to be done. The priority of the pilot-norm to ethical commands is distinctive of moral norms when compared to other types of commands that represent merely social pressure without a grounding in the broader norm (e.g., when we say you *must* use this brand of toothpaste or you *must* buy this brand of clothes).[69]

In addition to viewing the norm of moral action as both a measure and as a precept or command, Maritain also notes that in our moral experience it is encountered as a constraint. He argues that this is a result of the theological fact that living under the burden of sin, our nature has been corrupted. A purely natural morality would not lead one to experience fear and trembling at the moral law; it would merely be the means best suited to the human end. But for real human beings in a state of sin, the law is experienced as constraint to such a degree that many sociologists see coercion as an essential aspect of the notion of a norm or rule. This is due to the fact that coercion is the most empirically obvious characteristic of law, while being in relation is the least fundamental or essential to its intrinsic character.[70]

The fact that morality is a constraint is particularly important in the more practical and immediate dimensions of moral reasoning. This is seen easily enough in a particular case. I see that murder is bad. Even though this murder fits my anger, I realize that if I do it I shall be bad, and I cannot wish to be bad, for I can only will the bad under the aspect of the good. This recognition binds me in conscience as a moral

---

68 *An Introduction to the Basic Problems of Moral Philosophy*, 148–49.

69 *An Introduction to the Basic Problems of Moral Philosophy*, 153.

70 *An Introduction to the Basic Problems of Moral Philosophy*, 155. There is a profound meditation on the relation between our experience of the moral law as a constraint and God's love by Raïssa Maritain that was very important and meaningful to Jacques. See Raïssa Maritain, "The True Face of God and the Law," in *Raïssa's Journal* (Albany, NY: Magi Books, 1974), 389–94.

obligation.[71] But this is an abstract consideration at the level of moral essences taken in themselves (i.e., given the nature of murder and my nature as a human agent). There is another level of consideration that concerns not abstraction, but my actual choice, my act of freedom. At this (practically practical) level I can make a choice that runs against my conscience and moral obligation that was established at the level of abstract (speculatively practical) considerations. In this case I am considering murder not in its essence or nature, but with respect to my own personality, desires, and preferences. In this light I can say that although this act is bad and forbidden by the law, it is my own private good that I love to satisfy, and this is my anger. Accordingly, I make this evil of murder what I love best and do not care for the law that I have acknowledged. "Then I choose murder not because it is bad, but because in respect to concrete circumstances and to the love which I freely make prevalent in me it is good for me. But not morally good!"[72] In this way the mind recognizes a rule in the abstract that gives rise to a moral obligation, but disregards that rule in the moment of acting. This entails that it is vital that moral rules not only be intellectually recognized as true and binding, but the moral agent must also recognize in them an urgent demand of his most intimate and personal desire for ends that he has made central to his life. If not, he will not do the good that he purports to love.[73]

Accordingly, Maritain argues against a Kantian emphasis on universality as an essential aspect of being a norm. To the contrary, for Maritain universality is merely a consequence of a norm's rationality. As we have seen, this universal norm needs to be applied to the individual case through a prudential interiorization that applies it to the person's pursuit of subjectively pursued ends. The truth of this position and the limits of rationally demonstrated universal duties so emphasized by

---

71 *An Introduction to the Basic Problems of Moral Philosophy*, 172–73.

72 *The Responsibility of the Artist* (New York: Charles Scribner's Sons, 1960), 34–35. See also the helpful schema in *An Introduction to the Basic Problems of Moral Philosophy*, 174. This is a graphic instance of the non-consideration of the relevant moral rule that is the first cause of evil discussed in chapter five.

73 *Existence and the Existent*, 45.

Kant can be seen when one looks at the acts of the saints and the gifts of the Holy Spirit. These gifts are higher than the merely natural moral virtues. When a saint strips naked before his bishop to show his love of poverty, he is performing an act that cannot be made into a rule. When another becomes a beggar and shocks people by his free embrace of poverty and filth, or when another abandons his responsibilities to become a galley slave out of love for the captives, in these cases we have acts at the height of moral greatness, but which are not capable of being generalized into a rule that others could follow in any obvious way.[74]

The connection of prudence to the metaphysics of Thomistic Existentialism are explicitly drawn out in the chapter entitled "Action" in Maritain's 1947 work *Existence and the Existent*. In this chapter Maritain argues that in the sphere of ethics Thomistic existentialism is ordered not toward things, but to the act that the liberty of the subject brings into existence. This contact with existence, through the focus on the act of choice, arises in terms of two fundamental doctrines: the first concerning the perfection of human life, and the second concerning the judgment of moral consciousness, which is a focus of the earlier treatments we have already explored.

The perfection of human life consists in charity. Our life is perfected insofar as we love according to our condition and power. The measure of our ethical conduct and virtue is ultimately the measure of our love:

> All morality thus hangs upon that which is most existential in the world. For love (this is another Thomist theme) does not deal with possible or pure essences, we love that which exists or is destined to exist.[75]

Given the doctrine of divine simplicity, that every property affirmed of God is fundamentally identical with his act of existence, and thereby with one another, we are enabled to say that ultimately it is because God is his act of existing that love of him is better than all other goodness through which man is perfected. In loving God we love the good

---

74 *Existence and the Existent*, 46–47.
75 *Existence and the Existent*, 49.

itself and for itself and as a result this is also our highest good. This love brings us to fullness of perfection through the complex and often messy dialogues and relationships between persons. Through this act of love we become gods by participation in grace in a single "spiritual super-existence of love."

On the second point of doctrine Maritain notes that in the judgement of moral conscience the appetite contributes to the regulation of the moral act by way of reason. This action occurs "at the heart of concrete existence." Maritain explains:

> Not only is the truth of the practical intellect generally under-
> stood to be conformity with right appetite (not, as in the case of
> the speculative intellect, conformity with extra-mental being,)
> because the end is not to know that which exists, but *to cause
> that to exist which is not yet*; but also the act of moral choice is so
> individualized (both by the singularity of the person from whom
> it emanates and by that of the context of contingent circumstance
> in which it takes place) that the practical judgment in which it is
> expressed and which I declare to myself, "this is what I need," can
> only be right if actually, *hic et nunc*, the dynamism of my willing is
> right and tends towards the genuine goods of human life.[76]

For Maritain this existential approach allows him to balance universal moral norms with the demands of the particular situations where competing duties often complicate a simplistic deontological approach. In contrast to Kierkegaard he insists that there is no suspension of ethics, but rather, lower laws give way in the face of higher ones, as the gifts of the Holy Spirit come into play, which move the soul in ways that transcend the virtues, while not conflicting with them. Accordingly, even in the case of Abraham, he knew by the Holy Spirit that the sacrifice, were he called to make it, was not a transgression of the law against killing, since it was commanded by the Master of life.

While there is more to be said to explicate the relation between the natural law, the virtues, and the gifts of the Holy Spirit, it is clear that Maritain recognizes the limitations of the natural law. The universality of

76 *Existence and the Existent*, 43–44.

its precepts makes it inadequate to determine action. What is required is contact with real existence, which comes through love—which always regards the existent—and prudence, which applies the precepts of law to the real cases before us in view of the hidden and connaturally known subjectivity of the moral agent.

CHAPTER 8

Political Philosophy

Hard experience has taught us that the kingdom of God is not
meant for earthly history, but at the same time we have become
aware of this crucial truth that it must be enigmatically prepared
for in the midst of the pains of earthly history.

Christianity and Democracy, 34

M aritain's many reflections on political philosophy originated
out of practical concerns. After years of writing predominantly theoretical philosophy, he turned to the study of
politics in the wake of Pope Pius XI's condemnation of reac-
tionary political movement Action Française, with which he had been
loosely associated, and the overwhelming events of the Second World
War. Yet he situates his political thought in a context that is not so much
personal as it is historical.

The fundamental background to politics, for Maritain, is the concept of the human person; this provides the metaphysical framework
for the broader culture within which political action takes place. Maritain identifies a historical transition from the theocentric image of man
found in the medieval era, to a degenerate and pessimistic image of man
in the Christian Reformation, to a more autonomous and secular notion

of man in the Enlightenment. In light of this history Maritain challenges the overly simplistic assumption that humanism is equivalent with *secular* humanism. To the contrary, he argues that proposing a merely secular and human view of the person is to betray the deepest dignity of the human person. It would be to ignore the principal part of humanity, namely, the spiritual, since we are called to more than a merely human life. Accordingly, he argues that one's understanding of humanism is contingent upon one's understanding of human nature. If human nature is spiritual, then a merely anthropocentric humanism would be a profound aberration—and indeed, anti-humanistic at its core.[1]

Hence, he defines humanism in a manner that is more nuanced than is customary, writing:

> To leave the whole discussion open, let us say that humanism (and such a definition can itself be developed along very divergent lines) tends essentially to render man more truly human, and to manifest his original greatness by having him participate in all that which can enrich him in nature and in history (by "concentrating the world in man," as Scheler said approximately, and by "dilating man to the world"); it at once demands that man develop the work to make the forces of the physical world instruments of his freedom.[2]

This definition leaves open the dispute between a theistic or anthropomorphic humanism, but points to the fact that the decisive factor in deciding the matter will be our understanding of the human person. However, humanism cannot be understood apart from culture and civilization.

Maritain insists that anthropocentric humanism in the Western world, as a matter of historical fact, arose from Christianity. This is not merely a question of origin, but affects the very nature of humanism even in its atheistic and anti-Christian forms, for "Western humanism has religious and transcendent sources without which it is incomprehensible to itself." This is an important point that is especially emphasized in

---

1   Jacques Maritain, *Integral Humanism, Freedom in the Modern World, and A Letter on Independence*, Revised Edition, Vol. XI of *The Collected Works of Jacques Maritain*, trans. Otto Bird (Notre Dame, IN: Notre Dame University Press, 1996), 169.

2   *Integral Humanism*, 153.

Maritain's early works, especially *Integral Humanism*. In this work he argues that the medieval historical ideal was a *sacral* Christian conception of temporal realities. While clearly recognizing there is no turning back of time to that conception, he argues for the development of a "New Christendom," which would be a *profane* Christian conception. This is not to argue for a less religious model of Christianity compared to the past, or for a separation of the temporal from the spiritual. Rather, as the Italian philosopher Augusto Del Noce has pointed out, "He is saying that the transcendence of Christianity with respect to all civilizations rules out every univocal conception of the Christian temporal order."[3] This development of a New Christendom was profoundly affected by his experience of modern Europe prior to World War II, which was to raise deep questions for his vision of a relatively unified Christian Europe. After the war we find further reflection making room for pluralism within the framework of a shared Christian heritage, in contrast to the twin threats of Eastern communism on one extreme and of Western capitalist individualism on the other.

While this ideal of a new Christendom is never discarded, Maritain's personal experience of the United States during and after the war, as well has his active role in the formative years of the United Nations, give his later work a different emphasis. In his book *Man and State*, based upon his postwar Walgreen Lectures, Maritain focuses more directly on clarifying a series of concepts relating to the community and society. He maintains that there is nothing more important for a sound political philosophy than the correct understanding of these concepts.

Political Concepts: Community, Society, and the Body Politic

The most basic distinction is between the community and society. These are distinct concepts; while community is a work of nature and emerges spontaneously, society is a work of reason and, accordingly, a matter

---

3   Augusto Del Noce, "The Lesson of Maritain," *Maritain Studies* 31 (2015): 76.

of convention.[4] Community is a fact prior to determinations of human intelligence and will that create a common spirit and mores, while society has a task to be done or an end aimed at; thus, society is formed through human activity informed by intelligence and will. Communities, however, consist of regional groups, ethnic or linguistic groups, and social classes. They are formed spontaneously through instinct and heredity or historical circumstances, while societies require reason and exhibit the moral character of its members. A corporation, a labor union, a scholarly or scientific association, are examples of societies. Even natural societies like the family and political body remain societies as well as being communities, since they arise from and are sustained by the exercise of human freedom.

Much like Aristotle, who had held that the political community, the polis, was a natural form of association, Maritain argues that the modern nation is a community, not a society.[5] The nation is, in fact, the most complete and complex community in modern life. It is a human community based on birth and heredity along with moral connotations of these facts: the activities of civilizations, the inheritance of family, social, legal and cultural traditions, etc. It is distinct, however, from an ethnic community, which is a community of patterns of feeling rooted in the physical origin of the group and in the moral unity of its history.[6] An ethnic community becomes a nation when this factual context gives rise to self-awareness and the group becomes aware that it constitutes a community and organizes itself as such. The nation is simply a community that has become aware of itself in its common history and imagination. In this sense the nation has rights and a common heritage, a historic calling that is a particularized specification of the universal human calling.

Yet Maritain insists the nation is *not* a society. It doesn't enter the political realm as such. Rather, it is a "community of communities," a self-aware network of common feelings. Here Maritain seems to be

4 *Man and the State*, 2.
5 *Man and the State*, 4.
6 *Man and the State*, 5.

speaking about the nation as a sociological reality, rather than a polit-
ically organized state. A nation in this sense has no formal leader or
governance. It may have elites and opinion makers, but it possesses no
formal structures. The nation is not a rational formal juridical structure. One's national identity is not a result of freedom and responsibility
of personal conscience, but of heredity and cultural formation around
one's instinctual living. A good example of this would be the province
of Quebec in Canada, which has historically insisted on the importance
of its distinctive French language and culture within the Canadian state.
In 2006 the Canadian government formally recognized Quebec as a
nation, in a sense similar to how Maritain uses the term, through a
motion in the House of Commons. However, Maritain argues a national
group cannot transform itself into a political society, for a political society is something essentially different. A political society arises through
distinguishing itself from the confused social life of the multitude, taking the place of community activities that had been mingled with other
social functions. As the example of Quebec shows, however, the distinction is not as clear in practice. In fact, the cultural reality of the Quebec
nation has spawned a political movement for separation from Canada
and the establishment of Provincial and Federal political parties in Quebec whose main concern is the preservation of French interests while
working toward an independent Quebeçoise state. Nevertheless, in
Maritain's view the body politic is something distinct from and beyond
the nation in this sense.[7] Yet it is unclear that the insistence that the
nation is not a political category can evade the risk of "balkanization"
once multiple nations are recognized within a broader state.

In light of his analysis, Maritain argues that the entire concept of a
nation-state is a myth that should be seen as a simple oxymoron resting
on the confusion between the nation and the state. Such a concept erroneously presupposes that each nation must establish a separate state.
This would be to reduce the state to the clan, party, or chief and would
absolutize the political realm. Maritain denies that a nation necessarily
becomes a state, arguing that the state can, and often does, contain

7   *Man and the State*, 6–7.

within itself a plurality of nationalities.[8] For Maritain the state and the political society (or body politic) differ from each other as part and whole. Political society is a whole, while the state is a part—even if the highest part—of this whole. This is necessary to recognize the rich diversity that exists in any body politic while accommodating for the unity required in governance.

Political society is required by nature. It is a concrete and human reality tending to the concrete achievement of the common good and human good of its members. It is a work of reason establishing a rational order, bringing about a society. The body politic tends to establish justice and civic friendship. It requires historical continuity and traditions that establish common feeling, a common inherited experience and moral and intellectual instincts. The body politic contains family units and a multiplicity of other societies. Accordingly, pluralism is inherent in and a normal part of any political society. In contrast, the state is the part of political society that maintains law and the promotion of the common welfare and public order, administering public affairs. The state is the part of the community that specializes in the interests of the whole. It is for this reason that the state rightfully has powers to act for the common good, although those powers are limited by various factors such as human rights.

The Person and the Common Good

Whereas Maritain's early work *Integral Humanism* presented a historically informed account of political society, very much influenced by the prewar European scene, *Man and the State* is deeply informed by American political considerations, as we see in the more conceptual and less historically concrete framework Maritain provides. However, his political thought forms a unity insofar as his understanding of the person and the common good, the very the aims of political life, remains constant throughout his career. In the late 1930s into the 1940s, Maritain became an ardent defender of universal human rights, articulating

8 *Man and the State*, 8.

this in an innovative way within the framework of a Thomistic theory of natural law. While this may seem non-controversial today, when Catholicism is frequently a vocal supporter of human rights issues, it is important to remember that the language of rights did not become a familiar aspect of the Church's official teaching until Pope John XXIII's encyclical *Pacem in Terris* in 1963, and was later cemented by the teaching of John Paul II.[9] Accordingly, the debate over the person and the common good was not merely an isolated academic concern, but a part of a larger dispute that would determine the course of the Church's future engagement with the modern and post-modern world.

By the early 1940s Maritain had long been seen as both a Thomist and a personalist, associated with the leading French personalist Emmanuel Mounier and others writing in the journal *Esprit* (although he expressed concerns with aspects of Mounier's project).[10] It is in this context that Charles De Koninck, the Dean of the Philosophy Faculty at Laval University, published a little book in 1943 entitled *The Primacy of the Common Good against the Personalists*. The book was published with a preface written by the Archbishop of Quebec, Cardinal Villeneuve, who used the occasion to condemn the personalists of reviving the "polychephalus monster of Pelegianism." Interestingly, De Koninck himself did not identify who these problematic personalists were, preferring to simply present what he took to be characteristic arguments of this school of thought for refutation. However, many supporters and critics of Maritain saw his thought as the target, and indeed the very title *The Primacy of the Common Good* can easily be read as an allusion to an earlier book Maritain had written, entitled *The Primacy of the Spiritual*.[11] The polemics were increased substantially when a Dominican professor of philosophy at the Pontifical Institute of Mediaeval Studies at the University of Toronto, Fr. Ignatius Eschmann, published

---

9   Steps towards this full recognition of rights had been taken by earlier pontiffs, especially Leo XIII and Pius XII, which Maritain is also building upon.

10   See Bernard E. Doering, *Jacques Maritain and the French Catholic Intellectuals* (Notre Dame, IN: University of Notre Dame Press, 1983). See also Dries Deweer, "The Philosophical Theory of Personalism: Maritain and Mounier on Personhood and Citizenship," *International Journal of Philosophy and Theology* 74, no. 2 (2013): 110.

11   This allusion is lost in the title of the published English translation, *The Things that are Ceasar's*.

a scathing article attacking De Koninck's work, entitled "In Defense of Jacques Maritain." In it he held that if the book's arguments were true, "then the personalists, and with them all the Christian Fathers and theologians and philosophers, should close their shops, go home and do penance in sackcloth and ashes for having grossly erred and misled the Christian world for almost two thousand years."[12] De Koninck replied to this passionate critique with an article—"In Defense of St. Thomas"— that was longer than his original book, while still shedding no light on the issue of who the personalists in question were or whether Maritain was the target of the critique or not.

The vehemence of this debate may seem somewhat surprising, given that all parties to the dispute share a number of fundamental philosophical positions. Indeed, Mary Keys has gone so far as to argue that there are few, if any, substantive differences between Maritain's and De Koninck's positions.[13] This is a view that was first suggested by Maritain's own close friend and collaborator Yves Simon, who reviewed De Koninck's book, arguing that while the views he refuted were erroneous, they were certainly not the views of Maritain.[14] For his own part Maritain did not address the dispute until 1946 in his book *The Person and the Common Good*. In a footnote, he thanks Fr. Eschmann for coming to his defense, while at the same time stating that the views De Koninck criticizes do not reflect his own positions.[15] Noting the diversity

---

12 Ignatius Eschmann, OP, "In Defense of Jacques Maritain," *Modern Schoolman* 22, vol. 4 (1944): 181.

13 Mary M. Keys, "Personal Dignity and the Common Good: A Twentieth-Century Thomistic Dialogue," in *Catholicism, Liberalism, and Communitarianism: The Catholic Intellectual Tradition and the Moral Foundations of Democracy*, ed. Kenneth L. Grasso, Gerard V. Bradley, and Robert P. Hunt (Lanham, MD: Rowman and Littlefield, 1995), 179 and 183.

14 See Yves Simon, "On the Common Good," reprinted in *The Writings of Charles De Koninck*, Vol. 2, ed. and trans. Ralph McInerny (Notre Dame, IN: University of Notre Dame Press, 2008), 165–72. This volume provides translations of De Koninck's book, Eschmann's article, De Koninck's response, and Simon's review. There was also a significant correspondence between Simon and Maritain on the consequences of this dispute between 1945 and 1946. See Jacques Maritain, Yves Simon, *Correspondance, T.2 : Les années américaine (1941-1961)*, ed. Florian Michel (Tours: CLD Éditions, 2012).

15 *The Person and the Common Good*, 6n6.

of personalist views, he holds that what is at issue is not a personalist doctrine, but a personalist aspiration.[16]

While there are certainly broad areas of substantial agreement between the two Thomists, Maritain does go significantly beyond De Koninck in his understanding of the metaphysics of the human person and in the manner in which he draws upon this to defend a largely modern framework of natural human rights that is utterly foreign to De Koninck's position. These differences are crucial ones, as they are precisely those aspects of Maritain's thought which contributed most directly to the development of Catholic social thought and the Church's own—rather late—embrace of human rights discourse in the twentieth century.

De Koninck's defense of the primacy of the common good is particularly concerned with refuting two major errors. The first of these is the modern tendency to reduce the common good to an aggregate of individual goods.[17] Such an approach would entail that the common good is not a shared and communicable good, but a mere collection of individual goods. To the contrary, De Koninck insists that the common good is not primarily the good of individuals, but the good of the collectivity. Otherwise it would only be common accidentally, but would remain properly singular.[18] De Koninck's second major objection to the personalist doctrine is that it entails that the good of the singular person is superior to the good of the community—contrary to Aquinas's doctrine that the common good is more lovable and superior to any private good. Accordingly, he argues:

> A society made up of persons who love their private good above the common good, or who identify the common good with the private good is a society, not of free men, but of tyrants—"and thus

---

16   *The Person and the Common Good*, 2.

17   Such a view is, however, advocated more recently by John Finnis, *Aquinas: Moral, Political, and Legal Theory* (New York: Oxford University Press, 1998), chapter 7. In his work on natural law Finnis defines the common good as "a set of conditions which enables the members of a community to attain for themselves reasonable objectives, or to realize reasonably for themselves the value(s), for the sake of which they have reason to collaborate with each other (positively and/or negatively) in a community." John Finnis, *Natural Law and Natural Rights* (Oxford: Clarendon Press, 1980), 155.

18   *The Primacy of the Common Good* reprinted in *The Writings of Charles De Koninck*, Vol. 2, ed. and trans. Ralph McInerny (Notre Dame, IN: University of Notre Dame Press, 2008), 75.

the whole people become as one tyrant"—who would use force on one another and whose eventual chief would be the shrewdest and strongest of tyrants, his subjects being only frustrated tyrants. Refusal of the primacy of the common good proceeds, at bottom, from the distrust and scorn of persons.[19]

Maritain's position on the person and the common good is strikingly similar to De Koninck's on these points. He explicitly denies that the common good is merely an aggregate of the individual goods of the persons who constitute it. He rejects this as a dissolution of society for the benefit of its parts, entailing that society become "an anarchy of atoms." Such an anarchy would simply be a bourgeois materialism that insists the freedom of each be respected to the point that the strong have the freedom to oppress the weak.[20]

Neither is the common good holistic and separate from the individual members of society. Like De Koninck, Maritain insists that while the common good cannot be reduced to the private goods of the persons who are members of society, it must nevertheless be a good they share in fully. As Maritain states it:

It is the good human life of the multitude, of a multitude of persons, the good life of totalities at once carnal and spiritual, and principally spiritual, although they more often happen to live by the flesh than by the spirit. The common good of society is their communion in the good life.[21]

To this point there is little difference between our two authors.

Yet Eschmann had taken De Koninck's position to entail that the common good had primacy over the personal good, and that the human person's end was subjected to the order it had as a material part in the cosmos. The implication of this, which Eschmann finds so objectionable, is that it risks interjecting the political or social common good as an intermediary between the soul and its attainment of God as its

---

19   *The Primacy of the Common Good*, 80.
20   *The Rights of Man and Natural Law*, 7–8.
21   *The Rights of Man and Natural Law*, 10. See also *The Person and the Common Good*, 3.

ultimate end. Accordingly, in a passage quoted favourably by Maritain, Eschmann writes:

> The most essential and dearest aim of Thomism is to make sure that the personal contact of all intellectual creatures with God, as well as their personal subordination to God, be in no way interrupted. Everything else—the whole universe and every social institution—must ultimately minister to this purpose; everything must foster and protect the conversation of the soul, every soul with God. It is characteristically Greek and pagan to interpose the universe between God and intellectual creatures.[22]

De Koninck, for his part, repudiated this implication, while holding that personalism entailed the mistake that the private good of the individual trumped the common good of the community. The logical implication of this would be an unmitigated anarchy of private goods reminiscent of Hobbes's war of each against all. Accordingly, the task Maritain's theory has is to show what the dignity of the person consists in, and the implications it has for the political order, without turning the common good into a mere aggregate of individual goods, or allowing the good of the individual to override the higher good, the common good of the political community.

The source of the differences between these views seems to arise not so much from competing understandings of the common good, but from the account of the person that Maritain offers. For Maritain the human being exists in a tension between a material pole of individuality and a spiritual pole of true personality.[23] This distinction between the individual and the person is drawn out of the work of earlier Thomists, such as Schwalm and Garrigiou-Lagrange. However, Maritain argues that it is a part of the common wisdom of humanity, seeing it as analogous to the distinction between ego and self in Hindu philosophy and being expressed in different ways in the thought of Aquinas, Proudhon, Berdyaev, and others—particularly among the existentialists.[24]

---

22 Eschmann, "In Defense of Jacques Maritain," 192. It is important to note that Fr. Eschmann is concerned about inserting an intermediary between the person and God in the natural order. In the supernatural order there is such mediation through the Church.

23 *The Person and the Common Good*, 23.

24 *The Person and the Common Good*, 3 and 24.

The distinction between individual and person rests on the fact that human beings are unique in the entire universe in being both physical and spiritual beings. Maritain draws on Aquinas's understanding that the individuality of a material being is rooted in matter. According to Aquinas, a material being is an individual in its own right and distinct from others because it is made up of unique matter that marks its dimensions in space and time as quantitative entity with a position distinct from every other material entity. This is developed within the hylomorphic theory that Maritain inherits from Aristotle and Aquinas, in terms of which matter is a mere potency or capacity to receive form. As Maritain describes it, matter is a kind of non-being (i.e., a potential for being) that nevertheless possesses an "avidity for being." In the order of actual existence, every material being is structured by a form or soul that, as the principle of actuality, makes it a substantial unit and reduces the material potency to actuality. Because of its union with matter the substantial form that is common to all beings of the species is particularized into an individual member of its species; it is the same common nature shared with all the other members, but manifested in a unique and particular way.[25]

For Maritain the human being's rootedness in matter as the basis of its individuality has important ethical and social implications that become clear in the way he sums up his understanding of human individuality:

We have characterized matter as an avidity for being, having of itself no determination and deriving all of its determinations from form. In each of us, individuality, being that which excludes from oneself all that other men are, could be described as a narrowness of ego, forever threatened and forever eager *to grasp for itself.* Such narrowness in flesh animated by a spirit derives from matter . . . As an individual, each of us is a fragment of a species, a part of the universe, a unique point in the immense web of cosmic, ethnical, historical forces and influences—and bound by their laws.[26]

25 *The Person and the Common Good,* 25–26.
26 *The Person and the Common Good,* 27–28.

Consequently, the human being is not only an individual, a particular substance limited by matter, and as such, a part of the social whole. Rather, due to the fact that each of us has a spiritual core of intelligence and freedom, we are also persons. This means each human being is an integral whole in his or her own right, and not merely a part of any of the communities of which they are members. Maritain describes his understanding of person by saying:

> Personality is the subsistence of the spiritual soul communicated to the human composite. Because in our substance, it is an imprint or seal which enables it to possess its existence, to perfect and give itself freely, personality testifies to the generosity or expansiveness in being which an incarnate spirit derives from its spiritual nature and which constitutes, within the secret depths of our ontological structure, a source of dynamic unity of unification from within. Personality, therefore, signifies interiority to itself.[27]

It is this spiritual reality that makes one a person, through subsistence and subjective interiority. But for Maritain this doesn't make each person self-enclosed and inward focused, as one of the defining characteristics of a person is self-expression through knowledge and love. Accordingly, personality has a deep need for dialogue, in which there is a genuine communication in knowledge and love. Yet this communication is often incomplete and stammering, for the person is "directly related to the absolute." Vital to this account is the continued emphasis upon integral humanism. Only in relation to God is the person able to encounter entirely the range of goods to which she or he is called. Maritain sees this implied in the Christian doctrine of the person as created in the image of God, and that we are thus called to participate in the very life of God through knowing and loving him as he knows and loves himself.

Maritain explains this distinction between person and individual further clarifying four points to avoid potential misunderstandings:

---

27   *The Person and the Common Good*, 31. For a reliable guide to the nuances involved in Maritain's theory of subsistence, see chapter three of Raymond Dennehy, *Jacques Maritain's Philosophy of Action* (CreateSpace Independent Publishing Platform, 2017).

1. The person and the individual are not two separate things, but rather the same thing is in one sense an individual, insofar as it comes from matter, and in another sense a person, insofar as it comes from the spirit.[28]

2. Individuality, coming from the material aspect of the human being, is not something evil in itself. Since matter is a condition of the existence of human beings, it is in itself something good. Rather, evil arises when our actions, which involve our whole being as both an individual and a person, give undue priority to the individual aspect of ourselves. In this way we will only be fully a person insofar as the life of spirit and freedom reigns over our senses and passions.[29]

3. In education it is essential to avoid confusing the person with the individual. It is a grave danger to try to bring about the development of personality and the expansive freedom it requires by rejecting asceticism and self-discipline. Rather than self-fulfillment such false trails only lead to dispersion and disintegration that atrophies the heart or leads to frivolity.[30]

4. Finally, it is a mistake to exalt the person at the expense of the individual. To deny the individual aspects of the human being is to undermine his personality as well. Instead of contributing to the grandeur of the person in the image of God, one who follows this path is more likely to create the "austere mask of the Pharisee."[31]

To this point Maritain's position is relatively consistent with that of De Koninck. However, the latter does not develop a philosophical anthropology grounded in the distinction between the individual and person in the way that the former does. It is this additional philosophical resource that allows for Maritain to present a Thomistically inspired theory of human rights in a way that would conflict with, or at least go beyond, De Koninck's more limited view.

---

28 *The Person and the Common Good*, 33.
29 *The Person and the Common Good*, 33–35.
30 *The Person and the Common Good*, 35.
31 *The Person and the Common Good*, 35–36.

Natural Human Rights

Maritain resolves the tensions that arise within the relation between the person and the common good using this distinction between the human being considered as individual and as person. He arrives at this through a consideration of two apparently contradictory principles found in Aquinas:

1. "Each individual person is related to the entire community as the part to the whole."[32]
2. "Man is not ordained to the body politic according to all that he is and has."[33]

Far from finding these positions contradictory, Maritain holds that the second qualifies and balances the first. He arrives at this through holding that the self is discovered in a dynamic tension between two poles, material and spiritual. He holds that every human being can be understood as an individual insofar as she or he is a material being, individuated from other members of the species through the unique body through which each lives. In light of this, every individual is merely a part of its species and accordingly, a part of the society of which it is a member. As a part of this society the body politic has a claim over the individual and can make demands of the individual for the benefit of the common good of the whole; taxes can be levied, soldiers conscripted, etc. Interestingly, Aquinas appeals to this sort of part/whole reasoning in various contexts (for example, when arguing in favor of capital punishment), in ways that seem to undercut a full recognition of dignity of the person.[34]

However, in virtue of their rational nature each intelligent being is also a person. Personality gives rise to the subjective interiority of self that is found in human beings. It is the subsistence of the spiritual soul that is communicated to the human composite. In virtue of this personal dimension each human being is the source of the activity of

32 *S.T.*, II-II, q. 64, a. 2.
33 *S.T.*, I-II, q. 21, a. 4 ad. 3.
34 *S.T.*, II-II, q. 64, a. 3.

its intellect and free will, and as such is not merely a part, but also an autonomously functioning whole. As a whole, the person cannot merely be subordinated to the interests of the political community—as if he or she were but an instrumental part—in the way that the Fascist totalitarian governments at the time of Maritain's writing were doing. Rather, Maritain holds that because each human being is a person and a whole, each is directly related to God as an absolute.

By distinguishing the individual from the person, Maritain is able to assert that each citizen has various duties as a part of the political community—and that since the political community is a whole, its good is superior to, though not separable from, the good of its individual parts. This does not mean that the individual is only partially at the disposal of the political community (since, for example, the state can in time of war even conscript a citizen for military service and expect him to put his life at risk for the sake of the political community). Yet at the same time, Maritain holds that the good of the human person, in certain respects, takes priority over the common good of the political community, precisely because it is directly ordered to a good of a higher order, namely, to God as the common good of all that exists. Accordingly, the political authority can make demands of the citizen that require that citizen's complete engagement, but not with regards to all that the person is. In a similar way a girl running a race is completely engaged in the act of running, yet it would be false to say that a runner is all that she is.

It is precisely Maritain's move to give primacy to the good of the human person over the common good in some respects that differs from De Koninck's anti-personalist stance—for Maritain's position seems to entail making the good of the person superior to the common good of the political community, at least in some respects. However, what De Koninck fails to give sufficient attention to is the fact that the common good is an analogous concept that functions in different orders. In this light Maritain is not exalting the private good over the common good, but rather recognizing that the political common good is subordinated to higher common goods: namely, God as both the common good of the material cosmos and of all that is even in the natural order.

In this argument Maritain lays particular emphasis on Aquinas's doctrine that God's providence cares for each individual intellectual creature *for its own sake*, not merely as a piece in the larger whole of the universe. This is the case even though intellectual creatures are, as any creature, ordered first and absolutely to God, and secondarily to the order and perfection of the created universe as its most noble parts.[35] Accordingly, Maritain finds that every intellectual creature is created for three orders of good: (1) for God as the separate common good of all creation, (2) for the perfection of the order of the universe, and (3) for its own good, that is, for the immanent and spiritual action through which it perfects itself and achieves its end.[36]

Accordingly, there is a common good to be found at the level of animal life—in speaking of the good of a beehive, for instance—in which each member of the community is merely a part and nothing more than a part. However, this is quite different from the common good of the purely rational and spiritual order, which is found in each rational being's direct relation to God and to others through God. Between these two is found the political common good, which exists in a dynamic tension, for the members of the political community are at once material and thus parts of a social whole, yet not ordered to this social whole by way of all that is in them.

This allows Maritain to say that the political common good is indeed superior to the good of the individual citizen, while at the same time insisting that, as a person, one is ordered to a good that transcends the political order. It is to this that Maritain appeals in arguing for a theory of universal human rights upon which the political community cannot impose, for the entire political order is, in one sense, a means disposing the human person towards the achievement of its ultimate end: union with the uncreated common good of the Blessed Trinity:

> Together God and the soul, are two in one; two natures in a single vision and a single love. The soul is filled with God. It is in

---

35 *The Person and the Common Good,* 7 noting *Summa Contra Gentiles,* III, 112.
36 *The Person and the Common Good,* 7n7.

sociability with God. With Him, it possesses a common good, the divine Good Itself.[37]

Accordingly, in his book *The Rights of Man and the Natural Law* Maritain gives two arguments for rights. The first is from the concept of the human person:

> The human person possesses rights because of the very fact that it is a person, a whole, master of itself and of its acts, and which consequently is not merely a means to an end, but an end, an end which must be treated as such.[38]

Here we find Maritain arguing in a personalist and almost Kantian vein that the very nature of a person as a whole entails that the person can never be a mere means but must be treated as an end. This fact demands that her inviolable rights be respected.

The second argument follows from this consideration, arguing that since the natural teleology of the human person entails obligations under the natural law, one must have the rights commensurate with fulfilling these obligations:

> The notion of right and the notion of moral obligation are correlative. They are both founded on the freedom proper to spiritual agents. If man is morally bound to the things which are necessary to the fulfillment of his destiny, obviously, then, he has a right to fulfill his destiny; and if he has a right to fulfill his destiny he has the right to things necessary for this purpose.[39]

Both of these arguments appeal to the human person being by nature ordered to an end that transcends the political community, and thus are framed in distinctively religious and Christian terms.

This defense of universal human rights has, of course, been critiqued from various perspectives; however, the most persistent criticisms tend to arise from Maritain's coreligionists, such as De Koninck, who argue

---

37 *The Person and the Common Good*, 12.
38 *The Rights of Man and Natural Law*, 65.
39 *The Rights of Man and Natural Law*, 65.

that Maritain's move to the higher plane of the person's spiritual destiny ends up undermining the doctrine of the primacy of the common good. For his part, Maritain finds this objection unconvincing, as the political common good is only superior in its own order, while the human person is ordered to a good of a yet higher order in virtue of his or her spirituality.

More recently, a further concern similar to De Koninck's has been raised by a number of scholars, such as Frederick Crosson, Ralph McInerny, and Deborah Wallace. These scholars question whether Maritain's attempt to incorporate a largely liberal and Lockean notion of pre-political universal human rights really fits within the broader conception of the primacy of the common good within which he tries to situate it. These authors find Maritain's project of attempting to accommodate Thomist natural law theory to modern political pre-suppositions contradictory.[40] Yet arguably the reason De Koninck and others fail to make this connection to a universal theory of rights is because they lack the distinctive philosophical anthropology that Maritain offers.

---

40 While these generally traditional Catholic critics fail to mention the point, this is at least indirectly a critique of the Catholic Church's social teaching, which has largely taken up a strong defense of universal human rights as following from natural law in a manner similar to Maritain and is not merely a coincidence. See *Compendium of the Social Doctrine of the Church*, 140. The most prominent contemporary Catholic philosopher to reject the notion of rights is Alasdair MacIntyre. For a critical assessment of Maritain's position on rights in light of MacIntyre, see Ralph McInerny, "Maritain and Natural Rights," in *Art and Prudence: Studies in the Thought of Jacques Maritain* (Notre Dame, IN: University of Notre Dame Press, 1988), 123–36. This line of criticism has been renewed in the light of the more recent development of post-liberal and integralist political thought in Catholic circles. Tracey Rowland has argued that Maritain's attempt to use natural law as a *lingua franca* with liberal secularists and Protestants made some sense in the largely Christian culture of the twentieth-century, but was largely a failure due to the massive societal changes that began towards the end of his life and which have accelerated since. Tracey Rowland, "Natural Law: From Neo-Thomism to Nuptial Mysticism," *Communio* 35 (2008): 374–96. Her argument fails to acknowledge the degree to which the basis for Maritain's argument is metaphysical and anthropological and informed by his method of Christian philosophy, rather than a program for political practice. Maritain frequently sounds a pessimistic note with respect to prospects of practically implementing political philosophy. The post-liberal and integralist discussion to date is largely one of public discourse and has not yet received much sustained scholarly discussion. However, it can be noted that critics who accuse Maritain of seeking a reproachment with liberalism from this perspective fail to note his emphasis on the fact that a modern culture depends on Christians freely exercising holiness to transform the social and political orders. They also tend to ignore his significant critiques of liberal thought in areas such as free-market economics, international law and politics, and the rights of workers and of the poor—perhaps as these are areas where post-liberal intellectuals have found their own reproachment with the liberal order they claim to oppose.

Without Maritain's distinction between the individual and the person, it is natural to take such rights claims to be an assertion that the good of individual citizens trumps the common good. However, for Maritain, rights claims only suggest that the individual citizen is ordered to a good superior to the state which the state itself must recognize and cannot legitimately impede; it does not in any way undermine the citizen's obligation to serve the common good with a complete engagement even to the sacrifice of his or her life. It simply means that there are aspects of his or her life that are not the province of the state. Any account of universal rights inspired by Maritain would insist that these rights be situated in the context of social obligations to promote the common good, which in some cases can demand real sacrifices of citizens. Further, it would have to recognize that rights and moral obligations are, to use Maritain's term, "correlative." There can be no question of appealing to human rights as trumping the political common good authentically understood, nor of exalting the person's good at the expense of the community. Nor can such rights be taken to be minimal rights to non-interference. Rather, universal human rights, in Maritain's account, follow from the teleological ordination of the human person to the divine. Accordingly, a Catholic understanding of human rights in light of Maritain insists that rights have an objective grounding in the ontological order and that they cannot be considered in abstraction from the commensurate duties that give rise to them in the first place.[41]

For Maritain human rights follow from the fact that the person is ordered to God as an end that transcends the political order. Accordingly, they are possessed due to the fact that we live in the context of an ordered world amongst creatures of different natures, and because we have a nature that is ordered to goals that are spiritual, we have rights in relation to other human beings and creatures. In *Man and the State* Maritain makes explicit that he sees the metaphysics of human nature as the only adequate foundation for rights:

---

41 As will be seen below, it is also important to note that Maritain's list of human rights is considerably narrower, and closer to that of classical liberalism, than one would expect today.

It [the concept of natural rights] is only valid and rationally tenable if each existing individual has a nature or essence which is the locus of intelligible necessities and necessary truths, that is to say, if the realm of Nature taken as a constellation of facts and events envelops and reveals a realm of Nature taken as a universe of Essences transcending the fact and the event. In other words there is no right unless a certain order—which can be violated in fact—is inviolably required by what things are in their intelligible type or their essence by what the nature of man is, and is cut out for: an order by virtue of which certain things like life, work, freedom are due to the human person, an existent who is endowed with a spiritual soul and a free will.[42]

Yet this cannot be dismissed as merely religious and of no concern to those who don't share Maritain's Catholicism, because his claims about God are grounded in natural reason and are not limited to any particular creed. Accordingly, he argues, "Every human right possessed by man is possessed only by virtue of the right possessed by God, which is pure Justice, to see the order of His wisdom in beings respected, obeyed and loved by every intelligence."[43] Maritain clearly intends this not as a theological claim, but as a philosophical one.

Indeed it is not merely in regards to God that the person transcends the state, but also in apprehending truths of science, of wisdom, and of art. Here the state cannot dictate the results of such inquiries. Maritain insists that while the state can, in some circumstances, require a person whom it has educated as a philosopher to teach philosophy, it cannot force that person to adopt a particular philosophical doctrine, as that relies upon the truth of the matter as apprehended through that person's study.

This should be understood in contrast to various modern theories, taking their roots from Rousseau and the liberal philosophical traditions, that hold that the person is subject to no law but his own will and freedom. For Maritain such a view is an inadequate basis for human rights, as these rights then lack any logical limit. One is inevitably

---

42 *Man and the State*, 96–97.
43 *The Rights of Man and the Natural Law*, 66. *Man and the State*, 96.

entitled to develop one's own possibilities even at the expense of other creatures. Any attempts to limit this pursuit of self-fulfillment through a social contract or a principle against harm are illusory, as these too only have force insofar as the free will endorses them. When people formed in the philosophy of freedom encounter the impossible, they turn against rights or fall into skepticism. [44]

These abstract rights, however, need to be embodied in particular communities subject to various social and historical dynamics. Accordingly, Maritain distinguishes the natural law, which derives rights and duties from the first principle to do good and avoid evil in a necessary manner in virtue of our human nature itself, from both the law of nations (which he understands philosophically to mean the rights and duties that follow from that same first principle in a necessary manner, supposing the factual social conditions of civil society) and from positive law (the body of laws actually in force in a particular community that follow from the same first principle, but in a contingent manner, in virtue of the customs and culture of this or that community). However, the fundamental point is that both the law of nations and positive law have binding force upon the moral consciences of persons precisely because they flow from the natural law. Indeed, they are "prolongations or extensions of the natural law," passing into areas that are less determined directly by the mere consideration of human nature, and more or less informed by particular contexts.[45]

Human rights concern issues that are related to the first principle of moral reasoning, to do good and avoid evil, in a way that is directly related to human nature. Thus, the right to follow one's conscience in religious matters, to choose one's own vocation to pursue for work, to form a family, and to educate one's children are all rights of this order. Beyond this, however, there are rights that belong to one as a citizen or, as Maritain puts it, a civic person. These are political rights that come directly from the positive law and the constitution of particular political communities and depend only indirectly on the natural law. Here the

---

44 *The Rights of Man and the Natural Law,* 67. *Man and the State,* 82–83.
45 *The Rights of Man and the Natural Law,* 69–70.

goal sought is of the natural law, but the natural law leaves indeterminate the manner in which that goal is to be attained. So there is, for instance, a right to universal suffrage through which every adult citizen has a right to participation in the political life of society. However, the precise manner of this participation—the frequency of votes, the methods of forming political parties, and so forth—legitimately vary from one society to another.[46] Fundamental among these rights of citizens are (1) political equality that assures each citizen his status, security, and liberties in the State; (2) equality of all before the law, which requires an independent judiciary; and (3) equal admission of all citizens to public employment according to ability and free access to all professions without racial or social discrimination.[47]

Beyond these civil rights Maritain finds another more distinct category of rights: those of the social person, and in particular, of the person as a worker. Here he argues for the right to a just wage, to organize and form a union, etc. Underlying these rights is the view that the human person as a worker is in a relationship of justice to his or her employer as an adult, not a child or servant.[48] This is obviously opposed to slavery, but also to servitude in a more general way, such that authority over persons ought to be exercised for the benefit of the common good and not the particular good of the person in authority.[49]

Maritain is quite aware that the range of rights he has articulated will often find themselves in tension with one another. The various rights of the person limit each other, and this is perfectly normal (and indeed, necessary). He notes that in weighing these and making such judgments we are no longer addressing a merely philosophical issue about the different categories of human rights. Rather, we are concerned with the dynamic unification of these rights. This will take place in different types of societies that may give priority to individualist, communist, or personalist tendencies. Maritain implies that each society will have

46 *The Rights of Man and the Natural Law*, 83–87.
47 *The Rights of Man and the Natural Law*, 88.
48 *The Rights of Man and the Natural Law*, 96.
49 *The Rights of Man and the Natural Law*, 106. *Man and the State*, 104–6.

some supreme value or set of values, in light of which it limits and orders other considerations.[50] Accordingly, Maritain does not provide a fully worked-out way for communities to address the tensions that arise between competing rights claims. Rather, he seems to suggest that any resolution of such difficulties will depend upon how one prioritizes the range of goods being sought, and that frequently this is a prudential judgment in which one is guided by broader philosophical emphases that vary between cultures.

Pluralism, Rights, and Democracy

This issue of the tension between human rights raises the broader challenge of philosophical pluralism to a theory of rights. How do we achieve practical political collaboration in a world that is divided between people and cultures that have radically different conceptions of the good, human nature, and society? How do Christians, communists, libertarians, and others co-exist and collaborate in achieving common public goods between nations and even within a particular state? Maritain's fullest treatment of this question is presented in an inaugural address given to the second international conference of UNESCO on November 6th, 1947. In this lecture he notes that there is a basic paradox in UNESCO's mission, for the collaborative mission it envisages is to be carried out in a way that implies intellectual agreement among people who have radically different—and even opposed—visions of the world, culture, and knowledge. So different are these philosophical positions that we do not just have disagreement on substantive issues, but a failure at times to even understand the ideas one another use to express their views: "Every man's voice is but noise to his fellow-men."[51]

However, Maritain refuses to just give up on the task and counsels against limiting the aim to merely collecting documents, statistics, and surveys. Rather, he argues that a solution can be found by setting aside

50 *Man and the State*, 106.
51 *The Range of Reason*, 179.

theoretical differences, as important as these in fact are, in areas where there is a practical agreement about the ends to be pursued:

> Precisely because, as I pointed out at the beginning, Unesco's goal is a practical one, agreement among its members can be spontaneously achieved, not on common speculative notions but on common practical notions; not on the affirmation of the same conception of the world, man and knowledge, but on the affirmation of the same set of convictions concerning action. This is doubtless very little; it is the last refuge of intellectual agreement among men. It is, however, enough to undertake a great work, and it would mean a great deal to become aware of this body of common practical convictions.[52]

Accordingly, he notes that in reality people of very different theoretical positions can find in common a "practical ideology" and basic principles of action. Each party to this practical work will engage in it for different reasons. They will have their own rational justifications drawn from their own traditions. So long as they lead to the same conclusions about what must be done to agree upon fundamental human rights and to engage in the humanitarian work of providing food, health-care, basic education, etc., to those in need, these speculative differences do not need to be an obstacle to practical collaboration.

This does not mean that one doesn't need philosophical concepts and argumentation or that those differences are unimportant, but it does mean that we do not need to wait to resolve all of these differences before cooperating to address commonly recognized evils and to pursue commonly recognized goods:

> I am fully convinced that my way of justifying the belief in the rights of man and the ideal of liberty, equality, fraternity, is the only one which is solidly based on truth. That does not prevent me from agreeing on these practical tenets with those who are convinced that their way of justifying them, entirely different from mine, or even opposed to mine in its theoretical dynamism, is likewise the only one that is based on truth. Assuming they both believe in the

democratic charter a Christian and a rationalist will, nevertheless, give justifications that are incompatible with each other, to which their souls, their minds and their blood are committed and about these justifications they will fight. And God keep me from saying that it is not important to know which of the two is right! That is essentially important. They remain, however, in agreement on the practical affirmation of that charter and they can formulate together common principles of action.[53]

However important philosophical and theological disagreements are, in order to make science, culture, and education work towards the aim of peace and human well-being, all that is needed is a consensus on practical principles. What we demand is an agreement on a set of practical principles for action and a respect for fundamental human rights. We are not entitled to demand that others agree with our own justifications of these practical principles on which all agree. These principles form the basis of a common charter which is the basis for collaborative action among people of opposed intellectual and cultural frameworks. Maritain notes in particular that the Universal Declaration of Human Rights, which was, at the time, in the process of being drafted, is a vitally important example of this sort of practical agreement.

This approach is also at work in Maritain's justification of democracy. Intellectual pluralism is, of course, not only found between states but also within states, however unified they may be. While he allows that there may be within the body politic a group, even a substantial majority, that is inspired by a common world view (by the Christian faith, for instance), he notes that there is a need to recognize those belonging to other philosophical or religious creeds.[54] This diversity is not a problem so long as there is an adherence to the basic tenets of a society of free people. Here Maritain rejects a merely procedural liberal approach which would see government as a neutral arbiter of citizens with no substantive commitments of its own. Rather, there is a need for society to defend its conception of political and social life through acceptance of "a common human creed, the creed of freedom." Having

---

53 *The Range of Reason*, 180–81.
54 *Christianity and Democracy*, 28–29.

witnessed fascism arise from democratic systems he has no patience for a democracy that does not safeguard the freedom and rights its very existence presupposes. The content of this secular faith includes the broadly agreed-upon code of universal human rights and their commensurate responsibilities: human equality, ideals of fraternity, and mutual tolerance of various spiritualties and schools of thought. They are simply the broadest principles—implicitly, the most universal principles of natural law—upon which we can expect virtually universal agreement in modern societies.[55]

Democracy, therefore, requires a common faith in order to function. This is a secular faith, not a religious one. It is precisely those practical tenets that people of diverse and opposed theoretical dispositions can mutually adopt that form the basis of this secular faith. While these commitments have been historically awakened by the Gospel, they can be accepted independently of that source on other grounds. Thus, democracy requires acceptance of practical conclusions that are shared by all, while leaving open the issue of their theoretical justifications through philosophical or religious argumentation:

> The body politic has the right and the duty to promote among its citizens, mainly through education, the human and the temporal— and essentially practical—creed on which depend the national communion and civil peace. It has no right, as a merely temporal or secular body, enclosed in the sphere where the modern State enjoys its autonomous authority, to impose on the citizens or to demand from them a rule of faith or a conformism of reason, a philosophical or religious creed which would present itself as the only possible justification for the practical charter through which the people's common secular faith expresses itself. The important thing for the body politic is that the democratic sense be in fact kept alive by adherence of minds, however diverse, to this moral charter. The ways and the justifications by means of which this common adherence is brought about pertain to the freedom of minds and consciences.[56]

---

55 *Man and the State*, 112.
56 *Man and the State*, 111–12.

In protecting this moral charter from "political heretics" who reject the secular faith of the community, Maritain distinguishes between political activity and illegal activity of dissenters. Political activity ought to be met by opposing political activity freely developed by citizens in the body politic who are sufficiently enlivened by the community's ideals to defend them. Illegal activity, however, should be checked using the authority of the state.[57]

Oddly, however, Maritain argues that free expression may at times need to be restricted to protect the secular faith of the community. While he notes such coercion is the worst way to counter harmful ideas, he thinks it is sometimes necessary. He insists, however, that such interference cannot be of a doctrinal nature; it must be solely practical. For instance, the state should not be in the business of judging a work of art to be moral or immoral, but it can judge that an author or publisher is planning to make money selling obscenities. Likewise, the state need not judge theoretically if a political theory is "heretical" or counter to democratic faith; it is sufficient to make a practical judgement that the political heretic's action threatens the democratic charter through his or her action or propaganda.[58] These examples do not seem to be sufficient to draw a very clear distinction. His point is that the state is not equipped to deal with matters of intellectual truth and must restrict itself to the practical sphere of action that threatens its existence. But this seems to be at odds with his claim that political activity of those who reject human rights and the core values of democratic society should be met by the opposing—but free—activity of citizens. If this is the case, it is hard to see why speech and writing opposing these ideals should not also be met by freely produced arguments defending them. In this respect his encouragement of positive means, and in particular democratic education, seems a more coherent solution to the problem of those who dissent from human rights and democratic ideals.

It is important to understand that Maritain views his defense of democracy as a consequence of his Christianity. With the dissolution

57 *Man and the State*, 115.
58 *Man and the State*, 118.

of cultural and religious unity in the medieval period, modernity has had to face directly the fact of pluralism. The democratic spirit that rejects all forms of servitude is the one most in keeping with the Christian vision of human dignity. This doesn't mean that Christian faith requires every sincere Christian to be a democrat. Rather, it means that the democratic impulse has, as a matter of historical fact, arisen as a temporal manifestation inspired by Christian commitments. Beyond its commitments in the Creed, Christianity has acted as a leaven in social and political life, bringing temporal hope to humanity.[59] Further, Christian faith is needed to sustain the democracy, for we need to have confidence in the abilities of our all too fallible fellow citizens to govern the temporal order.[60]

Maritain's defence of democracy is quite simple:

> Once the man of common humanity has understood that he is born with the right to conduct his own life by himself, as a being responsible for his acts before God and the law of the community, how can the people be expected to obey those who govern unless it is because the latter have received from the people themselves the custody of the people's common good?[61]

If one has a right to conduct one's private life, then there is no justification to demand that one obey the rulers of a community unless the people have granted those rulers responsibility.

In view of this Maritain examines how authority is given and functions in a democratic state. He begins by distinguishing authority (the right to command and be obeyed), from power (the force that can be used to compel others to obey). In a well-functioning state these go together. To separate them is to divorce power from justice.[62] Maritain sees this right to govern as flowing from the natural law. Since human nature requires life in a community to achieve its natural ends, and since the state of social communities requires that some structure give

---

59 *Christianity and Democracy,* 29.
60 *Christianity and Democracy,* 49–50.
61 *Christianity and Democracy,* 41.
62 "Democracy and Authority," in *Scholasticism and Politics,* 94.

commands for the common good, then this commanding function is a requirement of the natural law and implies a right to command and govern. If this right is clear in direct democracies, it is also clear in larger and more diverse societies, in which a decision of the people entrusts to representatives the right to rule so long as the process of their selection is open and free. In such a case, their right to govern is of the natural law and the obligation to obey just directives from them is binding in conscience. Accordingly, the obligation to obey the laws and directives of a legitimate democratic authority does not arise merely because they have been formed in keeping with the right procedure. That is indispensable; nevertheless, those laws and directives must also be just.[63]

Consequently, Maritain's account of democracy is radically opposed to that of Rousseau, which he refers to as a "democracy of the individual" in contrast to his own "democracy of the person." For Rousseau democracy arises out of a desire to obey only oneself. Through participation in a democracy the citizens hand authority to the "general will," which is to be obeyed precisely because it is the will of the people. For Maritain, commands not only need to be democratic, but they must also be just—and thus be participations in, and expressions of, the natural law.

Thus, Maritain sees democratic governance as having its true authority from God. While authority in a democracy derives immediately from the agreement of the people through their right to govern themselves, it does so "as from a channel through which nature causes the body politic to be and to act."[64] This occurs in the way that the authority of self-governance is not just held by the people in a transitory way, as mere instrumental causes that invest the government with authority. Rather, the people are possessed of this right and authority inherently. Further, in giving authority to those who govern, the people do not divest themselves of their right to self-government and authority.

63 *Man and the State,* 126–27. "Democracy and Authority," in *Scholasticism and Politics,* 103. For further development of these ideas in keeping with Maritain's approach also see Yves R. Simon, *A General Theory of Authority* (Notre Dame, IN: The University of Notre Dame Press, 1991).
64 *Man and the State,* 127.

In giving democratic authority to a government the people do not transfer and thereby lose this right.[65]

Crucial to this explanation is the distinction between the possession of a right and the exercise of it. In exercising the right to self-government the people choose rulers to be invested with authority. In doing so they restrict the future exercise of their right to govern themselves for a specified time and for the purposes of a particular office, etc. This in no way, however, ends or lessens the possession of that right as such. It only entails that future uses of this right may be limited by the present exercise of it.[66] This is crucial, since the rulers are not vicars or images of God, as the proponents of the divine right of kings may have supposed. Rather, they are vicars of the people. Hence, democratic rulers possess *per participationem* (by participation) the very same authority to govern that exists in the people *per essentiam* (essentially) given by God.[67]

It is common to interpret Maritain as though his thought were motivated by concrete political concerns and to see him as trying to establish a theoretical framework for Catholics to participate in action against fascist ideologies through a Catholic minimalism founded upon a historical ideal of a Christian, but profane, conception of temporal conditions.[68] In this manner his thought is seen as providing the conditions for a political program of collaboration with the secular world. This view sees his rationale for collaboration with the UN's Charter as the central point of his political thought. While there certainly are political goals and implications to his thought, his aim is certainly not to present a compromised or watered-down Christianity that is at ease in the modern liberal world. Rather, what Maritain recognized was that the problem of history itself imposes on us the need for a humanism of the person—indeed, of every person. Historical reality presents us with the concrete historical ideal of a profane Christian conception of temporal realities in a way that cannot be a simple return to God's sacral

---

65 *Man and the State*, 128–29.

66 *Man and the State*, 135.

67 *Man and the State*, 135.

68 See Robert Song, "Jacques Maritain and the Liberal Defence of Pluralism," in *Christianity and Liberal Society* (Oxford: Oxford University Press, 2006), 128–75.

empire over things, "but the idea of the *holy freedom* of the creature whom grace unites to God."[69] Thus, in Maritain's way of thinking, neither human rights nor democracy can survive, let alone thrive, for long without a new resurgence of Christian spirit and thought, for the freedom offered by the liberal political order on its own is but a caricature of this authentic freedom.

Maritain's political philosophy is notable for the way in which he adopts traditional Aristotelian and Thomistic concepts, such as the common good and the natural law, and adapts them to support very modern notions of human rights and democracy. It is quite clear that he consciously goes beyond his sources. Nevertheless, he remains faithful to his project of creative appropriation of Aquinas, as he is trying to draw out what he sees as the logical consequences of the principles he finds in the medieval tradition. It remains a hotly disputed point whether his philosophy is successful in bringing traditional concepts to bear upon modern political discourse, or whether he gives too much ground to forms of classical liberalism that are being called into question in this postmodern age. However one answers this question, no one can deny that his attempt to engage the dialogue opens upon new possibilities to correct some of the challenges of each tradition in light of the other.

---

69 *Integral Humanism*, 256.

CHAPTER 9

Philosophy of Education

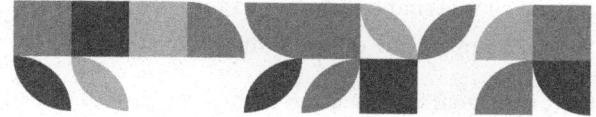

It is by virtue of the allure of beautiful things
and deeds and ideas that the child is to be led
and awakened to intellectual and moral life.
Education at the Crossroads, 61

P hilosophy of education occupies a unique place within Maritain's thought, as it is a locus where the principles of knowledge, ethics and political philosophy come together in practice in the formation of a society's children. Accordingly, it provides a helpful instance to see how Maritain would envision the application of his philosophical principles in practice. In this chapter, three aspects of his philosophy of education will be explored: (1) his account of the aims of education, (2) the means of education, particularly, the dispositions to be fostered in students and the broad rules educators should follow in order to successfully achieve the aim of their task, and finally, (3) his reflections on the moral dimensions of education. These themes are primarily addressed in his 1943 book *Education at the Crossroads* and in a collection of his addresses on the topic under the title *The Education of Man*, which was edited by Donald and Idella Gallagher in 1962.

The Aim of Education

Maritain describes the aim of education in a way that captures its centrality for human life, writing: "Thus the chief task of education is above all to shape man, or to guide the evolving dynamism through which man forms himself as a man."[1] He later describes this primary aim evocatively as "the conquest of internal freedom."[2] In this context he further specifies his earlier account of the end of education, stating:

> Thus the prime goal of education is the conquest of internal and spiritual freedom to be achieved by the individual person, or, in other words, his liberation through knowledge and wisdom, good will, and love.[3]

The task of education is nothing less than to prepare the person to achieve his or her ultimate goal in life. It is important to note that in speaking of the "spiritual" here, Maritain indicates that he is referring to intentional activities directed toward an object with an objective goal that measures and rules these activities. Accordingly, he is not concerned with the merely natural actualization of one's potential or a merely moral preparation for the sake of social order. Rather, education aims to prepare the student to learn the truth and to live in light of that truth, which is to open the person to the infinite which transcends us, while leading us to a "conquest of being" through the progressive attainment of new truths or the renewed understanding of the significance of truths already attained.[4] Education apprentices the student in the art of the humanities' two highest activities: knowing and loving.

---

1   *Education at the Crossroads* (New Haven, CT: Yale University Press, 1943), 1.
2   *Education at the Crossroads*, 10.
3   *Education at the Crossroads*, 11.
4   *Education at the Crossroads*, 12. See also Mario O. D'Sousa, *A Catholic Philosophy of Education: The Church and Two Philosophers* (Montreal & Kingston: McGill-Queen's University Press, 2016), 91–98.

This account of the aim of education is articulated in the context of discussing what Maritain takes to be seven misconceptions about education. The first problem is a general lack of awareness of what the genuine ends of education are. The problem with this is that it leads to a disordered focus on cultivating the means of education, without a clear sense of what those means are ultimately meant to achieve. This leads education to lose its practicality, however more refined its educational techniques may become. Maritain sees this tendency to give supremacy to the means of education over its end as the "main reproach" to contemporary education. In general, he recognizes the most current pedagogical means are typically an improvement over the previous ones, but his worry is that we become so fascinated with them because they are efficient and measurable that we lose sight of the real ends that they are to serve:

> The child is so well tested and observed, his needs so well detailed, his psychology so clearly cut out, the methods of making it easy for him everywhere so perfected, that the end of all of these commendable improvements runs the risk of being forgotten or disregarded.[5]

Maritain compares this to the case of a physician who is so fascinated with a careful analysis and monitoring of the patient's condition that he forgets to administer the medicine he needs to heal his disease.

The second misconception arises from false ideas of the end of education. Here Maritain has in mind those whose view of the end of education abstracts from philosophical considerations. Since the end of education is to aid the human person in attaining the end of the person as such, education is necessarily bound up with one's philosophical anthropology. In fact, the primary end of education as articulated above is determined by human nature itself.[6] In this context Maritain considers the contrast between a merely scientific conception of the person and a philosophical-religious one. A purely scientific idea of humanity

---

5   *Education at the Crossroads*, 3.
6   *The Education of Man*, eds. Donald and Idella Gallagher (New York: Doubleday and Co., 1967), 50.

can provide us with valuable insights and information that assist in refining the tools we use in education. But in itself it is inadequate to ground a theory of education, for this requires that we know "what man is" and what scale of values human development involves. The scientific method, as we have seen, of its very nature has no resources to deal with these issues that are philosophical of their very nature.[7] In contrast to this Maritain develops his distinction between the individual and the person, which was explored in the previous chapter. In this context this distinction is used to show the danger of educating children as if they were merely individuals, paying insufficient attention to their spiritual capacities of knowing and loving. By virtue of being persons they are not merely parts of some collective but autonomous wholes each with a distinctive end. This again points the educator to the child's interior life as the primary concern:

> Thus what is of most importance in educators themselves is a respect for the soul as well as the body of the child, the sense of his innermost essence and his internal resources, and a sort of sacred and loving attention to his mysterious identity, which is a hidden thing that no techniques can reach. And what matters most in the education enterprise is a perpetual appeal to intelligence and free will in the young.[8]

The third misconception is that of pragmatism. While acknowledging there are many good things that arise from a practical disposition, Maritain rejects pragmatism as a viable foundation for education. Life is not just a matter of pursuing particular goals of career, wealth, etc. Rather, life exists for an end that makes it worthy of being lived. In this sense pragmatism will always be guilty of misconstruing the goal of education. More basically, however, Maritain insists that human action always springs from some awareness of the truth:

> At the beginning of human action, insofar as it is human, there is truth, grasped or believed to be grasped for the sake of truth. Without trust in truth, there is no human effectiveness.[9]

In placing the real at the disposition of the useful, pragmatism ironically renders itself ineffective rather than useful. While it has brought about innumerable benefits, particularly through renewing focus on the human subject, it goes wrong in giving priority to the learning subject at the expense of the object to be learned. Accordingly, the pragmatist ends up disregarding the primacy of the object to be taught and fostering a "cult of means without an end," only to result in a "psychological worship of the subject."[10]

The fourth misconception that he identifies is sociologism. This misconception seems to involve two errors. The first is to take the primary aim of education to be shaping the student to lead a normal and useful life in the community. This is obviously a necessary aim for education, but it is only a secondary aim. Education must first and foremost be concerned with making the student a mature and responsible person; it is only secondarily concerned with making him or her a productive citizen. These goals are, of course, not unrelated, for one becomes a mature and fulfilled adult only in the context of one's society and culture through living civic virtues.[11] The second and fundamental problem is to take standards of the purposes and values that form the student to have no firmer basis than the intellectual conventions that emerge through the particular social dynamics at play in any given time. This is itself closely related to the pragmatic theory that requires perpetual reconstruction of the educator's goals. Such an approach "teaches educational recipes but gets away from any real art of education." In losing sight of the actual goals of education and replacing them with a vague goal such as "continuous and further growth," sociologism leads back to the original error of losing sight of the goal of education. To educate

---

9   *The Education of Man*, 47. *Education at the Crossroads*, 13.
10 *Education at the Crossroads*, 14.
11 *Education at the Crossroads*, 15.

in this way would be like an architect trying to plan a building without knowing its purpose.[12]

Maritain's fifth misconception is the error of intellectualism. This error can take two forms: classical and modern. In its classical form, intellectualism views the highest goals of education to lie in cultivating dialectical and rhetorical skill. In its modern guise it involves the repudiation of universal values, emphasizing instead scientific and technological achievements. This leads to a misplaced emphasis upon specialization at the service of the technological organization of life. Under such a conception education is at risk of being replaced by job training. Maritain insists, in contrast to Plato, that specialization on a single functional task is more characteristic of non-rational animals than it is of human beings. Accordingly, an intellectualism that reduces education to functional training also reduces human life to the pursuit of economic values, empirically scientific inquiry, and cheap pleasure or social entertainments: "The overwhelming cult of specialization dehumanizes man's life."[13]

This modern form of intellectualism is a particular threat to a democratic society, since democracy requires a faith in the intelligence and good will of ordinary citizens to make judgments about society and our common life in a way that defies restricting one's judgment to one's own specialized vocational competence. Accordingly, such an intellectualist vision of education would suggest political judgments be left in the hands of experts.[14]

The sixth misconception—and one of the most influential—is that of voluntarism. Voluntarism has its roots in the philosophy of Schopenhauer, particularly, in the claims that the intelligence is subservient to the will and that the will is guided by irrational forces. In practice this means one of two things: either education ought to focus upon disciplining the will to some national standard, or it should be open to the free expansion of natural capabilities. The best forms of voluntarism

---

12 *Education at the Crossroads,* 15.
13 *Education at the Crossroads,* 19.
14 *Education at the Crossroads,* 19–20.

were presented as correctives to intellectualist errors, recalling the importance of voluntary functions of morality, virtue, and generosity in education. After all, preliminary education is more ordered towards producing a good person rather than a learned one.

However, this ideal was rarely realized in practice, its greatest successes occurring in the service of evil in the Nazi training camps, disregarding truth in the mind to make the intellect merely an instrument of the of the state. When Maritain was writing in 1943, this was more than an academic worry. Voluntarism was subject to this abuse, since it works best in the context of technical training. Accordingly, the greatest objection to voluntarism is that it fails to produce the moral development it so enticingly offers. Moving beyond intellectualism to educate feelings and form the character of the student is all well and good, but there is no generic recipe by which the educator can reliably achieve such goals. In fact, having disregarded the appropriate role of the intellect, voluntarism leaves itself inevitably open to abuse. It does not succeed in forming the will, but in undermining the intellect by exaggerating the role of the will and extending it into the sphere of thought. Maritain eloquently sums up his rejection of this error in writing,

> We believe that intelligence is in and by itself nobler than the will of man, for its activity is more immaterial and universal. But we believe also that, in regard to the things or the very objects on which this activity bears, it is better to will and love the good than simply to know it. Moreover it is through man's will, when it is good, not through his intelligence, be it ever so perfect, that man is made good and right. A similar intermingling of roles is to be found in education taken in its broadest sense. The upbringing of the human being must lead both intelligence and will toward achievement, and the shaping of the will is throughout more important to man than the shaping of the intellect. Yet, whereas the educational system of schools and colleges succeeds as a rule

in equipping man's intellect for knowledge, it seems to be miss-
ing its main achievement, the equipping of man's will. What an
infelicity![15]

Maritain's position is that education deals *directly* with the formation
of the intellect, and through this intellectual formation it bears *indirectly*, but most importantly, upon the will. As Mario D'Souza, CSB
has pointed out, this establishes a critical relationship between education and wisdom that is rooted within the contemplative dimension of
education, where a desire for knowledge for its own sake is cultivated.[16]

The seventh and final misconception is the presumption that everything can be learned. The final challenge for education is for Maritain
a paradoxical one, namely, that the most important task in education is
not education or learning. This leads him to confront the presumption
that everything can be learned. Maritain gently mocks this view, saying
it implies colleges ought to propose courses on how to acquire creative
brilliance, consoling those in sorrow, or becoming generous.

Yet he notes a great emphasis in education ought to be given to how
to rightly resolve practical cases and to shape the power of judgement
through a will that is rightly ordered. But this experience of the virtue
of prudence cannot be replaced through a lesson. It requires experience
for which there is no merely cognitive replacement. This is why a college can offer courses in philosophy, but not in wisdom. Intuition and
love are the greatest things in a person's life, and maturing in these is a
principal aim of education, and yet there is no training or learning to
be had in these matters; they are "gift and freedom."[17]

In this respect, Maritain is also clearly aware that education occurs
outside of the school. In fact, the family and the Church are the most
important spheres of learning for the child, particularly in terms of
forming moral character. He is certainly not Pollyanna-ish about these

---

15   *Education at the Crossroads,* 22.
16   Mario O. D'Souza, CSB, "Maritain's Philosophy of Education and Religious Education," *Catholic
     Education: A Journal of Inquiry and Practice* 4, no. 3 (2001): 377. See also *Education at the
     Crossroads,* 28.
17   *Education at the Crossroads,* 23.

institutions either, recognizing that poor experiences of family life or the Church have led to much trauma for many children. However, he argues the solution to this is not to dispense with these natural and prior forms of association, but to rectify and support them to serve their aims more fruitfully.

The school itself is primarily concerned with knowledge and education, even if there are more important experiences in terms of moral maturing that happen partly there. In the educational process itself the central concern of the educator is attentiveness to and in collaboration with the mind of the child, who is the active agent in her own education:

> From the very start the teacher must respect in the child the dignity of the mind, must appeal to the child's power of understanding, and conceive of his own effort as preparing a human mind to think for itself. The one who does not yet know must believe a master, but only in order to know, and maybe to reject at this very moment the opinions of the master; and he believes him provisionally, only because of the truth which the teacher is supposed to convey.[18]

Accordingly, moral education occurs primarily in an indirect way through the manner in which the school teaches and conveys knowledge to the student, not by merely giving speculative reasons. Rather, the student will become prudent and learn the ways of practical wisdom by being part of a community of mature and virtuous teachers. The will is not as likely to be moved by a regimen of training under a set of rules as it will be by the cultivation of practical reasoning in the company of those experienced in its exercise.

The Student and the Teacher

Turning from the theoretical questions around the aim of education to its practice in the classroom, we find Maritain giving consideration to the dynamic between the teacher and student. Maritain expresses the role of the teacher rather poetically: "Teaching is an art; the teacher is an artist." However, he immediately qualifies this judgment with further

---

18 *Education at the Crossroads*, 26.

analysis. The appropriate understanding of this metaphor is not to think of the teacher as a fine artist, such as a sculptor or a painter, whose task is to impose the form to be known upon the passive matter of the rock or canvas. Rather, he sees the teacher being an artist in the way that a craftsman is an artist who has to cooperate with the nature of the subject upon which he works. In this sense the teacher is like a physician who does something that is genuinely effective in restoring the patient to health, but who must carry out this healing art through applying dietary guidelines, exercise, and medicine that work in keeping with the nature and activity of the patient. Accordingly, teaching is an art of ministering to the student and must be subservient to the student's nature.[19]

Maritain naturally rejects the Platonic view that the teacher does nothing but draw out knowledge that is already present within the student. Instead he holds that the active principle that gives rise to knowledge is present within each person. This is the inner ability of the intellect to see, which from the very start of our intellectual life, originates in sense experience and through eidetic visualization (i.e., abstraction) arrives at the first principles and notions upon which all knowledge depends, allowing reason to move from what it knows to what is yet to be known. The role of the teacher is to cooperate with and foster the work of this activity of the intellect:

> This inner vital principle the teacher must respect above all; his art consists in imitating the ways of the intellectual nature in its own operations. Thus the teacher has to offer to the mind either examples from experience or particular statements which the pupil is able to judge by virtue of what he already knows and from which he will go on to discover broader horizons. The teacher has further to comfort the mind of the pupil by putting before his eyes the logical connections between ideas which the analytical or deductive power of the pupil's mind is perhaps not strong enough to establish by itself.[20]

---

19 *Education at the Crossroads*, 30. See also Mario O. D'Sousa, *A Catholic Philosophy of Education: The Church and Two Philosophers* (Montreal & Kingston: McGill-Queen's University Press, 2016), 155–58.

20 *Education at the Crossroads*, 31.

While the teacher has a critical role to play, it is nevertheless secondary and at the service of the student's own intrinsic principle of understanding. Accordingly, any method of teaching that resorts to force or sees the teacher as the primary agent in the learning process is a bad method.

In reflecting upon the appropriate relation of teacher to student it is important to recall Maritain's distinction between the individual and the person, which we explored in the previous chapter. While being two aspects of one and the same reality (i.e., the human being), these designate two distinct spheres that can be fostered. Individuality designates the "material ego," namely, the instinctive tendencies that one has due to one's physical body and heredity. By contrast, personality designates the mastery and independence of the spiritual self. If the despotic method of education fails by suppressing the student's personality, an anarchic model that fosters free spontaneity and eschews self-discipline risks letting the student's true personality be submerged within and overrun by her individuality. Accordingly, it is important that the educator not confuse the spontaneous expression of individuality, one's base instincts or ill-formed habits, with a genuine development of the person as such. Personality grows insofar as reason and authentic freedom dominate over instinct and sensual desire; it is most typically expressed in self-sacrifice and a striving toward self-improvement and love. In an anarchic form of education the development of personality is confused with a self that is torn between base desires and passions that it can neither understand nor control.

The authentic growth the educator seeks to cultivate is rather one of self-perfection in knowledge and love. Further, the discipline required is not a matter of submitting oneself to rules or standards from outside, but rather a development towards a fuller realization of one's own identity:

> Man's perfection consists of the perfection of love, and so is less the perfection of his "self" than the perfection of his love, where the very self is in some measure lost sight of. And to advance in this self-perfection is not to copy an ideal. It is to let yourself be led by Another where you did not want to go, and to let Divine Love

Who calls each being by his own name mold you and make of you a person, a true original, not a copy.[21]

In keeping with this insight, Maritain notes five basic dispositions that the teacher ought to seek to foster in the student and four rules for the teacher.

Dispositions to be fostered in the student:

1. Love of truth: this is the basic disposition of an intellectual nature.
2. Love of the good and justice: this is also a natural disposition for the human person and is expressed in love of heroic action.
3. Openness to existence: the disposition of a being who exists gladly, is unashamed of what he is, and accepts the natural limitations of his existence with simplicity.
4. Satisfaction in a job well done: this is not just a matter of working hard, but a sense of respect for the task to be done and an acceptance of responsibility for it.
5. A sense of cooperation: a willingness to play an active part in the social and political life of one's community.

Norms of education for the teacher:

1. Foster the fundamental dispositions that enable the student (i.e., the principal agent in education) "to grow in the life of the mind." Encouragement and liberation of what is best in the student is vital and is the most effective means of repressing any negative tendencies. Encouragement is as necessary as humiliation is harmful.
2. Center attention on the inner dynamism of the student's own personality. Stress needs to be given to the internalization of education. This is not to be understood as a training of the subconscious of the student by means of scientific technique, which would be to undermine both reason and freedom. Rather, it is a matter of unlocking the creative potential of the student's intuitive and conceptual resources,

---

21 *Education at the Crossroads,* 36.

without stifling it with an overemphasis on memorization or assimilation of overly specialized and detailed information. The overriding concern is to free the intellect's intuitive power: "The great thing is the awakening of inner resources and creativity. The cult of technical means considered as improving the mind and producing science by their own virtue must give way to respect for the spirit and the dawning intellect of man!"[22]

3. The entire work of education should be ordered towards the internal unity of man rather than his dispersion. This is, above all, achieved by having the student bring together intellectual and physical forms of work, particularly manual training in mechanics and crafts. In addition to its intrinsic benefits, it helps undermine the social tendency to distinguish the learned from the laborer and underscores the truth that all education begins from experience.[23]

4. Teaching must liberate intelligence instead of burdening it. This simply means that effective teaching liberates the mind by giving it a mastery through reason over the things that are learned. Here Maritain quotes the method of Pascal's father, who reportedly insisted that the child must always "be kept above his work." The child must be able to master the lessons that are given and to actually understand, rather than merely successfully repeat, whatever is presented. Knowledge cannot be passively received as dead information. It needs to be actively transformed into understanding by the life of the student's mind: "Reason which receives knowledge in a servile manner does not really know and is only depressed by a knowledge which is not its own, but that of others."[24]

In view of these dispositions it is helpful to compare Maritain's approach with that of the American pragmatist philosopher John Dewey (1859–1952). Dewey was unquestionably the most influential philosopher of education of the twentieth century and his ideas remain profoundly important for educators even today. Dewey's philosophy of

---

22 *Education at the Crossroads*, 43.
23 *Education at the Crossroads*, 45–46.
24 *Education at the Crossroads*, 50.

education advocated progressive methods that would engage the student's own interests and make the student an active participant in the learning process. Accordingly, he was a critic of more traditional pedagogies that focused primarily on an objective content in the curriculum that the student passively received, with an emphasis on skills such as memorization and recitation. In this respect his view shares deep similarities with that of Maritain, who saw the educator as an instrumental aid to the student's own educational activity, and saw the first task of the educator as providing a context in which the student can come to love the subject at hand. However, these superficial similarities at the level of method risk obscuring the deeper differences between their respective philosophies of education.

The root of their differences lies in radically distinct philosophical anthropologies. For Dewey, human beings are to be understood primarily in biological terms as living organisms in a process of evolution. Living is a matter of growing and life itself needs no defense or rational justification.[25] Thus, the child to be educated is viewed primarily from the scientific viewpoint, whereas for Maritain, it is important to insist that we view the child from the widest and deepest possible perspective, as a person who is both material and spiritual. Further, for Dewey, in sharp contrast to Maritain, education has no end beyond itself. It is its own end.[26] As Laurence Stott has pointed out, it may appear that Dewey's appeal to science grounds his anthropology in a more public form of evidence than that of Maritain. However, Maritain can also appeal to the equally public acknowledgment of the universal quest for beauty, which cannot be explained in terms of environmental selection. The universal phenomenon of love also suggests, both privately and publicly, that survival is not life's only, or most important, value. While the stomach does indeed hunger for its daily bread, so, too, does the human spirit long for and need Truth, Beauty, and Goodness.[27] By contrast, in Dewey's philosophy of education is for the sake of growth, but if one asks

25 John Dewey, *Democracy and Education* (New York: MacMillan, 1916), 2 and 285.
26 Dewey, *Democracy and Education*, 49.
27 Laurence Stott, "Dewey a Disaster?" *Westminster Studies in Education* 18, no. 1 (2006): 28.

towards what goal, Dewey can only reply, growth towards more growth. On this view, life is empirically given and its development requires no justification, nor does it appear to require any objective purpose.

The different views of education result from this deeper anthropological difference. For Dewey it is natural that the interests of the child be the primary drive behind educational growth. Natural biological interests such as activity and self-expression should be used by schools as a basis to encourage social intelligence. Since growth towards maturity is fundamentally biological, the role of the teacher is simply to guide it, not to act as an authority figure. Where Dewey relies on interest to foster education, Maritain relies on conscience. Whereas Dewey finds knowledge always provisional and dependent on testing, Maritain holds that we can directly know spiritual values through a connatural affectivity for the good. This is important, for the book was written in the midst of World War II. Accordingly, Maritain was rightfully horrified by a pragmatic approach that would see evil as a mere social shriveling or an extinction through a lack of growth. Rather, such evil was a violation of the spiritual absolute and a tremendous distortion of the human being.[28] This is not to say that certain elements of Dewey's theory of education— such as his transformation of scientific method into pedagogy by using problem-solving approaches in active learning to engage students—are without value. However, Maritain would insist that problems should be resolved in an intellectual apprehension of truth that provides some content to be known, not merely a provisional process to be superseded by some more sophisticated method in the future.

Moral Education: A Shared Responsibility

We have already noted that the school has an important role in moral education. However, the direct and primary responsibility of the school is the cultivation of knowledge in the student. The school must primarily teach the student how to think. However, in virtue of this function the school also indirectly has a role in forming the student to think

---

28 Stott, "Dewey a Disaster?" 29.

and act in a morally mature manner. The primary responsibility for moral education rests with the student's family and religious community, should she have one.

The family is the natural context for moral education. This is natural because education in love is the primary basis for any sort of authentic development in morality, and love is not something that can be learned through a training program. Rather, love is primarily a gift of God that comes to us through nature and grace. Love of God is a communion in friendship and virtue that grows through its own activity:

> There are no human methods or techniques of getting or developing charity, no more than any kind of love. There is nevertheless education in this matter: an education which is provided by trial and suffering, and which primarily consists in removing impediments and obstacles to love, and first of all sin, and in developing moral virtues.[29]

While educators have a role to play in this, it is primarily in the family where the pattern of love is imbibed. Maritain is not blind to the shortcomings and deficiencies that can arise in family life. He is aware that the economic and social pressures of the modern world often bring negative—and even tragic—consequences to the family in many cases. Yet he holds that it is an essential dimension of the natural course of events that love develops in the family and that the normal beginnings in one's moral and religious formation occur in the context of the family, however problematic this may be in particular instances. The examples of one's parents, the stories of one's ancestors, the experience of common trials, sufferings, and hopes bring about a daily experience of love and labor in the midst of tenderness and discipline that naturally acquaints the child with love and gives ethical guidance. While the history of the family is no better than the history of any other social group, while there are cases of abuse and neglect, Maritain insists that family life is something that is part and parcel of human nature, so in the ordinary case the role of the family is paramount:

29 *The Education of Man*, 118.

Even at the most mediocre average level, nature at play in family life has its own spontaneous ways of compensating after a fashion for its own failures, its spontaneous processes of self-regulation, which nothing can replace, and provides the child with a moral formation and an experience of mutual love, however deficient it may be, which nothing can replace.[30]

A flawed family is, in all but the worst cases, better than no family at all. To want to repudiate the family because we find dramatic cases of failures would be like noting that many baby birds fall out of nests, and trying to remedy the problem by destroying all the generally well-prepared nests mother birds make in order to replace them with artificial cages.

Nevertheless, the family's efforts will usually be supplemented by the child's experience at school. Maritain, however, notes that the school is not a mere instrument of either the family or of the state. It has its own autonomy over its sphere of concern, that is, education in the various disciplines it teaches. While the school can demand that a teacher teach mathematics or physics, it cannot demand that the teacher teach something except in accordance with the principles of these disciplines. When it comes to morals the school does not ordinarily engage in a direct training of the will, but in the formation and enlightenment of the student's practical reasoning. As we have seen, the school's involvement in moral education is indirect, and typically a consequence of its direct responsibility for intellectual formation. In this respect, Maritain's thought is in keeping with that of Dewey, who also argues against the folly of introducing courses that would teach one how to be moral. Rather, both philosophers would agree that morality is conveyed to the student not through the curriculum, but through the lived activity and community of the school.[31]

In this respect, Maritain introduces a paradox. The school must be involved in the moral education of the child, but knowledge of morality,

---

30 *The Education of Man*, 121.

31 John Dewey, *The Moral Principles of Education* (Boston: Houghton Mifflin Company, 1909), viii.

while necessary, is insufficient to bring about the moral development of the student. As Aristotle rightly argued against Socrates and Plato, virtue is not merely knowledge. One can be an expert in morality and yet be a rascal. Knowing alone does not produce virtue. Rather, what produces virtue is love. However, love requires overcoming our powerful tendencies towards egoism and selfishness. This requires a depth of love that transcends love of oneself or the love of one's own group to embrace all persons. Such a love he finds plausible only when it is rooted in a love of God, which has God as its very source.[32] Thus, he finds a vital connection between morality and religion; consequently, there is a role not only for the school and the family, but also for the Church, in the moral education of youth.

In carrying out its functions in this area, Maritain warns against the temptations for a school, felt with particular strength in a pluralistic context, of a sociological approach that would aim to educate the student to be merely a useful citizen familiar with and compliant to the mores of her culture. Such a method would be gravely inadequate, if only for the simple reason that a vital dimension of moral education is to be true to one's conscience in commitment to the moral truth one has apprehended, even should it fly in the face of an erroneous culture, even if one must suffer persecution for one's convictions. There would be no place for a hero of the calibre of Socrates or Gandhi in a school whose moral teaching was aimed merely at functioning well and fitting in with society. Moral teaching, regardless of the tradition in which it occurs, must aim to be grounded in truth rather than in mere social convenience.[33] Here Maritain is again challenging the mainstream views of the prominent secular philosopher of education John Dewey. Although he held that education did not serve a moral end or any end beyond itself, Dewey did clearly hold that the role of the school was to prepare

---

32 *The Education of Man*, 115. While he recognizes a non-believer may be ethical, he questions whether such ethical living is not itself influenced by having unwittingly imbibed Christian values to some degree from a shared history and culture with Christians, and also whether a rich moral life can persist in a community for many generations without some religious basis. See page 117.

33 *The Education of Man*, 106 and 117. See also *Education at the Crossroads*, 93.

students for their future life as citizens in democratic society. As Dewey writes, "Apart from participation in the social life, the school has no moral end nor aim."[34] By contrast Maritain clearly held that education has a vital moral purpose, even if it is best approached only indirectly in the school.

For Maritain the need to offer students education implies a role for religion, however informal and indirect this may be. This gives rise to a need for both religious education and moral formation, as well as a need to educate children to take their place in a society that is inevitably diverse. He notes that this will obviously require different treatment in a denominational school than it will in one that is public or nonreligious. In denominational schools the need for religious and moral education is obviously provided for through the faith tradition to which the school adheres. Maritain has quite high expectations here, insisting that the entire life and outlook of the school's activities be framed by the school's religious and spiritual point of view. The challenge in such a context is to avoid the student's being ignorant or distrustful of those educated in other traditions who share the common life of broader society with them. There is a need to ensure students will be capable of the mutual understanding needed for civic friendship and cooperation in pursuit of the civic common good. This should be addressed by establishing regular contacts between diverse schools through youth camps or organizations, sports teams, conferences, and so forth. In the case of public schools the challenges are somewhat reversed. In a nondenominational school the issue of mutual understanding of people from diverse spiritual families is resolved naturally by the interaction, ordinary friendships, and resolution of challenges that occur daily. Here, it is providing for religious and ethical education that is a challenge. It is interesting that Maritain's proposal for such schools is not to offer neutral educational

---

34 Dewey, *Moral Principles in Education*, 12. For a more detailed comparison of Maritain and Dewey on moral education, see Madonna Murphy, "Maritain Explains the Moral Principles of Education to John Dewey," *Educational Horizons* 83, no. 4 (2005): 282–91. For contrasting views between these two philosophers on the role of the school in promoting the democratic charter and preparing the student for life in democratic society, see Walter Schultz, *Jacques Maritain in the 21st Century: Personalism and the Political Organization of the World* (Newcastle upon Tyne: Cambridge Scholars Press, 2022), 68–75.

material about various religions. To the contrary, he advocates an exposure to a diverse range of teachers who are committed proponents of the diverse creeds shared by the students.[35] However, given the diversity and the objections of many parents to any religious teaching being offered at all, a considerable emphasis should be placed upon natural morality in its relation to our common civic and political life, without overlooking that which is of greatest importance: the uprightness of will and conduct. An essential component of this is Maritain's insistence that modern schools be mandated with providing a liberal education for all. This is envisioned not as a preparation for a life of an idle gentleman, but the basic familiarity with one's cultural tradition and the broad artistic, historic, and intellectual resources that make possible a basic understanding of what constitutes a fulfilling human life.

However, as we saw in Maritain's treatment of politics, the political community cannot legitimately demand agreement with any philosophical or religious creed as a condition for belonging to the body politic. Nevertheless, he insists that there must be a basic set of convictions in the practical order that are demanded of all citizens in order for a pluralistic society to function. As he explains in *Man and the State*:

> The body politic has the right and the duty to promote among its citizens, mainly through education, the human and temporal—and essentially practical—creed on which depend national communion and civil peace. It has no right, as a merely temporal or secular body, enclosed in the sphere where the modern State enjoys its autonomous authority, to impose on the citizens or to demand from them a rule of faith or a conformism of reason, a philosophical or religious creed which would present itself as the only possible justification of the practical charter through which the people's common secular faith expresses itself.[36]

Consequently, the modern state needs to be concerned, in Maritain's view, not only with providing a liberal education for all, but also with inculcating a moral commitment to the democratic charter itself. It

---

35 *The Education of Man*, 126.
36 *Man and the State*, 111–12.

is vital that this teaching be restricted to the practical principles that constitute the basis for the common life citizens have agreed to share despite their diversity of opposing spiritual or philosophical traditions. Yet this raises a paradox, for it is impossible that a democratic charter, such as that represented by the US constitution, be taught compellingly and win adherents if it is taught in artificial isolation from the real intellectual and religious commitments that animated its acceptance in the first place. Maritain's solution to this challenge is that teaching of the democratic charter should be founded in the teacher's own convictions or, ideally, a plurality of teachers with different religious and ethical convictions. But such teachers would also seek to engage the moral and religious ideals the students themselves have already acquired from their family lives, in order to allow them to see clearly how these moral principles coincide with and support the democratic charter the state has a practical need and moral responsibility to support.[37] Maritain sums up his position, writing:

> The goal aimed at by the educational system and the State is unity—unity in the common adherence to the democratic charter. But for the very sake of attaining this practical unity a sound pluralism must obtain in the means; inner differentials must come into force in the structure of the educational system so as to afford an efficacious teaching of the democratic charter. On the one hand the State—or groups and agencies in the body politic which are concerned with education, or the authorities that govern the educational system—should see to it that the democratic charter be taught—and taught in a comprehensive, far-reaching, and vitally convincing manner—in all the schools and educational institutions. On the other hand, and for the very sake of fostering the democratic faith in peoples' minds, the educational system should admit within itself pluralistic patterns enabling teachers to put their entire convictions and most personal inspiration in their teaching of the democratic charter.[38]

---

37   *Man and the State*, 120–21 and 123.
38   *Man and the State*, 122.

In this manner, Maritain defends a substantive but restricted teaching of public mores in a pluralistic society, one which emphasizes acknowledging the shared commitments that make public life possible in a liberal democracy. What is distinct, is that the particular way this defense is formulated will be left open to the various religious and moral commitments the members of the community actual have.

CHAPTER 10

Aesthetics

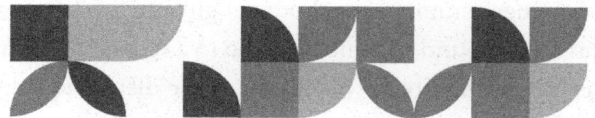

Artistic creation does not copy God's creation, it continues
it. And just as the trace and the image of God appear in His
creatures, so the human stamp is imprinted on the work of
art—the full stamp, sensitive and spiritual, not only that of
the hands, but of the whole soul.

Art and Scholasticism, 60

Maritain is one of the first Thomists to write a significant body
of work on aesthetics. Scholastics seldom took interest in
questions about the nature of the fine arts at all. When
they did it was usually limited to a note about the relation
between beauty and goodness.[1] In part this is due to the fact that medieval writers such as Aquinas only treated the arts in general, with a
focus on the liberal arts, and even in this area such accounts were often
sporadic and indirect. There is no medieval treatise on the fine arts;
rather, one finds discussions in works of logic that address the nature
of reasoning in the liberal arts, or in works of moral theology where

---

1   For example, Josephus Gredt, *Elementa Philosophiae Aristotelico-Thomisticae* (Freiburg: Herder
    & Co., 1937), 642–44.

prudence is contrasted with art, or in works of metaphysics that treat of beauty as a transcendental. However, the medieval period was a sacral age, where all was ultimately ordered to God. In our own secular times pragmatism is often the attitude that underlies our common life. We are caught up in the quest for more and more efficient means, yet we are less and less clear about the ends those means are to serve. Thus, the human need for beauty is obscured. This need is rooted in the fact that human beings cannot live without delight and joy. In this regard the fine arts have a profound spiritual mission in a secular age. The fact that Maritain is one of the first to disengage these disparate insights from their original medieval contexts and use them as sources to develop a philosophy of art is undoubtedly a response to this deep, if forgotten, human need.

It is also worth noting that, unlike so many philosophical theories of art, Maritain's work in this area was not only read by philosophers; it also had a significant impact on working artists. Painters, composers, and literary authors read his early work on art and in many cases were deeply influenced by it. Jean Cocteau, Julien Green, Eric Satie, Igor Stravinsky, Georges Rouault, and Flannery O'Connor are some of the notable figures that testify to being influenced through Maritain's work.[2] The work most commonly noted in this connection is his early and very short book *Art and Scholasticism* (1920). However, the positions taken in it are developed more fully in a range of later writings on these topics, especially in his late masterpiece of aesthetics *Creative Intuition in Art and Poetry* (1953). While this is undoubtedly Maritain's mature and more nuanced account of aesthetics, it never had the kind of broad influence on the artistic community—likely due to its considerable complexity and length—that his earlier *Art and Scholasticism* had.

Although Maritain treats a wide range of topics in his thought on art, two primary themes emerge that will be treated in the present chapter. The first is his insistence that art is a virtue of the practical intellect. This is the context in which all of his writing on aesthetics

---

2   For a study of Maritain's influence, especially in literature, see John M. Dunaway, *Jacques Maritain* (Boston: Twayne Publishers, 1978), 139–54.

must be understood; it is also where his theory evolves most significantly. As his later works related to the modes of knowing of the human
agent explore the themes of the spiritual preconscious and connatural
modes of knowing more deeply, his views of the role of the intellect in
art naturally result in richer explorations as well. Second, Maritain's
understanding of the beauty of the work of art and the "rules" of making
beautiful art will be explored.

Art as a Virtue of the Practical Intellect

Central to Maritain's view of art is that it is a virtue of the practical
intellect. Clearly, art is not only speculative, since it aims at a work to
be made. Without this act of production there would be no genuine
art, although the work can obviously incorporate diverse elements or
objects. It might be a novel, a painting, a poem, a symphony, etc. Indeed,
Maritain uses the term "art" in the ancient sense of τέχνη. While his
primary concern is what we today call the fine arts, he does recognize that art as such is a broader category including any work of skilled
craftsmanship. With the scholastic tradition, Maritain distinguishes
two spheres within the exercise of the practical intellect: doing and
making. Doing concerns the free use of our facilities, precisely with
regard to freedom. It is concerned with the exercise of free will itself,
not with respect to the work to be accomplished, but with respect to the
use of our freedom. This area of activity—that of doing—embraces the
sphere of morality or the human good as such; it is governed through
the virtue of prudence, which is right reason in doing.[3] Making is to be
understood in contradistinction to doing. It is concerned with productive action, and relates to the action precisely in regards to the thing to
be produced, the work in itself.[4] Due to this distinction between doing
and making, Maritain can insist that an action of making is to be understood and judged in its own right. The standard of that judgment is the

---

3   *Art and Scholasticism* in *Art and Scholasticism and The Frontiers of Poetry*, trans. Joseph W.
    Evans (New York: Charles Scribner's Sons, 1962), 7. *Creative Intuition in Art and Poetry* (New
    York: Pantheon Books, 1953), 36.

4   *Art and Scholasticism*, 8.

rules of making in keeping with the proper end of the work that is being produced. This is to say we are judging the goodness of the act of making the work in relation to the end of the work itself, not in relation to the good of the human person as such. This is why an artist can be a bad person, yet a great artist.[5] For the sphere of art is the sphere of making, while the sphere of morality is the sphere of doing:

> Art, which rules making and not doing, stands therefore outside the human sphere; it has an end, rules, values, which are not those of man, but those of the work to be produced. This work is everything for Art; there is for Art but one law—the exigencies and the good of the work.[6]

Maritain is quite insistent that the spheres of art and of morality are distinct and autonomous. The artist in her work must follow relentlessly the relevant artistic principles in pursuit of her creative vision. To compromise the work in view of moral concerns would be to fail as an artist, every bit as much as compromising one's artistic integrity for any extrinsic consideration (e.g., money, popular acclaim, institutional acceptance, etc.) would be. Morality doesn't teach us how to become good artists any more than Art in its own sphere can teach us how to become morally good human beings. If it does so, it is a happy result of the moral integrity of the artist's vision, but it is due to the artist's moral insight, not merely his or her artistic skill. However, since the artist is not just an artist, but a human being, he or she is obliged to take into consideration moral principles as well as artistic ones and unite them in artistic activity. Human life has need of the Beauty and creativity of the artist, and in this, art has the final say. Yet art only arises in human life in the context of human needs and goals where morality has its proper authority:

> In other words it is true that Art and Morality are two autonomous worlds, each sovereign in its own sphere, but they cannot ignore or disregard one another, for man belongs in these two worlds, both

---

5   *The Moral Responsibility of the Artist,* 26.

6   *Art and Scholasticism,* 9. I shall return to this relationship between art and morality in section three of this chapter.

as intellectual maker and as moral agent, doer of actions which engage his own destiny.

The unity of the human person requires that even though we distinguish the spheres of art and morality from one another and assign each their own proper principles and ends, these two spheres are nevertheless both applicable to the human person who happens to be an artist. Since an artist is essentially human, irrespective of his particular professional vocation, the principles of morality that are bound up with his humanity are prior and more fundamental. While he can choose not to become an artist after all, he cannot choose not to be human. Accordingly, the principles of art should be less significant to the artist than the principles of morality. However, insofar as he is acting as an artist, it is the principles of art that matter, and those of morality remain extrinsic to the work of art as art:

> And because an artist is a man before being an artist, the autonomous world of morality is simply superior to (and more inclusive than) the autonomous world of art. There is no law against that law on which the destiny of man depends. In other words Art is indirectly and extrinsically subordinate to morality.[7]

Thus, Maritain rejects the view that art has to serve only artistic aims and that its impact upon the life of the artist or the community is irrelevant. He agrees that it is not relevant to the assessment of the work's artistic excellence, but this is not the only way—nor always the most important way—to assess the work. Neither does he accept the view that art should simply be produced for the sake of the people or what they like. While he certainly thinks it is a good thing that art be made available to the community, it is not for the community to dictate what the artist's creative vision should be. In a similar way the state might reasonably expect those it has trained in mathematics to teach in its schools. However, it cannot tell its mathematics teachers to teach what they know to be contrary to the truths of mathematics (as we find suggested in Orwell's novel *1984*, for example). The tensions arising between

---

7   *The Moral Responsibility of the Artist*, 41.

the principles of art and morality are only ever fully worked out in the particular life of the artist, who like all human beings has an obligation to order all of his or her activities and works toward God and to find sanctity in the midst of these everyday realities. While the occupation of the artist presents special challenges to this task, the task itself is the same one that we all share.[8]

Accordingly, Maritain is very clear that the making of art is a virtue of the practical intellect. Yet what is unique in his treatment is the emphasis on the role of the intellect in the production of a work of art, since art arises through a virtue of the practical intellect. Appropriating Aristotle's hylomorphism, Maritain insists that the artistic act consists in imposing form upon matter. The form exists initially as an idea of the work to be produced; it then is imposed upon matter through the creative act of artistic skill to produce the object of art, whether that be a poem, a painting, a string quartet, etc. Thus, while the work is practical, for Maritain it is first and foremost an act of the intellect:

> The work of art has been thought before being made, it has been kneaded and prepared, formed, brooded over, ripened in a mind before passing into matter. And in matter it will always retain the color and savor of the spirit. Its *formal* element, what constitutes it in its species and makes it what it is, is its being ruled by the intellect . . . *The work to be made* is only the matter of art, its form is *undeviating reason.*[9]

Consequently, in *Art and Scholasticism* Maritain defines art as "the *undeviating determination of works to be made.*"[10]

In his late work the notion of the spiritual preconscious plays an increasingly significant role. As we saw in the earlier discussion of Christ's knowledge, Maritain developed this concept through his critique of Freud's work on the subconscious (the material and instinctive responses that take place below the level of conscious life). Maritain

---

8   Maritain offers a sustained reflection on this theme in chapter IV of *The Moral Responsibility of the Artist*, "Poetry and the Perfection of Human Life."

9   *Art and Scholasticism*, 9.

10 *Art and Scholasticism*, 9.

postulates that in addition to these there are also incidents of unconscious intellectual activity that grasp truths affectively in ways too direct
and sublime to be articulated discursively. In *Creative Intuition in Art
and Poetry* this becomes the central theme, so much so that an entire
chapter is devoted to the relation between the creative intuition that
emerges from the spiritual preconscious and poetic knowledge. In
many ways this is a refinement of his early discussions of connatural
knowledge.

Maritain finds a basis for his theory of the spiritual preconscious
in the thought of St. Thomas, who had held that in the order of natural
priorities the more perfect powers give rise to the others. This is to say
that the more perfect powers are the rationale for the lower, being both
their end and their active principle. Intelligence, for example, does not
exist for the sake of the senses, but rather the senses exist for the sake of
the intellect. Likewise, imagination and emotional affectivity proceed,
or flow, from the essence of the soul through the intellect. Maritain
creatively adopts Aquinas's view to see this central and primary activity
as the work of the spiritual preconscious, which underlies the activities
of the intellect, the imagination, and the senses, providing a common
but hidden root for all the powers of the soul.[11]

This common source of spiritual activity is the birthplace of poetry
in Maritain's unique sense of the term:

> And because poetry is born in this root life where the powers
> of the soul are active in common, poetry implies an essential
> requirement of totality or integrity. Poetry is the fruit neither of
> the intellect alone, nor of the imagination alone. Nay more, it pro-
> ceeds from the totality of man, sense imagination, intellect, love,
> desire, instinct, blood and spirit together. And the first obligation
> imposed on the poet is to consent to be brought back to the hidden
> place, near the centre of the soul, where this totality exists in the
> estate of a creative source.[12]

---

11 *Creative Intuition in Art and Poetry*, 76–79; note especially the diagram on 77.
12 *Creative Intuition in Art and Poetry*, 80.

Maritain generally uses the term "poetry" not to mean the particular form of art that consists in writing in verse, but rather to indicate the creative intuition that animates the making of any genuine work of beauty—and it is best explained through distinguishing it from art. This sense of poetry did not appear in *Art and Scholasticism*, but was first introduced in an essay added to the second edition, entitled "Frontiers of Poetry," where he explained this unique sense of poetry by saying, "This divination of the spiritual in the things of sense, and which expresses itself in sense, is precisely what we call POETRY."[13] Accordingly, in this sense poetry is obviously not merely writing in verse, but the creative intuition that animates a work of art whatever its medium. Art is the making of the work itself in keeping with right reason. By the time of his mature work, Maritain draws the distinction between art and poetry more strongly in relation to the dialogue between the self and the realities the artist contemplates. Accordingly, he begins *Creative Intuition in Art and Poetry* by saying,

> By Art I mean the Creative or producing, work-making activity of the human mind. By Poetry I mean, not the particular art that consists in writing verses, but a process both more general and more primary: that intercommunication between the inner being of things and the inner being of the human Self which is a kind of divination (as was realized in ancient times; the Latin *vates* (seer) was both a poet and a diviner). Poetry, in this sense, is the secret life of each and all of the arts; another name for what Plato called *mousiké*.[14]

Accordingly, as Maritain often notes, poetry is to the various arts what grace is to the moral life.[15]

Again, in this later work the role of reason is emphasized, with the emphasis that the relevant mode of reason is not logical discourse. Poetry, in this unique sense, comes to take on the central role in the

---

13 "Frontiers of Poetry," 128.

14 *Creative Intuition in Art and Poetry*, 3; see also 130–31. See also John G. Trapani, *Poetry, Beauty and Contemplation: The Complete Aesthetics of Jacques Maritain* (Washington, DC: The Catholic University of America Press, 2011), 71–74.

15 e.g., "Frontiers of Poetry," 129.

creativity of the artist; it is simply the particular way in which the spiritual preconscious manifests itself in the creative life of the artist irrespective of her medium. By contrast, in the early work *Art and Scholasticism* there was a simple insistence upon art as a virtue of the practical intellect (right reason in making) in contrast with the virtue of prudence (right reason in doing). While this view is not rejected, it is substantially complemented by a new emphasis upon the preconscious life of the intellect, which leads Maritain to introduce poetry as a distinct concept.

Poetry in this sense is what allows for the work of art to be a medium that communicates the connatural knowledge of the artist, for poetry unleashes the intercommunication between the inner being of things and the inner being of the human agent who gives rise to the work of art. In this respect, Maritain insists that there is a poetic form of knowledge that is genuinely knowledge and cannot be arrived at in other ways. As he explains,

> Poetic knowledge, as I see it, is a specific kind of knowledge through inclination or connaturality—let us say a knowledge through affective connaturality which essentially relates to the creativity of the spirit and tends to express itself in a work. So that in such a knowledge it is the object created, the poem, the painting, the sympathy, in its own existence as a world of its own, which plays the part played in ordinary knowledge by the concepts and judgments produced within the mind.[16]

Maritain is careful to clarify that even though this is knowledge by connatural affectivity, it is the intellect that knows. Human emotions do not know; only the intellect does. Further, the emotion that he appeals to here is not merely subjective or brute emotion, which falls outside of the proper scope of art. Nor is it an emotion that is expressed or portrayed by the artist, which would treat the emotion as a thing to be the subject of the work of art. Neither is it an emotional response the artist hopes to elicit from the audience of the work. In contrast to all of these Maritain instead holds: "It is an emotion as *form*, which, being one with

---

16 *Creative Intuition in Art and Poetry*, 86.

the creative intuition, gives form to the poem, and which is intentional [in the Thomistic sense], as an idea is, or carries within itself infinitely more than itself."[17] This is to say that poetic intuition is born in the spiritual preconsciousness of the spirit by means of a spiritualized emotion.

Since things do not only exist as they are, but always point beyond themselves, as creatures they are always signs of their Creator. As Augustine put it evocatively in the Confessions, even the earth, the sun, and the heavens call out "we are not Him, but He made us."[18] For Maritain the analogy of being entails that the thing that is known through poetic knowledge opens up to an awareness that goes beyond itself, for each thing is "permeated on all sides" by the influx of the activating first cause, namely, God.[19]

Accordingly, Maritain often explains the intuitive insight of poetry by contrasting it with metaphysical knowledge. Metaphysics is directly a form of knowing, while poetry is a form of making and regards delight found in beauty. Accordingly, metaphysics arrives at the spiritual through an idea in the most abstract forms of intellection possible for the human intellect, while poetry reaches spiritual insight through its work in the particular and sensible refined by intelligence. This contrast is artfully expressed in the opening chapter to *The Degrees of Knowledge* where Maritain writes:

> The metaphysician breathes an atmosphere of abstraction which is death for the artist. Imagination, the discontinuous, the unverifiable, in which the metaphysician perishes, is life itself to the artist. While both absorb rays that come down from creative Night, the artist finds nourishment in a bound intelligibility which is as multiform as God's reflections upon earth, the metaphysician finds it in a naked intelligibility that is as determined as the proper being

---

17 *Creative Intuition in Art and Poetry*, 87. In Thomism, "intentional" refers to the tendential existence through which a thing comes to be within the mind in an immaterial manner. An idea of a thing is intentional insofar as the idea, though immaterial, serves as a sign of the thing. Here the claim seems to be that the emotion gives form to the poem and is intentional in the same sense that the emotion that forms the poem is also that present in the artist's creative intuition.

18 St. Augustine, *The Confessions*, trans. Henry Chadwick (Oxford: Oxford University Press, 1991), X, 6, 9.

19 *Creative Intuition in Art and Poetry*, 92.

of things. They are playing seesaw, each in turn rising up to the sky. Spectators make fun of their game; they sit upon solid ground.[20]

This is to say metaphysics is directly intellectual but arrives at its ideas by way of the senses, while poetry is directly concerned with crafting the material particular work, through intellectual activity guiding material production. Both seek the real, but metaphysics has to attain it in the natures of things while poetry touches it through whatever signs it finds at its disposal.[21]

With regards to the poetic intuition animating any true artist, two themes are important to recognize here. The first is the understanding of the work of art as a self-expression of the artist. This is introduced through an analysis of the differences between Western and Oriental art. The second is the breadth of reason and the role of the preconscious life of the intellect as a dimension of reasoning in the work of the artist. This theme is encountered through a comparative analysis of the different critiques of reason found in surrealism and Platonism.

For Maritain the work of the artist is to be understood as the fruit of a dynamic encounter between the World and the Self. By Self, he understands the artist in her inner subjectivity as an individual.[22] In terms of the World, he refers to the things of the world that the Self encounters. The relation between these two has had distinctive and differing emphases in Eastern and Western art. Maritain accepts the then-prevailing view that the art of the Orient is generally opposed to Western individualism. The artists of the East would traditionally have been ashamed to think of the work of art as an opportunity to express their own personal subjectivity. Rather, the Oriental artist has a duty to forget herself, mediating the mystery of Things in their visible appearance and meaning, for pleasure or in the service of religious worship:

---

20 *The Degrees of Knowledge,* 2. See also the similar passage at *Creative Intuition in Art and Poetry,* 173.

21 The concept of poetic knowledge is further explained in "Concerning Poetic Knowledge," in *The Situation of Poetry* (New York: The Philosophical Library, 1968), 51–52.

22 *Creative Intuition in Art and Poetry,* 88. There is further discussion of subjectivity in general in *Existence and the Existent,* 80–84.

But because Oriental art is essentially religious or religious-minded, this art is in communion with Things not for the sake of Things but for the sake of some other—invisible and adorable—reality whose signs Things are, and which, through Things, art reveals together with Things. In actual fact religion, not art has lifted art to that level of life which is the very life of art, basically needed for its own truth and greatness, and which is the life of symbols. Oriental art is only intent on Things; but, like every genuine art, it loathes realism.[23]

Yet, this art is nevertheless a form of communication, for the work is only brought to completion in becoming a meeting place where minds join together. While the Oriental artist is focused on Things, she is focused on Things in order to make them communicable to the minds of others, and this adds another reason in support of the artist's self-forgetfulness.

Maritain finds that this focus on Things manifests differently in Indian and Chinese art. Indian art is "captured by Things"; here the soul is given up to the energy present in Things exploding in sensual luxuriance. In this, Indian art is ordered to a practical purpose of spirituality. The work of art is itself an instrument to move the mind of the audience to a spiritual goal, producing peace and contemplation in the beholder. Chinese art is also intent on things rather than on the artist's self-expression, but in a different way. Rather than being captured by Things, it captures them. It aims to bring out the inner meaning or "soul" of the things that it depicts, which are enclosed within their material forms: "The Chinese contemplative painter becomes one with Things, not to be carried along by their generative torrent, but to seize upon their own inner spirit."[24] Whereas the Thing in Indian art is a dream mediating the Absolute, within Chinese art the Thing has its own reality, and the spirit that they contain can be set free through our contemplative searching, which is captured in the creative insight of the artist.

---

23 *Creative Intuition in Art and Poetry*, 10. The realism that is relevant here would appear to be that associated with a narrow and excessively academic approach to art in such a way that inevitably stifles poetic expression.

24 *Creative Intuition in Art and Poetry*, 14.

The point of this comparison is to show that the differences between Indian and Chinese art stem from the human and cultural dimensions of the artist, rather than the Things that they depict:

> The typical difference between Indian art and Chinese art does not proceed from the Things that man contemplates. It proceeds from men who contemplate Things. All the distinctive features on which I have laid stress are but an expression of the invisible human fabric, spiritual and carnal, religious, intellectual, or emotional depending both on nature and history, on conditioning and freedom, which is rooted in the subjectivity of the Indian people and the Chinese people.[25]

This focus of early art of varying cultures upon Things is also true of Greek art with its emphasis upon idealized form in its presentation of objects, particularly the human figure. Further, Maritain argues it is not repudiated by Islamic art in its rejection of representation; rather, it is manifested differently in its mathematical harmony and rhythmic order. The ornamental dimensions of Islamic art show what Maritain calls "a sensuousness, burned by the intellect's refined fire, of the creative subjectivity from which it proceeds."[26]

The distinctively Western understanding of art as a form of self-expression emerges from its encounter with the Christian doctrine of the person as articulated in the theology of the Trinity and the Incarnation. Additionally, St. Paul's doctrine of the inner man as the true self in its struggle to overcome the external man gave impetus to this new focus. Thus, it emerges in the distinctively Christian emphasis upon the spiritual dignity of the person in contrast with the mere individuality of the human being, which is more bound up with its merely material dimensions. The history of Western art undergoes an evolution from the Self first grasped as an object in the exemplar of Christ's divine self, to a sense of self grasped as subject, in the creative subjectivity of the person both as such and as artist.

---

25 *Creative Intuition in Art and Poetry*, 16.
26 *Creative Intuition in Art and Poetry*, 18.

Maritain analyzes this development of the role of the Self in Western art in terms of three distinct phases. In the first phase the Mystery of the person is encountered merely as an object that is among the world of Things while transcending them. Man emerges above the world of nature, seeking to overcome it. Maritain sees Byzantine art as an archetype of this phase. Its freedom from things is exemplified in its presentation of Christ as glorified and without suffering, among other ways. The human soul is present, but it remains shadowed behind the intellectual and universal as sacred symbols of dogmatic mysteries: "The Divinity of Christ soars over everything."[27] The second phase also presents the mystery of the person as a mere object, in the world of things while transcending them, but disclosing more deeply the human dimension. Maritain has in mind the humanistic tendency of artists like Giotto and Fra Angelico. Like the first phase, art is predominantly sacred with Christ at the center. But here Christ's humanity and suffering are more directly in the forefront. The saints and the Blessed Virgin in their unique and individual features become central focuses for the artists. The human soul is glimpsed through the objective world and the human Self is more central to the artists' concerns. Finally, with the third stage the human self and human subjectivity enter a process of internalization and the artistic focus is no longer solely taken up with the object depicted, but passes to the manner in which the artist develops the work. Here there is a new focus of the self-awareness of the artist in her own creative artistic activity, which brings the poetic dimension of artistic work to the fore. Maritain sees this as revealing an important truth: namely, that the artist unconsciously imposes her individuality upon the object she is concerned with in nature, and this fact becomes gradually more prominent and freely represented in the artistic work.[28] The historian of art could trace examples of these developments. For instance, by the early seventeenth century Diego Velázquez was able to paint the *Road to Emmaus* with an unknown serving girl as the central subject. Here Christ and the disciples are seen in the background of

---

27 *Creative Intuition in Art and Poetry*, 21.
28 *Creative Intuition in Art and Poetry*, 20–22.

the painting in an adjoining room. Christ is present, but the focus is the ordinary humanity of an unknown and uncomplaining "Martha" laboring while the disciples converse. A case like this seems to be transitional. Christ is no longer at the center and the artist has greater scope to introduce his own priorities. Yet the artist's concepts are mediated by the representation of ordinary things. Once we are fully into the third stage, which is characteristic of modernist painting, the artist's self-expression takes on a greater role as the origin and often the subject of the painting.

Accordingly, Maritain rejects viewing art as an attempt to simplistically reproduce or present as close of an approximation to its real objects as possible. The work of art is never merely a copy of the object, but always an interpretation of it.

> Nature for him [i.e., the artist] is the inspirer of an imaginary world which he draws from Things with her assistance and collaboration. And the subject on which he is intent is a fruit of imagination born of nature and permeated with nature, which he tries to make present to our eyes.

In Maritain's view, the work of art remains bound to Things and, consequently, to nature—even when poetic intuition leads the artist to present the Thing in a way quite different from the way it appears when we merely take a look at it. While making room for modern art, even a high degree of abstraction, he insists that the artist and her work remain captured by the object they portray:

> Thus on the one hand he remains subjected to the primacy of the object—become, in the sense I just specified, the "subject represented." But on the other hand he definitely imprints on it the mark of his own individuality, of his own style, even if it is true that he aspires to achieving "style" rather than to "having a style." The work bears more openly than ever, it bears of necessity, by virtue of the typical relationship prevalent in those times between the artist and Nature, the imprint of its maker.[29]

29 *Creative Intuition in Art and Poetry*, 23.

This context set the stage for the diverse forms of expression modern art explored in the twentieth century in virtually all of its forms—whether in painting, music, or poetry. All forms of art experienced a revisioning in view of this growing emergence of self, prompted by Romanticism and radicalized by modernism and post-modernism in the arts.

Maritain remains deeply sympathetic to this emerging focus, and indeed makes the creative subjectivity of the artist the central feature of his own theory of art. Yet it is crucial to recognize that he rejects any attempt to separate the artist from Things, from the objects that spur on her artistic vision. Thus he scorns the "art for art's sake" movement, if it is to be understood as an attempt to free art from Things as its proper objects and pretend that artistic activity is not part of the moral life of the artist. Rather, he advocates a different formula; namely, "art for the sake of the work."[30] Without a connection to the Things found in reality, the creative subjectivity so vital to the artist would become impossible: "Creative subjectivity cannot awaken to itself except in community with Things. Thus the relationship with Nature has been changed but not abolished."[31] The artist inevitably reveals herself within any genuine work of art, while at the same time sacrificing herself for the good of the work.[32] Accordingly, Maritain sees the great modern painters, whether Cézanne or Klee, as bringing about a genuine revolution, while not breaking their relationship with the greatest painters of history. Their work was rather to highlight and set free the relation of Things and creative subjectivity in the work. This is entirely in keeping with Maritain's aesthetic theory, the fundamental position of which he expresses as follows:

> Our descriptive and indirect inquiry suggests that at the root of the creative act there must be a quite particular intellectual process, without parallel in logical reason, through which Things and the Self are grasped together by means of a kind of experience or

---

30 *The Moral Responsibility of the Artist*, 48.

31 *Creative Intuition in Art and Poetry*, 26.

32 *The Moral Responsibility of the Artist*, 52.

knowledge which has no conceptual expression and is expressed only in the artist's work.[33]

We have already seen that Maritain adapts Freudian psychology to complement Freud's theory of the unconscious with a spiritual precon-scious element in the human intellect. He sees the creative intuition that is manifested in art as being an instance of this spiritual precon-sciousness, this ability to see and grasp in a connatural manner what cannot be discursively and consciously expressed. For Maritain this is the realm in which the genuine artist is most at home. Accordingly, while making use of insights of Plato and the surrealists he ultimately rejects their antirational views of artistic inspiration. For Maritain the work of art ultimately remains a work of practical reason, even if it is guided by insights that arise intuitively. These are not *ir*rational, but if anything, *supra*rational: reason of a form that is too direct and simple to be expressed in the limited manner of discursive and logical forms.

In view of this difference Maritain gives significant attention to sur-realism among the modern approaches to painting. While recognizing that there is genuine poetic intuition to be found among the surrealists, Maritain is ultimately critical of their tendency to assert that this comes through an abandonment of reason. With surrealism it is not only log-ical or discursive reason which is left behind (which is necessary if the artist is to enter into the realm of the poetic at all). Rather, the surrealist seeks an absolute liberation from reason as such. This complete break with reason is characteristic of the surrealist's project. The automatic writing of André Breton is a central example of this approach.

However, for Maritain such a method is fundamentally illusory, for automatism does not give rise to freedom but only dispersion. No longer bound to the light of the intellect, unconscious impulses on their own are utterly impotent to reveal anything genuinely creative or new. When we find genuine poetry in the surrealists it is only because they have violated the principles of their own dogmatism and "obey despite

---

33 *Creative Intuition in Art and Poetry*, 29–30.

themselves the secret music of intelligence."[34] For Maritain the surrealists quite simply are lying to themselves when they claim to have broken
free of reason in the sphere of art, just as we may be tempted to lie to
ourselves by attempting to deny that poetry is nothing more than a
rational process that does not break in any fundamental way from conceptual, logical, or discursive modes of reasoning.

These considerations return us to the comparison with Platonism.
While it shares with surrealism the view that the poet abandons reason
for some form of inspiration, in other ways surrealism and Platonism
are opposites. For the Platonist holds that art's primary mission is a participation in and a making present of the transcendent form of Beauty
and thus of Goodness. In this respect Maritain notes that his own project could be construed as a restructuring of Platonic aesthetics: "I think
that what we have to do is to make the Platonic Muse descend into
the soul of man, where she is no longer Muse but creative intuition;
and Platonic inspiration descend into the intellect united with imagination, where inspiration from above the soul becomes inspiration from
above conceptual reason, that is, poetic experience."[35] This is, in fact,
a good summary of Maritain's project for aesthetics, to show how the
modes of artistic knowledge that go beyond our ordinary powers of
discursive reasoning are in fact a result of human reasoning operating
creatively in modes that are intuitive and preconceptual through the
spiritual preconsciousness. Again, this is not the instinctive or material
unconsciousness articulated by Freud but a supraconscious intuition,
one too intensely intellectual to be articulated fully in discursive terms.
As Maritain describes his broader understanding of reasoning:

> Reason does not only consist of its conscious logical tools and
> manifestations, nor does the will consist only of its deliberate con-
> scious determinations. Far beneath the sunlit surface thronged
> with explicit concepts and judgments, words and expressed res-
> olutions or movements of the will, are the sources of knowledge
> and creativity, of love and above-sensuous desires hidden in the

---

34 *Creative Intuition in Art and Poetry*, 59.
35 *Creative Intuition in Art and Poetry*, 66.

primordial translucid night of the intimate vitality of the soul. Thus it is that we must recognize the existence of an unconscious or preconscious which pertains to the spiritual powers of the human soul and to the inner abyss of personal freedom, and of the personal thirst and striving for knowing and seeing, grasping and expressing: a spiritual or musical unconscious which is specifically different for the automatic or deaf unconsciousness.[36]

Here we see Maritain developing the same principle he had presented in criticizing Bergson's theory of intuition as a non-rational insight in his first book. Throughout his career this focus on the broad range of modes of reasoning and the fight against reducing reason to its most common and explicit forms of activity is apparent. Yet by the time he wrote *Creative Intuition in Art and Poetry*, his account had been notably deepened by treating it in terms of his developing insights into the spiritual preconsciousness. Accordingly, the creative intuition that is so characteristic of the poet in the act of artistic creativity adds significant nuance to his account of artistic production as a virtue of the practical intellect. While this insight is defended from his first work, it is progressively deepened without ever escaping his focus.

Beauty and the Rules of Art

Drawing on St. Thomas Aquinas, Maritain defines beauty as *id quod visum plactet*, or that which pleases when seen.[37] He rephrases this from a passage where Aquinas is responding to an objection that the good is not a final cause (i.e., an end or a goal), because the good and the beautiful are the same. Rather, beauty is a formal cause, found in the way things are structured and appear, rather than a final cause. However, it would be completely erroneous to interpret this in a subjective sense, as entailing that beauty can be reduced to whatever pleases the appetite,

---

36 *Creative Intuition in Art and Poetry*, 94. For a thorough discussion of Maritain's development of the notion of poetic knowledge, see Trapani, *Poetry, Beauty and Contemplation*, 83–87. A helpful summary of the historical development of this idea through his thought is found from 116 to 118.

37 Aquinas's text reads: *Pulchrum autem respicit vim cognoscitivam, pulchra enim dicuntur quae visa placent.*

as if beauty was no more than mere titillation or that the standard of a beautiful work of art could possibly be just the size of its appreciative audience. This is clear from the context in Aquinas, as he introduces this phrase by noting that "beauty relates to the cognitive faculty; for beautiful things are those which please when seen."[38] In this passage Aquinas is actually using this cognitive dimension of beauty to distinguish it from the good, which relates directly not to cognition but to appetite. Aquinas also considers beauty in the context of love while arguing that the good is the only cause of love. An objection draws on a passage of Pseudo-Dionysius that the beautiful is loved by all just as much as the good is. In reply Aquinas distinguishes beauty from goodness in a way that again emphasizes the cognitive dimension of beauty. Both beauty and goodness calm our desire. However, beauty not only calms our desire, but also delights us when it is seen or known. Here Aquinas also notes that this cognitive dimension is further demonstrated by the fact that something is called beautiful when it is seen or heard, and beauty is not, strictly speaking, applied to the other senses, to what is tasted or smelled.[39] If we happen to speak of a beautiful meal, we are either speaking about more than the particular tastes or else using the term "beauty" in a metaphorical sense.

As we might expect, Maritain strongly emphasizes this cognitive dimension of the beautiful. It is certainly true that beauty gives rise to delight. But he holds that a genuine encounter with beauty is not associated with every delight whatsoever; rather, it is specifically a delight in knowing: "Beauty consists of intuitive knowledge, and delight. Beauty makes us delighted in the very act of knowing—a delight which overflows from the thing this act attains."[40] Hence, the beautiful is not associated with just any act of knowing, the way I might delight in getting the right answer on a quiz. Instead, the beautiful is most properly "a delight which superabounds and overflows from this act [i.e., the act of knowing] because of the object known." This is to say, it is delight that

---

38 *S.T.*, I, q. 5, a. 4 ad 1.
39 *S.T.*, I-II, q. 27, a. 1 ad 3.
40 *Creative Intuition in Art and Poetry*, 122.

has its source in the object and that I apprehend through my apprehension of it. Its source is the thing that is apprehended, and it is beautiful precisely because it is good to apprehend it. Accordingly, Maritain writes: "Beauty is essentially an object of *intelligence*, for that which *knows* in the full sense of the word is intelligence, which alone is open to the infinity of being. The natural place of beauty is the intelligible world, it is from there that it descends."[41] This is not to deny that there is a sensory element, for we are human beings and not angels. But the senses serve the intellect and thus can lead to delight in knowing. Here he again notes Aquinas's position that sight and hearing are more cognitive than the other senses. Due to the fact that human understanding requires abstraction, it is clear that the senses have an indispensable role for us in perceiving the beautiful:

> Thus man can doubtless enjoy purely intelligible beauty, but the beautiful that is *connatural* to man is the beautiful that delights the intellect through the senses and through their intuition. Such is also the beautiful that is proper to our art, which shapes a sensible matter in order to delight the spirit.[42]

This should be sufficient to make clear that Maritain's definition of beauty as *id quod visum plactet* doesn't in any way entail a subjective notion of beauty as merely a pleasant sensation or experience. Pleasure is a property that accompanies beauty, but it is not its essence. In fact, in an endnote addressing this definition Maritain notes that it is not an essential definition, but a definition through an effect.[43] That is to say, it does not tell us the nature of beauty, but merely notes an effect that is manifest when beauty is apprehended. A scientific definition of the nature of beauty cannot be given. Since beauty is identical with goodness in reality, differing only in its intelligible character (i.e., in the concepts and language we use to understand it), it transcends the various categories. Accordingly, a definition by genus and specific

41 *Art and Scholasticism*, 23.
42 *Art and Scholasticism*, 24.
43 *Art and Scholasticism*, 161, endnote 47.

314 | THE CHRISTIAN PHILOSOPHY OF JACQUES MARITAIN

difference—e.g., Man is a rational (specific difference) animal (genus)— is not possible, for there is no higher genus that beauty shares in that we could use to distinguish it from members of the same genus. Rather, beauty, like goodness, runs throughout all that is.

Yet neither are we limited to noting beauty's effect. The fullest definition of beauty possible, according to Maritain, is found through noting the three essential characteristics of beauty set out by St. Thomas Aquinas: namely, integrity, proportion, and clarity (or radiance). These are articulated in the context of explaining how, although properties (strictly speaking) belong to the whole Trinity, some terms are "appropriated," or especially fitting, to one of the divine persons. Beauty, St. Thomas explains, is suitably appropriated to the Son:

> For beauty includes three conditions, "integrity" or "perfection," since those things which are impaired are by the very fact ugly; due "proportion" or "harmony"; and lastly, "radiance" or "clarity," whence things are called beautiful which have a bright color.[44]

Maritain interprets each of these characteristics with reference to their relation to the cognitive power, in view of the position above, that beauty, being formal, pertains to cognition, while the good, being a final cause and thus purposive, pertains to the appetites. Accordingly, we can compare Aquinas and Maritain on the essential properties of beauty as follows in table 10.1 below:

Property	Aquinas's Explanation	Maritain's Explanation[45]
Integrity or perfection	For a thing that is impaired is ugly	Intellect is pleased in fullness of being
Due proportion or harmony	N/A	Intellect is pleased in unity and order
Clarity or radiance	Bright colors are called beautiful	Intellect is pleased in light and intelligibility

---

44 *S.T.*, I, q. 39, a. 8 c.

45 *Art and Scholasticism*, 24. *Creative Intuition in Art and Poetry*, 123.

Integrity or perfection pertains to beauty because a thing is beautiful when it possesses all of the characteristics it ought to have. A dog that has been injured and has had its tail or a leg cut off strikes us as less beautiful than a healthy member of the species whose physique is in fine shape. Maritain infers that this implies that when we encounter a thing that has integrity the intellect is pleased in the recognition of this "fullness of being." Nothing is lacking that should be there, and thus, experiencing a thing in this condition is pleasing to the intellect that recognizes this fact. In a work of art this fullness of being needs to be understood not just in relation to the thing's ordinary and familiar composition, but also to the artist's purpose, the creative intuition animating the work. A lady with half an eye—or three eyes—may have integrity in a cubist painting, for instance, so long as this is what is needed to communicate the artist's intuition.[46]

Due harmony or proportion is another essential aspect of beauty. Aquinas seems to take this to be obvious and gives no further explanation. If we take a beautiful painting, the various parts of it will be found to have a due proportion to each other and to the scene as a whole. Consider da Vinci's mural *The Last Supper*, which is a famous example of perspective. Each of the apostles is presented in a way that gives a balance throughout the painting; additionally, their lines of vision, and the placement of the other objects in the work, all lead to Christ at the center. The fact that the people and objects are properly proportioned to each other creates a harmony in the work that is naturally pleasing. Here again, harmony has to be assessed in relation to the objects and ends in view.[47] The proper proportion of an infant is different from that of an adult. The complex proportions of music in a symphony are not proportionate in a simple folk song. According to Maritain, harmonious features are pleasurable, since the intellect finds a natural pleasure in that unity and order. When we apprehend a thing as unified and ordered, it is experienced by us as pleasing.

---

46 *Art and Scholasticism*, 27.
47 *Art and Scholasticism*, 28.

Finally, what is beautiful is always radiant; it grabs our attention and is noteworthy. Maritain emphasizes that this dimension of clarity is related to beauty being something that is recognized through the apprehension of form. Beauty is a "splendor of intelligibility," because it is, in Aquinas's phrase, a "splendor of form," and form is the principle that constitutes the proper perfection of each being. As Maritain describes it in his characteristically evocative language, form is "the ontological secret that they [i..e., things] bear within them, their spiritual being, their operating mystery—the form, indeed, is above all the proper principle of intelligibility, the proper clarity of every thing."[48] Maritain also insists that clarity is an ontological, rather than conceptual, feature of the beautiful thing. The beautiful is clear, luminous, and intelligible in itself. It need not be clear, luminous, and intelligible to us. In fact, its intelligibility can often remain hidden from us, because it is obscured by the matter that exhibits the form or because the form is so transcendent and related to the spirit that our awareness of such things is too dim to apprehend it. This is why form is at one and the same time the principle both of intelligibility and of mystery, for mystery exists when there is more to be known than what we have grasped: "To define the beautiful by the radiance of form is to define it by the radiance of a mystery."[49] Beauty is not a matter of conforming to an ideal, as Plato seems to have construed it. Rather, there is beauty whenever some form pleases the intellect. Further, this beauty is always relative. This is not to say, as I have already pointed out above, that beauty is relative to the subjective dispositions of the viewer or audience in the way we would take for granted today. Rather, he means that beauty is relative to the proper nature and end of the thing under its formal conditions. Any work can appear beautiful to some and not others. This is not because it is all just a matter of taste, but rather because it is beautiful only in relation to various aspects (which some apprehend while others do not).[50]

48 *Art and Scholasticism*, 24–25.

49 *Art and Scholasticism*, 28n.

50 *Art and Scholasticism*, 29–30.

Accordingly, beauty arises from the intellectual apprehension of form, which is found when we experience and intellectually apprehend the intelligible order present in structured and unified matter. This is ultimately Maritain's rationale for emphasizing so strongly the cognitive and intellectual dimensions of beauty:

> The intelligence delights in the beautiful because in the beautiful it finds itself again and recognizes itself, and makes contact with its own light.[51]

Given our human nature, which is both material and spiritual, beauty is not purely intellectual for us. Whereas scientific knowledge is only attained by abstracting away from sensible knowledge of the particular, in artistic beauty the light of being radiates and stimulates intelligence through the apprehension that takes place in sense experience. Since beauty is essentially delightful, it naturally gives rise to love, which in turn sparks ecstasy in various analogous ways, whether it be in the form of one caught up in the beauty of a work of art, a lover struck by the beauty of his beloved, or the mystic caught up in the contemplation of God.

In his explanation of the fixed rules of art, Maritain is careful to avoid any suggestion that the artist merely dutifully applies the rules of his or her particular craft in some sort of routine way to produce a work. The rules of any art, whether it be a servile, liberal, or fine art, are in fact a vital and spiritual condition of the artist. Here he returns to the notion of art as a habit. The rules are nothing other than the habits and virtues of the artist's intellect. Accordingly, the artist is never acting in a merely instrumental manner, slavishly following rules. Rather, she is a ruler making use of the rules as a means to achieve her ends:

> Through the *habitus* or virtue of art superelevating his mind from within, the artist is a ruler who *uses* rules according to his ends; it is as senseless to conceive of him as the slave of the rules as to consider the worker the slave of his tools.[52]

---

51 *Art and Scholasticism*, 25.
52 *Art and Scholasticism*, 39.

Hence, the master of an art will use the rules to his artistic ends. He will not, as is often said, break the rules to serve his purposes. Rather, he will transcend them, moving beyond them in those occasional moments of genius. Thus, there is a difference between a living and acting habit, and a method in the modern sense of a formula (which is to be followed blindly, and which largely dispenses one from the difficulty of thinking). The first rule of the artist, then, is not a matter of a technique to be followed in the particular medium the artist is working in; rather, it is fidelity to the artist's own creative intuition:

> Now what is this primary rule in the case of the fine arts? I have said that in this case the appetite, together with the intellect, basically tends to the release of the pure creativity of the spirit, in its longing for beauty. Consequently, the primary rule is the vital actuation or determination through which this free creativity of the spirit expresses itself first and foremost—and to which, therefore, the mind and the hand of the artist must first of all be loyal.[53]

Fidelity to this rule is primary and fundamental and takes precedence over all other rules of art, however important they are. Other rules deal with the manner of operation through which the artist carries out her work, while this primary rule deals with the very conception of the work in the spirit of the artist, which is to be carried out to create something beautiful. In the absence of this creative intuition, a work—however perfectly it may be made from the perspective of the artist's craft and technique—amounts to nothing.[54] Accordingly, following the rule of art can never be reduced to a matter of unthinking activity, as if one were following the instructions of a recipe. At the same time, the artist disregards the rules that govern the operation of her particular form of art at her peril. To mock them through an appeal to the liberty of art is, Maritain asserts, "an excuse provided by foolishness to mediocrity."[55]

---

53 *Creative Intuition in Art and Poetry*, 45.
54 *Creative Intuition in Art and Poetry*, 45.
55 *Creative Intuition in Art and Poetry*, 48.

At this point, we can see why Maritain is far more sympathetic to modernist poets and painters, and far more critical of academic neo-classical revivals in the arts than many other Thomists are. He clearly rejects the notion that it is the artist's job to merely reproduce the things he encounters in nature. Such a position can only breed a stale academicism that he holds in contempt. It would be the death of the spirit. Rather, as we saw in the previous section, the work of art is the result of a dynamic encounter, through which the artist's self-expression occurs through his expression of the things he represents in his art. Accordingly, imitation—or making a copy—is not the appropriate aim of the artist. This is not to say that Maritain rejects the Aristotelian doctrine that "art imitates nature." It would be fundamentally wrong to take Aristotle to mean that one could produce a better landscape than Cézanne's *Mont Sainte-Victoire Seen from the Bibemus Quarry* merely by painting it more accurately and precisely. Rather, in its appropriate context, this phrase does not mean that art is a copy of nature. Rather, the phrase occurs in the *Physics*, where it is clear that Aristotle has in mind the productive arts rather than the fine arts. He is, in fact, exploring how nature and art both act in producing things for the sake of an end. His example is a house, which he argues would be made the same way by nature as it is now made by art. The conclusion of his line of thought is that art often completes the works begun by nature.[56] The point of the claim that "art imitates nature," then, is that art imitates nature in its operations. The artist in creating a work of art follows similar operations in acting as an agent cause as would take place in a natural causal process. In this manner even the abstract painter must be an imitator of nature.[57]

If the artist does not create a beautiful work simply through following rules or imitation, neither is this a result of an untutored natural gift. In fact, Maritain cuts through the false dichotomy of leaving the artist to choose between seeing her art as a matter of either following sterile academic rules or possessing such a gift. No set of rules or formulae

---

56 Aristotle, *Physics*, in *The Complete Works of Aristotle*, ed. Jonathan Barnes (Oxford: Oxford University Press, 1984), 199a10–19. *Creative Intuition in Art and Poetry*, 164–65.

57 See Maritain's discussion of non-representational painting in *Creative Intuition in Art and Poetry*, 160–62.

produces an actual work of art; if anything, it merely serves to set the conditions of a potential work, while a natural gift of talent is not art at all but merely a precondition of becoming an artist (for art can only function through an intellectual and living habit).[58] Thus, art has a necessary, but not sufficient, spontaneous origin in the instinctive natural gift of the potential artist—but in order to rise to the level of art this natural impulse must be crafted and guided by the discipline of artistic training. However, this training is really a matter of cultivating the internal principle within the artist; it is not a matter of forcing it into subservience to any external principle. It is always the interior principle within the student that is the primary cause or agent in education. The master or instructor is but an external assistance to the nourishment and growth of this interior light, allowing for the formation of good habits in keeping with the old insight that "art cooperates with nature."

Maritain sees the fine arts as having a special relationship to their rules, for they aim more directly at Beauty, and Beauty—like being—has an infinite fullness and range. However, an artistic work always exists in some limited genus; it is some kind of thing and not another. Thus, the work of the fine arts is a paradox: it is a limited and concrete work, yet it dares to bring into being an instance of a transcendental, Beauty. Outside the genre of any particular work of art there remains an infinity of other ways of being beautiful. Thus, there is a tension between the transcendence of beauty and the material narrowness of the work of art. Yet this paradox is not an impediment to the work of the artist. The artist's task is not to do the impossible, manifesting the infinite in the finite. Rather, it is a humbler work of discovering a new mode of expressing the beautiful analogously:

> The creator in art is he who discovers a *new analogate* of the beautiful, a new way in which the radiance of form can shine on matter. The work that he makes, and which as such exists in a certain genus, is from then onwards a new genus and requires new rules—I mean a new adaptation of the fundamental and perennial rules, and even the use of *viae certa et determinatae* (certain and

58 *Art and Scholasticism*, 41.

determinate rules) not hitherto employed and which at first disconcert people.[59]

In this sense the artist does not create a copy of God's creation, but continues God's work of creation.[60] Here we confront the fact that beauty is a transcendental, a specific way of conceptualizing what is in reality good, one, and true. This is the fundamental reason why art is a basic human need, both for the individual and for society, as Maritain puts it eloquently in *Art and Scholasticism*:

> The moment one touches a transcendental, one touches being itself, a likeness of God, an absolute, that which ennobles and delights our life; one enters into the domain of the spirit. It is remarkable that men really communicate with one another only by passing through being or one of its properties. Only in this way do they escape from the individuality in which matter encloses them. If they remain in the world of their sense needs and of their sentimental egos, in vain do they tell their stories to one another, they do not understand each other. They observe each other without seeing each other, each one of them infinitely alone, even though work or sense pleasures bind them together. But let one touch the good and Love, like the saints, the true, like an Aristotle, the beautiful, like a Dante or a Bach or a Giotto, then contact is made, souls communicate. Men are really united only by the spirit; light alone brings them together, *intellectualia et rationalia omnia congregans, et indestructibilia faciens*.[61]

Accordingly, art has an indispensable spiritual mission within society.

In this chapter we have seen how Maritain articulates the nature of art as a virtue of the practical intellect, consisting in right reason in making. The work of the artist is reducible neither to an expression of emotion, nor an attempt to provoke an emotional reaction in the audience. Rather, it is always a work of practical reason. This certainly does not exclude the emotions, which have important roles to play in

---

59 *Art and Scholasticism*, 45.
60 *Art and Scholasticism*, 60.
61 *Art and Scholasticism*, 32–33.

the arts, but it does entail a rejection of the many theories that see art as an escape from reason—whether ancient, like that of Plato, or modern, like that of the surrealists. In the second section Maritain's development of Aquinas's understanding of beauty was explored. This led to a reexamination of the central role of creative intuition, itself a mode of reasoning in the arts. Finally, the relation of art to beauty considered as a transcendental was highlighted.

This last point is suggestive of the vital mission that art has for humanity. As Maritain sees it, nothing less than our connection to our fellow man and to God is at stake, for our grasp of the transcendentals is a fundamental characteristic of human nature: "Man is an animal who lives on transcendentals."[62] In this respect it would be a fatal mistake to dismiss beauty as unimportant. Such a mistake is not fatal for art— which never fully relinquishes its quest for beauty in spite of the uses to which it is put by some of its aspirants—but for humanity. Maritain here relies on an insight from Aquinas that human beings cannot live without delectation, so that when we are lacking in spiritual delights we are likely to turn toward carnal ones.[63] This is of particular concern in the modern world, where the cult of the useful has overtaken the transcendentals, in a culture where money and efficiency is valued over the beautiful, the good, and the true—indeed, over human life itself. Maritain poignantly reflects on this fact:

> One of the vicious trends which outrage our modern industrial civilization is a kind of asceticism at the service of the useful, a kind of unholy mortification for the sake of no superior life. Men are still capable of excitation and relaxation, but almost deprived of any pleasure and rest of the soul—a life which would seem insane even to the great materialists of antiquity. They flog themselves, they renounce the sweetness of the world and all the ornaments of the terrestrial abode, *omnem ornatum saeculi,* with the single incentive of working, working, working, and acquiring technological empire over matter.

---

62 *The Responsibility of the Artist,* 73.

63 *S.T.,* II-II, q. 35, a. 4 ad 2.

Here Maritain shows a deep sensitivity to the ever-increasing functionalism of modern society. The quest for more and more efficient technical means—without any sense of ultimate ends—leads to a life that is not only meaningless, but full of self-imposed hardship, without this burden being for the sake any greater good. While work, of course, has its place, it needs to be subordinated to the fundamental human goods that make life fulfilling, notably, friendship, love, and contemplation. Yet so many of our contemporaries scoff at the notion that some values could transcend the sphere of what is useful:

> Their daily life lacks nothing so much as the delectations of the intelligence-permeated sense; and even the churches in which they pray are not uncommonly masterworks in ugliness. Then, since we cannot live without delectation, they have no other resource left but those arts and pleasures which satisfy "the brute curiosity of an animal's stare"—all the better as they produce stupefaction and obliviousness, as a substitute for Epicurean ataraxy. No wonder that other kinds of drugs, from alcohol or marijuana to the cult of carnal Venus, occupy a growing place in the process of compensation.[64]

To overtake this relentless functionalization of all human activities, a process that makes life gradually unlivable and deaf to spiritual delight, art is a basic necessity. It has a spiritual mission of the first importance in putting us in touch with the transcendentals in the most accessible and natural manner available to us, through beauty: "It is the most natural power of healing and spiritualization needed in the human community."[65]

---

64 *Creative Intuition in Art and Poetry*, 146–47. See also Josef Pieper, *Leisure: The Basis of Culture*, trans. Alexander Dru (New York: The New American Library, 1963).

65 *Creative Intuition in Art and Poetry*, 147.

CHAPTER 11

Philosophy of History

If, in fact, human freedom plays in the history of the world a part which seems all the greater as the level of activity considered is more spiritual, and all the smaller as the level of activity is more temporal, this is because man, collectively taken, lives little of the properly human life of reason and freedom.

On the Philosophy of History, 16

M aritain's incursion into the philosophy of history is somewhat limited. He came to treat the topic explicitly only rather late in his career, giving a series of four lectures on the subject at the University of Notre Dame in 1955. These were published as a book two years later, after having been edited by Joseph Evans, CSB, and then corrected by Maritain himself. Maritain had come to consider this field explicitly only after having been surprised to learn that he had a philosophy of history at all, after Charles Journet had written a paper drawing together Maritain's writings on the topic that had arisen in the context of treating other subjects.[1] While

---

1 Charles Cardinal Journet, "Maritain's Sense of History," in *Jacques Maritain: The Man and His Achievement*, ed. Joseph W. Evans (New York: Sheed & Ward, 1963), 180–91.

this is a subject upon which Maritain wrote relatively little, it is a fitting topic with which to end this study of his philosophy, for a main theme we have traced throughout his treatment of every area of philosophy has been related to the question of the relation between the individual and the universal. Indeed, I would characterize Maritain's work as a whole as an attempt to reconcile the formal, objective, and universal approach of St. Thomas Aquinas and the scholastic tradition to the distinctively contemporary concern with the concrete dynamism of the individual in the various domains of philosophical knowledge. This assessment is in keeping with the judgment of noted philosopher Augusto Del Noce that "he was before anything else a philosopher of history."[2] In this respect, it is in the development of his philosophy of history that his philosophy as a whole finds its culmination and, to some extent, its justification. His thought on the matter, accordingly, provides an appropriate topic with which to conclude the present study of his philosophy.

Is a Thomistic Philosophy of History Possible?

Thomistic philosophy, as indeed any scholastic philosophy, has a problem recognizing the possibility of a philosophy of history, in large part due to its dependence upon Aristotelian principles. For Aristotle, philosophical knowledge is scientific. It proceeds logically, and its objects are not particular facts about this or that individual, but the universal. As Boethius pointed out, there is no definition of "Socrates" as such, but only of "human." History, however, deals entirely with individual contingent states of affairs, not universals. Aristotle draws out this implication in his *Poetics*, when he explains the difference between poetry and history. This is not just a matter of poets writing in verse, while historians write in prose (for, as Aristotle points out, even if Herodotus had written in verse, he would have been writing history). Rather, the true difference between the poet and the historian lies in two related facts: (1) The poet treats of what might happen, whereas the historian is concerned with what did happen; and (2) poetry is more philosophical

---

2   Augusto Del Noce, "The Lesson of Maritain," *Maritain Studies* 31 (2015): 72.

and more important than history, as its pronouncements concern what is universal, whereas the statements of historians are always about singulars.[3] Since history is concerned with individuals and events as they happened, it seems that by definition it is unable to rise to the level of knowledge or science in the Aristotelian sense. This suspicion of history is also found in St. Thomas Aquinas. In arguing that sacred doctrine is a science, Aquinas considers an objector who holds that a science does not deal with individual cases, but that sacred doctrine deals with the particular deeds of Abraham, Isaac, Jacob, and the like. Aquinas's answer is that individual facts are used by the theologian to provide examples of how to live well or to establish the authority of particular individuals to transmit divine revelation.[4] Yet this reply seems to significantly undermine the role that history plays in Christian theology, where several key doctrines have a historical dimension, notably, those related to the birth, life, and death of Jesus.

Maritain articulates the problem of history's unscientific character and answers it directly. History, he admits, is quite clearly concerned with the individual. It aims to explain the singular through the singular and its object is the singular or individual: "The explanation given by an historian, as historian, is an explanation of the individual by the individual—by individual circumstances, motivations, or events. The historical elucidation, being individual, participates in the potential infinity of matter; it is never finished; it never has (insofar as it is elucidation) the certainty of science."[5] If history is not a suitable subject matter for science, how can there possibly be a philosophy of history?

Maritain gives two related lines of response to this problem. Most significantly, even though the discipline of history itself is not a science, the *philosophy* of history is a science, since philosophy by its nature is "scientific knowledge," in the Aristotelian sense of the phrase, and a formal systematic discipline of wisdom. There is no need for philosophy to

3   Aristotle, *Poetics* in *The Complete Works of Aristotle*, ed. Jonathan Barnes (Oxford: Oxford University Press, 1984), 1451b1–7.

4   *S.T.*, I, q.1, a.2 ad 2.

5   *On the Philosophy of History* (New York: Charles Scribner's Sons, 1957), 2–3.

restrict itself to subjects that have been previously known and worked out scientifically by some other science. Philosophical principles can be brought to bear to develop a philosophy of art or a philosophy of law, yet neither art nor law are sciences. In dealing with history, art, or law, philosophy deals with the same subject matter as those disciplines, but from the point of view of philosophy's own distinctive method or perspective. Accordingly, in the philosophy of history we have a "scientific" object, since the object of history is being considered philosophically, but not through the subject matter being previously studied and scientifically articulated by some other discipline. To put it more formally in scholastic terms, history and the philosophy of history have the same material object (i.e., they both study the same content), but they have different formal objects (i.e., they view this content through different perspectives or in light of different methods).[6] History is a potential subject matter for philosophy, as it provides factual certitude, every bit as much as science does. Here Maritain notes and endorses the renowned philosopher of science Pierre Duhem's thesis that the data of the senses or the common knowledge of people can be more certain than the findings of science, though they are less precise and not useful for the scientific task itself.[7]

Maritain's second line of argument in defense of a philosophy of history is to point out that the appeal to Aristotelian science's restriction of knowledge to the universal is understood too simply in this context. In fact, unless there is a distinction between the individual thing and the universal essence, it is impossible for us to understand how an event can be contingent while the law is known through science (be that science a natural science, a philosophy of nature, or a philosophy of history). Only with this distinction can we grasp how individual events flow and change, while the laws governing this change remain immutable and enduring. This is, in fact, the basis upon which history itself is possible. As Maritain argues in *The Degrees of Knowledge:*

6   *On the Philosophy of History,* 4–5.
7   *Philosophy of Nature,* 60–62.

Every existing thing has its own nature or essence. But the existential positing of things is not implied in their nature, and amongst them there are encounters which are themselves not natures, the necessity for which is not prescribed in any nature. Existing reality is therefore composed of nature and adventure. That is why it has a direction in time and by its duration constitutes an (irreversible) history—these two elements are demanded for history, for a world of pure natures would not stir in time; there is no history for Platonic archetypes; nor would a world of pure adventure have any direction; there is no history for a thermodynamic equilibrium.[8]

This mutual dependence of the individual upon the universal also manifests itself in Maritain's discussion of the philosophy of history. He explains that while Thomist science aims at the universal, it does not—indeed cannot—ignore the particular. Rather, science as it is understood by Aristotle and Aquinas not only has its origins in the individual, from which the universal is abstracted, but also is terminated and brought to completion only in the singular individual. The senses are not only necessary to provide the basis for abstraction of our concepts; they are also necessary to come to a resolution through a judgment. While judgment obviously doesn't occur through the sense organs directly, it cannot take place without reference to them. In this regard Maritain quotes from the *Summa*, where Aquinas is arguing that the suspension of the senses impedes judgment:

> Now the Philosopher says (*De Coel.* iii), that "as the end of a practical science is action, so the end of natural science is that which is perceived principally through the senses"; for the smith does not seek knowledge of a knife except for the purpose of action, in order that he may produce a certain individual knife; and in like manner the natural philosopher does not seek to know the nature of a stone and of a horse, save for the purpose of knowing the essential properties of those things which he perceives with his senses. Now it is clear that a smith cannot judge perfectly of a knife unless he knows the action of the knife: and in like manner the natural philosopher cannot judge perfectly of natural things, unless he

---

8 *The Degrees of Knowledge*, 29.

knows sensible things. But in the present state of life whatever we understand, we know by comparison to natural sensible things. Consequently it is not possible for our intellect to form a perfect judgment, while the senses are suspended, through which sensible things are known to us.[9]

To take Aquinas's example, the knowledge of a smith will be imperfect unless he is able to apply the universal principles that he has to the particular uses that they have. Likewise, philosophers of nature will not be able to judge rightly about the things of nature unless they are able to reduce and apply the universals they have abstracted to particular sensible things. It is by this return to the singular and contingent things that the universal is realized and, with the aid of the senses (which reintegrates the intelligible in the particular thing that exists), the intellect completes its apprehension of the real. This return to the particular is necessary whether the thing to be known is a sensible existent or a spiritual one.[10] From this Maritain concludes that at every degree of knowledge there must be a return to the singular, although this will take place differently in each discipline.

Having established the philosophy of history as a genuinely scientific dimension of philosophy, it is important to note where Maritain sees it fitting within the structure of the philosophical sciences. For him it is a dimension of moral philosophy, in which the breadth of the natural law can be seen in more specified and applied ways. Further, it shares with moral philosophy the need to be understood in a theological context if it is to be adequately considered. The Christian philosopher of history will miss essential aspects of his or her topic if ignorant of basic theological data (such as the Fall) or the difference between the historical development of humanity and the mission of Israel under the old law, and how these change under the new law, etc.

---

9   *The Degrees of Knowledge*, 140. See also *S.T.*, I, q. 84, a. 8 c.
10 *The Degrees of Knowledge*, 139.

Spurious Philosophy of History

As is well known, practicing historians have a general distrust for the philosophy of history. Maritain shows considerable sympathy with this attitude. He cites with agreement four objections to mainstream philosophies of history, be they those of Hegel, Marx, Comte, or others, as set out by Henri Marrou:

1. They display an oversimplified and arbitrary approach to the choice of historical materials, assuming their value for the sake of supporting an already accepted philosophical position.
2. They have a self-deceptive ambition to achieve an *a priori* explanation of the development of human history.
3. This self-deceptive ambition also extends to an ambition to have an all-embracing explanation of the meaning of human history.
4. They reveal a self-deceptive ambition to offer a supposedly "scientific" explanation of human history, in the sense that such an explanation would give our thought intellectual mastery over the historical subject matter.[11]

These problems are especially prevalent in various nineteenth-century philosophers of history, particularly the greatest of them, namely, Hegel. Hegel's reading of history as an evolution of rational progress through dialectical contradiction is well known. In his preface to his *Philosophy of History*, this is famously articulated through the development of the idea of freedom. In a society without law we have anarchy. While this may appear to be absolute freedom, in reality it is not, as each individual is subject to the arbitrary whim and power of the others. Accordingly, our freedom is limited because others can harm us or take from us insofar as they are stronger. In order to ensure freedom against anarchy, there first arose authoritarian forms of government, which provided law that ensured some degree of freedom for citizens, who could now be assured of a somewhat stable context in which to act freely. However, this form of freedom is limited, as one remains subject

---

11   *On the Philosophy of History*, 30, summarizing Henri-Irénée Marrou, *De la connaissance historique* (Paris: ed. du Seuil, 1954), 16.

to the authority of a government one has not chosen and has no control over. Accordingly, we find again a contradictory tension for freedom which needs to be resolved in a higher synthesis. This occurs with the development of democracies that give citizens a say in government, since democracy secures freedom found through law with a higher freedom that allows for a say in the formation of that law.[12] While Hegel is cautious not to speculate about the future, we can see with hindsight that the democratic movement itself is subject to further dialectical development in various ways, as the mechanisms of democratic politics are not equally available to all, etc.

Accordingly, it is easy to see the challenges noted by Marrou and endorsed by Maritain in Hegel. Here we have a philosophy of history that is rather arbitrary and self-serving with its choice of historical events, yet also a philosophy of history that claims to offer an explanation of human history that is *a priori*, all encompassing, and scientific.

For Maritain, Hegelian philosophy of history is nothing less than a delusion. He forthrightly rejects the claim of progress or necessary dialectical development in history, which is central to the Hegelian approach. He holds that Hegel's central intuition is that reality is history; reality is fundamentally motion, change, and progressively rational evolution. Here Hegel takes rationalism to an absolute through his dialectical understanding of history advancing rationally through the logical resolution of lived contradictions. In contrast, although he does not develop the insight, Maritain explains this development alternatively, by noting that each new apparent triumph in history is nothing other than an exhaustion of the very potentialities that gave rise to it, and which, in the process of succeeding, discloses and provokes in "the abyss of the real the opposite tendencies."[13] The apparent similarity of historical development to the general nature of his philosophy misled Hegel to think that logic, in the Hegelian sense, was the only factor involved. In Maritain's view Hegel's dialectic turns facts into material

---

12 G. W. F. Hegel, *The Philosophy of History*, trans. J. Sibree (New York: Willey Book Co., 1944), 19–26.

13 *On the Philosophy of History*, 21.

for the *a priori* exercise of thought. As he puts it, "Since the real is no longer the rule and exercise of thought, but simply the furnisher of materials for the *a priori* exercise of thought, this off-center dialectic can make the real say anything it wants it to, provided only that the materials in question are chosen with sufficient astuteness and perspicacity."[14] However, Maritain points out that there are many other historical aspects and general laws of historical development that are even more important and closer to reality. Hence, Hegel's philosophy of history is seen by Maritain to be "a modern form of Gnosticism, that is a pure Gnosticism."[15]

It is important to add that Maritain, correctly, sees the Marxist notion of history as one that is directly inherited from Hegel, with the qualification that Marx transforms the Hegelian idealist dialectic to a materialist one. Whereas for Hegel the evolution of the world of the Idea drove history, for Marx, by contrast, the conflict of economic interests plays a more vital role.[16] While Maritain criticizes Marxism on several fronts (e.g., for adopting atheism with a quasi-religious faith), it is its flawed philosophy of history that is at the forefront of his attack. In this context Maritain sees Marxism as a philosophy of resentment, pursuing a process of substitution of a new Marxist society for the previous Christian one. The first step in this process is to denounce exalted ideas of idealism and metaphysics and to substitute these with an absolute realist immanentism. (This is to say that Marx focuses only upon material causality.) Thus, the principles and processes are entirely immanent or within history. Further, for the Marxist, philosophy should become practical, not in the Aristotelian sense, but in the sense that speculative philosophy should be replaced by thought wholly given to *praxis* (i.e., practice). In keeping with this, Marx not only asserted the importance of material causality, but made it purely and simply primary. Here Maritain

---

14 *Moral Philosophy*, 133.

15 *On the Philosophy of History*, 23. For a full analysis of Maritain's critique of Hegel see Stephen Rocker, "Maritain on Hegel," *Maritain Studies* XXXVI (2020): 19–29. Rocker argues that a Hegelian God's role in history is not as far from Aquinas's model as Maritain thinks if we consider the way in which God's divine ideas are a pattern for historical events. See Rocker, 22.

16 *Philosophy of History*, 24. *Moral Philosophy*, 229–34.

is sensitive to note that it is not (as is popularly thought), economics that is the sole source of Marxist history, but rather the full range of material causality. Marx integrated his practical insight about the dehumanization of work conditions into an anthropocentric metaphysics in which work became the constituent element of human nature.

Maritain's "New Christendom" would call for an end to economic servitude and the inhuman condition of workers in the name of the fundamental dignity of the human person who, as spiritual, has a destiny that relates him to transcendent goods and rights. By contrast, Marxism calls for an end to these same dehumanizing conditions, but in the name of collective man: for the sake of his collective life and in order to free him for his collective work through which he can find deliverance.[17] The second moment in this process of substitution is Marxism's expectation of salvation from merely material causality. Given the dynamic of Hegelian dialectic is limited to matter, Marxists expect the economic process in conjunction with the energies of the revolutionary mindset to lead to the rule of reason, the elimination of disenfranchisement, and the making of man as the master of history. In the third and final moment, the question is posed concerning what mediator will bring about this redemption. The Marxist answer is to see this role as fulfilled by the proletariat, that is, by the oppressed and alienated in society. In this way, Maritain sees Marx as replacing God with the social process.[18]

In this context, it is important to note that dissatisfaction with Maritain's thought on some of these points played an important role in the evolution of liberation theology. In his landmark book *The Theology of Liberation* the theologian Gustavo Gutiérrez traces the history of the Church's engagement with the political order. At the culmination of this history is a critical appraisal of Maritain's notion of a "New Christendom," which provides the point of departure for Gutiérrez's own theological view. He notes that Maritain's thought on this topic marks a new approach in which the long-outdated understanding of the Church operating in a sacral culture—in which all is ordered to God—is at last

---

17 *Integral Humanism*, 182.
18 *Integral Humanism*, 185.

given up. For Maritain the question is how to form a Christian culture and politics in a context where the Church no longer provides the central common point of reference. Accordingly, Maritain advocates for a move from Christians acting in society explicitly as an arm of the Church under the guidance of the hierarchy, to a notion of the Christian as a free citizen carrying out a social apostolate *as* a Christian, through his own free initiative in the temporal order. Thus, there is a basic distinction between the Church and her spiritual mission that happens to be carried out in history, and the Christian who also has a temporal mission and for whom the change of temporal history and civilization is of great importance. Maritain's conception of a New Christendom was a significant influence upon the Christian Democratic movement in Europe and Latin America.

While Gutiérrez admits that many generous souls were inspired by Maritain's thought to work towards a Christian transformation of the social order and even suffered from the enmity of Church authorities,[19] he raises two objections. His first objection is practical. Maritain's position in practice gave rise to "fundamentally moderate political attitudes" that combined nostalgia for the past with a modernizing mentality. It did not entertain a desire for radically new social forms.[20] However, it is scarcely a reasonable criticism of a political theory that it does not produce the results that a proponent of a fundamentally different theory would prefer. Moreover, Gutiérrez's practical objection is not directly aimed at Maritain or his ideas, but at how others inspired more or less by him implemented these ideas in political practice. Maritain himself was not a politician and consistently resisted attempts to have him engage in partisan politics, as he felt the loyalty needed to be a member of a political party was inconsistent with the liberty of thought his vocation as a philosopher demanded. This is to say his contribution

---

19 Gutiérrez, *A Theology of Liberation*, 15th anniversary trans. and eds. Sister Caridad Inda and John Eagleson (Maryknoll, NY: Orbis Books, 1988), 36.

20 Gutiérrez, *A Theology of Liberation*, 36. In *The Cambridge Companion to Liberation Theology*, ed. Christopher Rowland, 2nd ed. (Cambridge, UK: Cambridge University Press, 2007), 213, the objection to Maritain is expressed in terms of a concern about his emphasis on the "primacy of the spiritual." While less precise, this is clearly related to his distinction of the spiritual and temporal planes of activity.

to politics was a philosophical one; the responsibility for its practical applications clearly rests with those who tried to appropriate his ideas. In this respect, it is worth noting that in his late work Maritain himself expressed deep dissatisfaction with the attempts to apply his thought to politics. In fact, he notes that in his own view there are only three revolutionaries worthy of the name: Eduardo Frei, the Christian Democratic President of Chile; the American Saul Alinsky; and himself in France (though he mentions that his own work is directed towards philosophy rather than political action).[21] Accordingly, one could argue that Gutiérrez's objection does not touch Maritain's thought at all, but rather is directed towards incompetent attempts to realize this political theory in practice.

The second objection raised is theological. Maritain's New Christendom is rooted in a fundamental distinction between the spiritual and temporal planes of activity. Gutiérrez holds that this distinction allowed for too strong a separation between the Church and the world. The autonomy of Christians in the temporal sphere was asserted, not only with respect to ecclesial authority, but also with regards to the Church's mission. Accordingly, the Church's role as an institution in the world was limited in temporal matters to moral teaching. In practice, this meant that the Church could only act in the temporal sphere through mediating the conscience of the individual Christian. As a result, the Church's function in the world was limited to two missions: evangelization and the inspiration of the temporal sphere. This also meant a clear division of responsibility between the clergy and the laity. The priest's task being primarily sacramental and evangelizing, with no responsibility or role for direct intervention in political action (this being a responsibility of the lay person). The laity would engage in the temporal politics of the world in cooperation with others, whether Christian or not, for a more just human society. This work would be a work of sanctity if it was to come to anything, but a sanctity directed toward the resolution of secular and profane problems.[22]

---

21 *The Peasant of the Garonne*, 22–23.
22 *Integral Humanism*, 227–29.

For Gutiérrez this distinction between the spiritual and temporal planes of activity leads to a perception that the Church has two different missions. It also emphasizes a sharp division between the role of the priest and lay people that hampers pastoral action, leading to a Church whose spiritual mission is divorced from its temporal responsibility of working towards justice in the world. The entire thrust of his liberation theology is to bring these two into a deeper unity. However, from the perspective of Maritain's thought, such a unification presupposes a naïve view of the philosophy of history. Identifying the spiritual and the temporal dimensions of the Church's activity results in committing the cardinal sin associated with Marxism, namely, seeking to bring about the kingdom of God within history.[23] Such an attempt is pure folly, for even granting to the Marxist or the liberation theologian a society organized in the most just manner they can imagine, it will nevertheless give rise to evil and misfortune, simply because these are forever within man in this temporal life. History is fundamentally in process; it is moving towards the Kingdom of God, and while we must work tirelessly toward justice, we must be aware that every improvement to instantiate justice will leave some behind. As Maritain argues:

> To my mind, it is to betray both God and man not to understand that history is in movement toward the kingdom of God, and not to wish that this kingdom come about. But it is nonsense to think that it will come about *in* history, which is invincibly made up of good and evil. Prepared by the growth of history, and by the mixing and progressive exhaustion of the human being that are accomplished there, it will come at the end of history; I mean in the time of the resurrected into which history will open.[24]

Laws of History

Spurious philosophy of history—whether it be that of Hegel, Marx, or Comte—goes astray by attempting to offer philosophical explanations

---

23 Gutiérrez, *A Theology of Liberation*, 43–46.
24 *Integral Humanism*, 189.

338 | THE CHRISTIAN PHILOSOPHY OF JACQUES MARITAIN

of history, and thus inevitably slipping into a gnostic view of history that frustrates the practicing historian, who is ever alert to the contingencies inherent in his or her subject matter. It is in contrast to this common failing that Maritain sets out his understanding of a "genuine" philosophy of history, writing:

> Let us then state as our first principle: history can neither be rationally explained nor reconstructed according to necessitating laws.
> But history can be characterized, interpreted or deciphered in a certain measure and as to certain general aspects—to the extent to which we succeed in discussing in it meanings or intelligible directions, and laws which enlighten events without necessitating them.[25]

Just as in the realm of nature the laws that govern nature are necessary, while the particular course of events is contingent, so too in the realm of history we deal with contingent events—and even more—due to the factor of human freedom.

Philosophy of history can be neither the purely inductive work of a historian arriving at historical laws by generalizing solely on the basis of the particular cases she happens to have encountered; neither is it a purely rational process of philosophical deduction in the way Hegel at times suggests. Rather, Maritain sees two phases within philosophy of history:

1. An inductive step of abstraction from the historical data of an age or of an essential element of human history in general, and
2. The philosophical verification of the results of the inductions arrived at in the first step through a critical comparison with philosophical truths that have been previously acquired.

In this manner the philosopher joins together induction with the results of philosophical demonstration to arrive at the objective content of philosophy of history. The vital second step stabilizes historical knowing by grounding it within the broader scope of a philosophical account of human nature, politics, and culture. It is this step that Maritain seems

---

25 *On the Philosophy of History*, 32.

to think justifies us in saying that the laws of history are laws rather than mere inductive generalizations. The verification of the inductively generated insight with the philosopher of history's metaphysics, philosophical anthropology, political philosophy, etc. renders the historical induction a law or formula.

Further, Maritain distinguishes two kinds of historical laws to which this twofold method of analysis applies. The first are axiomatic, or functional, laws. These laws express a functional relationship between various intelligible characteristics that can be verified at various stages in human history. In this context we can only touch on each of these through a brief explanation below:

1. *The law of twofold contrasting progress*: This law states that history advances in the direction of good and evil simultaneously. Here Maritain points to the allegory in the Gospels that the cockle grows up amongst the wheat, and the wise farmer waits to separate them when the wheat has fully grown. This lesson is as true for the world of history as it is for the world of grace. While one or the other may predominate for a time, both always exist together to one degree or another.[26]

2. *The ambivalence of history*: If the previous law holds, it follows that each moment or event in history presents to us two faces, both good and evil: "No period of human history can be either absolutely condemned or absolutely approved." Each era has its own unique glories and characteristic errors. Each event taken in the totality of its consequences will advance both good and evil. Accordingly, even the worst evildoers serve the purposes of God: "He is served by the martyrs, and He is served by the executioners who made them martyrs."[27]

3. *The law of the historical fructifications of good and evil*: This law concerns the relations of ethics to politics. It reminds us that the good or harm that is immediately evident is not necessarily characteristic of the long-term impact political actions will have. This law flies in the face of those who would do injustice so that some good or other might

---

26 *On the Philosophy of History*, 43–52.
27 *On the Philosophy of History*, 56.

come from it. Rather, justice and righteousness in themselves tend to the preservation of human society and success in the long run, while injustice and evil in themselves tend to destroy society and bring real failure in the long run. Accordingly, it is impossible to separate the political order from the moral order.[28]

4. *The law of the world-significance of history-making events*: Maritain notes that he struggled to find the proper articulation for this law. He wants to argue that there is in the natural order of history a basic connectivity between all human beings and human groups. This is nothing as deep or significant as the unity of the Church or the communion of saints. There is a "vital unity," which is not political, organized, or explicit but which is still real. In view of this natural and oft-hidden solidarity, the major events of history are significant not only for those who are immediately involved, but affect the entire world. Maritain's example is the French Revolution, which brought about age-old potencies. This overthrow of the *Ancien Regime* was a response to absolute monarchy. While it happened in France, it happened for the world as well, and it affected other parts of the world in different and even opposing ways. Likewise, the Communist Revolution in Russia, though as a matter of contingent historical fact motivated by a false philosophical system, nevertheless happened "for the world." While another type of social revolution, founded not on Marx but on the Christian principles of a thinker like Péguy, might have taken place instead, it no longer can as the historical moment has happened. Now the aim of the Christian is not to dream of a Christian social revolution, but to work towards the Christian ideal through gradual adjustments as opportunities present themselves to manifest social justice.

5. *The law of prise de conscience*: This is a law of growth in self-awareness as a sign of human progress. However, Maritain is careful to note that it involves dangers as well. While the history of civilization manifests a growing consciousness, it takes place very slowly. In ancient Greece, there was, for instance, an awareness of the political freedom of the

---

28 *On the Philosophy of History*, 59–62.

citizen, but not the inner spiritual freedom of the person in relation to the city. In the history of philosophy, epistemology was not developed as a distinct organized discipline before Kant, as prior thinkers addressed epistemological questions in the context of either logic or philosophical psychology.

6. *The law of the hierarchy of means*: This law has a dual dimension, the first is the law of the superiority of humble temporal means over rich ones when it comes to spiritual ends; the second law is the superiority of spiritual means over carnal means in the field of temporal activity and welfare. Maritain's central example of this latter law is that of Gandhi's peaceful non-conformity.

This second category of formulas and laws manifests the variety of historical ages or aspects found in human history. They show the ways in which history can be understood in terms of determinate segments of direction and significance:

1. *The theological notion of various "states" of human nature*: This concerns theological distinctions between the "state of pure nature," "state of innocence," "state of fallen nature," and "state of redeemed nature." The relation of these categories to any history is complex, as the state of pure nature never existed but is merely a possibility, and while we can distinguish the states of fallen nature and of redeemed nature, they cannot be understood as a simple succession, as there is no time at which grace was not at work in humanity. Fallen nature was always to be redeemed in virtue of Christ's Passion to come or subsequently in view of its having happened. While the Fall can't be proven philosophically, the Christian philosopher of history cannot ignore it, for the Fall didn't just deprive us of the supernatural, it also "wounded human nature"—and these wounds of nature are always present in the human race. So while these theological distinctions are prehistorical, they have significance for the moral philosopher and thus, the philosopher of history, if these philosophers are to deal with the real existential state of humanity.

2. *The theological notion of various "states" in the historical development of mankind:* This formula is now properly historical, as it concerns the

historical states of humanity as viewed from a theological perspective. For instance, theology can distinguish the state of Abraham (i.e., before the Law was given), the state of the Old Law after Moses, and the state of the New Law given through Christ.

3. *The destiny of the Jewish people*: This issue presents unique problems for the Christian philosopher of history. First, on a theological level there is the mystery of destiny of the Jewish people in relation to the Kingdom of God and eternal salvation. Here Maritain draws two lessons from St. Paul: (a) their failure to recognize the new law was permitted for the salvation of all mankind, and (b) their eventual reintegration.[29] From these considerations it follows that the mission of Israel continues in a new form even once the New Law is manifested. While Maritain sees the Catholic Church as having the task of the supernatural and supratemporal saving of the world, he sees Israel as having the work of the "earthly leavening" of the world. It is to prod the world and to teach it to be restless while it is not with God, and so long as justice has not been fully manifest on earth.[30]

4. *The law of the passage from the "magical" to the "rational" regime or state in the history of human culture*: A difference is noted between a logical sign that speaks primarily to the intellect and a magical sign that speaks to the imagination. History tends to pass from an early state in which imagination is the supreme and final law, to one in which the intellect has a growing role to play.[31]

5. *The law of the progress of moral conscience*: This is identified by Maritain as the most important law in the philosophy of history. It regards the purity of moral conscience, which is to be understood independently of explicit knowledge of moral laws. Maritain gives the example of Abraham, who was a great saint even though he was ignorant of various actions that we now condemn and that were prohibited by the natural law. Even a connatural knowledge of the natural

---

29 *On the Philosophy of History*, 86–89, drawing on Romans 9–11.

30 *On the Philosophy of History*, 85–93. A more extended reflection on this topic can be found in Maritain's essay "The Mystery of Israel," in *Ransoming the Time*, 141–79.

31 *On the Philosophy of History*, 96 and 99.

law beyond the first principle, to do good and avoid evil, is something that only comes with long experience and difficulty for both individuals and civilizations. Accordingly, knowledge of the moral law is progressive in nature. While the sense of duty and obligation is always present, the awareness of particular norms such as the law of monogamy comes only with time. It also seems to follow that this knowledge will continue to grow in the future. Maritain is careful to point out that this progress is progress in *knowledge* of the moral law, and not necessarily progress in better moral *behavior*. We may know very well that slavery or torturing prisoners of war is wrong, but that doesn't mean there are not nations in which these are still practiced.

6. *The law of the passage from "sacral" to "secular" or "lay" civilizations*: While this distinction has a universal relevance, it is of particular significance in a Christian context. Accordingly, Maritain speaks of a historical trajectory from a Christian sacral civilization to a Christian secular civilization. There was a sacral age of medieval Christendom characterized by the fact that political unity was based upon the unity of faith and that the basic frame of reference for social unity was religiopolitical in nature. In the modern age, by contrast we have a secular age in which temporal society has become completely differentiated from the religious and has gained full autonomy in its own sphere. Maritain sees this development as normal and, indeed, required by the Gospel in its distinction between God's domain and Caesar's. But he notes that, historically, that normal differentiation was in fact spoiled by a rejection of God and the Gospel in social and political life, the fruit of which is the "theocratic atheism" of the communist state.[32] Yet in itself this hostility towards God is not a necessary consequence of recognizing the secular as autonomous in its own sphere, but a historically incidental aberration from the way in which that autonomy should ordinarily develop.

7. *The law of the political and social coming of age of the people*: This law concerns the progressive tendency in modern history for political communities to move from a state of subjection to a state of

---

32 *On the Philosophy of History*, 111–12. This is also a major theme of *Integral Humanism*.

self-government—the movement to forms of civilization that are characterized by a democratic philosophy or mindset.[33]

With these fundamental laws and formulas of history Maritain provides the start of a framework for an authentic philosophy of history within the Thomistic tradition. While disputing the fundamental characteristics of Hegel's philosophy of history, Maritain does agree with him in seeing theodicy as the fundamental goal of a history of philosophy adequately considered. (Indeed, the later part of his book on the philosophy of history summarizes his own response to the problem of evil, which has been examined in an earlier chapter.) However, the fundamental difference between Maritain's laws of history and the alternatives—whether the dialectical logic utilized in the Hegelian analysis, the Marxist call for revolution, or the liberation theologian's attempt to collapse the spiritual and temporal spheres of action into one another—is most clearly seen in relation to the teleological fulfillment of history. For Maritain no theodicy can limit itself to history. Indeed, there is no adequate theodicy that is not ultimately an eschatology. That is to say, the moral tensions that history presents are never completely worked out in history itself. Every historical event or trend is inevitably morally ambiguous, a mixed bag of good and evil. While God will use the evil that occurs to achieve a greater good, that does not do away with the fact that there is evil and suffering, and that these will be with us always while we are in this world of matter. As he puts it in *Existence and the Existent*:

> The mortal danger run by those whose doctrine mounts towards the heights of unity and peace is that they may think they have reached their goal when they have only started on the path, and that they may forget that for man and his thought, peace is always a victory over discord, and unity the reward of wrenchings suffered and conquered.[34]

---

33 Also see *Christianity and Democracy* (San Francisco: Ignatius Press, 2012), 28–29.
34 *Existence and the Existent*, 144.

In contrast to Hegel and related theorists, for the Thomist peace and unity are not the result of some universal or culturally manifested reason working out ready-made answers. Rather, these can only be won by a constant struggle in recurring conflicts. They demand constant individual effort and fresh insights.

CHAPTER 12

Concluding Summary

n coming to the end of this study it is appropriate to ask, "Why read Maritain today, some fifty years after his death?" This is not an unreasonable question, as there are some significant obstacles that his writing poses to the contemporary reader. His argumentation, especially in his early works, is strongly polemical. Due to the conditions in which he wrote, many of his major works have the feel of a loose collection of diverse studies rather than systematic treatises unified by a clear argument or structure. As we have seen, he was in high demand as a public lecturer. Accordingly, many of his works, even the best known, were compiled from revised versions of lectures given over time, rather than from pre-established plans. He also follows the rather frustrating French custom of being quite loose with citing his sources, and has an annoying habit of including long quotations from his own earlier works when he revisits a subject in later years.

More significantly, Maritain was very much a man engaged with the problems of his own time, and on occasion some of these problems are not our own. The political thought of *Integral Humanism*, for instance, is often articulated in the context of the uniquely twentieth-century tension between Soviet communism on one extreme and American laissez-faire capitalism on the other. His arguments in favor of a global government in *Man and the State* made some sense in the optimism surrounding the United Nations that emerged after World War II, but may seem rather naïve from a twenty-first century perspective.[1]

Nevertheless, these shortcomings on the whole are incidental, and certainly don't undermine the very rich and deep treasures of philosophical thought he offers. Having reviewed his major contributions to the various branches of philosophy, we can now step back and appreciate the main strengths of his general approach to philosophy. In this regard, as we have noted at several points in this study, perhaps the most significant reason for an ongoing interest in Maritain is the fecundity of his thought. Unlike that of most philosophers, whose writings are only of interest to a select group of peers, Maritain's thought—however one decides to ultimately assess it—has as a matter of historical fact inspired theologians, politicians, artists, composers, and others in virtually every field to which he contributed. In this respect his work finds no parallel whether in the twentieth century or any other.

More substantive is his approach to philosophical and theological questions: his unique manner of blending the old and the new. While firmly based in the thought of Aristotle and Aquinas, and frankly defending this approach as the "perennial philosophy," Maritain is clearly committed to engaging the modern world in which he finds himself. While one of his earliest books is entitled *Antimodern*, he warns he could just as easily be called *ultramodern*. The true thoughts that St. Thomas Aquinas had in the thirteenth century can be the very same thoughts that the contemporary philosopher has when reading him. If they were true then, they are just as true today. This perennial philosophy provides a base of fixed principles that we can depend on throughout history. However, they do not form a closed system, but one that is open to organic development. By way of analogy he invites us to consider the growth of a baby to an adult. Its metaphysical personhood remains the same; no heterogeneous parts are grafted to it from outside. Yet everything in that human has been transfigured; he has

---

1   See *Man and the State*, Chapter 7. A clear example of this can also be seen in a late essay started in 1972 and published posthumously that reflects his economic views and was as wildly optimistic then as it is now, is in Jacques Maritain, "A Society without Money," *Review of Social Economy* 43, no. 1 (April 1985): 73–83.

become stronger and better proportioned. This is the kind of progress a Thomistic philosophy is open to as it evolves: "The novelty which it thus displays, though not seeking it for its own sake, is above all a novel approach to the same shores of being, a new distribution of the same wealth, the pregnant mystery of things."[2]

Appealing to a perennial philosophy in this sense does not imply that all of the important philosophical questions have been answered. Rather, it suggests that there has developed a philosophical framework that is "essentially grounded in truth" which provides an ongoing basis for the development of further philosophical knowledge. In making the claim to a philosophy essentially grounded upon the truth Maritain is not attempting to wave away the reality of philosophical pluralism. While insisting that such pluralism is not, strictly speaking, necessary *de jure*, he acknowledges that it is entirely normal and to be expected *de facto*. Additionally, he points out that upholding a philosophy essentially grounded in the truth actually presupposes a degree of pluralism, as any such doctrine must ever remain fundamentally open to new insights proposed through the progress of science and culture; further, it must never cease to struggle to free itself from the limitations and short-sightedness of the perspectives of the particular milieu within which it develops. Accordingly, a philosophy that is essentially grounded in the truth will always be facing the difficulty of integrating new truths into its structure. In this light, it is easy to see that the notion that some defenders and opponents have presented of Thomism as some sort of intellectual police force defending a closed system is utterly foreign to Maritain's entire conception to philosophy.[3]

---

2   *A Preface to Metaphysics*, 14. See also Lawrence Dewan, OP, "Antimodern, Ultramodern, Postmodern: A Plea for the Perennial," in *Wisdom, Law, and Virtue: Essays in Thomistic Ethics* (New York: Fordham University Press, 2008), 87–89.

3   "Concerning Truth," in *Untrammeled Approaches*, 55–58. In "Reflections on Wounded Nature," another essay in this collection, Maritain transposes Aquinas's discussion of obstacles that original sin creates for four cardinal virtues to the intellectual order. In doing so he proposes four intellectual virtues that can be used to assess the contribution of various philosophers: rational solidity that aids in interconnecting concepts coherently, exactness of expression that declares clearly what the philosopher sees; boldness of vision through which the philosopher is intuitive and discovers new insights; and, finally, limpidity of thought which frees the philosopher from unconscious pressures and subjective desires. See *Untrammeled Approaches*, 214.

As we noted in chapter one, Maritain is not interested in the thought of Aquinas as a historical artifact to be reconstructed as accurately as possible. Such intellectual archaeology misses the point of philosophical and theological study. In this he is a faithful disciple to Aquinas, the latter of whom wrote that we read the works of the great minds of the past not to know what great men have thought, but to know what the truth of things is.

Yet at the same time, and for the same reasons, Maritain is ever on guard against what he once called "epistemological time worship," the presumption that the new is the true. He clearly holds that Thomism, in its foundational principles and implications, provides a true philosophy and a true theology, since its doctrine is ordered in a manner that conforms to the real. Consequently, it is able to provide the philosopher and theologian not a checklist of established facts, but a framework to advance in each domain of inquiry toward a greater share of the truth: "But there are an infinity of truths that this possible true doctrine has not yet attained; and, such as it presents itself at a given time, it can itself admit a number of accidental errors."[4] Hence the perennial philosophy is ever open to new developments, without becoming a mere eclecticism. Rather than being a recipe book for solving philosophical problems, Maritain's Thomism draws on principles that are solid and well established within the tradition in order to open up new areas of inquiry and address current problems in an organic fashion.

A second major contribution of his philosophy is its careful working out of how to address the distinctively modern problem of history and the individual. Even a thinker as sympathetic to Aquinas as Bernard Lonergan, SJ, found that Thomism was developed within classical ideals in which knowledge aimed at what was necessary, universal, and known through essences. Modern thought, in contrast, he found had turned to a general empirical method which functions statistically and infers according to the best explanation of data available for the present.[5]

---

4 *The Peasant of the Garonne*, 96.

5 Bernard Lonergan, SJ, "The Transition from a Classicist Worldview to Historical Mindedness," in *A Second Collection* (Toronto: University of Toronto Press, 2016), 3–10.

Others, as we noted in the previous chapter, have gone so far as to find either Aristotelian philosophy's ahistorical character or its static "metaphysics of presence" a reason to reject it as incompatible with the needs of Christian theology, since this theology needs to be essentially historical given the centrality of Jesus's earthly life. Maritain not only succeeds in finding a way to address the role of the particular in human knowing and offering a coherent and realistic philosophy of history, but he is also very attentive to the dynamic between "nature and adventure." The individual can only exist and act within the context of its nature and the fundamental laws that follow from this. Maritain works out this delicate balance in virtually every area of thought he addresses, as we can see from the previous chapters. This focus offers a real advance in making the creative retrieval of Aristotle and Aquinas a living possibility for thinkers of the future.

Finally, at the core of all of Maritain's philosophy is a profound awareness of the "generosity of being." This realization of being is manifested through the analogical varieties of the degrees of being and is realized in a diversity of natures. As envisioned by Maritain, Thomist philosophy is a philosophy of the superabundance of being:

> Being superabounds everywhere; it scatters its gifts and fruits in profusion. This is the action in which all beings here below communicate with one another and in which thanks to the divine influx that traverses them, they are at every instant—in this world of contingent existence and of unforeseeable future contingents— either better or worse than themselves and than the mere fact of their existence at a given moment. By this action they exchange their secrets, influence one another for good or ill, and contribute to or betray in one another the fecundity of being, the while they are carried along despite themselves in the torrent of divine governance from which nothing can escape.[6]

If being itself is superabundant and communicative of itself, then love is justified. So too, Maritain asserts, is *eros*, a natural love coextensive with being instilling in all things at every level their natural drive towards

---

6 *Existence and the Existent,* 31.

their proper end. So, too, the aspiration to emerge from oneself to share the life of one's beloved is justified. Such an aspiration is fundamentally human, and one which no philosophy unaware of the rich generosity of being is capable of recognizing. To be is to act. Thus, the philosophy of being is the philosophy of the dynamism of being. According to Maritain, what the moderns sought for in Heraclitus, Darwin, Bergson and so many others—that is, a metaphysical dynamism that would be true to the changing reality we experience—was in fact awaiting to be rediscovered and appropriated from the thought of St. Thomas Aquinas without any of the confusion inherent in a philosophy of pure becoming. This ability of Maritain to uncover how the deepest aspirations of much modern philosophy, at its best, are fulfilled when situated in a Thomistic framework is one of his most significant gifts to future generations.

This fundamental position is also a reason to continue to turn to him as a model of intellectual life for Christian philosophy irrespective of one's judgment of his views on this or that particular topic, for in Maritain we find a way to live in the contemporary world as a Christian philosopher, as one loving wisdom and drawing on the tradition while ever attentive to the nuances of our own age. Maritain's insistence that philosophy be the result of lived experience is a clarion call to integrity and authenticity in the intellectual life in a discipline in which it is all too easy to fall into empty abstractions and irrelevant technicalities. Accordingly, his demand that philosophy be lived, and his unique ability to live as a Thomistic philosopher in the modern world, continues to be, and should ever remain, inspirational.

Bibliography

Primary Sources

Maritain, Jacques. *Antimoderne*. Paris: Éditions de Revue des Jeunes, 1922.

———. *Approaches to God*. Translated by Peter O'Reilly. New York: Harper and Brothers, 1954.

———. *Art and Scholasticism and The Frontiers of Poetry*. Translated by Joseph W. Evans. New York: Charles Scribner's Sons, 1962.

———. *Bergsonian Philosophy and Thomism*. Vol. 1 of *The Collected Works of Jacques Maritain*, edited by Ralph McInerny. Notre Dame, IN: University of Notre Dame Press, 2007.

———. *Challenges and Renewals*. Edited by Joseph Evans and Leo Ward. Notre Dame, IN: University of Notre Dame Press, 1966.

———. *Christianity and Democracy: The Rights of Man and Natural Law*. San Francisco: Ignatius Press, 2012.

———. *On the Church of Christ: The Person of the Church and Her Personnel*. Translated by Joseph W. Evans. Notre Dame, IN: University of Notre Dame Press, 1973.

———. *Creative Intuition in Art and Poetry*. New York: Pantheon Books, 1953.

———. [with Raissa Maritain] *De la vie d'oraison*. 2nd ed. rev. Paris: L'Art Catholique, 1925.

———. *The Degrees of Knowledge*. Vol. VII of *The Collected Works of Jacques Maritain*, edited by Ralph McInerny. Notre Dame, IN: University of Notre Dame Press, 1995.

———. *The Dream of Descartes*. Translated by Mabelle L. Andison. New York: Philosophical Library, 1944.

———. *Education at the Crossroads*. New Haven, CT: Yale University Press, 1943.

———. *The Education of Man*. Edited by Donald and Idella Gallagher. New York: Doubleday and Co., 1967.

———. *An Essay on Christian Philosophy*. Translated by Edward H. Flannery. New York: The Philosophical Library, 1955.

———. *Existence and the Existent.* Translated by Lewis Galantière and Gerald B. Phelan. New York: Pantheon Books, 1948.

———. *Formal Logic.* Translated by Imelda Choquette. New York: Sheed and Ward, 1937.

———. "Freudism and Psychoanalysis." *Cross Currents* 6, no. 4 (1956): 307–24.

———. *God and the Permission of Evil.* Translated by Joseph W. Evans. Milwaukee: The Bruce Publishing Co., 1966.

———. *On the Grace and Humanity of Jesus.* Translated by Joseph W. Evans. New York: Herder and Herder, 1969.

———. *Integral Humanism, Freedom in the Modern World, and A Letter on Independence.* Rev. ed. Vol. XI of *The Collected Works of Jacques Maritain.* Translated by Otto Bird. Notre Dame, IN: Notre Dame University Press, 1996.

———. *An Introduction to Basic Problems of Moral Philosophy.* Translated by Cornelia N. Borgerhoff. Albany, NY: Magi Books, 1990.

———. *An Introduction to Philosophy.* Translated by E. I. Watkin. London: Sheed and Ward, 1944.

———. *Man and the State.* Chicago: University of Chicago Press, 1951.

———. *Moral Philosophy.* Translated by Joseph W. Evans. New York: Charles Scribner's Sons, 1964.

———. *Natural Law: Reflections on Theory & Practice.* Edited and Translated by William Sweet. South Bend, IN: St. Augustine's Press, 2001.

———. *Notebooks.* Translated by Joseph W. Evans. Albany, NY: Magi Press, 1964.

———. *The Peasant of the Garonne: An Old Layman Questions Himself about the Present Time.* Translated by Micheal Cuddihy and Elizabeth Hughes. New York: Holt, Rinehart, and Winston, 1968.

———. *The Person and the Common Good.* Translated by John J. Fitzgerald. New York: Charles Scribner's Sons, 1947.

———. *The Philosophy of Nature.* Translated by Imelda Choquette Byrne. New York: The Philosophical Library, 1951.

———. *Oeuvres complètes de Jacques et Raïssa Maritain.* 16 vols. Fribourg (Switzerland): Éditions universitaires, 1986–2000.

———. *On the Philosophy of History.* New York: Charles Scribner's Sons, 1957.

———. *A Preface to Metaphysics: Seven Lectures on Being.* New York and London: Sheed and Ward, 1939.

———. *The Range of Reason.* New York: Charles Scribner's Sons, 1952.

———. *Ransoming the Time.* Translated by Harry Lorin Binsse. New York: Charles Scribner's Sons, 1941.

———. *The Responsibility of the Artist.* New York: Charles Scribner's Sons, 1960.

———. *The Rights of Man and Natural Law.* Translated by Doris C. Anson. New York: Charles Scribner's Sons, 1943.

———. *St. Thomas Aquinas.* Translated by Peter O' Reilly and Joseph W. Evans. New York: Meridian Books, 1958.

———. *Saint Thomas and the Problem of Evil.* Translated by Mabelle L. Andison. Milwaukee: Marquette University Press, 1942.

———. *Science and Wisdom.* Translated by Bernard Wall. New York: Charles Scribner's Sons, 1940.

———. *Scholasticism and Politics.* Translated by Mortimer Jerome Adler. New York: The Macmillan Company, 1940.

———. "A Society Without Money," *Review of Social Economy* 43, no. 1 (April, 1985): 73–83.

———. *Theonas: Conversations of a Sage.* Translated by F.J. Sheed. New York: Sheed & Ward, 1933.

———. *Three Reformers: Luther, Descartes, Rousseau.* New York: Charles Scribner's Sons, 1929.

———. *Untrammeled Approaches.* Translated by Bernard Doering, Ernst R. Korn, and Heinz R. Schmitz. Notre Dame, IN: University of Notre Dame Press, 1997.

———. *The Use of Philosophy.* Princeton, NJ: Princeton University Press, 1961.

Maritain, Jacques & Raïssa. *Lettres Intimes, 1901–1932,* T. 1. Edited by Dominique et Rene Mougel. Paris: Éditions Desclée de Brouwer, 2023.

———. *The Situation of Poetry.* New York: The Philosophical Library, 1968.

Maritain, Raïssa. *We Have Been Friends Together & Adventures in Grace.* Translated by Julie Kernan. Garden City, NY: Image Books, 1961.

———. *Raïssa's Journal.* Presented by Jacques Maritain. Albany, NY: Magi Books, 1974.

Maritain, Jacques & Simon, Yves. *Correspondance, T.2 : Les années américaine (1941-1961)*. Edited by Florian Michel. Tours: CLD Éditions, 2012.

Secondary Sources

Allard, Jean-Louis. *Jacques Maritain, Philosophe dans la cité/ A Philosopher in the World*, Ottawa: University of Ottawa Press, 1985.

Alberigo, Giuseppe, and Joseph A. Komonchak, eds. Vol. V of *History of Vatican II*. Maryknoll, NY: Orbis Books, 2006.

Aquinas, St. Thomas. *De Spiritualibus Creaturis*. Translated by Mary C. Fitzpatrick and John J. Wellmuth. Milwaukee: Marquette University Press, 1949.

——. *Summa Contra Gentiles*. 5 vols. Translated by Anton C. Pegis, James F. Anderson, Vernon J. Bourke, and Charles J. O'Neil. Notre Dame, IN: University of Notre Dame Press, 1976.

——. *Summa Theologica*. 5 vols. Translated by the Fathers of the Dominican Province. New York: Christian Classics, 1948.

Aristotle. *The Complete Works of Aristotle*. 2 vols. Edited by Jonathan Barnes. Oxford: Oxford University Press, 1984.

Arraj, James. *Mysticism, Metaphysics and Maritain*. Chiloquin, OR: Inner Growth Books, 2011.

Ashley, Benedict, OP. *The Ashley Reader: Redeeming Reason*. Naples, FL: Sapientia Press of Ave Maria University, 2006.

——. "Does Natural Science Attain Nature or Only the Phenomena." In *The Philosophy of Physics*, edited by Vincent E. Smith, 63–82. Jamaica, NY: St. John's University, 1961.

——. *The Way Toward Wisdom*. Notre Dame, IN: University of Notre Dame, 2009.

Augustine. *The Confessions*. Translated by Henry Chadwick. Oxford: Oxford University Press, 1991.

Ayer, A. J. *Language, Truth, and Logic*. 2nd rev. ed. New York: Dover Publications, 1952.

Báñez, Domingo. *In Iam Partem divi Thomae*, qq. 1–64. Salamanca, 1584.

Barré, Jean-Luc. *Jacques and Raïssa Maritain: Beggars from Heaven*. Translated by Bernard E. Doering. Notre Dame, IN: University of Notre Dame Press, 2005.

Bars, Henry. *Maritain et notre temps.* Paris: Grasset, 1959.

Bergson, Henri. *Creative Evolution. Translated by Arthur Mitchell.* New York: Random House, 1944.

——. *Introduction to Metaphysics.* Translated by T. E. Hulme. Indianapolis: Hackett Publications, 1999.

Bobik, Joseph. "The Sixth Way of Aquinas." *The Thomist* 42, no. 3 (1978): 373–99.

Bradley, Dennis J. M. *Aquinas on the Twofold Human Good: Reason and Human Happiness in Aquinas's Moral Science.* Washington, DC: The Catholic University of America Press, 1999.

Bréhier, Émile, "Y a-t-il une philosophie chrétienne?" *Revue de métaphysique et de morale* 38 (1931): 133–62.

——. "La notion de philosophie chrétienne." *Bulletin de la Société française de Philosophie* 31 (1931): 37–93.

Brock, Stephen L. *The Light That Binds: A Study in Thomas Aquinas' Metaphysics of the Natural Law.* Eugene, OR: Pickwick Publications, 2020.

Butera, Giuseppe, ed. *Reading the Cosmos: Nature, Science and Wisdom.* Washington, DC: American Maritain Association, 2011.

Cahalan, John C. "Thing and Object in Maritain." *The Thomist* 59, no. 1 (1995): 21–46.

Carnap, Rudolf. *The Logical Syntax of Language.* London: Routledge, 1937.

Chenaux, Philippe. "Maritain devant le Saint-Office: Le rôle du père Garrigou-Lagrange, OP." *Archivum Fratrum Praedicatorum*, Novum Series, VI (2001): 401–20.

Clarke, W. Norris, SJ. *Exploration in Metaphysics: Being, God, Person.* Notre Dame, IN: University of Notre Dame Press, 1994.

Colvert, Galvin T., ed. *The Renewal of Civilization.* Notre Dame, IN: The American Maritain Association, 2011.

Cooper, John M. "Contemplation and Happiness: A Reconsideration." *Synthese* 2 (1987): 187–216.

Compendium of the Social Doctrine of the Church. Ottawa: Canadian Conference of Catholic Bishops, 2005.

Congar, Yves. *L'Église: Une, sainte, catholique et apostolique.* Paris: Cerf, 1970.

Cottier, Georges, OP. "J. Maritain: Un philosophe travaillant comme 'research worker' au service de la theologie." *Notes et Documents* 62 (2001): 49–52.

Crane, Richard Francis. *Passion of Israel: Jacques Maritain, Catholic Conscience and the Holocaust.* Scranton, PA: University of Scranton Press, 2010.

Deely, John. *Intentionality and Semiotics.* Scranton: University of Scranton Press, 2007.

Del Noce, Augusto. "The Lesson of Maritain." *Maritain Studies* 31 (2015): 71–80.

Dennehy, Raymond. *Jacques Maritain's Philosophy of Action.* CreateSpace Independent Publishing Platform, 2017.

Descartes, René. Vol. II of *The Philosophical Writings of Descartes.* Translated by John Cottingham, et al. Cambridge: Cambridge University Press, 1984.

Dewan, Lawrence, OP. "History of Philosophy, Personal or Impersonal? Reflections on Étienne Gilson." *Maritain Studies* XI (1995): 7–31.

———. "Jacques Maritain, St. Thomas, and the Birth of Metaphysics." *Maritain Studies* 13 (1997): 3–18.

———. "Maritain, Einstein, and Special Relativity." *Maritain Studies* 18 (2002): 29–44.

———. *Wisdom, Law, and Virtue: Essays in Thomistic Ethics.* New York: Fordham University Press, 2007.

Deweer, Dries. "The Philosophical Theory of Personalism: Maritain and Mounier on Personhood and Citizenship." *International Journal of Philosophy and Theology* 74, no. 2 (2013): 108–26.

Dewey, John. *Democracy and Education.* New York: MacMillan, 1916.

———. *The Moral Principles of Education.* Boston: Houghton Mifflin Company, 1909.

De Koninck, Charles, *The Writings of Charles De Koninck.* 2 vols. Edited and translated by Ralph McInerny. Notre Dame, IN: University of Notre Dame Press, 2008.

Di Blasi, Fluvio. *God and the Natural Law: A Rereading of Thomas Aquinas.* South Bend, IN: St. Augustine's Press, 2006.

Doering, Bernard. "Jacques Maritain on the Church's Misbehaving Clerics." *CrossCurrents* 52, no. 2 (2002): 246–53.

———. *Jacques Maritain and the French Catholic Intellectuals.* Notre Dame, IN: University of Notre Dame Press, 1983.

D'Sousa, Mario O. *A Catholic Philosophy of Education: The Church and Two Philosophers.* Montreal & Kingston: McGill-Queen's University Press, 2016.

———. "Maritain's Philosophy of Education and Religious Education." *Catholic Education: A Journal of Inquiry and Practice* 4, no. 3 (2001). https://ejournals.bc.edu/index.php/cej/article/view/254.

Dougherty, Jude P. *Jacques Maritain: An Intellectual Profile.* Washington, DC: The Catholic University of America Press, 2010.

Dunaway, John M. *Jacques Maritain.* Boston: Twayne Publishers, 1978.

Dünkelsbühler, Ulrike Oudée. *Reframing the Frame of Reason: "Trans-Lation" in and Beyond Kant and Derrida.* Translated by Max Statkiewicz. New York: Humanity Books, 2002.

Einstein, Albert. *Relativity: The Special and General Theory.* Translated by Robert W. Lawson. New York: Henry Holt and Company, 1920.

Eschmann, Ignatius, OP. "In Defense of Jacques Maritain." Modern Schoolman 22, no. 4 (1944): 183–208

Evans, Joseph W., ed. *Jacques Maritain: The Man and His Achievement.* New York: Sheed & Ward, 1953.

Finnis, John. *Aquinas: Moral, Political, and Legal Theory.* New York: Oxford University Press, 1998.

———. *Natural Law and Natural Rights.* 2nd ed. Clarendon Law Series. Oxford: Oxford University, 2011.

Gallagher, Donald and Idella. *The Achievement of Jacques and Raïssa Maritain: A Bibliography 1906–1961.* Garden City: Doubleday & Co., 1962.

Garrigou-Lagrange, Reginald. *Predestination.* Translated by Bede Rose. St. Louis and London: B. Herder Book Co., 1939.

———. *Providence.* Translated by Bede Rose. Rockford, IL: Tan Books, 1998.

———. *The Three Ages of the Spiritual Life.* 2 vols. Translated by Sister M. Timothea Doyle. Rockford, IL: TAN Books, 1989.

Gilson, Étienne. *Being and Some Philosophers.* 2nd ed. Toronto: Pontifical Institute of Mediaeval Studies, 1952.

———. *The Christian Philosophy of St. Thomas Aquinas.* Translated by Laurence Shook, CSB. New York: Random House, 1994.

———. *Methodical Realism*. Translated by Philip Trower. San Francisco: Ignatius Press, 2011.

———. *The Spirit of Medieval Philosophy*. Translated by A. H. C. Downes. New York: Charles Scribner's Sons, 1940.

———. *Thomist Realism and the Critique of Knowledge*. Translated by Mark Wauck. San Francisco: Ignatius Press, 1986.

———. *The Unity of Philosophical Experience*. New York: Charles Scribner's Sons, 1950.

Grasso, Kenneth, Gerald Bradley, and R. Hunt, eds. *Catholicism, Liberalism, and Communitarianism*. Lanham, MD: Rowman and Littlefield, 1995.

Gredt, Josephus. *Elementa Philosophiae Aristotelico-Thomisticae*. Freiburg: Herder & Co., 1937.

Gutiérrez, Gustavo. *A Theology of Liberation*. 15th anniversary ed. Translated and edited by Sister Caridad Inda and John Eagleson. Maryknoll, NY: Orbis Books, 1988.

Feyerabend, Paul. *Against Method*, 3rd ed. New York: Verso, 1993.

Finnis, John. *Aquinas: Moral, Political, and Legal Theory*. New York: Oxford University Press, 1998.

———. *Natural Law and Natural Rights*. Oxford: Clarendon Press, 1980.

Hadot, Pierre. *Philosophy as a Way of Life*. London: Wiley-Blackwell, 1995.

Hanink, James G., ed. *Aquinas & Maritain on Evil: Mystery and Metaphysics*. Washington, DC: American Maritain Association, 2013.

Hannon, Urban. "Studying and suffering divine things: St. Thomas Aquinas on Hierotheus." *Medieval Mystical Theology* 31, no. 2 (2022): 80–90.

Hegel, G. W. F. *The Philosophy of History*. Translated by J. Sibree. New York: Willey Book Co., 1944.

———. *The Science of Logic*. Translated by George di Giovanni. New York: Cambridge University Press, 2010.

Henle, Robert, SJ. *Selected Papers from the Conference-Seminar on Jacques Maritain's "The Degrees of Knowledge."* Notre Dame, IN: American Maritain Association, 1981.

Hittinger, John. *Liberty, Wisdom, and Grace: Thomism and Democratic Political Theory*. Lanham, MD: Lexington Books, 2003.

———, ed. *The Vocation of the Catholic Philosopher*. Washington, DC: American Maritain Association, 2010.

Horkheimer, Max, and Theodor W. Adorno. *Dialectics of Enlightenment*. New York: Continuum International Publishing Group, 1973.

Hudson, Deal W., and Matthew J. Mancini, eds. *Understanding Maritain: Philosopher and Friend*. Macon, GA: Mercer University Press, 1987.

Hudson, Deal W. and Dennis W. Moran, eds. *The Future of Thomism*. Notre Dame, IN: University of Notre Dame Press, 1992.

Imhof, Paul, and Hubert Biallowons, eds. *Karl Rahner in Dialogue: Conversations and Interviews, 1965–1982*. Translated by Harvey D. Egan. New York: Crossroad, 1986.

John of St. Thomas. *Cursus theologicus in Summam theologicam D. Thomæ*. Madrid: Vives, 1883.

Journet, Charles. *The Church of the Word Incarnate*. Translated by A. H. C. Downes. London: Sheed & Ward, 1955.

———. "Jacques Maritain Theologian." *The New Scholasticism* XLVI, no. 1 (1972): 32–50.

Kernan, Julie. *Our Friend, Jacques Maritain: A Personal Memoir*. New York: Doubleday, 1975.

Kerr, Fergus, OP, ed. *Contemplating Aquinas: On the Varieties of Interpretation*. Notre Dame, IN: University of Notre Dame Press, 2006.

Kraut, Richard. *Aristotle on the Human Good*. Princeton: Princeton University Press, 1989.

Komonchak, Joseph A. "The Epistemology of Reception." In *Reception and Communion Among Churches*, edited by Hervé Legrand, OP, Julio Manzanares Marijuan, and Antonio García, OFM, 180–203. Washington, DC: The Canon Law Department, The Catholic University of America, 1997.

Lacombe, Olivier. "Jacques Maritain Metaphysician." *The New Scholasticism* XLVI, no. 1 (1972): 18–31.

Locke, John. *An Essay Concerning Human Understanding*. Edited by Peter H. Nidditch. Cambridge: Cambridge University Press, 1975.

Long, Steven A. "Providence, Freedom and Natural Law." *Nova et Vetera*, English ed. 4, no. 3 (2006): 557–606.

Lonergan, Bernard. *Insight: A Study of Human Understanding*. Edited by Frederick E. Crowe and Robert M. Doran. Toronto: The University of Toronto Press, 1992.

———. *A Second Collection*. Toronto: University of Toronto Press, 2016.

Marrou, Henri-Irénée. *De la connaissance historique*. Paris: ed. du Seuil, 1954.

McCauliff, Catherine M. A. "Jacques Maritain's Embrace of Religious Pluralism and the Declaration on Religious Freedom." *Seton Hall Law Review* 41, no. 2 (2011): 593–624.

McCool, Gerald A., SJ. *From Unity to Pluralism: The Internal Evolution of Thomism*. New York: Fordham University Press, 1999.

McInerny, Ralph. *Art and Prudence: Studies in the Thought of Jacques Maritain*. Notre Dame, IN: University of Notre Dame Press, 1988.

———. *The Question of Christian Ethics*. Washington, DC: The Catholic University of America Press, 1983.

———. *The Very Rich Hours of Jacques Maritain: A Spiritual Life*. Notre Dame, IN: University of Notre Dame Press, 2003.

MacIntyre, Alasdair. *After Virtue*, 2nd ed. Notre Dame, IN: University of Notre Dame Press, 1984.

———. *Whose Justice? Which Rationality?* Notre Dame, IN: University of Notre Dame Press, 1988.

Maréchal, Joseph. *A Maréchal Reader*. Edited by Joseph Donceel. New York: Herder and Herder, 1970.

Marion, Jean-Luc. *On Descartes' Metaphysical Prism*. Chicago: University of Chicago Press, 1999.

———. *Nineteenth Century Scholasticism: The Search for a Unitary Method*, 2nd rev. ed. New York: Fordham University Press, 1999.

Minerd, Matthew K., ed. *Facts are Stubborn Things: Thomistic Perspectives in the Philosophies of Nature and Science*. Washington, DC: The American Maritain Association, 2019.

Molina, Luis de. *On Divine Foreknowledge: Part IV of the "Concordia,"* rev. ed. Ithaca, NY: Cornell University Press, 2004.

Morrissey, Christopher S. "Dialectic and Demonstration in the Philosophy of Nature." *Maritain Studies* XXIII (2007): 63–74.

Murphy, Francesca Aran. *Art and Intellect in the Philosophy of* Étienne *Gilson*. Columbia: University of Missouri Press, 2004.

Murphy, Madonna. "Maritain Explains the Moral Principles of Education to John Dewey." *Educational Horizons* 83, no. 4 (2005): 282–91.

Nicolas, Jean-Hervé. "La permission du péché." *Revue Thomiste* LX (1960): no. 1, 5–37; no. 2, 185–206; and no. 4, 509–46.

Olivant, Douglas A., ed. *Jacques Maritain and the Many Ways of Knowing.* Notre Dame, IN: The American Maritain Association, 2002.

Owens, Joseph, CSsR. *Towards a Christian Philosophy.* Washington, DC: The Catholic University of America Press, 1990.

———. "The Need for Christian Philosophy." *Faith and Philosophy* 11, no. 2 (1994): 167–83.

———. *Some Philosophical Issues in Moral Matters: The Collected Ethical Writings of Joseph Owens.* Edited by D. J. Billy and Terence Kennedy. Roma: Editiones Acadamiae Alphonsianae, 1996.

Phelan, G. B., CSB. *Selected Papers.* Edited by Arthur G. Kirn, CSB. Toronto: Pontifical Institute of Mediaeval Studies, 1967.

Pieper, Josef. *Leisure: The Basis of Culture.* Translated by Alexander Dru. New York: The New American Library, 1963.

Piolanti, Antonio, ed. *San Tommaso e il pensiero moderno.* Citta Nuova: Pontificia Accademia Romana de S. Tommaso d' Aquino, 1974.

Porter, Jean. *Nature as Reason: A Thomistic Theory of Natural Law.* Grand Rapids, MI: Eerdmans Publishing Company, 2004.

Pugh, Matthew S. "Maritain, The Intuition of Being, and the Proper Starting Point for Thomistic Metaphysics." *The Thomist* 61, no. 3 (1997): 405–27.

Rahner, Karl. "Aquinas: The Nature of Truth." *Continuum* 2, no. 1 (1964): 60–72.

———. Vol. 6 of *Theological Investigations.* Baltimore: Helicon, 1969.

Ramirez, Santiago, OP. "De Philosophia Morali Christiana." *Divus Thomas* 50 (1936): 87–140 and 181–204.

Ramos, Alice and Marie I George, eds. *Faith, Scholarship, and Culture in the 21st Century.* Washington, DC: The American Maritain Association, 2002.

Redpath, Peter A., ed. *A Thomistic Tapestry: Essays in Memory of* Étienne *Gilson.* New York: Rodopi, 2003.

Rocker, Stephen. "Maritain on Hegel." *Maritain Studies* XXXVI (2020): 19–29.

Rowland, Christopher, ed. *The Cambridge Companion to Liberation Theology*, 2nd ed. Cambridge, UK: Cambridge University Press, 2007.

Rowland, Tracey. "Natural Law: From Neo-Thomism to Nuptial Mysticism." *Communio*, 35 (2008): 374–96.

Royal, Robert, ed. *Jacques Maritain and the Jews*. Notre Dame: University of Notre Dame Press, 1993.

Russell, Bertrand. *My Philosophical Development*. London: George Allen and Unwin, 1959.

Schultz, Walter. *Jacques Maritain in the 21st Century: Personalism and the Political Organization of the World*. Newcastle upon Tyne: Cambridge Scholars Press, 2022.

Shook, Laurence K., CSB. Étienne *Gilson*. Toronto: Pontifical Institute of Medieaeval Studies, 1984.

Simon, Antony O., ed. *Acquaintance with the Absolute: The Philosophy of Yves R. Simon*. New York: Fordham University Press, 1998.

Simon, Yves R. *Foresight and Knowledge*. Edited by Ralph Nelson and Anthony O. Simon. New York: Fordham University Press, 1996.

———. *A General Theory of Authority*. Notre Dame, IN: The University of Notre Dame Press, 1991.

———. *The Great Dialogue of Nature and Space*. Edited by Gerard J. Dalcourt. New York: Magi Books, Inc., 1970.

———. *An Introduction to the Metaphysics of Knowledge*. Translated by Richard Thompson. New York: Fordham University Press, 1990.

———. *An Yves R. Simon Reader: The Philosopher's Calling*. Edited by Michael D. Torre. Notre Dame, IN: University of Notre Dame Press, 2021.

Song, Robert. *Christianity and Liberal Society*. Oxford: Oxford University Press, 2006.

Suto, Taki. "Virtue and Knowledge: Connatural Knowledge according to Thomas Aquinas." *Review of Metaphysics*. 58, no. 1 (2004): 61–79.

Sweet, William. "Maritain's Criticisms of Natural Law Theories." *Maritain Studies* 12 (1996): 33–49.

Sweet, William, and Huang, Cristal. "The Metaphysical and Epistemological Foundations of Natural Law in Jacques Maritain." *Philosophy and Culture* 33, no. 9 (2006): 83–98.

Taylor, Charles. *Sources of the Self: The Making of Modern Identity*. Cambridge, MA: Harvard University Press, 1989.

———. *Philosophical Arguments*. Cambridge, MA: Harvard University Press, 1995.

Teilhard de Chardin, Pierre. *Hymn of the Universe*. Translated by Simon Bartholomew. New York: Harper & Row, 1961.

———. *Man's Place in Nature: The Human Zoological Group*. New York: Harper & Row, 1966.

———. *The Phenomenon of Man*, 2nd ed. New York: Harper Colophon, 1975.

Torre, Michael D. *Do Not Resist the Spirit's Call: Francisco Marín-Sola on Sufficient Grace*. Washington, DC: The Catholic University of America Press, 2013.

Torrell, Jean-Pierre. *Le mystère du Christ chez saint Tomas d'Aquin*. Paris: Cerf, 1999.

Trapani, John G. *Poetry, Beauty and Contemplation: The Complete Aesthetics of Jacques Maritain*. Washington, DC: The Catholic University of America Press, 2011.

Valente, Gianni. "Paul VI, Maritain and the faith of the Apostles: An Interview with Georges Cardinal Cottier." In *30 Days*, no. 4 (2008): https://www.30giorni.it/articoli_id_17898_l3.htm. Accessed October 18, 2023.

Van Steenberghen, Fernand. "Étienne Gilson, historien de la pensée médiévale." *Revue Philosophique de Louvain* 77 (1979): 493–507.

———. "La Ile Journée d'études de la Société Thomiste et la notion de philosophie chrétienne." *Revue néo-Scolastique* 35 (1933): 544–54.

Wallace, William A. *The Modelling of Nature*. Washington, DC: The Catholic University of America Press, 1996.

Wittgenstein, Ludwig. *Philosophical Investigations*. Translated by G. E. M. Anscombe. Oxford: Basil Blackwell, 1963.

Wippel, John F. *The Metaphysical Thought of Thomas Aquinas: From Finite Being to Uncreated Being*. Washington, DC: The Catholic University of America Press, 2000.

Zunic, Nikolaj. Editor. *Distinctions of Being: Philosophical Approaches to Reality*. Washington, DC: The American Maritain Association, 2013.

———. "Method in Philosophy: Maritain's Engagement with Modernity." *Maritain Studies* 22 (2006): 38–53.

Index

G

H

I

J

S

Science: moral, 203–12, 232;
natural or empirical, xi, 2, 4, 6,
12, 15, 20n30, 22, 46, 57–70,
70–94, 115–17, 167, 264, 283–
84, 328, 349; philosophical,
12, 27, 51, 58–70, 97–100,
110–11, 122, 163, 230, 327–30.
See also Physics; Theology

Second Vatican Council, 10–11,
160, 224n55

Semiotics, 44–50, 116–18

Sense experience, 28–30, 32,
38n22, 42–43, 45–47, 62,
64–65, 86, 95, 114–16, 126n12,
131, 168, 172, 280, 300, 317,
321, 323

Signs. *See* Semiotics

Simon, Yves R., 8, 52n56, 57n1,
80n55, 246, 268n63

Spiritual preconscious. *See*
Intuition, creative

Stott, Laurence, 284–85

Subalternation, 205, 209–12

Summa Theologiae, 4, 48n45,
51nn51–53, 127n13, 136n25,
144n39, 162n4, 163n5,
163n7, 170n24, 174n32,
185n57, 186n59, 202n2,
211n29, 212n30, 253nn32–34,
312nn38–39, 314n33, 322n63,
327n4, 330n9

T

Taylor, Charles, 27, 54n62, 202, 204

Theology, xii, 12, 21, 23, 63, 157,
162–69, 190–91, 199, 201–4,
205, 208, 209–13, 224, 231,
293, 305, 327, 334, 337, 342,
351, 357

Thing. *See* Object, and thing

Thomism, xi–xii, 4–5, 10, 11,
16–18, 20n38, 25, 31, 36n18,
37, 83, 227, 249, 257n40,
302n17, 349–50

Torre, Michael, D., 149n49, 160n1

Transcendentals, 106, 119–20,
322–23

W

Wisdom, 17, 19, 31, 53–54, 57, 59,
122, 159, 163, 167–69, 172,
176–77, 185, 202, 249, 259,
272, 278–79, 327, 352